STATE-BUILDING IN THE MIDDLE EAST AND NORTH AFRICA

STATE-BUILDING IN THE MIDDLE EAST AND NORTH AFRICA

One Hundred Years of Nationalism, Religion and Politics

Edited by
Mohammad-Mahmoud
Ould Mohamedou

I.B. TAURIS
LONDON • NEW YORK • OXFORD • NEW DELHI • SYDNEY

I.B. TAURIS
Bloomsbury Publishing Plc
50 Bedford Square, London, WC1B 3DP, UK
1385 Broadway, New York, NY 10018, USA
29 Earlsfort Terrace, Dublin 2, Ireland

BLOOMSBURY, I.B. TAURIS and the I.B. Tauris logo are trademarks of
Bloomsbury Publishing Plc

First published in Great Britain 2022

Copyright © Mohammad-Mahmoud Ould Mohamedou, 2022

Mohammad-Mahmoud Ould Mohamedou and contributors have asserted their right under the Copyright, Designs and Patents Act, 1988, to be identified as Author of this work.

Copyright Individual Chapters © 2021 Mohammad-Mahmoud Ould Mohamedou, Henry Laurens, Benoît Challand, Faleh Abdul Jabar, Ahmad Samih Khalidi, Jordi Tejel, Bruce Rutherford, François Burgat, Bertrand Badie, Ghassan Salamé

For legal purposes the Acknowledgements on pp. x–xii constitute an extension of this copyright page.

Cover design by www.paulsmithdesign.com
Cover image © TARIQ_M_1/Getty Images

All rights reserved. No part of this publication may be reproduced or transmitted in any form or by any means, electronic or mechanical, including photocopying, recording, or any information storage or retrieval system, without prior permission in writing from the publishers.

Bloomsbury Publishing Plc does not have any control over, or responsibility for, any third-party websites referred to or in this book. All internet addresses given in this book were correct at the time of going to press. The author and publisher regret any inconvenience caused if addresses have changed or sites have ceased to exist, but can accept no responsibility for any such changes.

A catalogue record for this book is available from the British Library.

A catalog record for this book is available from the Library of Congress.

ISBN: HB: 978-0-7556-0139-4
       PB: 978-0-7556-0140-0
       ePDF: 978-0-7556-0141-7
       eBook: 978-0-7556-0142-4

Typeset by Integra Software Services Pvt. Ltd.

To find out more about our authors and books visit www.bloomsbury.com
and sign up for our newsletters.

CONTENTS

Contributors vii
Foreword *Lisa Anderson* viii
Acknowledgements x

PART ONE FOUNDATIONS AND LEGACIES 1

1. A century of elusive state-building in the Middle East and North Africa
   Mohammad-Mahmoud Ould Mohamedou 3

2. The Western question
   Henry Laurens 25

3. From the twilight of the Ottoman Empire to the Caliphate redux: The tortuous journey of Arab statehood
   Benoît Challand 41

PART TWO IRRESOLUTIONS AND ABSENCES 65

4. A state in search of a nation: The case of Iraq
   Faleh Abdul Jabar 67

5. One hundred years of the Palestinian national movement
   Ahmad Samih Khalidi 81

6. Permanent irresolution of the Kurdish issue
   Jordi Tejel 93

PART THREE REINVENTIONS AND RETURNS 115

7 Egypt's post-Arab Spring neo-authoritarianism
   Bruce K. Rutherford 117

8 Armed militancy and alternative statehood: Al Qaeda, the Islamic state and revolutionary Islamism
   François Burgat 147

9 Authoritarianism, weakness and the new great game
   Bertrand Badie 165

10 Longing for the state, mistrusting the state
   Ghassan Salamé 179

Chronology 193
Glossary 252
Bibliography 255
Index 268

CONTRIBUTORS

Mohammad-Mahmoud Ould Mohamedou is Professor of International History and Politics and Chair of the Department of International History and Politics at the Graduate Institute of International and Development Studies in Geneva, Switzerland. He was the 2021 recipient of the International Studies Association (ISA) Global South Distinguished Scholar Award.

Faleh Abdul Jabar was the founder and Director of the Iraqi Institute for Strategic Studies. He passed away in February 2018.

Lisa Anderson is Professor Emerita of International Relations at the Columbia University School of International and Public Affairs in New York and former President of the American University in Cairo, Egypt.

Bertrand Badie is Emeritus Professor of Political Science at Sciences Po Paris, France.

Francois Burgat is Senior Research Fellow at the National Centre for Scientific Research (CNRS), France.

Benoît Challand is Associate Professor of Sociology at the New School for Social Research in New York, USA.

Ahmed Samih Khalidi is Senior Associate Member of St. Antony's College at Oxford University, UK.

Henry Laurens is Professor and Chair of History of the Contemporary Arab World at the Collège de France in Paris, France.

Bruce Rutherford is Associate Professor of Political Science at Colgate University in Hamilton, New York, USA.

Ghassan Salamé is the former Dean of the Paris School of International Affairs and Professor of Political Science at Sciences Po Paris, France.

Jordi Tejel is Adjunct Professor in Contemporary History at the University of Neuchâtel, Switzerland.

FOREWORD

Lisa Anderson

As the title of this volume suggests, scholars and policy-makers have been puzzling over the character of the state and state-building in the Middle East and North Africa for over a century. There were earlier efforts in the region to counter growing European power that we often characterize as state-building in retrospect – Mohammed Ali's military development and economic restructuring in Egypt, for example, and the Tanzimat reforms in the mid-nineteenth-century Ottoman Empire. But the political engineers of those efforts did not think of their work as 'state building'; they were merely borrowing ideas about how to govern in order to strengthen their domains and their own positions within them. It was not until after the First World War that deliberate and self-conscious efforts to construct states as such appeared with the collapse of the Ottoman Empire. Both local nationalists demanding independence – 'self-determination' – and European imperialists promising 'tutelage' to their mandatory charges did so within the legal and political framework of the new League of Nations and the modern European-style secular state that was its supposed constituent unit.

As the contributions in this volume eloquently detail, at that moment statehood became both an elusive aspiration and an impossible test. The state became, as Mohammad-Mahmoud Ould Mohamedou puts it, 'at once strong and weak, present and absent, visible and invisible.' The traces of this origin story are apparent a century later throughout the region but perhaps nowhere more poignantly than in Palestine. As this book goes to press, statehood remains both an elusive aspiration, an abstract symbol of victory, freedom and autonomy, and an impossible test, a compulsory demand to control a refractory population in the absence of resources to do so. Nowhere, except perhaps Israel or Turkey, however, did the state develop organically as a mechanism by which to resolve conflicts or distribute resources within a community.

Indeed, everywhere else in the region, thanks to their origin in this post–First World War context, states serve as the instruments of rulers, as they were intended to do by their European imperial designers. The nationalist rulers adapted the tools of civil administration and military force for their own purposes, promising, as the Europeans also had, to use them for the benefit of the people and deploying them instead, like their European predecessors, to extract resources and enforce compliance. Today's Middle Eastern and North African states are the instruments of local (and global) ruling classes, by design and in fact.

This is not the statehood which most of the region's people want, however, and it certainly does not afford democracy, which leads to another characteristic feature of the state in the region: it is an ever-receding target. The moment when these populations are – as the League of Nation's Covenant put it in creating the Mandate system – 'able to stand alone' unaided by 'the rendering of administrative advice and assistance' by outside powers never seems to arrive. Putative independence, a seat at the United Nations, the trappings of sovereignty proved not to mean self-reliant statehood, much less accountable government. Instead, state-building and democracy promotion, like the Arab–Israeli peace process, were transformed into ends in themselves and the 'rendering of assistance' came to serve as a device by which attainment of the ostensible goal was prolonged or perhaps even prevented. What are ordinarily understood as means to other ends – building, formation, promotion, process – became measures of success in themselves, obscuring failures to actually accomplish the supposed goals, statehood, democracy or peace.

Small wonder that the state seems both weak and strong, absent and too present, visible and invisible. Its rulers fail to provide adequate social services and yet are brutally and invasively coercive. Their constant activity – new reform agendas, aid projects and investment programmes – seems to bring little genuine change, as unemployment grows, education deteriorates and war and displacement become routinized. Conspiracy theories proliferate to explain these puzzling contradictions while scientific research languishes.

These features of the state in the Middle East and North Africa, its countenances as an instrument and illusion, are not easy to see and even more difficult to acknowledge. Students and scholars of the region are as susceptible to wishful thinking as anyone else; we want state-building to bear fruit and we want the states in the region to reflect the hopes and dreams of their citizens. This volume goes a long way to dispel misapprehensions born of good intentions and fond desires. It is a sobering, clear-eyed and necessary corrective to conventional wisdom and, in that alone, an important contribution to our understanding of the region.

ACKNOWLEDGEMENTS

This book originated with an international conference held on 27–28 September 2017 at the Graduate Institute of International and Development Studies in Geneva, Switzerland. Examining the question of 'Elusive State-Building: The Middle East and North Africa, 1917–2017', the conference was organized as part of the Annual Pierre du Bois Conference, an event jointly convened by the Pierre du Bois Foundation and the Department of International History and Politics at the Graduate Institute. The conference brought together a group of thirty-three scholars from the Graduate Institute Geneva, Oxford University, Harvard University, Columbia University, Princeton University, the City University of New York, the American University in Cairo, Sciences Po Paris, the University of Haifa, the University of Neuchâtel, the University of Saint-Joseph in Beirut, the European University Institute in Florence, the French Centre National de la Recherche Scientifique (CNRS), the University of Leeds, Exeter University, the New School, Tel Aviv University, the London School of Economics and Political Science and the Carnegie Middle East Center.

Building and expanding on these discussions, this volume is devoted to the question of state-building in the Middle East and North Africa in the period from the 1910s to the 2020s. It delves into the issue of the difficult, challenging and often elusive pursuit of modern statehood by Middle Eastern and North African societies. The book discusses this question as it played out over the past century, and in the context of a series of back-to-back largescale events – notably the colonial and postcolonial eras – and multiple conflicts that have characterized the contemporary history of the region. In recent decades as the Middle East and North Africa region went through the throes of the 1990–1991 Gulf War followed by the 11 September 2001 terrorist attacks and the Global War on Terror aftermath, notably in Iraq and Afghanistan, and then the 2011 uprisings of the Arab Spring and the associated civil wars in Syria, Yemen and Libya, one distinguishing feature remained visibly at the heart of these transformations, namely the challenge of establishing viable and functioning states. Decades after the modern-day state-making project was launched in the region, amidst new-old dynamics of neo-authoritarianism, coercive democratization, the rise of non-state actors and continuing socioeconomic strife, such active pursuit of statehood has remained the overarching aspect of the many perplexing features of the contemporary regional scene.

Over the past one hundred years, the quest for the state has in effect been at the heart of Middle Eastern and North African history and politics, as a frame of reference, an identity shaper and a force wielder. The states that have emerged in the area were incomplete, certainly not satisfactory from a political legitimacy perspective and in effect institutionally overall 'half-born' so to speak. These states suffered and continue to suffer an unshakable legitimacy crisis as a result of their predominantly authoritarian nature. Second, state-building in the Middle East and North Africa is importantly also part and parcel of 'world-making'. To extirpate the regional process from the global one, as has often been done, is to misconstrue the dynamics and the consequential interpenetration between the local, national, regional and international levels – all continuously affecting how a state is built and unbuilt in the Middle East and North Africa. Regional hegemony and global hegemony, in particular, are intertwined revealingly. Parcelling out our views of regions is indeed problematic, running the risk of depoliticizing eminently political issue. A third issue is the one of encroachments – colonial, imperial, economic and communal. As regards key diplomatic moments, such as the secret 1916 Sykes-Picot agreement, these intrusions can be looked at as consequential but must be put in the wider frame to avoid selectivity (or indeed the conspiratorial mindset so problematically prevalent in the region). What emerges is a 'MENA' state that is constantly *struggling* (often immersed in war-making) and, for the most, *dependent* (including in its rentier incarnation), subject to intervention or intervening itself (regional hegemon) and politically ever asymmetric with global powers. Therefore, state-building is an important and relevant paradigm for MENA, but equally it can be misleading in excessively and near-exclusively emphasizing the institutional façade of authority. In this fluid cartography, contestation is a staying feature in the 1910s, the 1960s, the 1990s and 2020s – anti-colonialists, nationalists, democrats, Islamists and modernizers, all in continuing dynamics of uprising, challenge and resistance.

The present collection of chapters by senior scholars examine these questions focusing on the overarching notion of state-building – understood here as those *actions undertaken by actors to establish or reform institutions and relationships in a given society with a view to generate an erect set of public structures meant to embody the general interest and further its development, notably through the delivery of services.* Other transversal issues tackled include the problematic role of interfering Western powers, the shaping and reshaping of social memory in the context of the competing nationalist and religious narrative, the political role of aesthetics and representation, the manipulation of state-building symbols and their distortion in the name of national security.

Part One, 'Foundations and Legacies', provides the background to this history with chapters by Henry Laurens, Benoît Challand and Mohammad-Mahmoud Ould Mohamedou, respectively, looking at the period before and after the fall of the Ottoman Empire and tracing the consequences of that transformative sequence over the next decades as statehood was unsuccessfully pursued across the region. Part Two, 'Irresolutions and Absences', delves into the specific key histories of Iraq, Palestine and the Kurdish issue. Faleh Abdel Jabar, Ahmad Khalidi and Jordi Tejel examine these different questions as vivid illustrations of the extent to which conflict and statehood were problematically entwined over this period. In Part Three, 'Reinventions and Returns', Bruce Rutherford, François Burgat and Bertrand Badie examine the ways in which the latter-day period in this search for statehood has featured different strategies with neo-authoritarian states, transnational armed groups and military interventions adding a new layer of complexity to that quest. Finally, a concluding chapter by Ghassan Salamé offers closing reflections on the trajectory so far of statehood in the region, and what can be envisaged in the next phase. The overall perspective put forth here is interdisciplinary with a central concern with international history and politics, and the necessary move beyond the 'area studies' dimension into international relations proper (as long called for by Bahgat Korany, among other). The chapters conclude not so much to the inevitability of the state but rather its centrality.

I wish to extend my appreciation to the president of the Pierre du Bois Foundation, Irina du Bois, for her funding of the conference. My heartfelt thanks go to the colleagues who took part and contributed so richly: Faleh Abdul Jabar, Anna Akasoy, Omar Ashour, Bertrand Badie, Joseph Bahout, Gopalan Balachandran, Amatzia Baram, Matthew Bamber, Jean-François Bayart, Karim Bitar, Riccardo Bocco, François Burgat, Benoît Challand, Stephanie Cronin, Hamid Dabashi, Jussi Hanhimäki, Ahmad Khalidi, Keith Krause, Bruce Maddy-Weitzman, Nadia Marzouki, Olivier Roy, Salman Sayyid, Adam Shatz, Jordi Tejel, Rim Turkmani and Maha Yahya, as well as Lisa Anderson for her kind foreword to this exploration. The discussions in which they all took part set this volume on its course.

I thank as well colleagues at the Graduate Institute for their valuable assistance, in particular my dear friend and colleague Davide Rodogno and my close collaborator Valérie Von Daeniken, as well as Atiya Hussain, Aditya Kiran and Catherine Fragnière. My thanks to Joel Alfred Veldkamp, a young scholar of the Middle East, for his kind assistance in the preparation of the chronology of events. Finally, my heartfelt thanks to my editor, Sophie Rudland, for her enthusiasm, support and patience all along.

This book is dedicated as ever to my parents, my beloved wife Shainese and my extraordinary children Bahiya, Kemal and Zaynab, and to the memory of Faleh Abdul Jabbar who, long ago, set me on this course.

Mohammad-Mahmoud Ould Mohamedou

PART ONE

FOUNDATIONS AND LEGACIES

1 A CENTURY OF ELUSIVE STATE-BUILDING IN THE MIDDLE EAST AND NORTH AFRICA

Mohammad-Mahmoud Ould Mohamedou

The period from the 1910s to the 2020s was a particularly important one in the long history of the Middle East and North Africa. From the Maghreb (the west) to the Mashreq (the east) reaches of the area, history seemed to accelerate during this century. History appeared to do so both in bringing long-festering, slow-building social and political tensions to a cusp and birthing new consequential ones, doing ever so indecisively and without a sense of closure. By the time the twentieth century closed and the twenty-first opened, the sequence had persisted. Analysis and study of the region remained as it had been, dominated by talk of unceasing armed conflicts, open-ended social crises, religious confrontation, ideological contestation and continuous political transformation. Though it had never really lost it all along, the region had in this new *fin de siècle* regained international policy and media attention, notably in the wake of the 1991 Gulf War following Iraq's invasion of Kuwait in August 1990 (an event coming ten months after the fall of the Berlin Wall). That crisis, which continued throughout the 1990s with the United Nations-enforced economic embargo on Iraq and its costly humanitarian consequences, then gave way to the 11 September 2001 terrorist attacks on the United States and the Global War on Terror, which in turn were followed by the 2011 Arab Spring and subsequent crises in the Levant, Egypt, Yemen and Libya. Following his election in November 2016, President Donald J. Trump added momentum to this sequence by adopting in January 2017 a so-called 'Muslim Ban', prohibiting citizens from seven Middle Eastern countries (Iran, Iraq, Libya, Somalia, Sudan, Syria and Yemen)[1] from entry to the United States, and launching in January 2020 a 'Deal of the Century' peace plan meant to solve the sixty-year-old Israeli–Palestinian conflict. For all their high-profile and urgent nature, these momentous events spanning the 1990s and early 2020s line up, however, more significantly in a historical sequence of developments, which can be traced back revealingly a century ago to the 1910s, and at the heart of which stands centrally the challenge of state-building combined with the primacy of foreign influence.

Against such latter-day and earlier backdrops, this book examines the question of statehood and its underpinnings in the Middle East and North Africa. Its starting point is threefold as it argues that, amidst nationalistic and religious contests and foreign interference, over the past one hundred years or so, the region of the Middle East and North Africa – in its generic understanding also referred to as the Arab world or the Orient[2] – has been wrestling primarily with the challenge of establishing cogent, performative, independent, representative and resilient states. This layered statehood conundrum played out in relation to several dimensions at the forefront of which stand three main founding historical developments: *regional imperial withdrawal, international colonial domination* and *domestic political struggles*. As the Mashreqi and Maghrebi Arab states, as well as the three non-Arab countries of the region (Iran, Israel and Turkey) all experienced a sequence of (i) end of the Ottoman Empire,[3] (ii) rise of Western colonial empires and (iii) emergence of local nationalist and religious movements, several questions that impact the search for statehood arose or were revealed problematically. The aim of this volume is to historicize this statehood trajectory by attempting an unpacking of the above three components against a dual interrogation: why so little statehood and why so much conflict?

Old orders and fleeting statehood

The past one hundred years can be characterized as a century during which the societies of the Middle East and the North African region have been overwhelmingly preoccupied with the project of the establishment of viable and functioning states. At times explicit and at times less so, that project was continuously crucial for them while constituting a distinct preoccupation for their larger international environment. In significant ways, the statehood project remains today a difficult, frustrating, divisive and incomplete endeavour. This shortcoming has also determined the imagery and phraseology resorted to in order to analyse the area. Problematic talk of 'fragile states', 'weak states', 'failed states', 'collapsed states', 'war-torn societies' and 'fractured lands'[4] continues to dominate representation of the region's political, economic and social scene. Where state apparatuses have been set up with a measure of stability, such apparent durability[5] was nonetheless achieved through the artifice of authoritarianism, which invariably – notably in Iraq and Syria, the twin enemy Ba'athist *mukhabarat* (intelligence services) states, or in Algeria and Egypt where the military continues to hold sway over all things political – sowed the seeds of its own crises to come.[6] For decades, these police state systems, divorced from their citizens aspirations for representation and better livelihood, seemed impervious to the internal and external pressures for socioeconomic and political change. In time, the deeply alienating dynamics the regimes had established only made the dead-end of these giants with clay feet more spectacular, as witnessed vividly with the fall of Tunisia's Zein Al Abidin Ben Ali, Egypt's Hosni Mubarak and Libya's Muammar Gaddafi 2011. Elsewhere, traditional so-called 'tribal-clanic systems', whether initially organized in the form of emirates, former Ottoman provinces or large regional confederations, evolved into state systems quite late during the second half of the twentieth century – doing so more in form than in substance, and often dragging a distinct 'tribes with flags' legacy into their uncertain statehood project, as the Egyptian diplomat Tahseen Bashir once termed it.[7] Similarly, the regionally all-important Palestine question itself – for all its identity, religious and geopolitical aspects – was and remains a state-formation dispute as well as an instance of quest for statehood for both Palestinians and Israelis.[8]

If Middle Eastern and North African statehood has been evanescent, it has been so not merely as result of the underperformance – real and consequential – of the local actors but equally and principally because of a specific historical configuration. The latter came into formation a century ago at the confluence of the three related-but-inherently distinct developments noted, namely the slow end of the Ottoman Empire, the violent encounter with the European colonial powers and the gradual rise of the local nationalistic and religious emancipation movements. In time, these three constellations came to preside over what we can term a *stateness deficit*, one that continues today to be determined largely by these strands. Eminently interrelated in their eventual consequences on statehood or the lack thereof, each of these three aspects of Middle Eastern and North African history, however, initially played out distinctly.

The so-called 'slow end' of the Ottoman Empire is the first and arguably most important of these stories, as it relates to the political and strategic milieu of the nascent, soon-to-be-elusive order. In retrospect, we can see that from about the mid-1860s the diminishing control of the Sublime Porte, as Istanbul was known, over the territories it had been administering directly or holding suzerainty over since the 1500s in the Levant, Arabia, the Nile Valley and the Maghreb both paradoxically enabled the rise of local autonomous movements for emancipation and rendered their project more arduous. The Ottoman twilight played out amidst a series of three successive failed attempts at reforming the empire: the military affairs-focused *nizam-i-cedid* or *nizam-e-jedid* (new order) in 1790–1807, the *tanzimat* (reorganisation) administrative reforms between 1830 and 1876 and the strategic political use of pan-Islamism in the period 1876 to 1908. Though it was ultimately unsuccessful – and fuelled the secular opposition to Sultan Abdul Hamid II led by the Young Turks movement known as the Committee of Ottoman Union, later renamed Committee of Union and Progress (CUP) – the combined historical territorial reach of the Ottoman provinces in the area and the nature of the transcendent religiously couched project, as well indeed as its 'reformist' claims, introduced a pattern whereby what can be termed 'backward-looking forward-moving' Islamist change could be articulated as a political project. One, too, that could be and would be pursued both by state and non-state actors alike. In time, it would be, as it were, precisely in those areas where Istanbul laid down the sword of the Caliphate in 1924 – in and around the Levant – that the organization of the Islamic State (IS) sought, in 2014, to reclaim it and re-establish that religious-territorial (by now also cyber-virtual) dominion.[9]

The Ottoman Empire's imprint – primarily present in the dynastic power matrix and heavy administrative structure that it left in the countries of the region (through the prisms of *sultan*, i.e. monarch, and *dawla*, i.e. state) – was accompanied by colonial experience at the hands of European powers. Often captured in reductionist ways in post-Arab Spring analyses heralding 'the end of Sykes-Picot' in the mid-2010s, the secret British-French-Russian agreement in 1916 and the League of Nations' Mandate System combined to introduce from the 1920s to the 1940s a second factor of structural historical disruption of the state-building project, namely external control and interventionism. To be certain, social and political events played out differently across the vast region, but the colonial impediment logic was more often than not systemically the same. In the Levant, the division of newly carved territories between Britain and France led to unrest starting in 1920 and running well into the late 1940s. Western action stunned and paralysed the domestic political power struggles, particularly between nationalists and Islamists – both now resultingly focused on the external arbiter – and cemented the role and place of violence as the chosen method to settle those struggles. Nowhere more than in Iraq (a country amalgamated in 1921 by the British from the former Mosul, Baghdad and Basra provinces of the Ottoman Empire, and given a Hashemite monarch, Faisal bin Hussein bin Ali al Hashemi, brought from the Hejaz by way of Syria, of which he was briefly king) were those dystrophies more visible. The trouble in Iraq built up continuously, ever more violently, during the monarchy years until the bloody revolution of July 1958, into the ruthless Ba'athi regime from July 1968 onwards and in the aftermath of the US invasion in March 2003. In the Maghreb, the Italian control of Libya (1911–1947) and the French one of Algeria (a department from 1830 to 1962), Tunisia (a protectorate from 1881 to 1956), Mauritania (a colony from 1904 to 1960) and Morocco (also a protectorate, from 1912 to 1956) yielded the same type of violent colonial dispossession experience formally ending in the early 1960s only to take new postcolonial forms. The brutality enacted by the British in Iraq was matched by both the Italian and the French, respectively in Libya and Algeria.

The past century was also importantly the scene of a virulent competition between societal projects throughout the region as nationalists and Islamists pursued different and antagonistic visions of nation and state. This existential contest played out amidst active external interference. Even if they tried by the mid-twentieth century to maximize their positions (individually as new states or jointly in regional organizations, notably through the League of Arab States established in 1945), the countries of the region were essentially in majority political systems set up by others and to the benefit of others. Dominated by a sense of peripherality in its very labelling (middle east, *medio oriente*, *moyen-orient*) and malleability (from the 'the Sick Man of Europe' in 1853 to 'the Greater Middle East' in 2004), the region's agency over its destiny and in particular its encounter with modernity was often hijacked by notions of alleged 'strangeness', 'dangerosity', 'volatility', 'instability' and 'violence', which became the familiar folkloric depictions of the area and simultaneously the geostrategic hallmarks of Orientalism. As Tarak Barkawi and Keith Stanski note:

> Orientalism [was here] not mere bias against Easterners; it [was] *a regime of truth*. Views that in fact amount to grotesque misrepresentation come to be accepted by the authorised experts and by those they communicate with. One such misrepresentation that sits at the core of historical and contemporary Orientalisms concerns the East as a site of disorder and the West as that which brings order to disorder.[10]

That site of disorder has often been identified as 'the Arab state'. These tenets also set the stage for the nationalist/military and the Islamist/insurgency dichotomous forces, which would come to compete indecisively in and for most of these theatres. As socio-historical entities in flux, these two camps – with many sub-fractions on either side (i.e., various denominations of nationalists and different Islamist currents) – were, in point of fact, none too different in their quest for forms of rule and political supremacy. They both sought to instrumentalize power structures for given projects rather than engineer actual states. Nationalists and Islamists were also similar in their populist appeals through ideologies of mass mobilization (in this case identity vs faith, i.e. 'who are you?' vs 'what do you believe in?'). As the post–First World War arrangements – encapsulated in the Sharif Hussein-Henry Mac-Mahon correspondence (14 July 1915 to 10 March 1916), the Sykes-Picot treaty (16 May 1916), the Balfour declaration (2 November 1917) and the Mandate System (inaugurated on 28 June 1919) – revealed themselves untenable, the next forty years would witness increasing clashes between nationalists and Islamists as they moved ever problematically towards the age of decolonization by mid-century.

Against the background of their respective intellectual trajectories during the nineteenth century,[11] nationalists and Islamists sought to present their societies with competing transocial conceptions about the nature of the state and the notion of political legitimacy. Whereas Arab nationalism was paradoxically at once a reaction to Western colonialism *and* a result of Westernizing reform – and therefore carried admittedly an element of statehood anchored in a feeling of cultural commonality (real or imagined) – Islamism in all its four configurations so far – early mobilization (e.g., Hassan al Banna's Muslim Brotherhood in the 1920s), post-independence militancy (from Egypt's Gama'at al Islamiya in the 1970s to Abassi Madani and Ali Belhadj's Islamic Salvation Front in Algeria in the late 1980s and early 1990s), globalized transnationalism (Osama Bin Laden's Al Qaeda in the 1990s and 2000s) and insurrectionary (post-Arab Spring in the 2010s, notably the Islamic State in Iraq and Syria) – invariably sought to reshape a legacy through (violent or non-violent) rupture from the classical Westernized view on the state.[12] In that sense, the Janus-faced ambition of Islamism has been to play out both as a liberating force (from the colonial West and then from the repressive states, often simultaneously) and as a restorative conservative movement (of the central place of religion in society, and of the Caliphate). It is important to remember that before jihadi Salafism, the contemporary version of Salafism (in North Africa notably) that emerged during the late nineteenth century and early twentieth century originally had a distinct anti-colonial expression and orientation (for instance, in Algeria and in Morocco).[13] With a violent armed group, the Islamic State in Iraq and Syria (ISIS), eventually overtaking that project in the 2010s to set up an 'Islamic State' – and doing so with an effective transnational influence on other militant groups across continents as well as on isolated individuals round the world – it remains to be seen in particular what lasting influence will that saga have on non-violent Islamist militancy in the countries of the region, and particularly so as the Middle Eastern and North African political transitions continue into the 2020s. Finally, the tentative set-up of states in the region also coincided with a period of global transformations intensifying and densifying during that same 1910s–2010s century.

A dual colonial mould

Why has the issue of the state remained such a gnawing question in the Middle East and North Africa? As noted, the period between the start of the twentieth century and the early twenty-first century marked a key moment in the history of region with a series of momentous transformations. During this phase, the foundations of the modern states of the region were to be established. This process was problematic, difficult and violent. Today, the systems that emerged stand as hollow structures filled almost solely by power and regularly assaulted by a variety of counter-power actors. The history of state-building in the Middle East and North Africa is a history of a colonially determined contest between nationalism and imperialism, and between nationalism and religion, but it is also a history of state versus society, and therefore time and again of power – a power struggle whose drivers were multiple.

The Middle East and North Africa experienced, as it were, a two-layered colonial experience: Ottoman and Western. Though the Ottoman presence in the countries of the Levant, in the Arabian Peninsula, in the Nile Valley and in the Maghreb is usually not understood as colonial in the same way as, say, the French or British ones – and if indeed the Ottoman Empire was itself a Middle Eastern entity – the fact is that Istanbul was a foreign occupying force in Arab lands and therefore clinically a colonial one in these regions. Whatever religious commonalities the Turkish occupiers enjoyed with the (Sunni) Muslim majority in these societies, these links did not alter the political fact of Istanbul's imperial projection over these territories and its political subjugation of their leaders. With such understanding in mind, we can see how much of the matrix, in which the Middle Eastern and North Africa state was designed, owes to the logic and practice of colonialism as a system. For instance, the naked and brutal language of power, which the new local authorities would themselves soon come to speak in the twentieth century, developed as the direct legacy of the combined and successive oppressive Ottoman and Western imprints. These two actors also regarded the Middle East and North Africa as a space (more precisely a number of related sub-spaces) onto which their power was to be projected, interests secured, populations subjugated, elites co-opted, culture and religion instrumentalized and economic benefits derived.

To be certain, the cultural traits the Ottomans shared with the Arabs and other local populations, and the religious authority Istanbul was exercising over Muslims, stand in substantial contrast to the exogenous European identity of the British, French, Italians and Spaniards who subsequently colonized different parts of the region. The alienating methods and violence of both Ottoman and Western empires were nonetheless similar in essence. Their combined effect on the socio-political milieu of Middle Eastern and North African societies and the mindset of their elites largely determined how power would be understood and how it would be practiced in the following decades – violently, arbitrarily, monopolistically and in the near-absence of accountability. Tracing the genealogy of the contemporary Middle Eastern and North African state, there is no overstating the importance of that influence and the reality of those links.

In truth, the driving force of the contemporary absence of the functioning, viable and cogent state in the region has been this *dual colonial authorship* which historically presided over the local state-building efforts. That exercise in (de)formation was launched amidst a history wherein the region was but destination, prize and bonanza. Such outlook, as brought on by both Ottomans and Europeans, would inevitably generate a similar outlook of exploitation on the part of the vast majority of the nationalist and post-colonial leaders. This was also the result of a far-reaching understanding of the 'purpose' of the region and its 'place' in the international system – that is the 'great game', as Henry Laurens termed it,[14] which it eventually came to represent. Just as was the case in North Africa, colonial expansion in the East was initiated as a combination of individual initiatives by so-called adventurers and by systemic logics of expansion. In the Maghreb, among many others, figures such as the Vendean traveller Paul Imbert exploring from Morocco as early as 1618 or the British Alexander Gordon pushing from Algeria in 1826 (in his case already using the Sahel as a destination for 'strategic depth') were among the forefathers of such logics of modern colonial penetration dictated by metropolitan policy concerns. 'Travelling' to the Orient has, in that regard, always been (and remained so quite late in the colonial sequence)[15] the entry point of indissociable mindsets of discovery and control. These two notions were reconciled and rationalized by a narrative also peddling the thought that the Middle East and North Africa area 'poses problems' to the West – and is thus to be controlled, or kept in check.

To this day, the idea of 'MENA' as a 'problematic' region of the world persists. On 20 January 2005, delivering the State of the Union address before the US Congress in the aftermath of Al Qaeda's 11 September 2001 attacks on New York and Washington, at the height of the inception of the Global War on Terror launched in response to those attacks, President George W. Bush declared: 'We have seen our vulnerability, and we have seen its deepest source. For as long as whole regions of the world simmer in resentment and tyranny – prone to ideologies that feed hatred and excuse murder – violence will gather, and multiply in destructive power, and cross the most defended borders and raise a mortal threat.' Then and now, calls for order abroad have always been coterminous with narratives about the 'barbarity of the native'.[16] Said dangerosity of the Middle East and North Africa – half-expressed here in cultural terms – is also linked to its alleged unreadability and its assertiveness, all of which, it is argued, need to be controlled and tamed. The Orient is a place – writes one analyst decrying the 'scandal of continuity' in analyses of the region – that is seen as 'too historical, literate, complex and self-confident to be turned into an ordinary subject matter'.[17] The lasting cultural constructions have incorporated the very geography of the region.[18] If the region is depicted in such an outlook, it is because the place fundamentally represented a political challenge, a contender long recognized by the West. As Tamim Ansary sums it: 'The Islamic world presented a particular complex psychosocial drama, first, because Western Europeans had a tangled history with Muslims already [since the Crusades at least], and second, because they started trickling into the Muslim world just as the three great Islamic empire were rising toward their peak of power and brilliance.'[19]

Informed by such historical depth demarcated by the end of the Caliphate, on the one hand, and an attempt to re-establish it, on the other, the 1910s–2010s period was the natural temporal arena on which these competitive dynamics landed. It is also where the respective armies of nationalism and religion – in part conjured up to push back against the occupiers, in part independently seeking supremacy over their societies-in-reconstruction – met and clashed. One should be wary, however, of the dangers of exceptionalizing this history, as it relates to the Ottoman Empire, Western powers, nationalists, Islamists or indeed statehood itself. Was, for instance, the 'fall of the Ottoman Empire' so clear-cut a decline as we often discuss it today, its imprint on the region so strong and therefore its influence over the local approach to statehood so consequential? As it were, the long 'decline' of the Ottomans was kick-started as early as 1536 with the signing of a series of commercial agreements, known as Capitulations or *ahidnâme* (bill of oath), between Istanbul and various European Powers, primarily France. These contractual agreements were largely beneficial to the Europeans. Importantly, they set in motion a sequence of Western gradual incursion into the Ottoman realm, with consuls, liaison offices and eventually military alliance with Germany notably. The shift was important and, in a Trojan Horse logic, arguably sealed the fate of the Ottoman Empire. It should be remembered that 'the Ottoman Empire [had] exercised considerable influence in European affairs, partly because of encroachments into European territory and partly because of its control of East-West trade routes. As a consequence, European states and particularly their merchants had always aspired to break the Ottoman monopoly on transregional trade and to appropriate profits for themselves.'[20] Later on, as noted, a lengthy period of attempted reforms generated political lethargy amidst growing discontent in Istanbul and beyond. By the early twentieth century, that discontent, best embodied in the Young Turks movement, had combined with four other key momentous series of events: the Great Arab Revolt led in Arabia by the Hashemites flanked by the British, the wave of nationalism in the Balkans, the virtual independence of the *bey* and *dey* chieftaincies and their principalities in North Africa and the turmoil and geostrategic competition from Russia. The important legacy of this lengthy sequence concerns centrally the sown seeds of division, the amorphous nature of the pre-national communities, the intensity and scale of rebellion as well as the pregnancy of identity and faith politics – all of which again landing squarely onto the statehood project in the region. It is important to stress anew that both the evolving structure of the Ottoman Empire (from a raiding *ghazi* state from the 1300s to the 1500s to a large administrative and bureaucratic entity subsequently) and its collapse were complex and multifaceted. This is key since the interpretation of the past taking place in contemporary Turkey, as well as in other post-Ottoman nation states, has often involved an exercise in selective memory presenting that empire in static and unchanging ways.[21]

Similarly, European colonialism to which most countries in the region were subject to is a determinant factor of the subsequent state-building sequence. European colonialism follows on, and in places overlaps with, the lengthy Ottoman control, but it is qualitatively different from it in its significant emphasis on violence, racism and de-humanization. In straightforward lineage, the post-colonial Middle Eastern and North African authoritarian state is the child of the dispossessive colonial state. The latter is the 'poisoned well', as one analyst called it,[22] from which these systems drank. Whereas the Ottoman Empire provided a matrix of authority and administration (*divan, vizir* and *awqaf*)[23] used by the predatory post-colonial state, European colonialism did also that but was most (de)formative of that state in its emphasis on security and the widespread and systematic use of repression. Italian concentration camps in Libya, British military campaigns in Iraq and French torture in Algeria determined that violence's choreography and tempo.[24] Such methods informed what in time emerged as the police state *mukhabarat* and *istikhbarat* systems of Muammar Gaddafi's Libya, Saddam Hussein's Iraq and the Front de Libération National (FLN) in Algeria, or those of Hafez al Assad's and Bashar al Assad's Syria or Hosni Mubarak' Egypt. Above and beyond the violence itself and more fundamentally, as Lisa Anderson remarks, is that, at independence, the rulers of the Arab world were not constrained by institutions actually designed to foster government accountability.[25] Such central trait of emancipation from democratic representativity further normalized the resort to power politics and the use of force; it in effect became second nature to these states.

Finally, there has long been a genuine danger of 'overstating the Arab state', to use Nazih Ayubi's phrase.[26] To be sure, many other forces determined and continue to define in different ways besides statehood what the Middle Eastern and North

African region emerged to be in the period from the late nineteenth century to the early twenty-first – and indeed whether this period is arguably so particular. Other explanatory variables attached to these variegated forces include political economy, civil society, identity politics and gender. All provide fundamental perspectives on this history allowing us to see the ins and outs of societal contests during the past decades. Similarly, the pursuit of statehood has at times been regarded as a one-dimensional political quest, whereas it was all along characterized by a diversity of perspectives and a plethora of actors; 'intellectual innovators during the formation of the modern Middle East were often landowners, merchants or professionals associated with the small but growing capitalist sectors that emerged, with variable orientations vis-à-vis the state, in the Ottoman Empire, Iran and Egypt'.[27] Because of such variety (a region 'too historical, literate, complex and self-confident' indeed), however, from the very beginning of this sequence, analyses of the region have also at time swung so far as to de-emphasize the role of statehood per se only seeing the role of groups. As Johann Büssow and Astrid Meier write:

> This tendency became even more pronounced when European powers institutionalised their rule over parts of the Ottoman Middle East in the age of colonialism. Many analyses of contemporary Middle Eastern culture and politics, as they are produced across the globe by academics and non-academic intellectuals today, still rely on easy but inaccurate representations of the importance of family, tribe and religious 'sect' as significant categories of social belonging in Middle Eastern countries, instead of confronting the difficulties of such categorisations.[28]

Or indeed replacing them under the umbrella of the state concept (an actor whose very *raison d'être* is to organize and control these actors). Similarly, the role of class has been de-emphasized ignoring what Adam Hanieh identifies as the intertwined development of class and society in the Middle East.[29] The state, however, has occupied and still occupies a particular *primus inter pares* place in this history. Immediately after the fall of the Ottoman Empire and throughout the rest of the century, it became successively a sacred objective, an object of detestation and a contested entity – all elevating its importance and endowing the issue with urgency. The centrality of the state in the region – and thus its inevitability and importance as an analytical lens – stems not so much from its actions but from the gaze so many had over it, the 'longing for it' as Ghassan Salamé argues.[30]

The quest for statehood in the region has been important for other reasons, chief among them is the naked use of force. To the extent that, as Stephanie Cronin remarks,[31] states are inherently coercive (principally by virtue of their activities related to taxation, order maintenance and legislation), such coerciveness was regarded by the Middle Eastern and North African elites as the way to turn their traditional, dynastic, religious or nationalist domination into an institutionalized supra-entity and a set of readily enforceable rule. Secondly, the very abstractness of the state – that entity that does not yet exist fully and which needs to be built – gave it useful malleability here. The new regimes could and would then align the design and functioning of that nascent state superstructure with their specific parochial interests. If, again, the focus on the state itself is not straightforward – 'the instability of much analysis of the region stems from the fact that it wanders from assessing an all-powerful state to unease about whether … it makes sense to talk of a state at all',[32] writes insightfully Fred Halliday – time and again, its centrality is unquestionable in this recent history.

The Middle Eastern and North African state is at once strong and weak, present and absent, visible and invisible. Its strength has rested in its capacity to impose itself brutally on its society and in its ability to weather all the storms of contestation and uprising for so many years. It is present in that obvious violent way, and yet it is weak and absent since such strength is superficial and such survival is ever so fragile, allowing it to remain merely alive from one crisis to the next. It is visible in the limits and demarcations it arrogantly puts before its populace, crowds standing at the gates of the insultingly grandiose palaces. It is invisible in the very way it functions, privately, secretly, nepotistically and incestuously. Accordingly, the history of the past century in the region has often been written as a series of political crises and conflicts revolving around the establishment of the state, the contest for it or attempts by domestic or foreign actors to influence it. For instance, one author identifies six such 'critical points':

> [T]he first … occurred between 1915 and 1922 with the McMahon-Hussein correspondence, the Sykes-Picot Agreement, the Arab Revolt, the Balfour Declaration, the Ottoman defeat during the First World War and the eventual partition of the Ottoman Empire and the establishment of the French and British mandates. The second critical turning point occurred in 1948 with the United Nations partition plan of Palestine and the 1948 Arab-Israeli war, which left Syria, Egypt and Jordan defeated. The third critical turning point occurred with the defeat of the Arab armies in the Arab-Israeli war of 1967. The fourth critical turning point occurred in 1979 with the Iranian revolution; the Israel-Egypt Peace Treaty; the seizure of the Grand Mosque in Mecca, Saudi Arabia; the Soviet Invasion of Afghanistan; and the sending of troops to help the Afghans. The fifth critical turning point occurred between 1987 and 1991 with the First Palestinian Intifada, the end of the Iran–Iraq War, the Soviet withdrawal from Afghanistan, the First Gulf War and the posting of US troops in the region and the dissolution of the Soviet Union. The sixth began with 9/11, the invasion of Afghanistan, the Iraq War and support of strategic partners … in the Global War on Terror.[33]

As events and phases, what these key moments point out to ultimately is the pre-eminence of the statehood factor. The primary drivers of this history are the design and composition of the state. Space is determined by borders and time is diplomatic, all derivative from state concerns and attributes. Revealingly, in the 2020s, not a single country in the region is immune from an overinflated external influence. Indeed, no other region in the world features such layered and multifaceted external interference.

Unsurprisingly, the history of the Middle East and North Africa over the past century can therefore be regarded as being bookended by two events symbolically signalling how the region has been and still is operating 'under influence' in international affairs; the 1916 British-French Sykes-Picot secret agreement to divide the Levant in their respective zones of influence with the agreement of Russia, and Donald Trump's 2020 so-called 'Deal of the Century' to bring peace between Israelis and Palestinians, also at a time of alliance between the American president and his Russian counterpart Vladimir Putin. Both events encapsulate the calculations and actions of external actors able to all-too-easily act dismissively of local political sovereigns, and establish, maintain or renew dominion over them, with the latter's complicity, naïveté, incompetence or corruption.

When in March 1915 a societally embattled Russia outlined its objectives for the survival of its empire as being 'strategic depth' towards Constantinople and the Dardanelles, this foreign set of concerns – driven by an accelerating, pre-revolutionary domestic crisis brewing since 1905 – was merely materializing to align with the designs of Britain and France over the region. These two countries' foreign policy objectives, which had existed since much earlier in both North Africa and the Middle East, could then logically come to coexist with Russia's, whose foreign minister, Sergei Dmitrievich Sazonov, signed on a year later on the agreement between Sir Mark Sykes and Monsieur François Georges-Picot. Much like the 1881 Berlin conference determined the political future of Africa for the next decades, the *longue durée* diplomatic time that followed that agreement (Moudros armistice in October 1918, conferences of San Remo and Treaty of Sèvres in 1920, creation of Israel in 1948, Suez crisis in 1956, oil shocks of 1973 and 1979, Iranian revolution that same year, 1990–1991 Gulf War, 11 September 2001 attacks, Arab Spring of 2011 and its aftermath) is largely in consonance with that impulse long ago.

When in December 2015 presidential candidate Donald Trump promised to declare a ban on Muslims if elected at the White House, he was weaponizing the sum of all hatreds towards Islam that a segment among the American population had been building up since the 11 September 2001 attacks on New York and Washington, as well as replaying and furthering a colonial imaginary. In North Africa, France had built an imperial republic whose vision and practices were anchored in a representation of Islam as inferior and dangerous,[34] and Italy had done the same in Libya. Elsewhere in the Middle East, the United Kingdom and France had acted similarly in the Levant. The 1920 allocation of the mandates over Syria and Iraq took place in a context of explicit and immanent racism, which persisted with the League of Nations.[35] All along and all over, the issue of power has presided over this sequence, and this has coloured the local statehood story.[36] Resultingly, the Arab state was forged in the matrix of the Western colonial state.

The latter's practice of power functioned on the basis of expansion, centralization, militarism and exceptionalism.[37]

Half-births

If the mid-1910s can be regarded as a founding moment of contemporary Middle Eastern and North African politics, it is because the events that played out during those years remained a forceful referential. Fifty years later, as the region would embark on a new moment led this time not by the colonial state but by its illegitimate postcolonial state offspring, the dispossessive vision set in motion at the start of the century had all along remained operational. In 1961, the success of the Hollywood film *Lawrence of Arabia* would symbolically reveal how much of that Orientalist vision was still appealing to Western military supremacy shrouded in alliance and emancipation. As David Barber remarked, '*Lawrence of Arabia* would be a *cri de cœur* from the dying colonial empire – an explanation for its death, a lament over its loss, a justification of its prior existence and a call for its enlightened continuation.'[38] Amidst such European desire for continuity – or active resistance to change, as seen in the case of Algeria where the Organisation de l'Armée Secrète (OAS) was organized to conduct terrorist operations to thwart French President Charles De Gaulle's independence agreement with the Algerian FLN – the next decades would witness the in-built fragility of these 'half-born' Middle Eastern and North African states. Such sequence would play out well into the early twentieth century. The consequential nature of this state incompleteness would be revealed to be initially the result of a disintegrative colonial project from without combined with the societal experience of authoritarianism which came to dominate these systems from the 1960s onwards. As noted, this would further strip the statehood project of its potential democratic representation component, as the new regimes would regularly and unabashedly exercise power on the mode of arbitrariness in lieu of accountability. To a large extent, the new state's centralized structure around a strong man (e.g., Gamal Abdel Nasser in Egypt, Muammar Gaddafi in Libya or Habib Bourguiba in Tunisia) was also the product of the patrimonial and patriarchal orders that characterized the societies of the region. As Diane King explains:

> In the twentieth century, as the modern state developed in the Middle East, patriliny became the basis of citizenship ... [Patriliny] lasted longer in the Middle East region than elsewhere.. [and] the Middle Eastern states recognised patrilineal succession in far more specific categories than citizenship: religion, sect, ethnicity and even residence itself ... Moreover, patriliny has served as a basis for legitimacy that is deployed in a wide variety of ways by state leaders.[39]

Today, a century after the modern-day state-building project was launched in the region, the stories continue to play out amidst neo-authoritarianism and coercive democratization.[40] During this whole period of the second half of the twentieth century, the process of state-building was difficult to observe as a cogent, viable and lasting experience with consistent, reliable and resiliently reproduced state structures. Rather, it remained eminently elusive, a journey whose waystations were but crises, wars and uprisings – all signposts of incomplete statehood fuelled first and foremost by its coercive nature. Importing the state after decolonization – or rather inheriting that Western version of it – of necessity meant boosting the military.[41] And so, liberated from the anti-colonial struggle, the new state was free to turn its attention to another venue of violence, its own society. In the late 1950s in Iraq, Egypt and Syria, and later in Libya, the 'military option' and authoritarianism were widely welcomed by the urban population as the only way of creating a national 'power' able to resist Zionism and imperialism. Likewise, in the three countries, wide sections of the intelligentsia legitimized the military coups and the resulting regimes (*al andhima*).[42] Within twenty-five years, the Algerian FLN had squandered the aura of legitimacy that the national war of liberation had bequeathed onto it. By 1988, a week of riots in Algiers in October of that year revealed vividly the dead-end of the empty project nationalism had become for most Algerians, notably the unemployed youth. In the same vein, whereas the early days of pan-Arabism had opened possibilities for an international 'third way', bringing together Arab, African and Asian nationalists, the postcolonial Arab states ultimately failed to engage with internationalist movements, such as pan-Africanism or Black-Palestinian transnational solidarity movements, leaving these imaginaries to civil society.[43]

In so doing, the postcolonial elites were fundamentally unable to link decolonization with the question of citizenship, namely to choose to help their populations shift from (colonial) subjects to (independent) citizens, politically as well as legally and indeed psychologically. Had this happened, it would have been the most resilient way to preserve the nascent states and bolster their legitimacy. Instead, the regimes opted for a superficial existence which relied on their largely symbolic opposition to Israel and their mere presence in international society. In that regard, Michael Barnett has argued that, in the second part of the twentieth century and notably as result of the 1967 defeat:

> Arab states, which are now routinely characterised as having a 'real' existence and basis in society, seemingly have agreed on some basic 'rules of the game' that are associated with the norms of sovereignty ... The consolidation of sovereignty and the emergence of a 'centrist' conception of Arab nationalism enabled Arab states to develop relatively stable expectations and shared norms, that is, to foster regional order.[44]

Yet this so-called Arab regional order that had emerged then – conservatively, negatively and with minimal expectations – was for all practical purposes a myth. Neither nationalism per se nor the League of Arab States as an organization[45] were ever able to produce a cogent and articulated vision of a common future beyond such passive presence in the international system. To separate the discussion of that 'order' from the notion of state-building is to extract the power issue of its natural and most consequential domestic context. In effect, as Avraham Sela noted, 'the capability of regional systems to establish normative order of security and stability should be perceived as a dependent variable of *entwined historical processes of state formation and international conflicts*.'[46]

Rather, the regimes were invariably on the lookout for new devices to control their populations. If, by the early twenty-first century, 'security' had become the be-all of politics, in the mid-twentieth century, the regimes were using myth and history itself, specifically nationalism shrouded as 'history', as a way to entrap their people. As Anwar Chejne wrote contemporaneously in 1960:

> [H]istory has become to some degree an instrument in the hands of the newly-arising states. It aims at the diffusion of an historical consciousness through the revival of the past and the glorification of its heroes and accomplishments. History has been approached with a definite orientation for improving the present and setting firm foundations for the future. The impact of the West has definitely played a role in this orientation, as a response to a challenge, a parallel development, an actual influence on Arab intelligentsia, or a combination of these three.[47]

Such nation-building chimeras serve primarily the regimes' survival throughout the first generation of post-colonialism. At the tail end of that sequence, the end of the Cold War opened a new phase in which all the dystrophies of the previous thirty years would come together, vividly illustrating the impasse of the postcolonial state. As noted, that entity had been the offspring of the colonial state. It used and abused a narrative centred around nation and identity, which rapidly showed its limits and alienated the economically aggravated societies. By the late 1970s already, popular culture in the form of comedic Egyptian theatre plays (*masrahiyyat*), televised around the Arab world, was sarcastically poking fun of public authorities and their dogmatic language of 'revolution' (*thawra*), 'reform' (*islah*) or 'opening' (*infitah*) – much like subversive Eastern European literature under Communism (e.g. Milan Kundera's *The Joke*) was subtly mocking the totalitarian state.[48] As noted, in October 1988 in Algeria, the 'children of the revolution' generation, youth born in the 1960s, rioted for days in Algiers – doing so literally on the grounds of the city's Martyrs' Square, erected in memory of the fallen for independence – demanding a better future. The FLN's obvious failure was that of all the region's regimes. Saddam Hussein's invasion of Kuwait less than two years later only served to further illustrate the collapse of Arab nationalism. Once again, interference accompanied the sequence as the US military intervention in 1991 and the subsequent embargo on Iraq were additional instance of domestic and external dispossession. But if the postcolonial Middle Eastern and North African state was stuck in looping authoritarianism – in 1992, in response to the riots and the successful political rise of the Islamic Salvation Front (FIS), the FLN yielded to the military who led a coup and unleashed repression on Algeria birthing the *décennie noire* (dark decade) civil war until 1998[49] – Western interventionism was, for its part, about to be rebooted.

The 11 September 2001 terrorist attacks on the United States conducted by Osama Bin Laden's Al Qaeda allowed the George W. Bush administration to launch a Global War on Terror (GWOT), which persists to this day. The military and imperial nature of that campaign spelled further impediments to the project of statehood in the Middle East and North Africa. The invasion of Iraq by the United States and the United Kingdom in March 2003 was the key moment in this sequence. Amidst a global moment of rising Islamophobia and anti-Arab feeling, the Middle Eastern state was shown for what it had come to be, or rather remains, half a century or so after decolonization, namely an object of direct or indirect control by Western powers. Over the next decade as transnational radical Islamism, led by Al Qaeda and its offsprings chief among them the Islamic State, raised hell across the region and around the world, the local states were becoming mere spectators to this sequence of regional political, social and security degeneration.

The 'war on terror' only served to fuel further the domestic uproar across the region. In time, the epitome of the Arab police state, Zein al Abidin Ben Ali's Tunisia, unexpectedly took the lead in a series of revolts known as the Arab Spring, which shook the region to its core in 2011 and within months caused the fall of Ben Ali, Libya's Muammar Gaddafi and Yemen's Ali Abdallah Saleh. Syria's Bashar al Assad managed to mount a resistance with the support of Russia, and the tacit acceptance of Western powers, which initially called for his removal, more concerned by Islamist radicalism than secular authoritarianism. The Arab Spring was an unprecedented moment of social empowerment in the region, notably as regards the youth and women. The movement also took place in the context of a changing grammar of transnational politics. This took the form of the rise of a new era of social activism, and particularly of solidarity politics, which were facilitated by innovations in information and communication technologies that allowed grassroots movements to connect with sympathizers around the globe.[50] For all their acuity and momentum, but for Tunisia, the revolts did not however succeed in reversing the course of the authoritarian state in the region. The Gulf monarchies brutally brought to a halt the uprising in Bahrain and pumped money into their societies further buying off their people's happiness and chasing out the question of a just and rights-respecting social contract. Arguably, because the monarchies had promoted neither populism nor pan-Arab nationalism, they were not as jeopardized by their failure.[51] The post–Arab Spring movement also revealed the extent to which the youth opposition movements could be creative and impactful during the uprising phase but inefficient, divided and often hollow politically during the transitions that followed. Mesmerized by the wizardry of their own technology, these e-revolutionaries used social media not so much to imagine alternative statehoods but merely to conduct guerrilla warfare on the regime – efficiently but often in politically sterile ways.[52]

By the mid-2010s, the authoritarian Middle Eastern state had staged a comeback. Saudi Arabia stood as the unassailable fortress of a despotism to which the United Arab Emirates also gave globalized, tech-savvy and modernized clothes. As the revolt in Syria turned violent and was overtaken by the Islamic State project – constructed simultaneously as quasi-state, insurgency and terrorist campaign[53] – Bashar al Assad played the 'bulwark against terrorism' card deftly, receiving the support of many in the West. He combined that survival tactic with protection he garnered from Russia's Vladimir Putin who was seeking to bring an end to the American Middle East.[54] A century after the Tsar, another Russian leader was similarly seeking strategic depth in the Middle East, equally with a view to protect his annexation of Crimea in March 2014. If the reassertion of the authoritarian state was well on its way before the Arab Spring at the occasion of the Global War on Terror,[55] the Arab Spring and the 2014 migration crisis allowed then that predatory state to renew its lease on Middle Eastern societies. What the Arab Spring fundamentally revealed was that the features of the military had in effect become part of the very mechanics of the state itself.[56] Force, hierarchy, implementation and bureaucracy were rebooting the cartography of that barren state supremacy installed midway into the twentieth century, only this time with the urgency of extraordinary measures, state of siege and the sacrosanct 'fight against terrorism' of the post-9/11 era.

Internationally, the great powers acted in variegated ways to reassert their power over the region, just as they had done a century ago. The 2011 Libya intervention was the opening salvo of a period wherein conflict would return to areas of imperial rivalry rather than isolated events of ruthless despots crushing subject populations.[57] Interventionism became a 'new game redux,' as Bertrand Badie argues.[58] As Dierk Walter sums it up:

> [M]ost informed contemporaries would doubtless concur that 'humanitarian interventions' and the 'War on Terror' of recent decades have few if any parallels in the campaigns of colonial conquest and punitive expeditions conducted during the 'age of imperialism', if only because there are no longer any Western empires that are taking possession of overseas colonies. Even in de facto protectorates like Iraq or Afghanistan, Western nations have refrained from redrawing the map of the world in the manner of the late nineteenth century. However, from the perspective of a longer-term history of the exercise of power and force in the modern world, such constitutional distinctions conceal certain fundamental structural continuities.[59]

Indeed, if, in the most immediate sense, imperialism manifests itself in the division of world among rival powers,[60] the newfound interventionism by both the United States and Russia in the region confirms the materialization of a new imperial moment.

With the Trump administration ascendancy to power, neo-authoritarianism was cemented in the Middle East and North Africa – even as a Muslim Ban was adopted in January 2016 with no protest on the part of the major Arab and Muslim countries' governments.[61] The United States turned a blind eye or directly supported reinvigorated autocrats such as Abdelfattah al Sisi in Egypt, Mohammed Bin Salman in Saudi Arabia and Mohammed Bin Zayed al Nahyan in the United Arab Emirates, while, in the Maghreb, Libya's post-Gaddafi chaos persisted, and in Algeria, the military was able to survive another wave of mass national protests in 2019–2020.

Conclusions and departures

Against this historical canvass, a series of questions arise. The main one concerns statehood itself: its past, present and future in the region. What, ultimately, is that state that somehow should be built in this region of the world? Beyond the lasting politico-security coerciveness and socioeconomic intrusiveness of the Middle Eastern and North African regimes, what sort of social contract can be engineered constructively so as to establish viable, lasting and representative states?

As the state's history is traced and its potential future is imagined, consideration of state elusiveness should not fall prey to a sort of fetishization of the Westphalian nature it would be expected to adopt or the Weberian traits it ought of necessity display. The particular nature of the half-born Middle Eastern and North African states provides us with an opportunity to think beyond Western statehood. There is more to the state in this region than dynastic lineage versus republicanism, regimes versus armed groups, civil society versus elites, or indeed nationalists versus Islamists.[62] For all its modernization dynamics and the demand for statehood, the state can lose currency even before achieving full supremacy. Similarly, statehood is not necessarily subject to a linear logic.

The 1910–2020 history of the state in the Middle East and North Africa is but a specific experience impacted by the given actions of domestic and foreign actors, in a context of transforming international relations. Ultimately, whether in the Middle East and North Africa or elsewhere, the state is fundamentally an umbrella notion and one that, here, has only been a subject of historical concern for a century. In the final analysis, as the chapters in this volume endeavour to, discussion of statehood in the Middle East and North Africa must embrace its complexity and its paradoxes.

Notes

1. Formally known as Executive Order 13769 Protecting the Nation from Foreign Terrorist Entry into the United States, the order was signed on 27 January 2017. On 31 January 2020, six other countries were added to the list of countries targeted with restricted travel: Eritrea, Kyrgyzstan, Myanmar, Nigeria, Sudan and Tanzania. In December 2020, President-elect Joe Biden promised to revoke the Muslim ban, and did so, once elected, on 20 January 2021.

2   As Giorgio Hadi Curti notes: 'As much as the region loosely stands together and endures in the popular and academic mind with somewhat simplified and essentialising representations, there is very little material extant coherency to its very geographical name'; see his 'The Middle of Where? Media Geography and the Middle East', *Aether*, VIII, B, September 2011, p. 2.
3   Mauritania and Morocco did not experience Ottoman rule. Morocco enjoyed a lengthy pre-colonial evolution in the stateness realm; see Susan Gilson Miller, *A History of Modern Morocco*, Cambridge: Cambridge University Press, 2013.
4   For an illustration, see the *New York Times* August 2016 series for the period 2003–2016, Scott Anderson, 'Fractured Lands: How the Arab World Came Apart', *The New York Times*, August 2016.
5   Eva Bellin, among others, covered this aspect in her article 'The Robustness of Authoritarianism in the Middle East: Exceptionalism in Comparative Perspective', *Comparative Politics*, 36, 2, January 2004, pp. 139–58.
6   See, notably, Eberhard Kienle's study, *Ba'th vs. Ba'th – The Conflict Between Iraq and Syria, 1968-1989*, London: I.B. Tauris, 1990; and Olivier Schlumberger, ed., *Debating Arab Authoritarianism – Dynamics and Durability in Nondemocratic Regimes*, Stanford, California: Stanford University Press, 2007.
7   The phrase inspired several works such as Charles Glass, *Tribes with Flags – A Dangerous Passage through the Chaos of the Middle East*, New York: Atlantic Monthly Press, 1990.
8   On that aspect, and looking at the Palestinian side, Rashid Khalidi speaks of 'two failures of state-building – one in the past and the other ongoing' (p. ix); see his 'Writing Middle Eastern History in a Time of Historical Amnesia', in *The Iron Cage – The Story of Palestinian Struggle for Statehood*, Boston: Beacon Press, 2007.
9   See the works of Reza Pankhurst (*The Inevitable Caliphate*, 2013) and Salman Sayyid (*Recalling the Caliphate*, 2014) on this issue.
10 Tarak Barkawi and Keith Stanski, 'Introduction: Orientalism and War', in Tarak Barkawi and Keith Stanski, eds., *Orientalism and War*, London: Hurst and Company, 2012, pp. 5–6, emphasis added.
11 Transnationalism was present even then with European influences (Johann Fichte and Giuseppe Mazzini impacted the thinking of the likes of Rifaa al Tahtawi, Abderrahman al Kawakibi and Sati al Husri) flavouring the Arab nationalism debate and Asian ones the Islamist discussion in the region (Jamal al Din al Afghani's views on a modern Islamic state fed into the philosophies of Muhammad Abdu, Rashid Ridha and Hassan al Banna).
12 See Mohammad-Mahmoud Ould Mohamedou, 'In Search of the Non-Western State: Historicising and De-Westphalianising Statehood', in Bertrand Badie, Dirk Berg-Schlosser and Leonardo Morlino, eds., *The SAGE Handbook of Political Science – A Global Perspective*, London: Sage, 2020, pp. 1335–48.
13 Ricardo René Laremont, 'Sufism and Salafism in the Maghreb – Political Implications', in Osama Abi-Mershed, ed., *Social Currents in North Africa*, London: Hurst and Company, 2018, p. 41.
14 Henry Laurens, *Le Grand Jeu – Orient Arabe et Rivalités Internationales depuis 1945*, Paris: Armand Colin, 1991.
15 See Ali Behdad, *Belated Travelers – Orientalism in the Age of Colonial Dissolution*, Durham, North Carolina: Duke University Press, 1994.
16 One such early political-security myth was the claim made by British agents that Ibn Saud's irregular forces had killed 400,000 to 800,000 people – a genocide, in effect – during their conquest of Arabian Peninsula. For a debunking of that claim, see Jeff Eden, 'Did Ibn Saud's Militants Cause 400,000 Casualties? Myths and Evidence

about the Wahhabi Conquests, 1902-1925', *British Journal of Middle Eastern Studies*, February 2018.
17 Judith Scheele and Andrew Shryock, 'On the Left-Hand of Knowledge', in Judith Scheele and Andrew Shryock, eds., *The Scandal of Continuity in Middle East Anthropology – Forms, Duration, Difference*, Bloomington, Indiana: Indiana University Press, 2019, p. 10.
18 See Diana K. Davis, ed., *Environmental Imaginaries of the Middle East and North Africa*, Athens, OH: Ohio University Press, 2013.
19 Tamim Ansary, *Destiny Disrupted – A History of the World through Islamic Eyes*, New York: Public Affairs, 2009, p. 219.
20 Tareq Y. Ismael and Jacqueline S. Ismael, *Government and Politics of the Contemporary Middle East – Continuity and Change*, London: Routledge, 2011, p. 23.
21 Stefano Taglia, 'Ottomanism Then and Now: Historical and Contemporary Meanings – An Introduction', *Die Welt des Islams*, 56, 2016, p. 288.
22 Roger Hardy, *The Poisoned Well – Empire and Its Legacy in the Middle East*, London: Hurst and Company, 2018.
23 Ministry, high official and philanthropy.
24 See Claudio G. Segrè, *Fourth Shore – The Italian Colonisation of Libya*, Chicago: Chicago University Press, 1975; Peter Sluglett, *Britain in Iraq – Contriving King and Country*, New York: Columbia University Press, 1976; and Alistair Horne, *A Savage War or Peace – Algeria, 1954-1962*, New York: New York Review of Books, 1977.
25 Lisa Anderson, 'The State and Its Competitors', *International Journal of Middle East Studies*, 50, 2, 2018, p. 319.
26 Nazih N. Ayubi, *Over-Stating the Arab State – Politics and Society in the Middle East*, London: I.B. Tauris, 1995.
27 Ewan Stein, 'Beyond Arabism vs. Sovereignty: Relocating Ideas in the International Relations of the Middle East', *Review of International Studies*, 38, 2012, p. 898.
28 Johann Büssow and Astrid Meier, 'Ottoman Corporatism, Eighteenth to Twentieth Centuries: Beyond the State-Society Paradigm in Middle Eastern History', in Bettina Graf, Birgit Krawietz and Schirin Amir-Moazami, eds., *Ways of Knowing Muslim Cultures and Societies – Studies in Honour of Gudrun Krämer*, Leiden: Brill, 2019, pp. 82–3.
29 Adam Hanieh, *Lineages of Revolt – Issues of Contemporary Capitalism in the Middle East*, Chicago: Haymarket Books, 2013, p. 9.
30 See Ghassan Salamé's chapter in this volume, 'Chapter Ten: Longing for the State, Mistrusting the State'.
31 See her *Armies and State-Building in the Modern Middle East – Politics, Nationalism and Military Reform*, London: I.B. Tauris, 2014.
32 Fred Halliday, *The Middle East in International Relations – Power, Politics and Ideology*, Cambridge: Cambridge University Press, 2005, p. 29.
33 Nayef R. F. Al-Rodhan et al., *Critical Turning Points in the Middle East, 1915–2015*, New York: Palgrave MacMillan, 2011, pp. 8–9.
34 See Olivier Le Cour Grandmaison, *Ennemis Mortels – Représentations de l'Islam et Politiques Musulmanes en France à l'Epoque Coloniale*, Paris: La Découverte, 2019; and *La République Impériale – Politique et Racisme d'État*, Paris: La Découverte, 2009.
35 See the discussion of this by Robert Vitalis, *White World Order, Black Power Politics – The Birth of American International Relations*, Ithaca, New York: Cornell University Press, 2015, notably Chapter Four, 'Imperialism and Internationalism in the 1920s'.
36 See, for instance, the analysis in Mehran Kamrava, *Inside the Arab State*, London: Hurst and Company, 2018.

37. See Fatemah Alzubairi, *Colonialism, Neo-Colonialism and Anti-Terrorism Law in the Arab World*, Cambridge: Cambridge University Press, 2019, especially Chapter One, 'On Imperialism, Colonialism and Neo-Colonialism', pp. 19–49.
38. David Barber, 'Lawrence of Arabia: A Dying Empire's Cri de Coeur', *Film and History*, 47, 1, Summer 2017, p. 28.
39. Diane E. King, 'Patriliny and Modern States in the Middle East', in John L. Brooke, Julia C. Strauss and Greg Anderson, eds., *State Formations – Global Histories and Cultures of Statehood*, Cambridge: Cambridge University Press, 2018, p. 311. Also see, notably on the Levant, Elizabeth Thompson, *Colonial Citizens – Republican Rights, Paternal Privilege and Gender in French Syria and Lebanon*, New York: Columbia University Press, 2000.
40. As discussed, for instance, in Juan Cole's chapter in Shahram Akbarzadeh, James Piscatori, Benjamin MacQueen and Amin Saikal, eds., *American Democracy Promotion in the Changing Middle East – From Bush to Obama*, London: Routledge, 2013.
41. See David B. Ralston, *Importing the European Army – The Introduction of European Military Techniques and Institutions into the Extra-European World, 1600–1814*, Chicago, Illinois: University of Chicago Press, 1990.
42. Hamit Bozarslan, 'Rethinking the Ba'thist Period', in Jordi Tejel, Peter Sluglett, Riccardo Bocco and Hamit Bozarslan, eds., *Writing the Modern History of Iraq – Historiographical and Political Challenges*, London: World Scientific, 2012, p. 143.
43. See, for instance, Noura Erakat and Marc Lamont Hill, 'Black-Palestinian Transnational Solidarity: Renewals, Returns and Practice', *Journal of Palestine Studies*, 192, XLVIII, 4, Summer 2019, pp. 7–16; and Alex Lubin, *Geographies of Liberation – The Making of an Afro-Arab Political Imaginary*, Chapel Hill, North Carolina: University of North Carolina Press, 2014.
44. Michael N. Barnett, 'Sovereignty, Nationalism and Regional Order in the Arab States System', *International Organization*, 49, 3, Summer 1995, pp. 480–1.
45. See, Mohammad-Mahmoud Ould Mohamedou, 'Arab Agency and the UN Project: The League of Arab States between Universality and Regionalism', *Third World Quarterly*, 37, 7, July 2016, pp. 1219–33.
46. Avraham Sela, 'The Vicissitudes of the Arab States System: From Its Emergence to the Arab Spring', *India Quarterly*, 73, 2, 2017, p. 147, emphasis added.
47. Anwar G. Chejne, 'The Use of History by Modern Arab Writers', *The Middle East Journal*, 14, 4, Autumn 1960, p. 383.
48. Among the key Egyptian plays were, notably, *Madrasat al Mushaghebeen* (The School of the Mischievous, 1973), *Shahad Ma Shafsh Haga* (The Witness Who Did Not See Anything, 1976), *Al Motazawegoon* (The Married, 1978) and *El Eyal Kebret* (The Children Have Grown Up, 1979).
49. See Mohammed Samraoui, *Chronique des Années de Sang*, Paris: Denöel, 2003.
50. Anne Garland Mahler, *From the Tricontinental to the Global South – Race, Radicalism and Transnational Identity*, Durham, North Carolina: Duke University Press, 2018, p. 203.
51. Michele Penner Angrist, 'The Making of Middle East Politics', in Michele Penner Angrist, ed., *Politics and Society in the Contemporary Middle East*, Boulder, Colorado: Lynn Reinner, 2019, p. 23.
52. On the digital activism, see Tarek El-Ariss, *Leaks, Hacks and Scandals – Arab Culture in the Digital Age*, Princeton, New Jersey: Princeton University Press, 2018. Also see Mohammad-Mahmoud Ould Mohamedou, 'Neo-Orientalism and the e-Revolutionary: Self-Representation and the Post-Arab Spring', *Middle East Law and Governance*, 7, 2015, pp. 120–31.

53 See Scott Englund and Michael Stohl, 'The World versus Daesh – Constructing a Contemporary Threat', in Michael Stohl, Richard Burchill and Scott Englund, eds., *Constructions of Terrorism – An Interdisciplinary Approach to Research and Policy*, Oakland, California: University of California Press, 2017, pp. 208–21.
54 See Brian T. Edwards, *After the American Century – The Ends of US Culture in the Middle East*, New York: Columbia University Press, 2017; and Steven Simon and Jonathan Stevenson, 'The End of Pax Americana', *Foreign Affairs*, 94, 6, November/December 2015, pp. 2–10.
55 On pre-Arab Spring neo-authoritarian dynamics in the region, see Oliver Schlumberger, ed., *Debating Arab Authoritarianism – Dynamics and Durability in Nondemocratic Regimes*, Stanford, California: Stanford University Press, 2007; and Stephen J. King, *The New Authoritarianism in the Middle East and North Africa*, Indianapolis: Indiana University Press, 2009.
56 Khaled Abou El Fadl, 'The Praetorian State in the Arab Spring', *University of Pennsylvania Journal of International Law*, 34, 2, 2013, p. 307.
57 Sagar Sanyal, 'Closing the R2P Chapter – Opening a Dissident Current within Philosophy of War', in C. A. J. Coady, Ned Dobos and Sagar Sanyal, eds., *Challenges for Humanitarian Intervention – Ethical Demand and Political Reality*, Oxford: Oxford University Press, 2018, p. 216.
58 See his analysis in Chapter Nine of this volume, 'Authoritarianism, Weakness and the New Great Game'.
59 Dierk Walter, *Colonial Violence – European Empires and the Use of Force*, London: Hurst and Company, 2017, p. 2–3.
60 Emanuel Saccarelli and Latha Varadarajan, *Imperialism – Past and Present*, Oxford: Oxford University Press, 2015, P. 57.
61 See Clara Eroukhmanoff, 'It's Not a Muslim Ban! Indirect Speech Acts and the Securitisation of Islam in the United States Post-9/11', *Global Discourse*, 8, 1, 2018, pp. 5–25. Eroukhmanoff remarks that 'security actors do not always need to invoke a security language of enmity to securitize. On the contrary, securitisation can be successful by mobilising a language of amity' (p. 22).
62 The latter opposition – Islamists versus liberals – was itself once a potentially bridgeable division in the name of democracy, as Elizabeth F. Thomson shows in her discussion of Syrian actors circa 1920. See her *How the West Stole Democracy from the Arabs – The Syrian Arab Congress of 1920 and the Destruction of Its Historic Liberal-Islamic Alliance*, New York: Grove Atlantic, 2020.

2 THE WESTERN QUESTION

Henry Laurens

In 1922, the young Arnold Toynbee published his first significant book, *The Western Question in Greece and Turkey – A Study in the Contact of Civilisations*, simultaneously the result of his field research the preceding year and a draft of what would become his major work, *A Study of History* (1934–61). In this initial text, the British historian undertook a kind of Copernican revolution by substituting the so-called 'Eastern Question' with the 'Western Question'. Toynbee began with a consideration that remains valid a century later: Near-Easterners – read Greeks and Turks – were certain that Westerners were fascinated by the course of events in the East. Unable to believe that one might feel distant from what is happening to them, Toynbee argued, the Near-Easterners insisted (of course erroneously) that the immense effects, which were being produced all the time in the East by Western action, must be the result of policy; it was inconceivable that they could be unintentional and unconscious.[1]

Toynbee did not linger on what could be an incipient definition of the 'Western Question', tacitly understood as the confrontation or cooperation of Western powers between themselves for possession of the East. He noted that the people of the region interpreted the Greco-Turkish War as an Anglo-French war. There is some truth to this affirmation; the Western powers were indeed the protagonists of this war from a distance and the suffering populations its pawns. Toynbee imagined a fictional drama titled 'The Patriots', portraying characters such as the Czechoslovak politician Tomáš Garrigue Masaryk, the Greek statesman Eleftherios Kyriakou Venizelos, the Bulgarian militant Aleksandar Stambolisky, the Polish leader Józef Pilsudsky, King Faysal I of Iraq and the Turkish field marshal Mustafa Kemal as men living in a dream like Britain's William Pitt and France's Napoleon Bonaparte, after which the scene would shift to a representation of reality in the offices and hallways of the Quai d'Orsay or Downing Street. To this he added the position of observers: a powerless chorus of commentators like himself.[2]

What interested Toynbee was the latter aspect: the Westernization of the East via the adoption of the nation-state formula. However, the absence of a homogenous population founded on a language community in the East transformed that formula into a factor of violence, as demonstrated by the conflicts in the Balkans and the massacres in Anatolia and beyond in the period 1913–22. A century later,

Arnold Toynbee's analysis remains just as relevant and pertinent as it was then. It defines a dual internal and external factor of transformation of so-called Middle Eastern societies, while simultaneously demonstrating their interdependence and the chorus of powerless commentators that have indeed spread to the research community.

The international relations factor

Academic literature on international relations in the Middle East and North Africa has largely been concerned with relations between external 'patrons' and internal 'clients'. The question generally posed is who ultimately 'manipulates' whom. There is no general rule, only specific cases. A strictly historical approach, which we will adopt here, has tended to be by and large absent.

Contrary to the Balkan part of the Ottoman Empire, the Arab provinces were long preserved from European political actions well into the eighteenth century. Europeans enjoyed access to a number of places of commerce, so-called 'Ports of the Levant' (*Échelles du Levant*),[3] but these actors' participation in the local political games was initially negligible. Consuls could accord 'protection', but this arrangement often carried little practical weight. On the contrary, they themselves needed protection to avoid being affected by the vagaries of power struggles within their provinces. Consular correspondence is filled with complaints of the 'slights' (exactions) inflicted by local powers, about which the central authority could generally do little, given the continuous progress of Ottoman decentralization. What tied the Arab provinces to the central authority in the eighteenth century was a common 'Ottoman-ness' bearing the weight of legitimacy. It was a sort of *avant la lettre* commonwealth system where Constantinople provided or withheld legitimacy to local authorities. In certain cases, the latter could take the form of proto-states (e.g. the neo-Mamluk in Egypt,[4] Iraq and the province of Acre).

The great shake-up came in 1770 with the arrival of a Russian fleet from the Baltic region in the eastern Mediterranean. After destroying the Ottoman fleet at the Battle of Chesme on 6 July 1770, the Russian force succeeded in maintaining and resupplying itself by striking alliances with local Ottoman powers: the Greeks of the Peloponnese and the Mamluks of Egypt (who had been attempting to take control of Syria). Eventually, the fleet retreated after the peace treaty in 1774. Significantly, for the first time, a foreign power had succeeded in building a formal alliance with local Ottoman powers. This event must be understood in its global context. During the Seven Years' War (1756–63), the British won the Battle of Plassey and on 23 June 1757 seized Bengal. From that event onwards, they began to build their Indian empire. During the same period, France lost its possessions in North America, and in the 1770s the British colonies of North America began to revolt. For the essayists of the time, it became clear that Europe's history in the New World was 'coming to an end'. These commentators also noted that after

Plassey and the Russo-Turkish war of 1768–74, no Eastern power was any longer in a position to resist a large-scale European military projection.

The question became then whether the Ottoman Empire would face the same fate as India. In that context, the Empress Catherine II initiated a so-called 'Greek Project' – the reconstitution of a Byzantine Empire to be handed to her grandson, Constantine – as well as an Orthodox Balkan state and the granting of 'compensations' to the other great European powers.[5] France could thus 'receive' Egypt, an enterprise King Louis XVI's entourage was rather hostile to. Indeed, the king's minister of foreign affairs, Charles Gravier de Vergennes, sought instead to reinforce the Ottoman Empire as a bulwark to Russian advances, which involved upgrading the Ottoman army by dispatching French military missions on location. However, the French soon enough reckoned that the military institution could not be separated from the rest of the Ottoman state. The French initiative thus turned to the set-up of printing houses and the teaching of modern military affairs science related to emerging so-called 'Learned Arms' (*armes savantes*; primarily artillery and engineering).

Fundamentally, however, the French proposal was concerned with the export of the modern European state project that the men of the Enlightenment, through 'enlightened despotism' and 'reforms', had undertaken. In the texts of the time, the Russian reference was constant: for all practical purposes, an Ottoman Peter the Great was anticipated. This perspective was not lost on Selim III and his entourage: the survival of the empire would pass through its integration into a European system of equilibrium and the modernization of its military apparatus, which included a reform of the state as a whole. By the end of the eighteenth century, the Western Question had now become endowed with intertwined internal and external aspects, and it featured centrally the question of statehood.

The revolutionary and imperial period defined the primary traits of this duality. The wars of the First Coalition (1792–7), which European powers fought against the new French Republic, momentarily suspended interest in the survival of the Ottoman Empire. It was, however, in this moment that the Europeans recognized that the secret to British strength lay in its Indian possessions, rather than in its financial capacities or indeed what would later become the Industrial Revolution. This evolved perspective was one of the motivations behind the French Campaign of Egypt and Syria (1798–1801). The British regarded that campaign as a major threat to their newly acquired territories in India, while Austria and Russia could hardly accept the seizure of the Ottoman Empire by the same revolutionary France they had been fighting.

The expanded wars of the Second Coalition (1799–1802) – still pitting European powers against France – then projected Europe's political space to the edge of the Indus Valley, making the regions that spread from the Mediterranean to India factors of European balance of power. For those who would defend the Ottoman Empire, in this case the British, it was necessary to modernize one's army. Those who would fight against it, in this case France, would stand as liberators of oppressed peoples and as the 'civilizing' instrument of the world. Again, the Eastern Question was given in terms of geostrategy, war and statehood. During the following wars, the Ottomans were on the side of the French, standing against the British and the Russians. The Ottomans' active diplomacy allowed them to escape the hornet's nest by concluding a peace treaty with the Russians, signed in 1812 in Bucharest. Their knowledge of Europe progressed in parallel, in particular, thanks to the reports sent back by the first permanent embassies before the European courts.

Dismantling the old order

As long as European superiority, expressed in terms of power, was analysed only as the product of technical factors, which one could simply borrow to confront a given danger, the old Ottoman order did not need to be questioned but only corrected according to the needs of the moment. Such was the essence of Ottoman military reforms under Selim III and Mahmoud II, as with their counterparts in the autonomous province of Egypt, Mehmet (Muhammad) Ali and his son Ibrahim Pasha. From the 1820s onward, the Muslim power then increasingly started adopting the phraseology of 'civilization' in the light of the various pressures exerted by the Europeans. As had been the case with the European *ancien régime*, the old order was doomed as a result of such changed mindset implying wider and deeper transformation. In particular, the military institution had to adopt a conscription system to satisfy the new military institutions' needs for men, which abolished the functional distinction between 'soldier-rulers' (*askeri*) and the governed.[6] Similarly, the establishment of an effective tax system implied an equal status of Ottoman subjects, abolishing the distinction between the governors and the governed.

The fundamental 'systemic' rupture came, however, from societal dynamics, notably from the opposition between Muslims and non-Muslims. In that respect, the so-called 'Greek Revolt of 1821' was first and foremost a revolt of the Orthodox against Muslim supremacy across the empire. Atrocities took place on both sides, motivated in part by the capture of the property of the vanquished. Accompanying the revolt was an ideological discourse of the resurrection of Ancient Greece, particularly useful in attracting the support of European public opinion. It then became an 'Eastern crisis', a political mobilization tied to humanitarian disasters and resting on ideological discourses including the necessity for urgent intervention.[7] This resulted in a marked shift in international diplomacy from mediation in search of a political solution to a series of military interventions between 1828 and 1831.

The 1820s constituted a critical moment. To satisfy the principle of nationalities, the Greek Orthodox and Philhellenists proceeded with the 'invention' of Greece, defining the movement as the resurrection of a people rather than an uprising of a religious nature. The impulse given to such 'invention of tradition' was then taken up by the different Balkan peoples – the Serbs, the Romanians, the Bulgarians and, later, the Albanians – who all undertook their own 'resurrections' in turn. The genesis of the new nation-state took place with terrible violence, including massacres and ethnic cleansing. Balkanization (the term itself first appeared in 1919) became a procession of appalling violence extending at least to the end of the twentieth century with the collapse of Yugoslavia.

Following the Greek revolt, the Ottoman civil war pitting Mahmoud II against Mehmet Ali was as much a struggle for power, as an opposition of civilization models, or in more contemporary vocabulary, modernization ones. In Syria, Ibrahim Pasha abolished de facto distinctions between Muslims and non-Muslims and established an identical taxation system for all sectors of the population. His attempt at a modern state set off a number of revolts which, between 1840 and 1841, rested on British military intervention. Mehmet Ali's propagandists thus opposed a pragmatic modernization to that of Mahmoud II, which was radical in the texts but often powerless in practice. As such the old order, which the 1839 Edict of Gülhane was meant to do away with, progressively gave way to a new society with significant discrepancies among the Empire's regions. From the 1840s, Ottoman decision-makers accompanied re-centralization work with a discourse in which they were bringing 'civilization' to more or less backwards provinces implicitly defined as barbarian. The critical factor is the understanding that the movement was as much exogenous (borrowed from Europe) as endogenous, with the emergence of new social groups competing for power. Added to this was a significant demographic growth constantly revising the composition of spaces, which continues to the present day. This growth was tied to the progress of the modern state, an entity looked upon as abolishing the secular obstacles to population increase.

The emancipation of non-Muslims

In defining the relationship between exogenous and endogenous factors, one must take into account evolutionary synchronism. The question of non-Muslims in the Ottoman Empire was tied to the exogenous through the protections offered by European powers (France thus claimed a 'protectorate for Catholics, Russia one for the Orthodox'), the ongoing emancipation model of non-Christians (primarily the Jews) for whom recognition was based on individual status and the freedom to worship. Simultaneously, this dimension was tied to the endogenous one through the prosperity of already well-structured non-Muslim groups which tended, particularly in the Balkans, to pass from the confessional to the ethnic through the invention of tradition (the non-Hellenists being unable to call upon a prestigious Antiquity, even for the Romanians who claimed descent from Daces, resorted to popular culture to define the ethnic group).

The Crimean War (1854–6) started as an Ottoman Empire 'rescue operation' in the face of Russian ambitions. The immediate issues concerned Christian populations. France and Great Britain therefore negotiated an emancipatory edict published in 1856, establishing a confessional community for non-Muslims as a state institution with a religious head (a Patriarch and, by extension, a Chief Rabbi), a community council of elected notables and specific personal status. Emancipation on community rather than individual basis led inexorably to community representation in public institutions, based on supposed demographics. Importantly, the edict of 1856 carried the seeds of a confessional political system. Far from being the inheritance of an ancestral history, the confessional community was now seen as the product of nineteenth-century modernity (although its foundations were laid much earlier) with, as response, Sunni Islam increasingly defining itself as state religion and religion of the state. In effect, Western and Eastern societies were facing the same questions at the same time: the emancipation of non-Christians (Jews) or minority Christians (Catholics in Protestant countries) was synchronous with the emancipation of non-Muslims. Evolutionary synchronism here underlines the fact that despite demands for the same order, responses took place on a significantly different basis.

The confessional community could appear as a means of coexistence for different groups in the same space. However, the Balkan Orthodox confessional community broke down into distinct and opposed nations, and the same process later extended to Anatolia where Christian communities defined themselves increasingly as nations with a territorial dimension. By the end of the nineteenth century, Balkan violence spread to Anatolia with a new flare-up of atrocities that resulted in the destruction of Anatolian Christianity during the fateful decade of 1912–22. Thus, in the Ottoman space, *the community gave birth to the nation*: a Turkish-speaking Armenian became an Armenian, a Greek-speaking Muslim a Turk. There were, however, two major exceptions: the Albanians and the Arabs who, not without difficulty, developed cross-community nationalisms.

The inevitable West

The opposition between European powers made it impossible to establish direct colonial dominance. Great Britain guarded jealously the fictitious line that was the imperial route to India, of which the Eastern Crises of 1832–3, 1839–41 and 1854–6 were the manifestations. The Arab provinces were subjected to a collective tutelage of the European powers represented by their local consuls. These representatives were in permanent competition for influence, creating a sort of constant agitation that, back home, the ministers of foreign affairs ironically called the 'consular illness' (*morbus consularis*). This played out at the lowest local level: a quarrel between a Maronite farmer (protected by France) and a Druze farmer (protected by Great Britain) risked sparking an international crisis.[8] The same occurred with a brawl between Catholic and Orthodox monks. In the relative insecurity ruling over certain regions at the time, local Muslim notables could establish alliances with consulates and receive a protected status.

After 1860, Ottoman authorities began a pacification process, providing populations with a new sense of security. At the same time, the central authority refused to recognize the protections accorded to Muslims, considering them an infringement on the Caliphate. A diplomatic dispute enriched the archives, but overall, this time, the Ottomans prevailed. Consular protection was essentially limited to non-Muslims, thereby completing the emancipation process. In the period after 1880, the Consuls and the Ottoman Governor would come to an understanding to limit damages in case of a confessional incident. The former would take charge of those they protected and issue sanctions as needed, while the latter would do the same for the Muslims involved. As the Anatolian violence echoed loudly locally, and putting aside the massacres of the Armenians,[9] it did not repeat itself thanks to the effectiveness of this mechanism.

The triangle of power constituted by the consuls, notables and the governor and his representatives allowed for the creation of alliance games under such governance scheme. The governor might need consuls in his relations with the central authority or, on the other hand, could ask them to act in coordination with the embassies to limit consular interventionism. Notables were now more on the side of governors but could seek out support from the Consuls.

It is amidst such statehood-in-the-making that the provinces entered the first wave of globalization. The global telegraphic network arrived at the tail end of the 1860s and in the early 1870s. Ports connected by rail with regions inland, although the interconnection of the networks would not be completed before 1914. These same ports were now linked with the northern bank of the Mediterranean through regular steamboat lines. From Beirut, it became easier to access Marseilles and then, through Paris, transatlantic ports. A significant Arab emigration took place, particularly Christian, heading to the Americas and later to West Africa and Australia. Jewish emigration from Eastern Europe was also able to reach the Holy Land. Emigrants discovered new lands and new ideas.[10] They remained in regular contact by mail with their villages of origin, which were better acquainted with world geography than French villages of the same period.

Arabs and Turks

The emergence of an Arab political identity is a complex phenomenon. Originally, Arab identity was based on genealogy, with a reference to the tribal groups of the Arabian Peninsula implicitly identified with Bedouinity. The Arabization of the Fertile Crescent regions led to the phrase 'children of the Arabs' (*awlad al 'arab*). During the classical Ottoman era (before 1800), religious identities were more important (between Muslim and non-Muslim) even if regions of Arab populations were sometimes defined as *Arabistan*. The social elites of these areas were tied only loosely with the Ottoman regime, with the exception of the officials who were in charge of controlling the local populations. All along, the Arabic language remained a language of cultural prestige, endowed with unique status in the Ottoman world and beyond.[11] The provinces which separated the Arab regions from the rest of the Ottoman Empire, before succumbing to European domination, such as Tunisia and Egypt, gradually developed a regional nationalism through a mechanism which precisely fused the Ottoman elite with local notables. The Arab provinces of the second half of the nineteenth century did not, however, have a state apparatus promoting regional nationalism, but rather an official doctrine of Ottomanism, that is to say a common Ottoman identity running in parallel with those nationalistic feelings.

The spread of printing led to the emergence of a more standardized modern form of the Arabic language (as was the case for Ottoman, which drew closer to spoken Turkish). Christians, who thanks to missionaries accessed modern education more easily, played an essential role in this intellectual renaissance. The confessional violence of 1860–1 in Lebanon and Syria brought out the necessity of going beyond a confessional framework to achieve the emergence of a common identity. The invention of tradition and of statehood drew from different sources. The European Enlightenment defined a historical narrative making the Arabs and the Middle Ages the predecessors of Europeans in the history of civilization. Philologists of the second half of the nineteenth century discerned a collection of languages and cultures with common traits that was to be defined as the Turanian whole. European Orientalism thus paradoxically provided the sociohistorical narrative essential to the genesis of the very Arab nationalism that would be opposed to it politically. At the same time, the combined action of archaeology and philology brought forth ancient civilizations which up to that point had remained, at best, distant legendary memory: Pharaonic Egypt in the 1820s, Assyria and Mesopotamia in the 1840s, Phoenicia in the 1860s, and Sumer and the Hittites around 1880. Intellectuals were thus faced with the necessity of taking into account millennia of supplemental history, with the added complexity that a great deal of these resurgent civilizations were grouped under an umbrella defined as Semitic.

The traumatic shock of European supremacy further put on the table the question of religion, which was also a sanctuary of identity. Reformers of Islam made use of the Protestant European reference, particularly as nineteenth-century Protestantism was regarded by many contemporaries as the epitome civilization, in contradistinction to Catholicism which was looked upon as having rejected 'modern civilization'.[12] If Protestants turned towards the first generation of Christians, Muslims could do the same for their own history, some argued. Here it was (divisively) noted that the first generations of Muslims were Arabs and that in some way, corruption arrived with the Persians and the Turks … The formulation of the Medinan utopia was thus inspired by a European model, claimed by the first generation of reformers who searched in the history of Europe itself a path to be followed.

At the beginning of the nineteenth century, the term 'Turk' served to designate the Anatolian farmer and 'Arab', the Bedouin. At the end of the century, progress in print technology, the associated widespread cultural renaissance, the simplification of language during the shift from manuscript to print and the use of references stemming from European orientalism led to the definition of two different types of peoples – those inclined towards modernity and those less so (even if, in this period, Arab nobility was associated with the management of the Empire). Arab identity was not alone in the running. The Lebanese, especially Christians, invoked a specificity that expressed itself in a Phoenician claim. The nomadic/sedentary binary found itself in the opposition between 'Syrians' and 'Arab Bedouins', and Syrianism would for a long time become a competitor to Arabism. A uniquely Palestinian identity emerged in the confrontation with Zionism.

The emergence of the new states

The Young Turks Revolution of 1908 established a more or less regular political life across the Ottoman Empire. One part of the Arab elite disassociated itself from the new regime and called for decentralization, which, if the Balkan examples were to be followed, could lead to autonomy and subsequently independence. That segment of the Arab population sought outside support and was compelled to turn towards France, the hegemonic power of the Syrian space (on 18–23 June 1913, an Arab Congress was held in Paris at the initiative of a group of Arab notables and students to discuss envisioned reforms in the region).

The Great War accelerated the ongoing events from the point of view of imperial projects, but it also gave momentum to national aspirations. In 1920, diplomatic arbitrage led to the materialization of the Mandate System. Britain and France determined the geographical borders within which the new states emerged. The local elites who participated in this action found themselves simultaneously or successively face-to-face with the might of imperial powers. Those powers undertook the real work of state-building, but had to contend with the logic of their own imperial system and the demands of European political alignments. The abolition of the Ottoman Caliphate, de facto in 1918 then de jure in 1924, made Sunni Islam the state religion, but other Muslims would not accept this domination and in turn demanded their own emancipation. (The Ottomans had held the Caliphate since 1517, and had claimed it since 1362.)[13] As a result, the Islam of the Near East (i.e., the non-Sunni Muslim communities of heterodox communities such as Shi'is and Alevis) structured itself on the model of nineteenth-century non-Muslim communities. The independent regional state thus collided incipiently with the problem of communitarianism.

Nonetheless, British hegemony temporarily suspended the games of implication and involvement which had prevailed prior to 1914.[14] The 'Middle East',[15] as it then began to be called, was no longer thought of by strategists in London as territories to be administered, but as a set of networks officially defined as the 'imperial communication routes': the Suez canal, straits, land and air routes, and pipelines. States needed now to pass treaties to attain greater autonomy, but the local British representative always exerted an influential force on internal political life – which manifested itself economically, politically, culturally and militarily.

Fascist Italy attempted to question this hegemony, but the Arabs rejected the colonial ambitions of Fascism. Nazi Germany and the Soviet Union attracted a few Arab personalities, but these two powers remained distant and without genuine ambitions in this part of the world. It was at this point that the Arab States' crisis of legitimacy developed. In the interwar period, Arab nationalism equipped itself with a doctrinal corpus that questioned the new states of the Great War. However, these states increasingly acquired a tangible reality that made strangers of the other Arabs. From the 1930s, any unitary project was *also* perceived as the hegemonic project of a local actor.

The geographical space of the region was now layered geopolitically. The creation of Saudi Arabia in September 1932 consecrated the independence of a large part of the Arabian Peninsula to the detriment of the Hashemites who were pushed further north in Transjordan and in Iraq. Egypt discovered itself as being of Arabic language and then Arab. North Africa began to feel the call of Arab nationalism. By the mid-1930s, this new reality took the name of the 'Arab world', spreading from the Gulf to the Atlantic Ocean. The Second World War bore the marks of a strong British determination to resist the enemy with an authoritarian steadying of control over these theoretically independent states. Some Arab nationalists saw in Nazi Germany the means of delivering themselves from Franco-British domination, but they were followed by few. On the other hand, the arrival of the Americans as of 1942 was perceived as that of a new reliable partner able to overturn that British and French colonial control.

The post–Second World War period was widely seen indeed as an opportunity to complete emancipation from foreign domination.[16] The independent Arab States, including Syria and Lebanon, were founding members of the United Nations in San Francisco in October 1945. This moment would, however, be short-lived. The British, supported by the Americans, sought at once to integrate the Middle Eastern region in their defence efforts against the Soviet Union. Regionally, that move was perceived, largely accurately, as a desire to perpetuate a now-unbearable British hegemony. Above all, it was the Arab–Jewish conflict over Palestine that demonstrated the limits of Arab means of action. The belligerent states of the 1947–9 conflict enjoyed no outside support, with the British withholding any assistance, the United States providing diplomatic support to Israel and allowing their nationals to provide it with considerable financial aid, as well as the Soviet Union and France delivering weaponry to the nascent State of Israel. Political isolation and inter-Arab rivalries were the direct causes of defeat.

After 1949, hope for independent sovereign states turned to resentment in the face of such persistence of international interference. Revolutionary movements fed off the sentiment and brought an end to what was retrospectively called the 'liberal era'. The new model for statehood became a modernist authoritarian regime with the declared ambition of social and economic development. The notion of catching up with the West remained present, and playing on the rivalries between the two great world blocs appeared even credible. Thus, the conflict with Israel had to go through an end to the Western 'monopoly on weaponry'. Turning towards the Eastern Bloc, the Arab States found the means to continue the fight but at the cost of embedding themselves in the Cold War – with the consequence that neither of the two blocs could accept a decisive victory of one of the parties. Likewise, a political solution implied a coming together of these two blocs, which was impossible to realize. The conflict was therefore condemned to persist in an enduring impasse defined as neither war, nor peace, and this framed further Middle Eastern statehood under international developments. This was illustrated further with several regional crises throughout the 1960s and 1970s in Kuwait, Yemen and Lebanon notably. Political engineering was implemented per an interventionist model: 'Arabization' (through Arab mediation) or internationalization (by way of UN or great powers mediation), or oftentimes both at the same time. The Western Question was simultaneously pursued in international rivalries (after all the Eastern bloc was only a second West) and in the proposed development models.

Largely on the basis of the Capitulations model, the nineteenth century had seen the institution of a colonial model of exchange in the Middle East: manufactured products for raw plant and eventually mineral materials. Foreign economic investment in the region was subsequently concentrated on the implementation of modern means of communication: ports, railways and roads, all completely reshaping the traditional space to the benefit of coastal areas. The inter-war period allowed for the definition of a new policy built on industrialization by import substitution. The region equipped itself with its first independent banks. However, the international financial crisis of the 1930s consolidated the attachment of the region to the Pound Sterling, with the exception of Syria and Lebanon in the Franc Zone. The Second World War favoured this industrialization, which was taken on by the private sector even if Great Britain had planned the entire regional economy during the war.

The revolutionary authoritarian regimes (in Syria, in Iraq, later in Egypt, Algeria and Libya) continued this industrialization by substitution but nationalized the modern sectors of the economy. The incapacity of these news Arab nations to create a common open economic area limited their industrialization to internal markets composed of state monopolies. Paradoxically, such inward-looking policy reintroduced mechanisms of dependence. Due to a lack of exports, the financing of intermediary goods came to depend heavily on foreign aid which, for a while, came from both Eastern and Western blocs in international competition with one another, a dynamic cynically coined 'positive neutralism'. Oil revenues began to affect the region as a whole at the end of the 1960s. The Arabian Peninsula became a centre encompassing all the Arab peripheries, if not beyond. Instead of importing capital, the area became a capital exporter in the name of recycling petrodollars. The strategic importance of the Gulf came less from its geographic position than from its wealth of hydrocarbons. By the end of the twentieth century, the rentier economy had triumphed.¹⁷ Oil producing countries provided financial assistance to their Arab partners to gain influence. Remittances from workers who immigrated from other parts of the Arab world to the Gulf (Egyptians, Palestinians, Sudanese, North Africans) became essential sources of funding for their countries of origin. In such a context, Western aid was calibrated according to the supposed geopolitical importance of Arab partners. Arms purchases allowed for making industrialized countries dependent upon purchasing states to an extent where one could speak of a political economy of 'mercenarization'.

The companies of the oil-producing states of the Arabian Peninsula were composed of social strata that, to a certain extent, could be considered 'ethnoclasses' (that is, an identification per a certain number of social functions to a geographically common origin). The associated Westerners belonged similarly to a relatively privileged group of so-called 'expatriates' who worked in industrial and commercial sectors and whose presence was temporary by nature. They consisted of the most important civilian population of Western origin in the Middle East as a whole.

Islamism and authoritarianism

The end of the Cold War could have marked a decline in geopolitical competition in this region of the world, and thus of the Western Question. This did not occur. Iraq's Saddam Hussein, struggling in its war against Iran (the First Gulf War of 1980–8), succeeded in provoking a Western coalition, assembled in the name of protecting access to oil. Hussein's subsequent invasion of Kuwait in August 1990 led to a new coalition under Saudi initiative,¹⁸ this time against Baghdad. This Second Gulf War created a second permanent region of tension that would lead to the Third Gulf War in 2003. After decades of independence, where the priority had been to remove Western military presence – the symbol of a hated past, the 1990s saw the return of Western military bases in the Gulf at the behest of some local states themselves, in the name of their own security imperatives. The distinction between implication and involvement is difficult to perceive here, as this situation re-energized opposition of the political Islam type.

Political Islamism had presented itself from the outset as much as a reaction to Western presence – in particular, its cultural influence – as an instrument of struggle for power. Contrary to the anti-imperialism of Arab nationalism, which had had a universal calling (Bandung Conference of 1955, the Tricontinental Conference of 1966 and the Non-Aligned Movement), the anti-imperialism of Islamism was distinctly limited to the world of Islam and the fight against 'cultural aggression' defined as a plot hatched against the *umma* (nation). Accordingly, Islamism was much more obsessed by the West than Arab nationalism. The 'Islam is the solution' (*al islam huwa al hal*) utopia is the demonstration of an omnipresent reference to the West. Despite references to the ancient Islamic corpus, Islamists desperately attempt to make Islam counter-Western, rather than a self-standing political project centred on itself. It may be said that this is the latest expression of the invention of tradition elaborated in relation to the West.

Jihadism transferred the struggle outside of the geographic limits of the Muslim world by using the weapon of terrorism. In turn, it has ignited a strong Islamophobia fed by references to discourses of identity. Beyond terrorist violence, the conflict has extended to women's bodies and the different forms of sexuality recently allowed for in the West. In the struggle surrounding the norms that the West continues to produce, it is possible to find contradictory alliances in the name of intersectionality, within a sort of alliance of minorities. This harkens back to the question of universality and its limits. The so-called 'exact sciences' of the Western nineteenth century, due to their effectiveness, had sublimated the ancient knowledge of other cultures (notably, the Arab legacy of mathematics, physics and astronomy). The only way to appropriate them was to define them as universal. It was more or less the same for the forms of social organization, which, for internal as much as external reasons, led to the creation of the modern state. What remain are the norms and values going back more or less specifically to the post–1945 renovated Western democracy. This democracy has found itself contested by resorting to specific cultural referents: Islamic, Indian, Asian or African values. However, there has been a resistance to see that these referents were themselves produced by the colonial system. The irony is that much of what claims to be 'decolonial' is enclosed itself into the colonial mould and its shaping vocabulary, particularly so with the notion of statehood.

The Middle East and North Africa is today largely dominated by authoritarian political systems. Some see this as a manifestation of idiosyncratic religious and cultural traits. Yet the former Ottoman Empire space had seen the materialization of a liberal era, which, even if it remained largely unrealized, had allowed for the constitution of a liberal intellectual corpus.[19] Contemporary Middle Eastern and North African authoritarianism is located at the juncture of multiple processes. The first is the raised consciousness of a 'delay' with regards to the West, leading to what could be defined as an 'authoritarian modernism' – a notion that essentially argues that access to modernity must be imposed by force on a recalcitrant society. This was the case of the Ottoman reforms throughout the nineteenth century, Kemalism in the early twentieth century and Arab and Iranian nationalisms in the second half of the twentieth century and into the twenty-first century. Under this logic modernity will be authoritarian, or it will not be.

The second determinant of the region's authoritarianism is a product of the game of implication and involvement. All pluralist systems reproduce within themselves regional and international political cleavages, as the Palestinian and Lebanese cases demonstrated. The result is to make a 'war of others'. As a result, dictatorship becomes the guarantor of national independence. Nasser theorized this perspective, a position incidentally favourable to him in his struggle for regional power. The third aspect is the rentier economy. The state finances itself through a number of funds that it redistributes, in part to purchase social peace.

The relative absence of taxation justifies the absence of representation. Rich countries can thus finance the authoritarian regimes in the region, which are subject to them. The final element is the one of security and stability. Authoritarian regimes define themselves as maintaining a stability perpetually threatened by recurrent threats such as terrorism and Islamism. When necessary, they trigger them. Today, practically all political regimes of the Arab East define themselves through their so-called 'fight against terrorism', an umbrella notion that engulfs all forms of real opposition.

To these general factors, a set of at least three Western demands is added. First is the security of oil provisions as demonstrated by the successive Gulf Wars. Second is the security cooperation against terrorism. This experience has demonstrated that once an Arab country is in a situation of instability, terrorist actions spread in Europe. This was the case of Algeria in the 1990s and Syria after 2011. Third is the fight against immigration. The Mediterranean Arab States are called on to act as barriers to African and Asian migration, and we have seen the extent the Libyan 'breach' of that deal could take since 2011. These demands support the constitution of a strong power and place us in the usual trap: authoritarian regimes are indispensable to face crises, but it is their very existence that provokes the crises.

Conclusion

One can only grasp the Western Question by simultaneously addressing its internal and external aspects. Externally, the issue plays out in a triangular set of relations: the state and the foreigner against the people; the state and the people against the foreigner; and the foreigner and the people against the state. We have seen these combinations take shape in the years after 2011. The Syrian War saw the multiplication of heterogeneous coalitions and, from a liberation struggle, it became a war for others. Internally, the temptation of the West continues despite the protests of Islamists. The profound will of the populations is for social and political rights. To the extent that this is frustrated by the regimes, the choice is emigration towards a largely fantasized West (it is sufficient to observe migrants' attraction to Great Britain to grasp the irrationality of certain choices).

In a sense, two twin utopias today translate the persistent Arab malaise. There is a Western utopia defined by political and social rights, and expressing a universality of human rights, and an anti-Western utopia – that of the Islamists – who claim authenticity while borrowing the idea itself from the West. The remedy to this situation lies in the demand for democracy on the ground, expressed by the whole of society in the face of authoritarian powers, where the only legitimacy rests on the maintenance of order and viable statehood. The counter-revolutions thought they had carried the day after 2011, but the resurgent pushbacks into the 2020s have demonstrated that this demand for democracy can always resurface.

Notes

1. Arnold Toynbee, *The Western Question in Greece and Turkey – A Study in the Contact of Civilisations*, Boston: Houghton Mifflin Company, 1922.
2. 'Perhaps the chorus of spirits would be composed of impotent Western observers like myself', ibid.
3. These cities and ports of the Ottoman Empire were managed under a regime wherein the Sultan – in exchange notably for the recognition of his rule over the Anatolian peninsula – had renounced to some of his commercial prerogatives to the benefit of European, mostly French, merchants. European port cities such as Marseille benefitted greatly from the economic consequences of this arrangement. See Michel Vergé-Franceschi, ed., *Guerre et Commerce en Méditerranée – IXe-XXe siècle*, Paris: Veyrier, 1991.
4. See, for instance, Il Kwang Sung, *Mamluks in the Modern Egyptian Mind – Changing the Memory of the Mamluks, 1919-1952*, New York: Palgrave Macmillan, 2017.
5. See Brian L. Davies, *The Russo-Turkish War, 1768-1774 – Catherine II and the Ottoman Empire*, London: Bloomsbury, 2016.
6. See Mesut Uyar and Edward J. Erickson, *A Military History of the Ottomans – From Osman to Atatürk*, Santa Barbara, CA: Praeger, 2009.
7. See Davide Rodogno, *Against Massacre – Humanitarian Interventions in the Ottoman Empire, 1815–1914*, Princeton, NJ: Princeton University Press, 2012.
8. See Leila Fawaz, *Occasion for War – Civil Conflict in Lebanon and Damascus in 1860*, Berkeley, CA: University of California Press, 1995.
9. See Benny Morris and Dror Ze'evi, *The Thirty-Year Genocide – Turkey's Destruction of Its Christian Minorities, 1894–1924*, Cambridge, MA: Harvard University Press, 2019.
10. This, of course, had also happened individually much earlier in the 1820s notably, as was the case with Rifa'a Rafi al Tahtawi when he visited France for five years as a part of the first Egyptian educational mission to Paris. His observations on European culture are consigned in his *Takhlis al Ibriz fi Talkhis Bariz*, also known as *Al Rihla al Bariziyya* published in 1834; see the translation by Daniel Newman, *An Imam in Paris – An Account of a Stay in France by an Egyptian Cleric (1826-1831)*, London: Saqi Books, 2016.
11. See Alexander Bevilacqua, *The Republic of Arabic Letters – Islam and the European Enlightenment*, Cambridge, MA: Harvard University Press, 2018.
12. See *The Muslim World – Special Issue: The Protestant Reformation and Islam*, 107, 4, October 2017.
13. The history of the Ottoman Caliphate is complex. In 1517, the Ottomans recovered the caliphal insignia from the Abbasid Caliphate of Cairo, as well as the Hajj organizational function. The formal claim of the full-fledged Caliphate only started, however, in the second half of the eighteenth century.
14. 'Implication' is understood here as an action coming from the exterior to the interior. By contrast, 'involvement' is an internal action to bring in an external action. All politics in the region are characterized by a combination of the two.
15. See C. G. Smith, 'The Emergence of the Middle East', *Journal of Contemporary History*, 3, 3, July 1968, pp. 3–17.
16. On the same day that Nazi Germany surrendered to the Allied powers on 8 May 1945, Algerians marched in the cities of Guelma and Setif in the name of independence only to be massacred by French colonial authorities. Estimates of the killed range from 6,000 to 20,000 civilians. See Marcel Reggui, *Les Massacres de Guelma – Algérie, Mai 1945*, Paris: La Découverte, 2008.

17 See Hazem Beblawi and Giacomo Luciani, eds., *The Rentier State – Nation, State and Integration in the Arab World*, London: Croom Helm, 1987.
18 See Mohammad-Mahmoud Ould Mohamedou, *Iraq and the Second Gulf War – State-Building and Regime Security*, San Francisco: Austin and Winfield, 1998.
19 See, for instance, Albert Hourani, *Arabic Thought in the Liberal Age, 1798-1939*, Cambridge: Cambridge University Press, 1983; and Ussama Makdisi, *Age of Coexistence – The Ecumenical Frame and the Making of the Arab World*, Berkeley, CA: University of California Press, 2019.

3 FROM THE TWILIGHT OF THE OTTOMAN EMPIRE TO THE CALIPHATE REDUX: THE TORTUOUS JOURNEY OF ARAB STATEHOOD

Benoît Challand

For three full decades now, Middle Eastern scholars have questioned the viability and durability of Arab states[1] and have engaged with the Anglo-Saxon political science debates about whether the state should be 'brought back in'.[2] In the wake of the Cold War, Arab states have continued enduring periods of turmoil and vulnerability but have also weathered, when not led, numerous local or regional conflicts. With neoliberal reforms, Arab states came under a new form of attack, one replacing public services with private enterprises.[3] With the wars in Syria, Iraq, Yemen and Libya, one can wonder whether we are not about to face a new round of Orientalist studies which foreground culturalist arguments about the 'weakness' of states in the region, and thus return to mid-twentieth-century views that ushered in the idea of Arab states as weak and artificial creations.[4]

For good or bad,[5] Arab states have been resilient and have borrowed many elements of statehood from their European peers (that is to say, governing elites have actively pursued reforms to mirror European, more recently American, policies). Despite the nefarious colonial distortions generated in the long nineteenth century and during the Mandate period, Arab states adapted to, and sometimes renegotiated, the contours (territorial, i.e. borders, or political, i.e. regimes, such as monarchy or republics) imposed by Western powers. Past the period of independence, many of these states have become tyrannical regimes. Only the recent rejection of colonial borders by the organization of the Islamic State has really challenged the frame of state interaction in the Arab Middle East by formally calling for the re-emergence of the Caliphate. Despite this 2010s Islamist-cum-Caliphate detour and the risk of secession in Southern Yemen, Arab states are well alive.

It is doubtful whether it is helpful to speak of the 'Arab state' as a homogenous category. After all, a mix of monarchies coexist next to republics; some benefit from massive rents, namely non-tax revenues such as oil, foreign aid or remittances from the Suez Canal, while others have remained largely orphans to these benefits. Some countries are socially homogenous, while others are highly fragmented, generating different political and social problems. Lastly, some have adapted a unitary legal code and are therefore secular, while other countries grant a certain autonomy to religious institutions and thus are closer to a model of legal pluralism, with religious courts operating along with secular ones.

Can we develop a general theory of Arab states? Beyond the common language – Arabic – and the existence of a loose inter-governmental entity, with the League of Arab States creating a common socialization for state affairs, two traits probably appear as common to all Arab states. First, the lack of an open, pluralist and inclusive formal political arena is a reality in most, if not all, Arab countries. In short, Arab states face a recurrent *democratic deficit* that translates into suspended or split parliaments, constitutions superseded by state of emergencies, a mockery of the rotation of power in republics or long-standing dictatorships. The second common problem is an oft-heard statement about the absence of the state. The colloquial phrase '*wayn al dawla?*' ('where is the state?') is heard over and over in places as diverse as Lebanon, post-Ben Ali Tunisia and Mubarak's Egypt. In each country, the context and the complaints are different: in Lebanon, one heard the objection during the garbage collection crisis of 2015 and again in the 2020 economic crisis; in Tunisia, it was when the state was not transparent enough about the redistribution of wealth generated from private licenses for oil extraction in 2016 and 2017; in Egypt, ten years ago, Salwa Ismail noted how, in the poor neighbourhoods of Cairo, people would repeat that there was no state: '*hina ma fish dawla, hina nas 'aysha fi dawla ghayr al dawla*' ('here there is no state, here there are people living in a state other than the state').[6] The question 'where is the state?' is of course a rhetorical one: people know too well that *certain aspects* of the state (policing, crushing dissent, intimidation) are always functioning. However, when it comes to guaranteeing functional services in education, health, waste management and the like, the state has either disappeared (leaving the stage for private actors) or does not fulfil its obligations. The question *wayn al dawla?* is thus a key prism to reveal inequalities and the acute perceptions by Arabs of 'a state' that chooses to intervene differently based on class, regional or sectarian basis.[7]

These two problems are at the core of this chapter. I argue that *the democratic deficit and the selective absence of the state can be subsumed under the same question of democracy*. The first common problem of Arab states relates to *formal* or *procedural* dimensions of democracy (elections, parties, checks and balances). The second predicament has roots in *informal* or *substantial* democracy (quality of citizens' lives, equality in everyday life, mechanisms to limit class or other social cleavages and so on). As we will see later from the definition adapted of 'the state', I argue that these two problems can be re-appraised from a discussion about state-making. However, far from posing an essentialist, a-historical and culturalist interpretation of Arab polities as 'backward', static or unchanging (what has been described as Orientalist depictions[8] and present since the nineteenth and early twentieth century as Asian despotism), I am offering a dynamic and multidirectional argument about what Arab citizens have offered and could offer to enhance democratic life, understood as the inclusion in formal politics of the demos (via class antagonism, civil society and/or political parties) and respect for pluralism.

Why focus so much on democracy? First, because the 'classical' texts of the 1980s did not deal with the quality of citizenship or the substance of democracy.[9] Their focus was on political economy, the role of elites, hard features of the state (coercion) or on the top-down capacity of the 'state' to 'penetrate' society.[10] Little was said about the actual aspirations of the Arab *demoi*,[11] let alone of their daily lives. This chapter hopes to propose vital questions about how ordinary people can be made bits and parcels of formal politics as well. It also discusses cases where radical projects of alternative state-building in the name of a community have created monstrous avatars, such as the case of Sunni believers with the establishment of the Islamic State in 2014.

Second, the need to include democracy in this reflection on the Arab states stems from the historic events that took place in the winter of 2010–2011 and which have since involved every single Arab country. The Arab Uprisings (a phrase I prefer over the problematic 'Arab Spring') were locally driven mobilizations to oust dictators and collective calls to defend the dignity of the Arab masses and abolish blatant inequalities at the heart of all Arab states. One of the slogans heard in Egypt, '*aysh, huriyya, karama insaniyya*' (bread, freedom [and] human dignity), is the perfect illustration of various agendas and political sensibilities merging, with an Islamist motto coexisting with those of leftist trade unions and liberal groups.[12] No one had a monopoly over attempts to pass democratic reforms (revolutionary routes having been quickly thwarted and closed by incumbents), and many shared in the call for a 'civil state' (*dawla madaniyya*) as a way forward to escape military or religious rule.

Third, my aim is to reclaim the ground for democracy, which, in the Middle East and North Africa, has become a tainted word after a decade and a half of 'regime change' in the name of Western democracy (i.e., American imperialism or European hypocrisy). To be sure, there has been too much political engineering by European and American actors to steer change as they wanted (even at the cost of more violence and destruction, for example, in Iraq), not to mention the blatant double standards of Western countries (think of the rejection of the electoral outcome of the 2006 parliamentary elections in Palestine, with Hamas, not considered a viable interlocutor by most of the international community, in spite of properly winning the election). The present consideration of democracy also implies being open to the contributions that (Islamic) religious groups and movements can have in democratic life (although, as we will see below, a clear line has to be drawn).

For many in the region, democracy has not only become a tainted Western idea but is regarded by many others as a dangerous project. Democracy is, in the etymological sense of the word, power to the people, or power of the demos. This is not merely my preference as a Swiss scholar based in the United States and working on Tunisian, Yemeni and Palestinian civil society and informal civic work. I focus on this political principle because Arab people have *themselves* embraced and made of this principle their own project. Democracy is too important a principle to throw out with the bathwater of colonial and imperial mingling in the region. Democracy also has an Arab pedigree, and a long one, a fact obfuscated by Orientalist and Neo-Con scholars alike. For more than a century, radical groups have engaged with alternative political practices to promote equality in the decaying years of the Ottoman Empire.[13] Communist parties have been de facto vehicles for the inclusion of marginalized groups, Shiites in Iraq, Kurds in Syria and Palestinians inside Israel,[14] in the first half of the past century. National projects have historically called for democratic solutions, for example, the Palestinian National Charter of 1968 demanding the establishment of a secular democratic state, with equality between Palestinians and Jews. More recently, Palestinian citizens of Israel have called to make Israel a 'state of all its citizens' for more than ten years now. This was a formulation coined around 2005 by the now-exiled Knesset Member Azmi Bishara and subsequently picked up by various Palestinian networks, most notably the Haifa Declaration.[15] Lastly, the 2011 'revolutions', which called for democracy, social justice and the foundation of a 'civil state' (*dawlah madaniyya*), suggest that the principles of democracy or of a democratic state representing the Arab demos are not only a Western priority. They figure high on the list of Arab citizens themselves.

The chapter therefore revisits some of the reasons why 'Arab states' have rarely been studied through the angle of democracy suggested here, which is a different principle from democratization.[16] After a discussion of the definitions and characteristics of the state, the chapter revisits classical texts on Arab states and discusses why leaving the people, that is, the demos, out of the equation has undermined certain findings of the main early texts on Arab states. The next section deals with the consequences of neoliberal reforms, while the following one turns to the nexus of secularism-Islamism, allowing a quick appraisal of the 'new form' of the Islamic 'statehood' as implemented by ISIS.

Defining the state in a way that captures Arab specificities

Important texts have been published on the question of statehood in the Middle East and North Africa and remain essential companions to historians, political scientists and political sociologists who want to make sense of the harsh competition that has characterized the last three decades of upheavals, conflicts and regime changes, some externally induced, others more democratically so. The present difficulty is to identify a definition of the state that is suitable for the context in which modern states emerged – in Europe, for instance – and for the Arab Middle East where the history of state-making has been and continues to be more tormented. The issue of taming and harnessing violence into a centralized and depersonalized government has been central to both European and Middle Eastern histories.[17] The main difference in these two trajectories has to do with the more recent and externally induced process for Arab states, which tells us to keep an eye on matters of external encroachments onto (Arab) states.[18] This is compounded with the existence of a rich array of non-tax revenues in the Middle East, some, again, externally controlled (such as foreign aid), which have made much of the historical trade-off between taxation and representation (and democratic enfranchisement), a conspicuously missing element in the process of Arab state-making. Bearing in mind these two Arab specificities (which contribute to the two common traits of democratic deficit and the perceived absence of the state identified above), let us see how general definitions of the state can be applied to the Arab Middle East.

Defining and studying the state is no easy feat. Timothy Mitchell, in his seminal 1991 article, provides a useful entry point for our discussion. He criticized the then-dominant question of 'bringing the state back in'.[19] For Mitchell, such approaches reduced the state to a subjective system of decision-making that presupposed a clear state–society division, which in reality is very elusive.[20] To tackle the subjective dimension (the state as policy-making) and to avoid the view of the state as an 'actual organization' with an interior and an exterior,[21] Mitchell proposed defining the state as 'the sum of the structural effects' generated by mundane practices and shifting relations of power in the name of what is perceived as the state.[22] This approach is helpful to avoid the hypostatization (of the state and of structures) and the reification of the state as a (living) entity, but it says nothing of the place of the demos, of the people in these relations of power. It resonates with other Foucauldian texts that insist on discursive powers or show the capillarity of domination (and resistance) but which fail to offer a robust theory of power. In Mitchell's (and Foucauldian) reading, it is as if power is reduced to gazes, discourses and cultural representations (visual, performative, etc.), but nothing is said about strictly political representation and mechanisms to connect the formal realm of politics (government, regimes, parties, judicial institutions) with simple citizens. Speaking of the bundle of (instrumental) effects does not tell us much about the place or role of the demos in state politics, except that it is the *object* of power.

The alternative, in my view, is to simply revert to the most famous definition of the state given by Max Weber. In its short version, the state is all about the use of legitimate violence. However, the actual definition, in his 1919 essay *Politics as Vocation*, needs to be stated in full. The state is 'the *human community* that, within a given territory, successfully claims for itself the monopoly of the legitimate use of physical force'.[23] In a nutshell, this definition reminds us that the power to use the means of coercion does not belong to an abstract supreme (governing) entity, an external state-as-organization but lays in the hands of a given human community, forming, all together, a polity. The state is thus a compact or a contract between this community and organizations meant to implement the exercise of just authority and the protection of a given territory.

Some will object that Weber was possibly not the most democratic or egalitarian person,[24] or that elsewhere in his writings, he was ambiguous about whether he saw the state as an organization or as a polity. At times, he seems to indicate that, say, France *is* a state (put differently the state is seen as a polity), while in others he speaks as if France *has* a state (state as an entity, as a formal organization).[25] It is also true that in certain historical moments (e.g., Bonapartism), the 'people' might come to think of violent measures as a necessary evil and therefore antithetical to the democratic quality. However, if this principle of collective decision remains open, the road to dictatorship can be averted through a renewed collective deliberation about how physical force can and should be used, not to mention the form and content of the preferred political regime (a monarchy, a republic, a unitary or federal state). The people are and should remain sovereign in the establishment of modern power.

Insisting on the polity component of the Weberian state definition has, in my view, numerous advantages: in general, to revisit the theme of the state and in particular, when it comes to the Arab Middle East. It circumvents the organizational fallacy of the state as an 'actual organization'. It undercuts the subjectivist view of the state (or personification). It puts the stress on legitimacy (a key Weberian theme) but allows one to not only reflect on what the proper uses of coercion are but to rethink the moral fundamentals of a social contract (e.g., envisaged on a secular or religious basis). Lastly, it connects the contours of these human communities to the existence of a territory and its international recognition. Thus, we can consider states beyond the danger of methodological nationalism,[26] namely the quasi-automatic, at times naturalized focus on phenomena limited by national borders. Arab states, like other postcolonial (or Third world) states, have suffered from different forms of external encroachments. A short list of these occurrences includes: Israel invading Lebanon in 1978 and 1982 and that country's occupation by Syria from 1976 to 2005; Iraq ruled by an American proconsul after 2003 (and which still remains hampered in its capacity to take sovereign decisions); Palestinians denied the right to self-determination by Israeli occupation and relentless colonization since 1948 or 1967. We can now add Yemen and Libya to this list of foreign interventions that show the power of external influence in undermining the ability of other populations (human communities) to claim for themselves and within a given territory, the monopoly of the legitimate use of physical force.

Shedding light on this oft-forgotten element of Weber's definition ('the human community') establishes a basis, in my view, for the discussion of a 'democratic state' and within this, from a transnational perspective. Each human community is or should be free to make its own decisions apart from privileged elites' vested interests or from external sponsors or patrons (euphemistically portrayed as 'protectors'). Put differently, the polity and its demos are autonomous in their effort to arrange various configurations of powers (economic, political, ideological)[27] in a way that tames, restrains and mitigates the use of physical coercion and turns the latter into legitimate violence (although violence will always be exerted in a way as to exclude some, be it in terms of gender, class or nationality). Let us now discuss the existing literature on Arab states in the light of this 'democratic' yardstick, namely assess how the demos appears, or not, as an integral component of the state as polity.

Revisiting classics on Arab statehood in the light of the democratic deficit

Among the seminal and 'classical' texts in the English and French languages, we can list Salamé (1987), Dawisha and Zartman (1988), Luciani (1990), Ghalioun (1991), Ayubi (1995) and Heydemann (2000). This is not an exhaustive list, to be sure. These are texts that have explained why we have the states we have known for a long time, that is, fierce or ruthless states which have been enemies to local societies. When this literature emerged, the situation of Arab states was best summarized by Burhan Ghalioun. In his 1991 book, the Syrian sociologist posited the following diagnostic: The domestic Arab predicament[28] comes from the opposition between state and society (*Le Malaise arabe: L'État contre la nation*). The state has remained alien to Arab populations and modernity, in Ghalioun's terms, and did not generate the same gradual acceptance among Muslim-majority societies as it did, for instance, in Europe.[29] Part of this argument might have made sense at the time of his writing but since then, a critical distance has emerged towards typical dichotomies in the literature of the 1980s and early 1990s: state versus society; western model of state-building versus Arab 'traditions'; secular versus Islamic routes to modernity; democratic West versus Asian despotism.

That frame has led many to question the legitimacy of the very idea of an Arab state in opposition to an unquestioned Western model. Salamé notes the paradox of Western-led or inspired bureaucratization in the Arab region: it reinforced and helped certain regimes survive, but at the same time it weakened state legitimacy.[30] The debate concerned not only the Middle East but also Africa, as in the famous debate between Bertrand Badie and Jean-François Bayard.[31] Was indeed the Arab state an alien 'import' with no historical basis? Many have toyed with the idea, but the reality is that the notion of a modern 'state' (*dawla*) existed since the early-to-mid nineteenth century, 1837 to be precise.[32] Furthermore, even if there were no formal Lebanese or Syrian states before the twentieth century, there certainly were pre-existing administrative units and provinces within the

Ottoman Empire that correspond, broadly, to these newly formed states.[33] It is therefore misleading to say that Arab states are totally artificial entities. Isa Blumi also revisited this idea that borders were mere impositions by external actors: in the Yemeni case, some local actors, in zones of authority disputed by the Ottomans to the north and to British protectorate in the south, were able to tease out the competition between state and colonial actors to gain some benefits.[34] They were assuredly limited but were nonetheless influential. As Blumi writes, 'the formal need for borders was the consequence of local politics'.[35]

Thus, rather than earlier interpretations in which local Arab actors were presented only as passive, one gets the sense that local agency has also been at play in times of border-making.[36] After decolonization, some Arab governments consciously perpetuated colonial management of borderlands. For example, in post-independence Tunisia, the country's first President, Habib Bourguiba, weakened by the internal opposition of the Youssefists, chose not to deploy state institutions equally throughout the territory. He opted to perpetuate the colonial type of border management with informal agreements with tribal leaders.[37] Thus, rather than placing modernity squarely on the side of Europe and 'traditions' at the Arab end, the literature of the last fifteen years has shown the ambiguous results of political modernity, with new concepts such as multiple modernities[38] and modern projects that emerged from within the (Arab) Middle East, in particular within the Islamic matrix.[39]

This does not mean that one should underplay the colonial fiats and interventions of the early twentieth century. All the dishonest promises during the last years of the Ottoman Empire created a terrible basis for inclusive and egalitarian citizenship and laid uneven foundations for a dysfunctional state system plagued by conflicts caused by these borders. That list is long and well known (and discussed in several chapters in this volume): Sykes-Picot and the set of artificial boundaries; biased support in Palestine for European Jews; imposition of a tiered system of citizenship[40]; imperial manipulation of 'minorities' to rule populations hostile to European control; redrawing of borders to make sure oil or other strategic assets would remain in European or American hands; and instrumental support for non-constitutional monarchies.[41] To be fair, one also needs to add the rapid disillusion after real independence, between 1952 and the early 1970s for most Arab states, with Arab states becoming the favourite object of predation for a select few: typically one-party regimes (Algeria, Egypt, Syria, Tunisia), often combined with the prominence of military or security elites (Iraq, Syria, Yemen, Sudan, Algeria after 1990). Even the soon-to-be Palestinian state suffers from an impossible opening of the Palestinian Liberation Organisation (PLO) to Islamist factions and a worrying concentration of political power in the hands of security *zu'ama* (Mohammed Dahlan being the most recent example, subsequently active for the neo-imperial Emirati security and intelligence).

If Arab states turned violently against their own citizens, this cannot be explained solely in reference to colonial or external influences. The legitimacy problem of ruling elites is a mixed problem, combining historical intrusions (colonial fiats in co-opting a given group) with sovereign political decisions taken by post-independence Arab regimes. Inspired by Charles Tilly's earlier work about the key relation between violence and state-making, Ayubi changed the focus to internal politics and was soon followed by Steven Heydemann in his study of war-making. These two texts are game-changers for our argument, because they pose the question of *how the formal end of the state relates to the demos*, or how citizens emerge, or not, during historical processes involving institutions of coercion.

Nazih Ayubi, in his early work on bureaucracy, observed how the building of bureaucratic apparatuses had been a key component of the post-independence developmental state.[42] Ayubi thus had the correct intuition in thinking about what connects the top aspects of politics to the demos, namely that legitimacy and popular support for Arab regimes was derived from hiring a vast number of public servants. The problem with this approach was that hiring was done along party or sectarian lines, rapidly turning bureaucracy into a barrier to overall inclusion.[43] The politicization of bureaucracy hampered the emergence of a rich party system and stifled the expansion of the kernel of Arab civil society, which had emerged at the turn of the nineteenth and twentieth centuries. Ayubi's monumental *Overstating the Arab State* (1995) pursues this question of the lack of political legitimacy and as such is helpful for a variety of reasons. First, he is the only author who gives the full version of the Weberian state as a human community,[44] and thus offers an important corrective to other classical texts which tend to reduce the state to an actual organization.[45] Second, his clustering of four types of state-making[46] is historically rich, well informed and proposes a synthesis of Arab and Western scholarship on the *longue durée* of state and sovereign entities, not just the colonial periods of artificial boundary-making. Third, his application of the Gramscian idea that the state ought to be the place for successful articulations between modes of coercion, production and interpretation opens a contact point for democratic theory. Finally, Ayubi was helpful for revisiting the language of strong and weak states inherited from authors such as Migdal (1988).

What emerges is that Arab states are neither strong nor weak. They are fierce and violent because they lack ideological hegemony (in the Gramscian sense of the term) that would enable them to forge a historical social bloc that accepts the legitimacy of the ruling stratum. As a result, the Arab states have taken the form of gendarme or corporatist states but have not managed to function as social aggregators, or in Gramscian terms, as political educators.[47] Ayubi follows the Moroccan historian Abdallah Al-'Arwi [Laroui] for whom the Arab states may be 'strong' in terms of 'body' (i.e., certain apparatuses of the state), but the violence of this state is in reality an indication of its weakness and fragility. The state as a whole is weak because it lacks rationality and educational supports.[48] The Gramscian perspective favoured by Ayubi (*en vogue* in the 1990s) dovetails with the view that the national human community should involve the definition of the use of coercion. It also fits with the view that civil society, a bourgeois and hence discredited institution for Marx and traditional Marxists, can be a place of emancipation and can be a vital element in the chain that connects the demos to the state. The problem remained, at the time of Ayubi, to see how the demos and working classes could actually disrupt these fierce states. Had Ayubi lived longer, he would have probably found lot of food for thought from the Arab Uprisings of 2011 and from the efforts from various strands of citizens to reclaim the state for themselves.

In his rich edited volume on war-making, Heydemann (2000) elucidated another aspect of the missed link between demos and state. In this work, which draws parallels with the Tillyian insight of state-making as war-making in Europe, Heydemann demonstrates that it is not futile to try to compare two very idiosyncratic paths of state-making, a process based on the relevance of revenue collection and culminating, in Europe, in gradual enfranchisement. Heydemann notes the fundamental difference that whereas in Europe war preparation led to the organization of centralized state revenues, in the (Arab) Middle East, the opposite is true: the organization and structures of state revenues, in particular the importance of (military) aid during the Cold War, and the existence of oil rent, influenced and encouraged patterns of war preparation.[49] In Europe, once a warlord emerged as powerful, he was able to extend his territorial basis and thus gradually pacify social relations. Over time, typically in the eighteenth and nineteenth centuries, this sovereign delegated the function of coercion to legal-rational institutions or new disciplining mechanisms, which developed interests in keeping a peaceful status quo with former enemies. On the other end of this model of state-making, domestic pacification rarely occurred: Arab statehood became a vector for personal enrichment and the consolidation of personalized power for a few dictators who would not hesitate to go to war to solidify their grip on power. Western military forces, usually kept in their barracks, differed from their Arab counterparts: the latter kept stepping out of their barracks and vied for power, turning their weapons not only against their external enemies but also against their own citizens. Thus the large number of wars and the hypertrophied presence of *mukhabarat* (security and intelligence units) are a fundamental reason for the democratic deficit in the Arab worlds: there cannot be equality in front of death (a substantial element of democracy) if Arab leaders play with the lives of their co-nationals (seen as cannon fodder) in order to cement their hold on power. Gradually, in fear of losing their grip on the economy, bureaucracy and resources, or to lose to (frequently) Islamist oppositions, Republican Arab leaders turned state institutions, typically coercive ones, against their own citizens and reinforced the control of the one-party system, while monarchies, notably the Gulf Cooperation Council (GCC), established pacts of self-defence that proved lethal to democratic aspirations in 2011. Let us now see how neoliberal reforms influenced these negative democratic records.

Neoliberalism and the deepening of the democratic deficit

With the systematic spread of neoliberal reforms from the 1980s onwards, the democratic deficit explained in classical texts was gradually compounded by a thinning out of the state that increased the second common trait of Arab states, namely their selective absence. Responsiveness to the agenda of economic reforms was a way for many Arab regimes to seem open to the language of democracy and pluralism (e.g. Sadat's *infitah* policy of 1973 or IMF pressure on Tunisia in the late 1970s). However, the substance of ruling regimes remained unaltered, as states based on a security rationale prevented the inclusion of the *demoi* in decision-making. International actors have a responsibility in this withering away of the Arab state, and by the same token the possibility for Arab *demoi* to be more involved. Three main international actors can be listed here. The IMF and World Bank have been initiators of the 'good governance' agenda as a way to grant formal political say to private institutions. Soon, this call to fight corruption turned into an unstoppable machine, geared by the so-called 'Washington Consensus'.[50] American think tanks and governmental funding schemes reinforced the dynamics set by international financing institutions. The story and impacts are well known and do not need rehearsing.[51]

The spread of these policies of structural adjustment programmes coincided with a new phase of European integration after the Maastricht Treaty and the establishment of the European Union (EU). In 1995, with the launch of the Barcelona Process, the EU sought to establish stronger political links with Mediterranean partners, mostly Arab but also Turkey and Israel. Behind the venerable objectives (and carrots) of establishing civil society and cultural exchanges, the EU used economic incentives and political conditionality (sticks) to impose free trade on European terms, the effects of which were particularly detrimental to North African economies, the agricultural sector in particular. Furthermore, requests for political cooperation in the fight against 'terrorism' (defined from a Western European perspective) or success of the 'peace process' in Palestine made the EU more complacent with authoritarian Arab regimes.[52] In Kienle's apt phrase, the politics of liberalization led more to de-liberalization than to democratization.[53]

Neoliberal 'success stories' – Tunisia under Ben Ali[54] or Egypt under Mubarak[55] – were in reality artificial ones. Using the tricks of debts unloaded on public workers in Egypt,[56] phoney privatization of enterprises actually sold to just-retired generals or security personal, spurious financial repackaging of 'growth',[57] or falsified statistics for Tunisia, neoliberal policies only accelerated the concentration of economic and political power in the hands of a happy few. Arab populations were receiving very little of the trickle-down or promised benefits from these policies. With neoliberalism, external encroachment shifted from the Cold War model of direct influence to more covert or indirect forms. Spaces of privileged economic exchange were taken out of public purview, leaving new spaces for international influence in these liminal spaces.[58] However, the trends of outsourcing to private actors in the security sector have been much more pernicious and detrimental for the democratic contract. Be it with mercenaries in Qaddafi's Libya or competing armed groups inside the Lebanese state (with Hezbollah and other factional paramilitary groups), the notion that the state should have the monopoly over the means of violence no longer had any currency.

According to Cihan Tuğal, it has become *passé*, after neoliberalism, to sustain the assumption that a Middle Eastern state can have a legitimate monopolization of violence.[59] The events of 9/11 and the ensuing 'War on Terror', combined with neoliberal reforms, have precipitated the surge of 'non-state warriors'.[60] Whether due to community policing (witness Shiite policing as distinct from the Iraqi army or police), the rise of private subcontractors or counterinsurgency as a method of population management,[61] the notion of the state as the normal depositary or organizer of the means of physical coercion has indeed become a hollow concept. For Tuğal, this 'rhizomatic' tendency can even explain the new form of violence spread by ISIS, which combines a revolutionary vanguard that Sayyid Qutb had proposed sixty years ago with a de-territorialized project of state-as-Islamic-community building.[62] In his comparison of security interventions in Brazil and Egypt's capital cities, Paul Amar would agree with Tugal's assessment that the effects of neoliberalism have had a serious impact on dealing with protests in large cities of the Global South, for example, by insisting on an individualized sense of human security.[63] Yet Amar argues that we are actually in a situation of 'post-neoliberalism': the focus of policy intervention is no longer based on market solutions. For him, the most pressing issue in contemporary politics is the securitization of subjects of morality, gender and sexuality. In this post-neoliberal situation, he describes a mix of moral communitarian actors (conservative religious groups), private security forces and state security forces acting to push for this new security agenda.[64] Another difference, according to Amar, is the origin of these neoliberal versus post-neoliberal policies. The former are thought of as coming from uniquely capitalist centre(s), the 'West', while for Amar, there are also political and moral entrepreneurs in the Global South who push for these reforms and thus thwart egalitarian activism in the region.

Here again, a careful reading of the evolution of 'Arab states' in (or after) neoliberal ages evidences that there is a tendency to reduce 'the Middle East' to an object of external decisions (as was the case so vividly during the first wave of studies of Arab statehood from the late 1970s to the mid-1990s). However, research such as Amar's or of Hanieh's[65] shows that some regional actors also prevent autonomous political projects and the aspirations of Arab citizens (Hanieh discusses the intensification of circuits of commodities and financial services from the Gulf region into Egypt and Tunisia). A multidirectional study of political influence is therefore needed. This brings us to a last case or model of Arab states, namely those based on religious principles and Islamic morality.

Islamic solutions to the problem of state-building

Can Islamist states or Islamist modes of governance be the solution to a greater inclusion of the demos in formal politics leading in turn to more resilient and representative statehood? Many Islamist intellectuals have made and continue to make the case for such an argument. Of the extensive literature, we will only address some of the key components of the state, as defined above. Actual instances of Islamic republics (Iran) or monarchies (Saudi Arabia) have existed, and their democratic record is far from convincing. We will therefore concentrate mostly on the latest iteration of such an Islamist revolution, that of the Islamic State.[66]

With regard to the place of the demos, a case can be made that Islamism per se, on paper, has historically granted a decisive place to the average citizen. Al-'Arwi [Laroui] noted that in Islamic society, freedom is linked with extra-state and/or anti-state (Sufism, tribalism, nomadism) and not with the modern state.[67] His interpretation converges with other sociologists of Islam who have observed that discourse on the "common good"[68] or social practice favouring forms of civility[69] are intrinsic to life in Muslim-majority societies. This has generated the view that the only path for effective citizenship among Arab-Muslim societies' involvement must come from socio-religious institutions, typically *tariqaat*, Sufi orders, and the emulation of Islamic traditions. Is not *shura*, an Arabic term for deliberation used in the Qur'an, an equivalent to democracy, and, too, a much older term? Was not Islam the first civilization that codified a theory of rights, for example, around *jus in bello*?[70]

The problems with such views are manifold. First, demos is equated with *umma*, therefore, excluding non-Muslim subjects, bringing a quick end to a claim of fully inclusive citizenship. Second, anthropologist Hammoudi underlines the patriarchal limitation of Sufism: a practice led by a master, Sufism confines authority to a religious and male figure and thus hinders modern and pluralistic forms of representation.[71] There have been cases of women Sufi leaders, but the vast majority of Sufi forms of socialization are patriarchal and male-centred. Third, Salvatore also notes that certain advantages of Muslim-majority society, for example, the inbuilt social capacity to assure civility and mutual neutralization of violence and despotism (in a triangular relation connecting the *umma* with *ulama* and the ruler), can only function when there are minimal external governing forces. As soon as Muslim lives under a centralized authority, these positive tools in Islamic history tend to become useless.[72] Fourth, the idea of mixing religious with other (secular) legal principles is bound to generate a clash where a hierarchy will have to determine which principles overrule the others.

The post-1979 Iranian state model shows the limitation of a hybrid system of a modern republic. There, an Islamic constitution was built on the French model of the Fifth Republic. It includes, on the one hand, a classical separation of power, and builds on modern notions of representative democracy, with the election of a parliament. On the other, one finds Ayatollah Khomeini's invention of the guardianship of the Islamic jurist (*vilayet-e-faqih*) enshrined in this same constitution. This invented institution grants *de facto* veto power for the supreme (Shiite) religious leader, short-circuiting other political principles. In a Sunni Arab context, the Sudanese experience of the late 1980s and 1990s shows the limits of formal Islamist politics. The Sudanese scholar Abdullahi An-Na'im has written a sharp criticism of the experience of establishing Islamic states: this can only create a dead-end for Islamists who call for these states to implement *sharia*. An-Na'im lucidly recalls that *sharia* is *not* a legal code, with a definitive or fixed interpretation. Rather, it is informal and 'plays a role in shaping and developing ethical norms and values'.[73] Enforcing *sharia* is a logical contradiction because religious compliance can only be voluntary. For An-Na'im, a just, democratic Islamic society can only exist within a secular state. Put differently, Muslims can observe *sharia* only if the state is neutral regarding all religious doctrines. Thus, the call for an Islamic state to enforce *sharia* is the crystallization of a confused and at times postcolonial discourse that perpetuates the view that only European notions of state and positive laws can be the basis of common political life. An irony not lost on An-Na'im.[74]

This paradox of mixed borrowings was similarly at play in the case of the Islamic State, under the self-proclaimed Caliph Abu-Bakr al Baghdadi. Even if ISIS, which changed its name to reflect this decision by insisting on being called 'Islamic State' (and thus abandoning the Syrian and Iraqi reference in its name), criticized the colonial imposition of the Sykes-Picot agreement and called for the erasure of all Arab borders, it was rapidly and inexorably caught up in the trappings of a modern state. When Mosul fell to the armed group in June 2014, the latter was quick to make sure that high school students could take their baccalaureate and receive their diplomas stamped by the 'Islamic State' rather than the 'Republic of Iraq'. In areas that were under ISIS control in Syria and Iraq, new centralized entities monitored and issued permits for movements (*tasaareeh*)[75] and organized a hierarchy of administrative units.[76] Keen to polish its political communication, especially to lure foreign fighters to join the rank of its army, the organization even issued advertisements for its health services mirroring the UK logo of NHS.[77] All in all, ISIS quickly assumed the form of a more or less normal state.

This trapping of the state is twice revealing: first, there seems to be no escape from the modern state. Large and complex polities require a degree of centralization, bureaucratization and delegation. Even a radical and revolutionary departure from the 'Western' state, such as ISIS, led to an organization that mirrored its principle. Second, and back to the core of the initial argument (democratic deficit and selective absence of the Arab states), the fact that the Islamic State acted like a (modern) state and even called itself a *state* is evidence of the idea of an absent state. The context of the emergence of ISIS is not innocent: the United States invasion of 2003 not only destroyed Saddam's regime, but it effectively destroyed the Iraqi state, with some of its ministries and its army disbanded, and the social cohesion of Iraqi society gone, replaced by an externally introduced federal structure fanning the flames of communitarianism. Not far from there, in Syria, and closer to us in time, the problem of an imploding state was identical. The Syrian regime was heckled by democratic protests in 2011 and 2012 and, to survive Bashar al Assad, did not hesitate to abandon parts of the territory (the Kurdish part in the northeast) to regroup in and around large cities in the west of the country. Thus, ISIS emerged because there was a selective (for Syria) or forced (Iraq) absence or collapse of the state in the years before ISIS's emergence.

A second blatant dimension of how un-Islamic and un-democratic ISIS has been from the onset is the extreme virulence the organization has shown to erase internal diversity. Non-Muslim populations or heterodox sects were victims of de facto ethnic cleansing, which are in total contradiction with the early days of Islam when new territories were conquered, often through military campaigns, but which accepted other monotheist populations. Luizard captured this strategy, describing it as the 'trap' of ISIS, namely the active pursuit of radical (Sunni) sectarianism as a way to establish a foothold in neighbouring countries (Syria, Lebanon). The Islamic State was only strong, argued Luizard, because of the weakness of its enemies or of their collapsing institutions.[78] The logic of purity, pursued by ISIS, corresponds to a top-down, hyper-Jacobinist strategy and is very much antithetical to the many Islamist and Salafi calls or programmes to return to the original Muslim community under the Prophet, or under the first four caliphs (the *Rashidun*), the so-called well-guided leaders who established the first Muslim dynasty. That logic is also largely influenced by the specifics of the Iraqi context, namely that of a Sunni community suddenly left with almost no power after 2003. No wonder that the large community of foreign fighters, many not even speaking Arabic or a local dialect, were sent by their leaders in Syria. Iraqi ISIS leaders did not want to be associated with this motley crew of converts and allophone militants on their own (national) territory.

The third and last component of ISIS credentials that could have provided an alternative to the modern Arab state system is the Caliphate. On this front as well, ISIS has been a failure. The notion of Caliphate has a long and complicated journey in Muslim-majority society[79]: a title given by the community of followers of the Prophet to his initial successors (*khaleefa* means successor, vice-regent in Arabic) became associated over time with the holder of temporal power (the Sultan). The Ottomans carried and merged the two titles together for several centuries and when the Ottoman Empire was formally disbanded in 1922, the title of Caliphate was abolished. The adoption of the title of Caliph by Abu Bakr al Baghdadi in June 2014 might reveal an attempt to revive an empire, but the greatest appeal of the title lay in the model of the original community of Muslim followers (the classical motto of Salafists, i.e. return to the golden times of the *ancestors*, or forefathers, *salaf* in Arabic). The Caliphate, Hamid Dabashi reminds us in his *Authority in Islam*, was an attempt at routinizing the charisma of the Prophet Mohammed, and at substituting 'brotherhood-in-faith for brotherhood-in-blood, which went against traditional Arab practices'.[80]

Calling for the Caliphate can be read as an alternative to the 'tradition' of modern times, namely to rule via the control of a modern state apparatus ('brotherhood-in-institution', one could say, as an extension of Dabashi's formulation). As such, Baghdadi was arguably trying to replace the legal-rational dimension of authority with a charismatic-religious one. The problem with this attempt is that, as noted, ISIS quickly realized that it needed a bureaucracy and functional hierarchies to rule large swathes of Iraqi and Syrian territories. Furthermore, there was little to be seen of al Baghdadi's charisma, or personal virtues in action, outside of being a ruthless military tactician. Invoking Sunni traditions to fan the flames of sectarian hatred against Shia Muslims, relapses (*murtaad*) or impious people (*kuffar*) were only successful in expanding the temporary territorial basis of the organization. It did not manage to fool more than a few confused persons willing to try out a new form of *takfiri jihadi* extremism.

Overall, the attempt of al Baghdadi and his followers to establish an alternative to modern states has not met with resilience. Most Western pundits have insisted on the predicate (Islamic) of the name of the organization, while we should have rather underlined the actual name, 'state', in the organization's moniker, for it revealed how deeply frustrated certain segments of Arab countries have felt vis-à-vis their own government and ruling institutions. Even if it represented a symbolically powerful *ersatz* to the (Western) state, the Islamic avatar or Caliphate Redux has not managed to find a solution to the issue of political legitimacy because of the issue of violence (returning thus to the Weberian definition of the state). Keen to appear as a just ruler, the neo-Caliph was outflanked by former Iraqi Baathist officers who were more interested in the 'management of savagery' and creating the conditions of sectarian hate to attain power than in exacting a model of social justice and a return to an imaginary pristine model of communal life. The idea of an Islamic State, in the ISIS iteration, was no more than a fig leaf to hide Iraqi Sunni frustration with the 2003 invasion.

Conclusions

Let us conclude by returning to the two common traits of all Arab states identified in the first pages of this chapter: the democratic deficit of Arab politics and the perceived absence of the Arab states are not separate issues. Rather they are two sides of the same coin, generated by a complex historical process. Political forces behind the shaping of these undemocratic Arab states are multiple. On the international level, we have seen the impact of European colonial decisions taken last century, and more recently, imperialist and capitalist encroachments have also left a debilitating mark on the democratic potential of Arab states.[81] However, it would be a mistake to ignore regional, intra-Arab forces (or for the pre-independence period, Ottoman influence) on state-making. Local actors have also had a say in the shaping of the current Arab state system. The essay has identified a definition of the state (stressing the Weberian definition) that allows us to compare the specificities of Arab state-making patterns. The analysis noted how past, 'classical' studies on Arab states of the 1980s and 1990s have by and large ignored the roles that Arab *demoi* have tried to play in order to make their respective countries a polity open to pluralism, equality in front of death and inclusion of all citizens in formal politics ('democratic life', as a shortcut). The wave of neoliberal measures has only increased the distance between well-off elites and the masses, leading to what Bayat described as the growing 'poor middle classes'.[82] Even attempts to establish a moral-religious alternative to modern states in the form of an 'Islamic state', as discussed, have failed.

This does not mean that the route to democratic Arab states is barred forever. The chapter has identified a steady stream of democratic calls by Arabs, women and men, in various moments of the last hundred years in active pursuit of such representative and legitimate statehood. These democratic aspirations were revived in the short-lived revolutionary moment of 2011, when mobilizations calling for political change, respect for human dignity and implementation of policies to promote social justice appeared in all Arab countries. Elsewhere, I have tried to describe the historical significance of these democratic upheavals.[83] Doing so showed that a positive sense of citizenship animated all of these protests. A direct involvement of Arabs in politics was at the heart of creative alternative political orders not only described in words or political manifestos but performed in such concrete actions as sit-ins, mutual protection, and direct enactment of social justice.[84] Along with other scholars,[85] I am persuaded that the kernel of revolutionary practices in the first months of 2011 was probably the closest thing we have seen in terms of citizens coalescing to show their reject of the past model of security *mukhabarat* states and their willingness to reshape 'Arab states' in a positive and constructive manner. Manifold calls for a civil state (*dawla madaniyya*) in the first months of 2011 were also proof that Arab citizens are not going to be satisfied with militaries at the helm, nor with Islamist leaders. Clearly more reformist than revolutionary, the protestors in 2011 have nonetheless shown that the link between demos and state can be democratic, in the full sense of the term.

To recap the main conceptual and definitional points underpinning the study of Arab states over the past one hundred years, let me offer a table, contrasting standard approaches to states (left column) and the alternative approach, which puts Arab people at the heart of their states (right column) (Table 1). This approach can enrich future studies and capture the originality of the Arab uprisings by summarizing the more open-ended and democratic potential of Arab states and identifying aspects of Arab statehood that have often been overlooked but identified in some of the literature discussed above.

Table 1 Old and new approaches to the study of Arab states

	Standard accounts on the Arab state and limitations of such studies	Suggested new approaches and themes
Metaphor	The state as an organization	The state as a polity
Population	Population following the state	Population being the state. Population as a collective force that cannot be dissolved in 'private initiative' (i.e. neoliberalism)
Demos	Object of state policies	Active participant in shaping the content and form of the state and debating symbolic questions of inclusion
Borders	Physical border	Borders as a lived and inhabited space (borderland)
Violence	As formal institutions with no democratic accountability	As a social contract that can be redefined
Legitimacy	Of the formal state and of the use of violence	Legitimacy stemming from an active link between the human community and the formal state institutions
International system	Methodological nationalism	Transnational perspective. Vulnerability of the state to external encroachment

This exercise in historical political sociology and democratic theory comes to an end with a few suggestions (summed up in the right column) but no clear solutions. It also raises multiple questions that future research, academic debates, such as the one that brought this collection of chapters together under the smart guidance of Mohammad-Mahmoud Ould Mohamedou, and actual practices by Arab actors will help settle, hopefully. At a time where 'a case for colonialism'[86] can be made shamelessly in (until then) reputable academic journals, and when new imperial or neo-colonial threats abound in the region (not only the United States but also Gulf monarchies, China, Russia and Israel), it is clear that Arab states are not stable entities, free from new forms of external meddling. The episode of an Islamic State in Iraq and Syria seems to come to an end, but then arises Benjamin Netanyahu's and Israel's statements that it sees the foundation of a Kurdish state with benevolence.[87] The scars of past colonial state-building are still with us on multiple fronts. We have to study these long-term historical continuities that generate a sense (within the Arab Middle East) of external manipulation and therefore distrust of Western political ideas and principles. This scepticism towards 'Western ideas' should not, however, distract us from the genuine and repeated aspiration of Arab nations and *demoi* to have more than a say every four or five years during elections. As seen with the outcomes of the 2011 uprisings, protests for more democracy and popular participation can open the door to external interventions (Libya, Yemen and Syria), thwarting hopes for new constitutions and democratic changes. Democracy is not a simple, positive and incremental progress. It comes at a cost, especially so in a region where various forms of encroachment (capitalist, neo-colonial and imperial) subsist at national and regional levels and thus undermine state sovereignty. The road to a democratic and inclusive citizenship and to representative and legitimate statehood in the Arab world was arduous over the past century, and it remains so.

Notes

1   See Ghassan Salamé, ed., *The Foundations of the Arab State*, London: Routledge, 1987; Adeed Dawisha and William Zartman, eds., *Beyond Coercion – The Durability of the Arab State*, London: Croom-Helm, 1988; and Giacomo Luciani, ed., *The Arab State*, Berkeley, California: University of California Press, 1990.
2   Peter Evans, Dietrich Rueschemeyer and Theda Skocpol, eds., *Bringing the State Back In*, Cambridge: Cambridge University Press, 1985; and Joel Migdal, *Strong Societies and Weak States – State-Society Relations and State Capabilities in the Third World*, Princeton: Princeton University Press, 1988.
3   Timothy Mitchell, 'No Factories, No Problems: The Logic of Neo-Liberalism in Egypt', *Review of African Political Economy*, 26, 82, 1999, pp. 455–68; Laura Guazzone and Daniela Pioppi, eds., *The Arab State and Neo-Liberal Globalisation – The Restructuring of State Power in the Middle East*, Reading: Ithaca Press, 2009; and Emel Akcali, ed., *Neoliberal Governmentality and the Future of the State in the Middle East*, London: Palgrave, 2016.
4   Dawisha and Zartman, *Beyond Coercion*, p. 1.
5   Marcella Emiliani, *L'idea di Occidente tra '800 e '900 – Medio Oriente e Islam*, Bologna: Rubbetius Editore, 2003, p. 11.
6   Salwa Ismail, *Political Life in Cairo's Quarters – Encountering the Everyday State*, Minneapolis: Minnesota University Press, 2006, p. 165.
7   Salwa Ismail notes how police forces intervene differently in poor quarters, targeting youth more than in other places. Her study of specialized and gendered sociability in one poor and marginalized section of Cairo, Bulaq ad-Dakrour, demonstrates that, there, the state is only perceived as a repressive entity where the term '*hukuma*' (government) becomes synonymous with police repression. See Ismail, *Political Life*, pp. 123–5 and p. 166: 'The citizens are aware that the state is not legal and that it is repressive but weak.'
8   Edward Said, *Orientalism*, London: Penguin, 1978; and Yahya Sadowksy, 'The New Orientalism and the Democracy Debate', *Middle East Report*, 183, 1993, pp. 14–21, 40.
9   There were books on Arab citizenship or issues of democracy, but they appeared much later. For example, Salamé published *Democracy without Democrats* in 2001, while Suad Joseph, who offered a much-needed perspective on gender and citizenship, published her edited volume in 2000.
10 Migdal, *Strong Societies*. This approach has been criticized by John Chalcraft, *Popular Politics in the Making of the Modern Middle East*, Cambridge: Cambridge University Press, 2016, pp. 10–14.

11 I use the plural form of demos to follow the call by Albert Hourani to speak of the Arab worlds in the plural form. See Albert Hourani, *A History of the Arab Peoples*, New York: MJF Books, 1991.
12 Killian Clarke, "Aysh, Huriyya, Karama Insaniyya: Framing and the 2011 Egyptian Uprising", *European Political Science*, 12, 2, 2013, pp. 197–214.
13 Chalcraft, *Popular Politics;* Ilham Khuri-Makdisi, *The Eastern Mediterranean and the Making of Global Radicalism, 1860–1914*, Berkeley, California: University of California Press, 2010; and Michelle Campos, *Ottoman Brothers – Muslims, Christians and Jews in Early Twentieth-Century Palestine*, Stanford, California: Stanford University Press, 2010.
14 Hanna Batatu, *The Old Social Classes and the Revolutionary Movements of Iraq – A Study of Iraq's Old Landed and Commercial Classes and Its Communist, Baathists and Free Officers*, Princeton, New Jersey: Princeton University Press, 1979; Zachary Lockman, *Comrades and Enemies Arab and Jewish Workers in Palestine, 1906–1948*, Berkeley, California: University of California Press, 1996; and Joel Beinin, *Was the Red Flag Flying There? – Marxist Politics and the Arab-Israeli Conflict in Egypt and Israel, 1948–1965*, Berkeley, California: University of California Press, 1990.
15 See Jonathan Cook, 'The Shin Bet and the Persecution of Azmi Bishara', *Counterpunch*, June 2007.
16 On democratization in the Arab world, see Oliver Schlumberger, 'The Arab Middle East and the Question of Democratisation: Some Critical Remarks', *Democratization*, 7, 4, 2000, pp. 104–32; Philippe Schmitter, 'Is It Safe for Transitologists and Consolidologists to Travel to the Middle East and North Africa?', in Roger Heacock, ed., *Political Transitions in the Arab World, Part One*, Birzeit: Birzeit University Press, 2001; Ghassan Salamé, *Democracy without Democrats? – The Renewal of Politics in the Muslim World*, London: I. B. Tauris, 2001; and Larbi Sadiki, *The Search for Arab Democracy – Discourses and Counter-Discourses*, London: Hurst and Company, 2004. All four offered stimulating texts on Arab democracy or issues of democratic transitions. In my understanding, democratization is the active pursuit of gradual reforms to make formal political institutions amenable with the principles of open and fair pluralist competition, power rotation and the rule of law. De facto, democratization concentrates on electoral components of democracy, focuses on political parties and emphasizes the separation of power. It therefore tends to be elite-focused, when not simply elite-driven. Democracy, understood as the power of the demos, entails a different focus on the quality of citizens' lives that is overlooked in democratization studies. Some of the following questions illustrate what studies of Arab democratic states should also ask, all of which are issues that do not emerge from democratization studies: Are all citizens (male and female, centres or peripheries, lower or higher social classes) equal in front of death? Do they have similar access to vital services? Can they be heard and listed to in various circuits and forms of deliberation?
17 Charles Tilly, ed., *The Formation of National States in Western Europe*, Princeton: Princeton University Press, 1975; Gianfranco Poggi, *The State – Its Nature, Development and Prospects*, Stanford, California: Stanford University Press, 1990; and Steven Heydemann, *War, Institutions and Social Change in the Middle East*, Berkeley, California: University of California Press, 2000.
18 I offer a brief account of this impact of external encroachment in 'Citizenship and Violence in the Arab Worlds – A Historical Sketch', in Juergen Mackert and Bryan S. Turner, eds., *The Transformation of Citizenship – Struggle, Resistance and Violence, Volume Three*, London: Routledge, 2017. In a longer book project, I distinguish three historical modes of external encroachment: capitalist, colonial and imperialist

attempts by external actors (ranging from Europe, then US and now Gulf countries, along with China and possibly Russia) to interfere in economic and political affairs of respective Arab states.
19 Evans et al., *Bringing the State*.
20 Mitchell, 'No Factories, No Problems', p. 77.
21 Ibid., p. 86.
22 Ibid., pp. 94–5.
23 Max Weber, *From Max Weber – Essays in Sociology*, Oxford: Oxford University Press, 1946 [1918], p. 78, emphasis added. Of course, Weber was not really a democratic scholar, in the sense that he did not care for the need to involve the demos or the masses. Furthermore, Weber never thematized the colonial and imperial ramifications of power that disqualified certain people to be below the par of (European) 'humanity'.
24 Wolf Hund and Alana Lentin, eds., *Racism and Sociology*, Vienna: Lit Verlag, 2014.
25 I am grateful to Jeffrey Weintraub for the discussions around these issues.
26 Ulrich Beck, 'Toward a New Critical Theory with a Cosmopolitan Intent', *Constellations*, 10, 4, pp. 453–68.
27 I owe this part (three forms of power) of the definition of the state to Poggi's *The State* (1990).
28 Beyond the international factors that were identified by Fouad Ajami in his *The Arab Predicament – Arab Political Thought and Practice since 1967*, New York: Cambridge University Press, 1992.
29 Burhan Ghalioun, 'Islam, Modernité et Laïcité: Les Sociétés Arabes Contemporaines', *Confluences Méditerranée*, 33, 2000, p. 25, 30.
30 Salamé in *Foundations of the Arab State* (p. 41) and Emiliani in *L'idea di Occidente* (p. 12) also notes that the *imitatio occidentalis*, the marked tendency in the last third of the nineteenth century to emulate the Western political and economic model was not only an external imposition but also, in part, a choice by the Sultan, the Egyptian Khedive or the Bey in Tunisia. In this light, we could also mention the earlier *Tajdeed* movement from the eighteenth century and which antedated the Napoleonic campaign and the start of the colonial rivalries in the nineteenth century. Thus, not every political process in the Arab Middle East is a reaction to the West. A lot of it is, but not all.
31 Jean-François Bayart, *The State in Africa – The Politics of the Belly*, London: Longman, 1993; and Bertrand Badie, *The Imported State – The Westernisation of Political Order*, Cambridge: Cambridge University Press, 2000.
32 1837 is the first occurrence of '*dawla*' with the modern meaning of the state as a juridical abstraction, endowed externally with sovereignty and internally with the function of organizing its society (see Ayubi, *Over-Stating the Arab State*, p. 22). Before that, the term, present in the Qur'an, indicated a dynasty, a system with a rotation of power.
33 In Doumani's account of a nascent Palestinian bourgeoisie, one sees that the geographical space corresponding to historical Palestine existed already back in the early nineteenth century as a space of socio-economic exchange. In Salamé's apt phrase, 'There are no *terra nullius*' (*Foundations of the Arab State*, p. 8).
34 Isa Blumi, *Chaos in Yemen – Societal Collapse and the New Authoritarianism*, London: Routledge, 2011, pp. 91–115. Blumi discusses the example of the Qa'tabah Valley, where local actors teased out the inability of the Ottoman and the British rule (under the formal control of the Lahj Sultan) to obtain benefits. Rather than imperial fiats, one has to consider the 'scramble to react to actual events taking place on the ground that were largely initiated by local forces' (p. 100).

35 Ibid., p. 104.
36 For a discussion of Arab agency in shaping economic policies in the twentieth century, see Aaron Jakes, 'Boom, Bugs, Bust: Egypt's Ecology of Interest, 1882–1914', *Antipode*, 49, 4, 2017, pp. 1035–59.
37 Moncef Kartas, 'The Tunisian-Libyan Border Space of the Jefara: Informality as Resistance to Post-Colonial State-Formation', unpublished paper, presented at the Middle East Law State and Society, Yale University, 2016.
38 Lara Deeb, *An Enchanted Modern – Gender and Public Piety in Shi'i Lebanon*, Princeton: Princeton University Press, 2005.
39 Bjørn Olav Utvik, 'The Modernising Force of Islamism', in John Esposito and François Burgat, eds., *Modernising Islam – Religion in the Public Sphere in Europe and the Middle East*, London: Hurst and Company, 2003, pp. 43–68; and François Burgat, *L'Islamisme en Face*, Paris: La Découverte, 1996.
40 Elizabeth Thompson, *Colonial Citizens – Republican Rights, Paternal Privilege and Gender in French Syria and Lebanon*, New York: Columbia University Press, 2000.
41 The problem continued well after independence. Samer Soliman describes how President Mubarak's social basis has been state employees. See his *The Autumn of Dictatorship – Fiscal Crisis and Political Change in Egypt under Mubarak*, Stanford, California: Stanford University Press, 2011, pp. 38–9, 60.
42 Nazih Ayubi, *Bureaucracy and Politics in Contemporary Egypt*, London: Ithaca Press, 1980.
43 This historical problem is now at play in Palestine, where two strands of public servants are paid by external sponsors, the European Union and the United States: the Fatah-led branch of the West Bank Palestinian Authority and the Hamas-led bureaucracy in Gaza. In Tunisia as well, access to state bureaucracy was excluding not only non-secular party members but also people from the south and the rural Hinterland. See Michaël Béchir Ayari, *Le Prix de l'Engagement en Régime Autoritaire – Gauchistes et Islamistes dans la Tunisie de Bourguiba et Ben Ali, 1957-2011*, Paris: Karthala, 2016.
44 Ayubi, *Bureaucracy and Politics*.
45 In *Beyond Coercion,* Dawisha and Zartman described the state as 'the authoritative political institution that is sovereign over a recognised territory' (p. 1). The works of Salamé and Luciani also focused on hard features of state politics and neglected the place of the demos in Arab politics. Salamé, in his effort to revisit the *Muqaddima* of Ibn Khaldun, focuses on the '*asabiya* of the ruling elite (*Foundations of the Arab State*, pp. 205–40). Roger Owen speaks of states as the nation-state, as the supreme coercive and rule-making body with external sovereignty and the internal duty of organizing society. See his *State, Power and Politics – The Making of the Modern Middle East*, Routledge: London, 1992, p. 3.
46 In *Over-Stating the Arab State*, Ayubi distinguishes analytically the Egyptian experience of state-building (98ff), from that of the Levant (Iraq included, 108ff), North Africa (117ff) and Arabia and the Gulf region (123ff).
47 Ibid., pp. 3–5. They also lack infrastructural power and ideological hegemony. Infrastructural power as described by Michael Mann is the power that 'enables states to penetrate societies affectively through mechanism such as taxation' (Ayubi, *Over-Stating the Arab State*, p. 3). See Michael Mann, *The Sources of Social Power, Volume 1 – A History of Power from the Beginning to AD 1760*, Cambridge: Cambridge University Press, 1986.
48 Abdallah Laroui, *L'Histoire du Maghreb – Un Essai de Synthèse*, Paris: La Découverte, 1982, pp. 146–58, 168.
49 Heydemann, *War, Institutions and Social Change*, pp. 22–4.

50 Ben Fine, Costas Lapavitsas and Jonathan Pincus, eds., *Development Policy in the Twenty-First Century – Beyond the Post-Washington Consensus*, London: Routledge, 2001.
51 For an overview of neoliberal impacts in Arab states, see Guazzone and Pioppi, *The Arab State* and Akcali, *Neoliberal Governmentality*.
52 The current burden put by the European Union on North African countries to limit 'illegal immigration' is likely to bolster another round of fierce Arab regimes.
53 Eberhard Kienle, *A Grand Delusion – Democracy and Economic Reform in Egypt*, London: I.B. Tauris, 2001.
54 Jean-Pierre Cassarino, 'Reversing the Hierarchy of Priorities in EU-Mediterranean Relations', in Joel Peters, ed., *The European Union and the Arab Spring – Promoting Democracy and Human Rights in the Middle East*, Lanham, Lexington: Lexington Books, 2012, pp. 1–15.
55 Mitchell, 'No Factories, No Problems'.
56 Soliman, *Autumn of Dictatorship*, pp. 44–5.
57 Mitchell, 'No Factories, No Problems'.
58 Pete Moore, 'QIZs, FTAs, USAID and the MEFTA: A Political Economy of Acronyms', *Middle East Report* 234, 35, 2005, pp. 18–23.
59 Cihan Tuğal, 'The Decline of the Legitimate Monopoly of Violence and the Return of Non-state Warriors', in Juergen Mackert and Bryan S. Turner, eds., *The Transformation of Citizenship – Struggle, Resistance and Violence, Volume Three*, London: Routledge, 2017, pp. 77–92.
60 Ibid., p. 77.
61 Ibid., p. 79.
62 Ibid., pp. 86–7.
63 Paul Amar, *The Security Archipelago – Human-Security States, Sexuality Politics and the End of Neoliberalism*, Durham: Duke University Press, 2013.
64 Ibid., p. 52 and p.100. This is what Amar describes as a 'parastatal' campaign, namely NGOs, policymakers, private-security agencies supported at times by police or military police (in the Brazilian case), morality campaigns and property developers (pp. 17–18).
65 Adam Hanieh, *Lineages of Revolt*, London: Haymarket, 2013.
66 Daʻesh is the Arab acronym for al Dawlah Islamiya fil 'Iraq wal Shaam, the 'Islamic state in Iraq and Syria' (Shaam is the historical name for the greater Syria region). The group abandoned this reference to Iraq and Syria during the summer 2014. To bolster its Islamic history credentials, ISIS insisted on holding on places such as Deir Ezzor, seat of an old administrative unit, a *sandjak* antedating colonial borders, or Dabiq, a village near Halib, Aleppo, where the last battle against the Antichrist is supposed to happen, according to a hadith. See Pierre-Jean Luizard, *Le Piège Daech – L'État Islamique ou le Retour de l'Histoire*, Paris: La Découverte, 2015 and Mohammad-Mahmoud Ould Mohamedou, *A Theory of ISIS – Political Violence and the Transformation of the Global Order*, London: Pluto Press, 2017.
67 Al-'Arawi, *L'Histoire du Maghreb*, pp. 11–86.
68 Dale F. Eickelman, *The Middle East and Central Asia – An Anthropological Approach*, Upper Saddle River, New Jersey: Prentice-Hall, 2002, p. 3.
69 Armando Salvatore, *Sociology of Islam – Knowledge, Power and Civility*, Malden, Massachusetts: John Wiley and Sons, 2016.
70 For a good overview of the arguments connecting Islam and democracy, see Michaelle L. Browers, *Democracy and Civil Society in Arab Political Thought – Transcultural Possibilities*, Syracuse: Syracuse University Press, 2006.

71 Abdellah Hammoudi, *Master and Disciplines – The Cultural Foundations of Moroccan Authoritarianism*, Chicago: Chicago University Press, 1997.
72 Armando Salvatore, *Sociology of Islam – Knowledge, Power and Civility*, Malden, MA: John Wiley and Sons, 2016.
73 Abdullahi An-Na'im, *Islam and the Secular State – Negotiating the Future of Shari'a*, Cambridge, Massachusetts: Harvard University Press, 2008, pp. 1–4.
74 Abdullahi An-Na'im, 'Sharia and the State in the 21st Century', video presentation for the conference 'Religion et État: Sécularisation et Citoyenneté en Islam', Graduate Institute, Geneva, http://iqbal.hypotheses.org/1010.
75 BBC, 'The Secret Lives of Young IS Fighters', 23 June 2017.
76 Aaron Zelin, 'The Islamic State of Iraq and Syria Has a Consumer Protection Office', *The Atlantic*, 13 June 2014.
77 Umberto Bacchi and Arij Limam, 'ISIS Mimics Britain's NHS with "Islamic State Health Service ISHS," *International Business Times UK*, 24 April 2015.
78 Luizard, *Le Piège Daesh*, p. 58.
79 Carool Kersten, *The Caliphate and Islamic Statehood – Formation, Fragmentation and Modern Interpretations*, Berlin: Gerlach Press, 2015.
80 Hamid Dabashi, *Authority in Islam – From the Rise of Muhammad to the Establishment of the Umayyads*, New Brunswick and London: Transaction Publishers, 1989, p. 49.
81 Hanieh, *Lineages of Revolt*, 2013.
82 See, when he speaks of the urban poor, Asef Bayat, *Life as Politics – How Ordinary People Change the Middle East*, Stanford, California: Stanford University Press, 2008, p. 44. See also Soliman, *Autumn of Dictatorship*, as regards his analysis of Egyptian civil servants and bureaucrats whose purchasing power and political relevance consistently diminished under Mubarak.
83 Benoît Challand, 'Citizenship and Violence in the Arab Worlds – A Historical Sketch', in Juergen Mackert and Bryan S. Turner, eds., *The Transformation of Citizenship – Struggle, Resistance and Violence, Volume Three*, London: Routledge, 2017.
84 Mohammed A. Bamyeh, 'Anarchist Method, Liberal Intention, Authoritarian Lesson: The Arab Spring between Three Enlightenments', *Constellation*, 20, 2, 2013, pp. 188–202.
85 Mouin Rabbani, 'The Year of the Citizen', in Bassam Haddad, Rosie Bsheer, Ziad Abu-Rish and Roger Owen, eds., *Dawn of the Arab Uprisings – End of an Old Order?* London: Pluto Press, 2012, pp. 33–6; and Farhad Khosrokhavar, *The New Arab Revolutions That Shook the World*, Boulder, Colorado: Paradigm Publishers, 2012.
86 Bruce Gilley, 'The Case for Colonialism', *Third World Quarterly*, April 2017, pp. 1–17.
87 'Israel Endorses Independent Kurdish State', *Reuters*, 13 September 2017.

PART TWO

IRRESOLUTIONS AND ABSENCES

4 A STATE IN SEARCH OF A NATION: THE CASE OF IRAQ

Faleh Abdul Jabar

Ethno-communal cleavages in Iraq seem so deep, so chronic and so intricate that the prospect of a peaceful symbiosis between state and nation appears remote, in fact elusive. The fierce politicization, and, since 2003, militarization of such schisms cast a gloomier look on the future. The disunion of state and 'national' community (read territorial) in Iraq, while not unique, was the first to erupt in the Middle East and North Africa. Today, this case seems to be present everywhere in the Mashreq (Syria, Yemen) and in the Maghreb (Libya). The Iraqi case, as well as those of Syria, Libya or Yemen, epitomize the basic problems of what has been labelled as the failure of 'state nationalism', a term that denotes a lack of unifying cultural, ethnic or other collective group markers, be they linguistic, religious or racial.[1] The term 'state nationalism' simply denotes that states in this case are *in search of* unified national communities, wherever this unity is wanting.

The politicization and militarization of subnational identities that disrupts unity is not an inevitable consequence of the mere existence of ethno-communal (religious or otherwise) differences per se. States may achieve success or may fail in building a national (again, primarily territorial) community. They may attain success at one point but may well take a step back in the next phase. Failure or success in the creation of viable state nationalism is not a once-and-for-all given status; rather it is constitutive of a fluid configuration sustained by a complex structural condition. And both are by no means essential, but in fact conjectural or situational.

This chapter explores this structural conditionality of success or failure in the quest for statehood in Iraq. First, the chapter addresses the general meaning of state, nation, nationalism and nation-building in the context of the Arab region. Second, it examines the sources of Iraqi nationalism and the causes of early phases of successful nation-building under the monarchy. Third, it turns to the gradual erosion of the 'national edifice' during the republican era. Fourth, the final failure of state nationalism due to successive wars and uprisings, and the rise of subnational identities under the successive military-authoritarian regime are discussed. Finally, the factors feeding into the persistence of ethno-communal breakup are analysed, ahead of tentative conclusions.

State, nation and nationalism

Nations, nationalism and nation-states are novel, historical and exclusively West European phenomena barely over two centuries old.[2] Since the end of the First World War, however, the nation-state pattern has become a universally recognized and accepted political model. It is the model of one nation-one state, based on a congruence of 'political and national unity', that is, the unity of the state and the national community, with the understanding that the political borders of the state should include all or the majority of the members of the nation as a community, as Ernest Gellner put it.[3] States and political borders are, in a sense, self-evident. A state is a system of governance, bureaucracy, army and economy with sovereignty over a demarcated territory and its inhabitants. The problem starts with defining 'the' nation as a community, as then a group-marker is required. Culture is put forward and further specification is required, notably language, religion (sect) or race, or a combination of any or all.[4] National community in India has none of these, while in Japan they all exist.

The general assumption is that 'national community', however defined, must have some form of cultural homogeneity which presumably allows cohesion and justifies integration into a single political unit: a state. When any of the three cultural markers is wanting, a substitute is fetched or even invented. The German cultural tradition of nationalism is paralleled by the French tradition of the will-of-togetherness. Culture and will can, nonetheless, be insufficient to form a state. Classical German thinkers such as Johann Gottfried Herder and Johann Gottlieb Fichte conceived lineage as the cultural unifying marker, that is, blood relation. They called it *stämme*, meaning tribe or clan. A national group is one tied by blood relations, by natural bonds, and the national *differentia specifica* becomes a natural trait just like having a nose or eyes. Perhaps this also is why the French went beyond 'ethno-naturalism' to what they termed the will to live together.[5] Togetherness is embedded in freewill and the freewill is in turn anchored in common interests, and the readiness, as Ernest Renan put it, to forget past subgroup reciprocal atrocities and focus on common interests at the present.[6] In all cases of cultural markers, or free-will-of-togetherness, a unifying space is created, one that gives birth to common identity, that equal of 'nationals' or equal citizens and a sense of meaning to the aggregation called 'nation.'

Non-ethnic nation-building is actually the universal rather than particular pattern. It is evident in the paradox of the plenty as there are worldwide at least 8,000 linguistic groups, implying 8,000 potential nation-states – and the figure is confined to linguistic markers. Imagine if religion, race and other indicators of ethnicity were to be added up. The conclusion would be simple: hundreds if not thousands of ethno-linguistic and/or religious groups would be trapped in the universal unit of political organization that modernity brought about: the centralized nation-state. Nationalism seems less problematic. It is sentiments, movements, discourses or political cultural ideology. These yearn for the unity of state and nation. Unless wedded with a state, a nation will remain a mere cultural conception, a would-be entity, a potential, a project. If not incarnated in a polity, with physical terrain, borders and sovereignty, a nation goes down in history as debacle, like Latin American or Arab nationalisms. Under heterogeneity, the clash between state and nation is a matter of course. Nations require what Renan ironically called a 'continuous referendum', a constant presence of this will-togetherness.

Attachment to empire

Iraq was born out of the 'sacred' Ottoman Empire. Like the Roman Empire, and other empires in Europe, the Ottoman Empire's existence was an aberration, and the states-nations (rather than nation-states) that emerged from it bore the birthmarks of this past. Empires, like the Ottoman, were large seemingly unified units. In actuality, they were fragmented from within into local emirates, city states, local ruling dynasties, warlords, autonomous tribal domains and self-contained sects and religious communities. Allegiance to the extended family, the clerical authorities, Sufi orders, Guilds, Aghas, tribal chiefs, in short a myriad of centres of power and authority, were factored in additionally. These all cut across ethno-linguistic-religious identities. Moreover, these segments were bereft of any organic connections that integrate modern societies. Their pre-modern fracture lines would face the drive to create a central modern state anchored in homogeneous, ethno-national bases.

Initiated by the state, modernization was rapid and sweeping where commercial economy, industrial centres and modern thought and culture rapidly developed. It resulted in the dismantling of the rigid, agricultural–artisanal division of labour and weakened and eventually removed the clerical monopoly of intellectual culture. State modernization standardized and generalized the local or native vernacular. It spread high culture through the educational system. The centralization of the polity brought about two formidable machines: the military and the bureaucracy, which worked in two ways: the ability to overcome and control societal segments, and the inclusion of these segments into institutions to become part of the state. With the growth of urban centres and modern communication networks, from print to audio media, a vast interactive cultural space emerged. This new cultural space birthed new loyalties for the new national community as a free, equal entity (citizenship and elections) with ideas of citizenship standing over and above old subnational (tribe, city) and supranational (religion) forms of allegiance.

Such was the general outline of the development of the new nation states in Europe, and to some extent in Turkey and its Arab satellites from the late nineteenth century to the mid-twentieth century. Looking from the vantage point of the nineteenth century at the Arab world in the next century, the rise of the 'national' (or *qutri*, i.e. regional, in the Arab nationalism jargon) statehood looks like a double-edged process. On the one hand, it is a 'separatist' entity materializing against the 'sacred' community of Islam (then embodied in the Ottoman Empire), and, on the other hand, it is an integrative polity against the segmented agrarian–artisanal communities. The transition from the age of empire to that of modern nation state was abrupt, hasty, compressed and complex. The modern state came to rest on citizenship, that is, the equality among individuals, irrespective of religious identity, be they Bedouins or urbanites, *effendi* or commoner. Such modernity necessitates the existence of strong central system, constitutional institutions, a dynamic economy, an open democratic system of representation and an all-inclusive national discourse.

In embryo, seeds of modern centralism, constitutionalism and nationalism grew at the heart of the Ottoman land (what then became Turkey).[7] Non-Turkish ethno-linguistic groups were stimulated along such lines. The historical process of centralization, constitutionalization and nationalism developed two major political trends: decentralization under some form of autonomy for non-Turkish ethnicities (Arabs and Kurds), and centralization of the state. The Committee of Union and Progress (CUP) military takeover in 1908 carried this line of modernization further. Although the idea of Arab autonomy had some reception in the Levant, it hardly had any recorded impact or significant trace in Iraq. In Albert Hourani's opinion, Arab and Turkish nationalisms were at that stage (1908) more geared towards the resolution of problems of identity and the political reorganization of the empire than they were directed against European colonial penetration. This latter anti-colonial pattern characterized more Egyptian, Algerian and other North African nationalisms, challenging the British and French colonialism.[8] The latter was 'patriotic', that is, native or local nationalism with strong territorial-political administrative unit and no trace of pan-Arabism. Compared to this Arab African case, Iraq had none.

Detachment from the empire

The newly born Iraq state, incepted by the British colonial administration throughout the mandate period (1920–1932), inherited all the intricate problems of modern centralization and nation-building that are usually associated with pre-national, agrarian–artisanal, tribal and communal 'society'. Nationalism – or the notion of the principle of nations – was in the air but not in society. The idea stemmed from two opposing source: the liberal president of the United States, Woodrow Wilson, and the revolutionary leader of the Soviet Union, Vladimir Lenin. That was the *geist* (spirit) of the age. Yet, in the Iraqi context, nationalism was a contradiction in definition since the country it was a *pre-nationalist* land. The Arab ideas embraced by Prince-then-King Faisal bin Husain or his Sharifian Officers were a vague concept of a thin elite. By contrast, Iraqi anti-colonial, responsive nationalism – triggered, as it were, by the British invasion and administration in 1920 – was widespread and popular, at least among wide segments of Baghdadi society.

In retrospect, to speak of nationalism in Iraq in 1920 may seem a contradiction in terms. Iraq – indeed the Mashreq in its entirety – was a pre-national region, bereft of unifying economic, cultural or political structures, not to mention the discourses of nationalism. The reaction against colonial penetration was the only manifestation of local patriotism, and it was confined to Baghdad, the tribal domains in mid-Euphrates and hardly beyond. Iraq social spaces were notoriously multiple: a myriad of identities and antagonistic social configurations. In ethnic terms, Arabs, Kurds, Turkmen and Assyrian (even Chaldo-Syriac) hardly intermingled, or had any meaningfully, unifying supra-identity. Arabs, and even Turkmen, were divided into Shi'is and Sunnis. The grand sociological cleavage was that of urbanites versus tribesmen. Towns and cities which may nurture some sort of local solidarity yet have social hierarchy with nobles (*sadah* or *ashraf*) at the helm, merchants a step below and further down the artisans, all organized in extended families and guilds, and revolved around solidarities of their relative quarters (*mahalla*).

The realm of tribes and clans was no less segmented. There was a rigid hierarchy that placed the camel-breeders (*ahl al bil*) at the helm as outstanding warriors; at a lower grade was the sheep-breeder (*shawiya*); next are land-tillers, the agriculturalists (*harratha*), down farther are the marsh Arabs (*mi'dan*), fisherman and buffalo-breeders. The last two categories are subdivided: the *harratha* are classified into rice and wheat growers at the top, and veg growers at the bottom, while marsh fishermen are subdivided into the superior spear-fishermen and lower net-fishermen. All these are status groups ordered in a hierarchy that confers superiority or inferiority of professional lineage. These segmented and fragmented communities are penetrated by traditional-religious values that tend to seclusion, differentiation and preference, rather than openness, equality and unification. Hence the need for integrative institutions, all-inclusive constitution and a unifying discourse of nationalist ideology.

None more than King Faisal I was painfully aware of the divided, pre-national reality of the Iraqi realm that was to be his kingdom. 'Iraq is bereft of the most important element of social life, that of ideological unity and millet (i.e., national) unity', he warned his entourage. He went on to specify what he considered the major segments of the nation: young innovators (modernists), fanatics (conservatives), Sunnis, Shi'is; Kurds, non-Muslim minorities, tribes, tribal chiefs and the bulk of ignorant who embrace any 'bad' idea.[9] Here with King Faisal we find the ethnic divide (Arab-Kurd), religious divide (Muslim and non-Muslims), the sectarian divide (Shi'is and Sunnis), the social divide (cities and tribes) and the intellectual divide (modernists vs. conservative). Faisal objected to the post–First World War British plans to have a Kurdish state in the northern part of the country, inclusive of what was then the Vilayet of Mosul. His argument was ethno-communal. As a Sunni Shafi'i, he was an alien *vis-à-vis* 'his' predominantly Shi'i populace; the Kurds, being Muslim Shafi'is like him, would create a balance of power enabling him to rule and build a viable state with some sense of patriotic union around the state, that is state nationalism.[10]

King Faisal dealt with the realities of religious identity but unwittingly created a multi-ethnic state at the very moment of the beginning of the rise of cultural-political nationalism in the region. The new state, the Kingdom of Iraq, had to embark on the process of integration to produce a 'national community'. It was a state in search of nationhood *par excellence*. The new kingdom was based on a constitutional-parliamentary system *à la* Westminster, headed by an Arab-Muslim king of noble Hashemite lineage. This arrangement wedded open and inclusive – that is, liberal – institutions of governance with the principle of Arabism and the nobility of lineage. Thus doing, it satisfied the major forces in action: the British colonial rulers and the Arab ideology of the Sharifian officers who had joined King Faisal. Faisal's Hashemite lineage also satisfied the values of the Shiite Sada, the Sunni Ashraf and, most importantly, the *mujtahid* (clerics) in Najaf, and was in harmony with tribal kinship ideology.

The referendum that gave birth to the monarchy showed massive approval among Shi'is and Sunnis but wide rejection by Kurds and Turkmen. This revealed the political gravity of ethnic divide and the political absence of sectarian (Sunni–Shi'i) rift, the opposition by Turkey notwithstanding.[11] Indeed this played out in tandem with the birth of Iraqi nationalism in 1920, before, during and after the 1920 anti-British revolt. It resonated with the *fatwas* from the religious dignitaries in Najaf who called for the inception of a Muslim-Arab monarch, with the Arab nationalist ideology of the military elite that joined King Faisal and with the activities of Baghdad merchants led by Ja'afar Abu Timmin, the founder of the first patriotic party, al Hizb al Watani, a Shi'i-Sunni outfit. The birth of Iraqi nationalism was thus the creation of Shi'i-Sunni understanding and agreement. It was in need of a side-track of accommodation of the Kurds and other minorities. In a word, Iraqi nationalism, as it stood in 1920, was not enough to hold the 'Iraqi' population in the integrative process of state formation. What followed was a two-track process of state-building and nation-building, with the first track used to enhance the second. Needless to say that state-building here refers to building institutions of governance and representation – from crown, cabinet, bureaucracy and security apparatuses (military and police, notably). Nation-building refers to the establishment of participatory and inclusive mechanisms to ensure the consent of the diverse ethno-communal groups, and to secure their proportionate participation in political, economic and cultural life.

The institutional build-up of the new polity was not smooth. It met with ethnic rebellions (by the Kurdish sheikh Mahmood Barzanji in 1920, 1924 and 1930; and the Assyrian revolt in 1933–1936), urban protests against the British Treaty (in 1924) and tribal insurrection against the conscription law (in 1934–1935). Yet the process received urban-tribal support across the land. Much of the success belonged to the 'liberal' nature of the polity and economy being introduced. Political, economic and administrative participation was wide open to all segments. As of the first cabinet and parliament, Arabic, Kurdish, Shi'i, Sunni, Jewish and Christian individuals were included. More importantly, the new state deployed its distributive power as the owner of land to create a multi-ethnic and multi-religious, unified landlord class and a capitalist class, who formed the social bases of the system. Both these strata included Arab, Kurdish, Sunni and Shi'i tribal chiefs, nobles and bureaucrats. Even the monarch himself turned into a landlord. The structure of the landlord class was 48 per cent Shi'is, 20 per cent Sunni Kurds and 18 per cent Sunni Arabs, in addition to Turkmen and Assyrian elements.[12] The structure of this class mirrors the Iraqi society at large, and it embodies the integration pursued by the state through political and economic participation. The liberal character of the political-economic system opened up all venues of representation, secured a share in the production and distribution of wealth, namely land and business, and allowed the state to mutate its function from a mere system of rule (*hukm*) into a system of governance representative of a national community in the making.

One should not nonetheless place too much emphasis on the political-economic aspects of the state-building process. Crucial as these aspects were and remain, the central educational system and other cultural aspects were equally important tools in the creation of an Iraqi 'imagined community'. After 1921, it took more than a decade to initiate and enhance this process of political, economic and cultural inclusion. It is this open-for-all or not-so-open-for all process that may explain much of the stability or instability of Iraq in ethnic and nationalistic terms. Before turning to the disintegration of this founding process, we need to register anew Renan's prophetic statement that nationhood is a constant 'referendum' – a flame that needs to be kept alive and to be maintained and repaired whenever damaged. In a word, this state-founding process is not a given that is taken for granted once and for all.

The republican disintegrative era

Against all odds, the Iraqi monarchy (1932–1950) had managed to create a state-nation, introducing viable state nationalism that had never existed before locally in sociological terms. That new polity established itself as a system of governance and a legitimate representative of the national Iraqi community. It shifted from military coercion to political consent, by dint of liberal polity, open market economy and inclusion of all segments and communal groups in the administration and the military. The monarchy also built a massive communication system and culturally cohesive institutions of education and learning that enhanced further the sense of Iraqi imagined community.

The republican era (1958–1968), which followed, gradually and unwittingly dismantled these basic pillars of an already fragile nationhood. As the military takeover opened up opportunities before hitherto disfranchised and excluded middle strata, it removed the landlord and upper business classes that had formed the backbone of the monarchy and the very grounds of the new Iraqi nation. The revolutionary soldier-politician shut the two-chamber parliament as a system of representation, and did the same to the constitutional court. While it improved the representation of the middle strata, the authoritarian nature of the new military regime dealt a heavy blow to the balanced inclusion and participation of the diverse communities. Unlike the landlord and upper business classes, the middle strata were united neither in purpose nor in interests, nor indeed in ideology. And with no parliament, no constitutional court and now crown, checks and balances no longer existed in the system. Blocked representation and participation opened up the venues of conspiratorial politics, coups and counter-coups, with thinner and thinner ruling elites at the helm monopolizing power by sheer coercion and violence.

Looking at the structure of the state elites after 1963, several features can be specified. These are the predominance of a mostly Sunni high brass; a decline in the representation of Kurds and Shi'is; a shift from upper, urban middle strata to provincial lower middle strata[13]; a cultural shift from state nationalism and organized mass politics to Arab nationalism and reliance on mostly tribal kinship networks; a shift of legitimacy and sovereignty from the ballot to the bullet, and from liberal election to self-claimed representation of the 'people' and the 'revolution'[14]; and lastly, the replacement of the liberal market economy by a command economy controlled by a thin ruling class. It is mostly in the second part of this period that the Kurdish rebellion and Shiite communal activism emerged, signalling the beginning of the decline of class-ideological politics. The disruption of nation-building never waned thereafter, suspending thereby the necessity of renewing this process via constant negotiations (the Renan syndrome).

War and the failure of state nationalism

The Ba'ath Party rule (1968–2003) opted for a totalitarian-patrimonial model anchored in a populist-statist form of nationalist socialism with its command economy, statist rentierism, single party system and a clan-class nomenclature at the helm. The Ba'athists used oil rent to buy consent and build crony networks of middle and business classes. They also used that rent to build a formidable security control over a notoriously restless, diversified and pluralistic society. By their very nature, totalitarian regimes monopolize the political field and impose a monist ideology, which is incompatible with a multi-ethnic and multi-cultural society. The end result is political exclusion and disfranchisement, unbalanced economic participation of regions and social segments, ethnic assimilation, cultural domination and coercive statist measures to hegemonize each and every autonomous space of cultural and social action.

What was materially lost was symbolically compensated. Along with the abstract concept of the Arab nation, the official creed of the regime became an Iraqi form of nationalism tailored further in the mid-1970s to better cope with realities. The new Iraqi nationalism was officially constructed out of diverse pre-Islamic, Islamic and modern elements. Historical symbols and myths from ancient

Sumerian, Acadian and Babylonian past were deployed.[15] Muslim symbols, like Shiite Imams or Kurdish Muslim leaders such as Salah al Din (Saladin), were incorporated into the fabric of Iraqi state nationalism.[16] All was meant to convey a sense of unity with a view to lend the modern Iraqi state-nation a semblance of historical depth overriding ethnic and religious divide. Perhaps more importantly was the bent to co-opt 'Iraqi patriotism', the popular sentiments of attachment to Iraq, which were strongly apparent among Arab and segments of other ethno-communal groups.

As noted, nationalism is of complex nature, resting on a major distinction between state nationalism and popular patriotism. In Ba'thi Iraq, the latter gradually diverged from the former, fuelling internal tensions. The seeds of this divorce were latent, and the Ba'ath regime had to remedy this illness. War – in fact wars – was the conceived therapy. In one decade (1980–1990), Iraq waged two devastating wars, against Iran and against Kuwait, the second of which culminated in massive anti-regime uprisings in April 1991.[17] Why these wars were ever waged is a matter of debate. The general assumption is that the first war was launched out of regional ambitions on part of Iraq's ruling elite, or to remove the national security threat Iran was seen as constituting after its 1979 Islamic revolution. The second war was started to remove the negative consequences of the first. The internal dynamics were overlooked,[18] namely the war as a means of nation-building in the face of the Shi'i-Islamic dividing influence Iran posed in 1980–1981, and in the face of changing regional and global conditions – notably the 1988–1990 uprisings in Jordan and Algeria and the collapse of single-party systems in Eastern Europe. Regional factors notwithstanding, Iraqi internal dynamics were the hotbed from which such grand, regional ambitions emerged: war was not only a means to outward expansion but also a cohesive instrument of state-building and regime security.[19]

No phenomenon more than war can ever make or break legitimacy of the state – in its capacity as a ruling system and representative of a national community – or nurture or disturb the fervour of nationalism both as an ideology and social movement. Iraqi war propaganda focused both on Iraqism with its various pre-Islamic, Islamic and modern aspects as much as it did on defaming the Iranian enemy on religious-ethnic grounds, as being Persian/Magus, that is, non-Muslims. Needless to say, the very logic of war similarly required the full-swing vitalization of nationalism as a space unifying divergent social groups and interests in one monolithic-like national community. The largest sections of the Arab populace showed unmistakable signs of support and pride in Iraq's military power and successes in the first years of the war, a testimony to the unity of state nationalism with popular patriotism.[20] In the interval between the Iran–Iraq war and the 1991 Gulf war tension were as high as expectations; the choice of reform in the manner Jordan or Eastern Europe were pursuing it was in the air. Reform was indeed offered but not delivered on, and the invasion of Kuwait followed overwhelming the nation. In the end, the bulk took up arms against their own government in March 1991.

If the strong union of statist nationalism and popular patriotism during much of the 1980–1988 Iraq–Iran war was evident, their clash during and after the 1990–1991 Gulf war was glaringly manifest. How and why did they diverge and, in the end, clash? In general, war usually demands unity of the nation, rebellion its discord. The logic of war, if prevailing, buries all schisms under thick, even monolithic layers of union of purpose and action and channels energies outwards. The logic of revolt hoists aloft the principle of dissent and directs fury inwards. Drained of their sense of loyalty to the state defined by their ruling class, large segments of the Iraqi population took to arms. All the twists and turns in official ideology – from Arabism to Iraqism and from secularism to religious symbols – had shifted political ideology away from notions of progress, vanguard-party and socialism, to tradition and tribe. Nationalist socialism changed direction from command economy, state-guaranteed employment and free social services to deregulation, commercialization and pauperism. The bulk of middle classes to which most of the Ba'ath generation belonged now plunged into the abyss. The Kurdish Province gained de facto autonomy, and Islamism and tribalism prevailed nationally, tailored on the model of the personality of the ruling dictator.[21] The state was never the same again, neither as a system of governance nor as a representative of a national-territorial community.

The rise and disintegration of identity politics

As the American and British armies swept into Iraq in March 2003, the totalitarian Ba'thist regime melted down in three weeks. It left an awesome void and a fragmented society bereft of cohesive social associations, save religion and kinship. And these latter two elements had become more divisive than ever. Religion, here Islam, was, unlike the Siamese twin, split into two warring creatures, Sunnism versus Shi'ism, or Islam versus non-Islam. Unlike the 1920 British invasion, the 2003 US takeover set in motion a process of dismantling rather than reforming what was left of the state system. This destructive logic impacted army, security, police, institutions of control and the essential condition of governance. Whereas the British based the newly set up monarchy in 1921 on a solid Sunni–Shi'i alliance, with a side accommodation of the Kurds and other groups, the United States birthed the new polity on a Shi'i–Kurdish alliance. This narrow base was gradually expanded with a sidetrack accommodation of the Sunnis.

The four scenarios envisaged by the United States to govern Iraq – direct military rule, civil US administration, civil Iraqi authority or interim Iraqi government – met the formidable currents of nationalism, Islamism and tribalism. However, all these trends evolved under a new sociocultural condition, namely, the rise of identity politics. Such identity factors had been a reinvigorated feature in the Middle Eastern polity since the second Gulf war of 1991. Ideological politics, the grand narratives of socialism, Marxism and Arab nationalism had sustained massive decline, which induced the reconfiguration of political blocs and outfits on the basis of communal group identity, be it sectarian (Shi'i or Sunni) or ethnic (Kurds, Turkmen, Assyrian and so on). To better understand the Iraqi strand of identity politics, it is instructive to cast a comparative look at other versions, for instance, in the former Yugoslavia or the former Soviet Union republics. This helps understand comparatively – and reasonably interpret – the Iraqi impasse of no-state-no-nation syndrome. In the former Yugoslavia and the former Soviet Union, the political crisis brought about the decline, in fact, the demise, of the official internationalist-socialist ideology. That official mantra was replaced by nationalism, which then triggered inter-ethnic conflicts across the two countries at the very moment their ruling elites were shaken and their command economy melting down.[22] In contrast, the decline of nationalist-socialism in Iraq was brought about by the 1991 military defeat, the degeneration of the state as a system of control and governance, and the collapse of the rentier-command economy. The official ideology was consciously replaced, and finally displaced throughout the 1990s, by reviving tribalism and Islamism. Retribalization was officially pursued as of 1993, and so were the so-called 'Faith Campaigns'. Both trends were launched to enhance a teetering regime strangled by the international sanctions imposed after the Gulf War. The informal institutions of religion and tribe took, however, a life of their own, and Sunni fundamentalism as well as Shi'ite identity conceptions spread across the Arabic part of Iraq. In Kurdistan, Kurdish ethno-identity politics induced other communities in the region to pursue the same line. In the end, Shi'i, Sunni, Kurdish, Turkmen, Assyrian and Chaldo-Syriac identities were in full politicization drive, fiercely or peacefully competing against each other.

The violent rise of Shi'i identity politics became a mass current following the return of Shi'i Islamic parties from exile in the summer of 2003. Shi'i symbols and images of Imam Hussain and Ali were deployed. Sunni groups responded by a counter-Sunni identity centred on the Prophet Mohammad. The war of religious and sectarian symbols spread across Baghdad and other cities. What occurred after 2003 was the massive spread of religious identities rather the creation thereof. Turning this into mass politics was only natural as the public sphere was flung wide open in the wake of the total collapse of the state. What also occurred was the militarization of identity politics, at least in the Sunni–Shi'i conflict. The conflict became complex, as opposition to the military occupation was incorporated in group competition over the levers of power and the lavish resources of a rentier economy.

Identity politics strive and partly succeed in painting the internal cracks in each and every community, but they never remove them. In this context, the protest movement that subsequently burst into social life in most Shi'i cities represented a rebellion of Shi'i middle and lower middle strata urbanites against a predominantly Shi'i government. This rift signalled a shift from identity politics to issue politics. This conception was embedded in differentiating the two aspects of communal identity, first, as a religious-cultural distinctiveness involving beliefs, rites, rituals, social networks and informal associations; and, secondly, as a group or collective political identity used to sustain unified political action and create an inclusive/exclusive discourse to mark and unite the community, feed collective action and manipulate the victimhood symbolism. This politicization of religious-cultural identity is similar in some respects to mass politicization by means of nationalism. Nationalism, like political sectarian identity, thrives on the notions of injustice – plunder and occupation – perpetrated by the Other, that is, the colonizer, Sunni/Shi'i community and so on. In brief, it thrives on external hazards and preys on internal dissent. When external threats subside and injustices are removed (say by the victim assuming power in place of the tyrant), the sense of internal unity created by the sectarian political discourse simply wanes. Indeed, the notion of 'Shi'i victimhood' has become largely, but not entirely, irrelevant and the notion of 'majority rule' stepped in.

Religious identities are solid, in fact perennial, and cannot vanish. They are simply cultural artefacts with historical depth, protected by a host of formal and in formal institutions, a system of rituals, traditions and social forces that produce them and reproduce them as rock hard monuments of identity. This cannot change. What may change are the forms, limits and modalities of turning these cultural entities and spaces into an exclusivist political discourse, i.e. politicization. In Iraq and elsewhere, these forms, limits and modalities are fluid and flexible since the communal space is in fact multiple spaces inhabited by various social, class, economic, cultural and political groups with conflicting views and interests that defy homogenizing in a single political discourse. The question is who has the right to represent the community – which party, what leader – is crucial. Rivalry sets in conflict over representation of the respective community. This conflict was well evident in the Iraqi national and provincial elections in 2009–2010 and 2013–2014, when each community, however defined, put forth multiple contenders. Rivalry reveals internal divisions along social, class, political, ideological, local, clan or even personal lines.

Identity politics are incompatible with nation-building or the re-creation of Iraq's state-nation (again, as different from the nation-state). The 'sect-centric' syndrome in both Shi'i and Sunni Islamic discourses has proved to be a recipe for failure.[23] The partial shift from identity to issue politics is, again partly, a recognition of this failure and a search for a way out of the dilemma. Thus far Iraq is a failed state. At least three criteria demonstrate this fiasco. First, the Iraqi state does not have a successful monopoly of the legitimate means of violence; there are seven armies in Iraq, four of which are autonomous of the central government. Second, the state does not enjoy full recognition as a representative of the 'national (territorial) community'. Lastly, the state has thus far failed to deliver public goods, notably services and internal security. It is still the case that the ruling elite thinks and acts in line with the German ethno-nationalism, whereas the complex realities may be more compatible with Renan's French model. The latter, however, requires more than recognizing common interests – which, in Iraq, spells forgetting past reciprocal atrocities.

Notes

1. Parts of this chapter incorporate earlier writings by the author. See Benedict Anderson, *Imagined Communities – Reflections on the Origin and Spread of Nationalism*, London: Verso, 1983, pp. 80–103.
2. This is in general agreement with most scholars examining nationalism. Some take a different route, that of perennial ethnicity that existed, so to speak, from time immemorial. See John Hutchinson and Anthony D. Smith, *Ethnicity*, Oxford: Oxford University Press, 1996.
3. Ernest Gellner, *Nations and Nationalism*, Oxford: Oxford University Press, 1983, p. 1.
4. Ibid., p. 35.
5. See Johann Fichte, 'Addresses to the German Nation', 1808; and Ernest Renan, 'What Is a Nation?', 1882. Gellner does not start his book on nationalism with examining the cultural theorem versus the free-will concept but leaves it to Chapter Five, despite the importance he attaches to the German versus French traditions.
6. Renan, 'What Is a Nation?', 1882.
7. Albert Hourani, *Arabic Thought in the Liberal Age, 1798-1939*, Cambridge: Cambridge University Press, 1962, p. 273; and Peter Malcolm Holt, *Egypt and the Fertile Crescent*, Ithaca: Cornell University Press, 1966, p. 52.
8. Hourani, *Arabic Thought*, pp. 309–10.
9. Abd al Razzaq al Hasani, *Tarikh al Wizarat al 'Iraqiyya* (The History of Iraqi Cabinets), Sidon, Lebanon: Matba'at al Irfan, 1953–1967, Volume 3, p. 315.
10. See Faleh Abdul Jabar, 'Artificial and Natural Nation-Building: The Case of Iraq', in Gérard Khoury and Nadine Meouchy, eds., *États et Sociétés de l'Orient Arabe en Quête d'Avenir*, Paris: Geuthner, 2007, Volume I, pp.122–3.
11. Ghassan R. Atiya, *Iraq, 1908-1921 – A Sociopolitical Study*, Beirut: Arab Institute for Research and Publication, 1973.
12. Hanna Batatu, *The Old Social Classes and the Revolutionary Movements of Iraq – A Study of Iraq's Old Landed and Commercial Classes and Its Communist, Baathists and Free Officers*, Princeton, NJ: Princeton University Press, 1979, pp. 47–8, Table of Landlords. For their role in the parliament, see p. 103.
13. Derek Hopwood et al., eds., *Iraq – Power and Society*, Oxford: St. Antony's College, 1993, pp. 20–30, 75–90; Roger Owen, *The Middle East in the World Economy, 1800–1914*, London: I.B. Tauris, 1993, pp. 197–200 and 206–12; and George Lenczoswki, *Political Elites in the Middle East*, Washington, DC: American Enterprise Institute, 1975, pp. 118–21.
14. Batatu, *Old Social Classes*; and Hazem Beblawi and Giacomo Luciani, eds, *The Rentier State – Nation, State and Integration in the Arab World*, London: Croom Helm, 1987, pp. 10–14.
15. On the restructuring of Iraqi nationalism under the Ba'ath, see Amatzia Baram, *Culture, History and Ideology in the Formation of Ba'thist Iraq, 1968-89*, London: St. Martin's Press, 1991; and Amatzia Baram, 'Mesopotamian Identity in Ba'thi Iraq', *Middle Eastern Studies*, 19, 4, 1983, pp. 426–55.
16. On the role of Islam in the first and second Gulf wars, see Falah Abdul Jabar, 'The Double-Edged Sword of Islam', in Haim Bresheeth and Nira Yuval Davis, eds., *The Gulf War and the New World Order*, London: Zed Books, 1991, pp. 211–18.
17. See Faleh Abdul Jabar, 'The War Generation in Iraq: A Case of Failed Etatist Nationalism', in Lawrence G. Potter and Gary G. Sick, eds., *Iran, Iraq and the War Legacies of War*, London: Palgrave Macmillan, 2004, pp. 121–40.

18   See Faleh Abdul Jabar, 'Roots of an Adventure', in Victoria Brittain, ed., *The Gulf Between Us – The Gulf War and Beyond*, London: Virago, 1991, pp. 27–42.
19   Perhaps the best analysis of the problems of nation-building and regime security involved in the war effort can be found in Mohammad-Mahmoud Mohamedou, *Iraq and the Second Gulf War – State Building and Regime Security*, San Francisco: Austin and Winfield, 1998.
20   There is general agreement that the uprising was triggered by the retreating soldiers in Basra, the most devastated city during the two Gulf wars. Prominent high-ranking officers confirmed this was the case. See, for instance, General Najib al Salihi, *Al Zilzal (The Earthquake) – What Happened in the Aftermath of Withdrawal from Kuwait*, London: Al Rafid, 1998.
21   See Faleh Abdul Jabar, 'The End of a Dictator', *The Financial Times*, 13 May 2003; and Faleh Abdul Jabar, 'Why the Uprisings Failed', *Middle East Report*, 176, May/June 1991, pp. 2–12. On 20 December 1994, General Jabar Muhsin, a veteran Ba'thist of Shi'i and rural origin, lamented about the 'middle classes which we have lost' in the Baghdad-based Babil. Muhsin was in charge of the Directorate of Morale Mobilisation in the Ministry of Defence, and his opinion reflected the state of mind of the ruling military and civilian elite.
22   Mary Kaldor, *New and Old Wars – Organised Violence in a Global Era*, Cambridge: Polity, 2006, pp. 81–2.
23   Sect-centric nationalism is coined by Fener Haddad in some of his essays on sectarianism in Iraq. See Fener Haddad, *Sectarianism in Iraq – Antagonistic Visions of Identity*, London: Hurst & Company, 2011, p. 143.

5 ONE HUNDRED YEARS OF THE PALESTINIAN NATIONAL MOVEMENT

Ahmad Samih Khalidi

Over the course of the past one hundred or so years of the struggle over the Holy Land, the Palestinian people have been driven by successive national impulses, aspirations and goals of varying influences and durability. Looking back, three distinct phases are discernible: 'independence', 'return' and 'statehood'. During the very earliest phase of the conflict, the Arab inhabitants of Palestine were subject to the push and pull of different and often conflicting tides, from Ottomanism, pan-Arabism and Syrian-centric nationalism, to regional, local, clan and familial loyalties, and finally to the more modern imports of self-rule and national self-determination. The 1917 Balfour Declaration and British occupation of Palestine began to clear the path towards a more coherent and definitive political stance, but the first national stirrings remained largely that of vocal protest and demonstrative opposition, grounded an appeal to the West's self-professed moral values and its Wilsonian claims to support the rights of the oppressed people of the Ottoman Empire to self-determination, matched with a native and visceral rejection of any attempt to hand the homeland over to European Jewry, such as that espoused by the new British rulers of Palestine.[1]

A broader and more cohesive national movement emerged slowly and in fits and starts over the next three decades under the British Mandate. The gravitational pull of Ottomanism naturally evaporated with the demise of Turkish rule, and the attraction of pan-Syrian-ism largely (but not totally) faded away after France's defeat of the Sharifist endeavour at Maysaloon in 1920. By the mid-1930s, the national movement had taken sufficient shape to give birth to the first experiments in organized party politics and, consequently, to the further development of clear national goals. The trajectory of Palestinian demands was not entirely linear, but there was an evident development from the proposals for various forms of 'self' or 'home-rule' under British dominion, to something more full-blooded and complete. Despite their often sharp, even violent differences, the various strands of the national movement thereby begun to coalesce around the classical mid-twentieth-century call for independence from colonial rule. By the late 1930s, the nascent political parties and independent personalities that articulated the Palestinians' aspirations were clear: What the Palestinians wanted was an *independent Arab state*, just like their brethren in Egypt, Iraq, Syria and elsewhere. The exact terms and moral and political bases of this state, and its relations with the then-Jewish minority and the rest of the Arab World were left largely vague, but the desire for independent statehood was openly and visibly pronounced in the various party programmes and platforms and was endorsed by the League of Arab States itself.[2]

The 1936–1939 Palestinian 'great revolt' against colonial rule and Zionist encroachment could have carved a putative path to independence. However, the brutal suppression of the revolt by the British (including British-sponsored armed Jewish actions against the Arab population), followed by the 1937 Peel Commission's recommendation for partition (the first abortive attempt at a 'two-state' solution), represented a severe setback to Palestinian aspirations, all but breaking the back of the indigenous population's armed resistance and opening the door to the their subsequent defeat at the hands of the Haganah and the other armed wings of the Zionist movement in 1947–1948.[3]

Yet the burden of the conflict was already beginning to weigh heavily on Whitehall's shoulders. As the storm clouds gathered over Europe and in a calculated attempt to pacify any further potential aggravation in the Arab region while otherwise engaged, the 1939 British White Paper finally conceded on the Palestinian Arabs' aspiration to independence, thereby effectively reversing the commitment to a Jewish state/'homeland' that had been integral to British policy in Palestine ever since the Balfour Declaration. The white paper offered full independence in ten years. Sadly, from the Palestinian perspective, the notion of an independent and 'complete' Arab Palestine was not to be. The outbreak of the Second World War, and the combination of single-minded Zionist dedication to a Jewish state eventually backed by the world's great powers and the United States in particular, foiled any prospect of a unitary independent Palestine, and this was set finally to rest in the 1947 Partition Plan and the outbreak of the 1948 war.[4] The shattering defeat of the Palestinian Arabs and the first sad and abortive experiment in an 'All-Palestine Government' in October 1948 finally put paid to any prospects of an 'Arab Palestine', then and possibly thereafter.[5]

Revolution and 'return'

The 1948 Nakba left the Palestinians in a state of national concussion. The war ended with roughly half the total of 1.5 million Palestinian Arabs as a defeated, dispersed and dispossessed and rudderless mass. The very term 'Palestinian' faded away: the inhabitants of western Palestine were incorporated into Jordan, the rump population of eastern Palestine fell under Israeli rule and the Gazans were left under Egyptian administration (not sovereignty). With their people scattered, their leaders discredited and their national movement broken, the Palestinians themselves seemed to fade into the regional background as but one element of the broader Arab–Israeli conflict.

Yet the Palestinians' cause remained very much alive, and the post-1948 'concussion' did not last long. While the Palestinians may have lost their status as a separate actor, the traumatic loss of their homeland gave birth to a lasting and powerful sense of injustice and a desire to undo the reality that had been forcibly imposed on them. From mid-1950s and from small beginnings, a new movement began to stir. Nurtured within the Gaza incubator, where a mass of voiceless refugees from 1948 was crammed into 1 per cent of Mandatory Palestine within eyesight of their lost lands and villages, a nascent activism began to take shape. After a decade of living in camps, concerned about the Arabs and the world's forgetfulness and determined not to slide towards oblivion, dissident Palestinian elements from within the Muslim Brotherhood and other factions born of Gaza's fertile revolutionary soil began to seek tangible restitution: armed struggle was the natural recourse of the oppressed and the goal was that of 'return'. This was the foundational core of the post-1948 national movement first established by Fatah in 1959 that eventually became that of the Palestinian people as a whole.[6]

There were, of course, other associated elements to the budding movement: the elemental forces that forged Fatah comprised re-building a shattered national identity, and that of self-assertion and the insistence on the independence of will (*istiqlaliat al qarar*). However, the movement itself remained largely non-programmatic. Fatah's call was mostly meant to mobilize, galvanize and re-awaken the people, but with no real discussion of modalities. That call expressed a powerful desire, part yearning, part-revenge, and its chosen means was 'armed struggle' as the appropriate vehicle for oppressed peoples at a time when China, Algeria and Vietnam seemed to offer a natural model of anti-colonial struggle. Despite this, Fatah's initial appeal remained limited and marginal within the broader and more comprehensive sweep of Arab nationalism (exemplified by Nasserism),[7] but the movement gained traction as it seeped into the communities of exile and the refugee camps in particular. Fatah's appeal was finally consolidated not so much by its own impetus but by the failure of the Arab regimes and their ignominious defeat in the war with Israel in June 1967. The great paradox of 1967 was that by their crushing victory over the Arabs, the Israeli helped to revive both the centrality of the Palestinians as independent actors and the saliency of the Palestinian cause itself. The appeal of armed struggle thus grew in direct response to the Arabs' failure.[8]

The turn to pragmatism

By 1969, Fatah had taken command of the Palestinian Liberation Organisation (PLO), which had been founded in May 1964, and effectively subsumed within its institutions. However, unlike its Zionist counterpart, the national movement represented by Fatah/the PLO had no real social content or vision of what kind of society would be built. The Marxist fringe, such as that of the Popular Front for the Liberation of Palestine (PFLP), established in December 1967 by Georges Habash, and the Democratic Front for the Liberation of Palestine (PDFLP), formed in 1968 by Nayef Hawatmeh and Yasser Abbed Rabo, that sought to answer such questions remained largely just that: a fringe that spoke the contemporaneous language of social transformation, but that had no real connection to the masses that were driven by other more basic impulses. Nonetheless, Fatah's course of armed struggle also began to be mired in the complexities of attempting revolution from exile, and particularly the fact that, in operating from foreign, albeit Arab soil, the Palestinians were generating a hostile response from their host environments, first in Jordan and then in Lebanon. Gradually, a second impulse began to take shape. This arose from a pragmatic reading of the consequences of the chronic friction with the Arab host countries, and the post-1973 war Arab/Israeli balance of power, whereby the limits of the Arabs' collective powers of coercion became painfully visible. This was matched with a conviction that the Palestinians could not afford to be absent from any United States/Soviet Union-sponsored peace deal as appeared to be in the offing at the time. From a visceral aspiration to 'return', Fatah and other Palestinian leaders began to move towards a broader notion of 'self-determination', as expressed in call for a Palestinian 'national entity' and then statehood even if only on *part* of the national patrimony.

The Lebanon War in 1982 was the first step in the journey towards a new pragmatism. The conflict, which began in June with the Israeli invasion of southern Lebanon and lasted until June 1985, ended in the PLO's defeat and semi-exile in Tunis, but it also freed the Palestinians from the constant friction generated by armed struggle from Lebanon and other proxy Arab arenas (i.e. Amman, Cairo, Damascus and elsewhere in the region). The 1987 Intifada was another critical turning point. The PLO/Fatah leadership sought to grasp the moment when the occupation had become an evident burden on Israel, and its international image as an oppressive power was resonating as never before. This finally gave birth to the November 1988 decision by the Palestinian National Council (PNC), the PLO's highest authority, in favour of a two-state solution along the 1967 lines as an implicit acknowledgement of the limitations of 'armed struggle', and in recognition of the global dictates of international legality. The necessary price was that this could only be achieved on that part of the Palestinian homeland that was occupied in 1967, and that the Palestinians would have to forego their claims to the 77 per cent of their national soil that had been lost in 1948. In seeking a state, the PLO/Fatah leadership recognized that their primarily tools had to be diplomatic and political. The hitherto centrality of armed action thus slowly faded away from the PNC's resolutions, and the PLO/Fatah's discourse; from what was once a sacred and unquestionable tenet of Palestinian action to Arafat's open renunciation of terrorism before the United Nations General Assembly assembled in Geneva in December 1988.[9]

Pragmatic as this shift was, it was also incomplete. Henceforth, the Palestinian national movement was ostensibly dedicated to statehood and state-building (if and when it acquired the territory required to do so). However, once again, as in the pre-1948 era, the ends were ill-defined; what sort of state, which real tools of state-building, how to acquire them and when to deploy them were questions hardly asked, let alone answered, by the leadership – or as part of the active and dynamic debate about whether the 'state' as such was desirable, and what the price would be to achieve it. In this sense, the Palestinians were more engaged in the political blueprint of their putative state than in its actual furniture and inner workings. Part of the reason stemmed from the origins of the movement and its roots in activism and armed action, which did not necessarily translate into the civil realm of state-building, which was never Fatah and its founders' primary concern anyway.

The experience of Lebanon was both debilitating and misleading in this respect: the years of civil war between 1975 and 1982 had forced what had begun as an underground/guerrilla movement to assume some of the characteristics of government and to develop rudimentary means of institutionalized representation and control. This, however, was largely reactive, extemporaneous and incapable of translation outside the specific Lebanese context. Whereas the Zionist movement in Palestine had set out to establish all the institutions of government designed for statehood (under British protection), the Palestinian experiment in Lebanon only served to create a false sense of Palestinian (read PLO) confidence that the product of one arena could be successfully transferred to the other.[10]

Statehood

The 1993 Oslo agreement should have marked a decisive point in the transition from revolutionary aspirations to meeting the concrete demands of governance and the prospect of setting the Palestinians down the path to statehood. Oslo failed to deliver or to foster such a change. There is no question as to Israel's responsibility for foiling Oslo's potential via its own conception of an open-ended endgame that would only be determined by Israel's own needs and demands. Whereas Israel perceived Oslo as a reversible experiment to be judged by the degree to which Palestinian performance matched Israel's expectations, the Palestinian construed it (or misconstrued) as a one-way ticket to statehood. Having conceded on 77 per cent of their homeland in 1988, the PLO leadership believed that it was 'owed' compensation in the return of the remaining 23 per cent to independent Palestinian sovereign rule. Israel's settlement policies were one manifestation of its concept of an 'open-ended' regime, and what it believed was the essentially reversible trajectory of Oslo. Settlement was, similarly, a reflection of the underlying political dynamic within Israel, and the politico-military establishment's unwillingness to confront the settler movement for, largely but not solely, electoral considerations, with the notable exception of the 2005 unilateral withdrawal Gaza that was only possible because of then-prime minister Sharon's previous commitment and stature within the right-wing and settler movements themselves.

Between 1993 and 2020, the number of settlers in the West Bank grew from 116,000 to 400,000 and in East Jerusalem from 150,000 to 200,000.[11] The settlers brought with them a dense network of communication hubs and legal entanglements, and have created a demographic/security reality that will be very difficult to unravel.[12] However, the Palestinians also failed to develop the appropriate means of challenging Israel's Oslo concept and its consequences. The PLO may have continued to call for an independent state, but this was largely perceived as the ripe fruit of ending the occupation, and as little more than a function of drawing agreed lines on the map. The one exception was best exemplified by the failed experiment in 'Fayyadism'. Salam Fayyad, the prime minister of the Palestinian National Authority (PNA or PA) established in 1994, sought to develop a new approach posited on 'statehood first'; that is, without waiting for the negotiations with Israel to produce any result or for a full final status agreement to be agreed. From this point of view and in a kind of 'Zionism-in-reverse', it was assumed that unilateral actions on the ground could lay the foundations for an independent Palestinian state, irrespective of Israel's demands or strategy. This approach was formalized in two successive plans in 2009 and 2011, which included an ambitious range of economic and developmental projects and were intended to converge with a growing international consensus on a two-state vision and a comprehensive Palestinian–Israeli settlement. This was in many ways the first real Palestinian attempt to articulate the means and mechanics of statehood beyond mere claims and aspirations.[13]

Fayyad's blueprints still stand as the only comprehensive Palestinian vision of a state. His 'statehood first' approach had a superficially attractive ring to it that won it traction among decision-makers in Washington and the European Union (EU), and he was feted and lionized by many in the West and Israel as the 'Palestinian Ben Gurion'. However, Fayyad's vision was fundamentally flawed.[14] The first problem with it was its assumption that a 'unilateral' exercise in Palestinian state-building was possible, at a time when every PA action was (and still is) determined by the Israeli occupation. The 2007 Fatah–Hamas split aside, the PA then (and now) was denied the most elementary tools of government; it could not independently trade on the world market, decide who can enter its soil, or deploy the smallest unit of its security services from one village to another; and its leaders then (and now) could not move without prior Israeli consent. In short (then and now), it had no means of freely exercising its authority over its citizens or its territory in any meaningful manner. At the heart of the PA's 2009/2011 programme was a basic contradiction: while it claimed to be building a state *against* the occupation, in practice it had no choice but to build state-like structures *with* the occupation. Yet Israel (then and now) was not committed to a truly independent and sovereign Palestinian state, at least not as understood and accepted by most Palestinians. It would, in fact, be hard to find a similar example of a genuine sovereign state built while still under occupation, and nothing in Israel's stance on the basic issues of Palestinian sovereignty (territorial extent, control over borders, the right to self-defence and so on) has suggested otherwise then or since.

The second problem arose from a misreading of history whether by omission or commission. The Zionist movement may indeed have developed a state-building capacity while under the British Mandate, but Britain, unlike the Israeli occupation, was legally 'mandated' by the League of Nations to foster such a capacity. Nevertheless, and despite the British embrace, Israel only finally came into being as a state by using *force* against British and Palestinians alike. By way of contrast, the only military capability the PA has been building under US/EU supervision has been directed against those who have sought to take up arms against the occupation. The 'Zionist' option of military self-reliance and readiness to use force for political-territorial ends was totally absent from the Palestinian National Authority's new approach and was (and still is) inimical to its political outlook. The state-first approach had other significant risks: Palestinian unilateralism could also have opened the door to legitimizing Israel's own brand of unilateralism such as formal annexation and unrestrained settlement building, and both historical precedent and the balance of power would suggest that it would have prevailed in such a contest. Rather than lay the foundations for a truly viable and sovereign Palestinian state with Jerusalem as its capital, so-called Palestinian 'Zionism' as conceived was only likely to produce a partial, *ersatz* entity; one that differed little from the kind of autonomous self-rule that has long been Israel's remedy for addressing the Palestinian problem.

Despite its apparent activism, Fayyadism was therefore incapable of building a state by stealth or undoing the occupation by other means. In spite of its grand design, its focus was largely apolitical: improving the Palestinians' living standards and encouraging them to state-like behaviour but without any of the advantages or rewards of a genuine state. This approach dovetailed all too neatly with Israeli Prime Minister Benjamin Netanyahu's notion of economic peace. The approach appeared as a pragmatic ambition to supplement the peace process and as path to a viable two-state solution. However, its danger was in circumventing this altogether – or, at best, in facilitating the outcome as determined by Israeli national interests alone. Arguably, the first and essential duty of any state is to defend its citizens against foreign incursions and threats. This part of the citizen–state contract was absent from Fayyad's plan, as was the ever-vexing and quasi-existential problem of how to prevent the further Israeli colonization of Palestinian soil. The net result was to devalue the already unconvincing currency of a two-state solution and leave the Palestinians suspended in yet another twilight zone trapped between a continuing occupation and a fake façade of empowerment.

Since Fayyad's failure, the Palestinian experiment in statehood has only suffered further retreat. Hamas in Gaza has also failed to provide an alternative Islamist mode that was able to deliver. It is hard to deny Israel's hand in all this, of course, or the terrible impact of the Egyptian siege of Gaza, particularly after 2013 and the advent of the Sisi regime. However, Hamas has also failed due to its own inexperience and ineptitude, and its inability to square between its claim to revolutionary armed action and its desire to build a new Muslim society in Gaza. Besides, and despite its religiosity, the Palestinian population at large was perceptibly unenthusiastic about adopting Hamas's Islamist discourse and its prescribed way of life, and has shown no propensity to change its mind after ten years of Hamas rule in Gaza. While it may be true that many of the basic services in much of the 1967 territories are in Palestinian hands on a daily basis, the fundaments of sovereignty are as distant a goal as ever. The ability to defend one's citizenry, to control one's borders external trade, to move freely at home, an agreed capital, to be free from outside harassment and detention, are all absent and there is nothing to suggest that Israel is going to relinquish its grip over Palestinian soil or stem the tide of settlement of Palestinian land anytime soon or in the foreseeable future.

Dislocation and protest

One hundred years or so on, none of the original national impulses retains its grip or evokes a response; the original desire for independence from Britain is irrelevant, 'return' remains as lingering and residual (if powerful) aspiration among the dispossessed people of Palestine, but it is no longer the primary driving force of Palestinian nationalism: neither the PLO/Fatah nor Hamas disavows it of course, but most people are not deceived by the failure to enact it and it has become more of a moral principle and stance than a motive for action. After more than half a century of occupation, 'statehood' as such has lost much of whatever allure it may have had more than three decades after 1988. Amidst such historical sequence, there is a genuine question to be asked as to why the project for statehood has failed. This is partly a reflection of Israeli obduracy and the continuing grip of its occupation, of course. This evolution also reflects a loss of faith in the instruments of action, whether peaceful *qua* 'international legality', or violent as in Hamas' belated attempt to pursue Fatah's path of armed struggle. It is also as reflection of the PA/PLO and Fatah's failure in governance, the equal failure of Hamas to demonstrate a viable alternative model in Gaza and the fading credibility of the Palestinian people's leadership and governing institutions. The curse of the Gaza/Ramallah Fatah/Hamas divide has also injected a severe dose of poison into the national project. Gaza's gradual secession has created an 'internal' political and psychological border that may be as difficult to erase, as the future 'external' borders with Israel will be difficult to define. The Palestinians as a whole may be genuinely hankering after 'national unity', but the rift has created a new reality that will require much more than pious mutual Fatah/Hamas proclamations to overcome.

What we have today instead is undoubtedly a moment of severe dislocation. None of the old ways have borne sustainable fruit – besides the post-1948 national movement's initial success in recreating a Palestinian identity and putting the 'cause' back on the map – an achievement that is not to be belittled. However, little else has worked since; the resort to arms has done nothing to produce political change or significantly deter Israel or raise the cost of occupation. The diplomatic path and PNA's President Mahmoud Abbas's dedication to negotiations and security cooperation have not undone an inch of occupation since the 1997 Hebron accord. Israeli unilateralism produced tangible change in Gaza (which remains the sole patch of Israeli-free Palestine), but the subsequent siege and suffering of its people are hardly alluring prospects for the rest of the Palestinian people under occupation or in exile.

By the late 2010s, the Palestinian national movement in its various components had retreated into protest. The political establishment as represented by the PLO/PA and Fatah/Hamas lost its status as legitimate interlocutor on the people's behalf, but even it had adopted protest as its predominant mode; protest against Israeli settlement activities, against the siege of Gaza, against the constraints of occupation and against international community's failure (with Washington at its head) to shift the trajectory of developments towards a viable two-state solution. Similarly today's popular actions are more a manifestation of the different faces protests than that of a national movement. The Boycott, Divestment and Sanctions (BDS) campaign, the ongoing (brave and persistent) protests against the Wall, the individual acts of frustration and violent resistance such as the stabbings and car-rammings, the vehement protests against Abbas's mode of government and the PA's security cooperation with Israel: all these forms of protest have become the default position of a shattered and incoherent national movement.

The new ways are uncertain. There is an undoubted need for a 'new language' and a new set of desirable and achievable national goals, but what this may be or what it really means is also unclear.[15] As the Abbas era ebbs, it is most important to revive and redefine the national project, rather than who or exactly what may succeed him, just as it is unclear how whatever successor or successor regime will be able to do any different or achieve any better result. There should be no misunderstanding here: the alternative is not the longstanding desire of the Israeli/US Zionist right to push for the free-reign settlement activity plus for 'economic peace' or improved living conditions for the Palestinians under occupation, as has long been touted by Zionist/Israeli leader from Theodore Herzl's *Altnueland*,[16] to Moshe Dayan's post-1967 'open bridges' policy, to Netanyahu's 'economic peace' and Donald H. Trump administration's Palestinian–Israeli centrepieces.

Outlook

Since 1988 at least, the national movement has assumed that a one-sized package will fit all; an end to occupation, national determination and independence via statehood and return for the 1948 refugees all in one fell swoop. The further assumption was that this comprehensive deal was negotiable with Israel on the basis of mutual recognition and agreed final borders between two states. Thirty years later, the idea of one overarching, comprehensive, negotiated resolution that incorporates all the basic elements of the conflict may have slipped out of reach. By adopting the notion of self-determination via statehood, the Palestinians' well-being was predicated on achieving sovereign state that will compensate for the loss of their homeland and the subsequent pain of exile and occupation. However, the Palestinians cannot remain shackled to the status quo and hostage to the absence of a state, living in permanent limbo while awaiting a salvation that is visibly retreating and may never appear. One possibility is that of disaggregating the various components of Palestinian reality and seeking parallel means of addressing them. In this context, the Palestinians may be said to be facing six circles of challenges: (i) the West Bank/East Jerusalem occupation, (ii) the Gaza secession, (iii) the question of civil and political rights in Israel, (iv) the rights of refugees, (v) the issue of good governance and last but not least (vi) the twin questions of security and a decent life for all Palestinians everywhere. These questions encompass issues of freedom, representation, legitimacy, national unity, the fate of the land, national identity, the fate of diaspora and the right to pursue a normal life.

This is a long, formidable and complicated agenda. Disaggregating its interconnected elements could also weaken them all. However, this may also be necessary so as to escape the persistent illusion of all-encompassing solution that resolves them all. There may be no other real path but to acknowledge it and seek a new discourse that incorporates these disparate goals, without sacrificing one at the expense of the other. There is an Israeli side to this as well. There are those who would claim Israel's victory and the Palestinians' defeat.[17] This is not just about seizing the moment for enforcing a one-sided peace on the Palestinians. It is also about deciding Israel's long-term relationship with its environment; at one stage it sought simply to be accepted (i.e. the right to exist), at another, it simply sought to be strong, and now the attempt for Israel is to secure the legitimacy of its historic claims to the land (a Jewish state). The real danger is that these three approaches play against each other: the right to exist requires true mutuality, which is not forthcoming. In the absence of a true peace, the second only produces an inevitable counter challenge. The third is all but impossible since it requires the abdication of the Palestinian Arab narrative.

Finally, and despite its long and apparent terminal decline, the two-state solution has yet to be officially pronounced dead. Furthermore, should an agreed/acceptable two-state solution materialize, the dynamic could change significantly: the traction of economic tools would grow. But barring that, the quest is for a new way to define the Palestinians' national aspirations. This will take some time and will not necessarily echo the path of the past one hundred years. The fundamental question facing the Palestinians today is whether any form of acceptable statehood is potentially achievable through a renewed negotiation process, or whether the future is that of permanent imprisonment within one form or another of the post-1967 status quo. Past experiences suggest that a renewed peace process based on the Madrid/Oslo parameters of 'land for peace' is unlikely to produce anything approximating the basic minimum acceptable to the Palestinian side, while Israeli settlements on the ground are steadily altering the political-demographic landscape in manner that consolidates an Israeli-dominated one-state reality. The Trump Plan and the subsequent spate of Israeli/Arab normalization should have awakened the Palestinian leadership and people to the harsh reality that an independent sovereign Palestinian state as envisaged in 1988 may be more of an anachronism than a feasible goal, and that the underlying dynamic of the conflict is that of further entanglement between the Arab and Jewish populations living between Jordan River and the Mediterranean Sea. Only time will tell whether this will lead to a better future to both sides or to yet another round of conflict in the 100 years of struggle over the land of Palestine.

Notes

1. The literature on the development of the Palestinian national movement is voluminous and all but immune to summary. The most comprehensive and balanced one-volume accounts can be found in Gudrun Krämer, *A History of Palestine – From the Ottoman Conquest to the Founding of the State of Israel*, Princeton, New Jersey: Princeton University Press, 2008; James Gelvin, *The Israel Palestine Conflict – One Hundred Years of War*, Cambridge: Cambridge University Press, 2014; and Neil Caplan, *The Israel-Palestine Conflict – Contested Histories*, Chichester, West Sussex: Wiley-Blackwell, 2010.
2. I have developed this argument in some detail elsewhere. See Ahmad Samih Khalidi, 'The Palestinian National Movement from Self-rule to Statehood', in Joel Peters and David Newman, eds., *The Routledge Handbook on the Israeli-Palestinian Conflict*, London: Routledge, 2013, pp. 20–30. For a broader view see also Haim Gerber's excellent *Remembering and Imagining Palestine – Identity and Nationalism from the Crusades to the Present*, Basingstoke: Palgrave, 2008. The one relatively clear and complete (but little-known) Arab vision of an independent Palestine was proposed by the League of Arab States in 1946. The plan included: citizenship for all those who had been legal residents of Palestine for the previous ten years; the use of Hebrew as an official second language; 30 per cent seats in parliament for the Jewish population commensurate with their percentage of the population at the time and a ban on further Jewish immigration; curtailed land sales to the Jews; and any changes to the rights of the Jewish population to be ratified by a majority of Jewish representatives. This was in effect the first Arab version of a bi-national or unitary Arab state. See Khalidi, 'The Palestinian National Movement', p. 25.
3. See Thomas Suarez, *State of Terror – How Terrorism Created Modern Israel*, Bloxham, Oxon: Skyscraper, 2016.
4. It may be worth recalling that the United Nations Partition plan also included a minority report that included a blueprint for an independent unitary Arab/Jewish state.
5. The shabby end of the British Mandate and its dramatic consequences are well covered in Walid Khalidi, 'The Arab Perspective', in William Roger Louis, ed., *The End of the British Mandate*, Austin, Texas: University of Texas Press, 1986, pp. 104–137. See also Avi Shlaim, 'The Rise and Fall of the All-Palestine government in Gaza', *Journal of Palestine Studies*, 20, 1, 1990, pp. 37–53.
6. The emergence of Fatah is covered in some detail in two separate pieces by Hussein Agha and Ahmad Salih Khalidi, 'Arafat: Why He Still Matters', *The Guardian*, 13 November 2014; and 'The End of this Road: The Decline of the Palestinian National Movement', *The New Yorker*, 6 August 2017.

7   See Peter Mansfield, *Nasser's Egypt*, London: Penguin, 1969; and Reem Abu El Fadl, 'Nasserism', in Amal Ghazal and Jens Hanssen, eds., *Oxford Handbook of Contemporary Middle Eastern and North African History*, Oxford: Oxford University Press, 2016.
8   I have touched on this in 'Ripples of the 1967 War', *The Cairo Review of Global Affairs*, Spring 2017.
9   For a review of the PLO's progression from armed struggle to diplomacy, see Mohammad Muslih, 'Toward Coexistence – An Analysis of the Resolutions of the Palestine Council', *Journal of Palestine Studies*, 19, 4, Summer 1990, pp. 3–29.
10 The best and most comprehensive account of the Palestinian national movement and its shift towards statehood can be found in Yazid Sayigh's monumental *Armed Struggle and the Search for State – The Palestinian National Movement, 1949–1993*, Oxford: Oxford University Press, 2000.
11 Peace Now data as of February 2019. See http://peacenow.org.il/en/settlements-watch/settlements-data/population and http://peacenow.org.il/en/settlements-watch/settlements-data/jerusalem.
12 Prime Minister Benjamin Netanyahu has made this clear: 'Alongside our desire to reach an agreement with our Palestinian neighbours, we will continue to protect the settlement enterprise and strengthen it. We are doing this responsibly and with discretion'. Netanyahu declared, in talks with world leaders, in addition to demanding the Palestinians recognize Israel as a Jewish state, 'that everyone has the right to live in their home, that no man will be uprooted from his home'. See *Times of Israel*, 6 June 2017. He similarly stated: 'We are building the land and we are settling it. In the mountains, in the valleys, in the Galilee, in the Negev, and yes, in Judea and Samaria [the West Bank] as well. Because this is our land. The homeland of the Jewish people. The only land promised to our forefathers. We were given the right to settle here. And we must guard it with caution.' See *UNSCO Daily Press Brief*, 14 September 2017.
13 See the PA's *Program of the 13th Government; Ending the Occupation, Establishing the State* (2009) available at https://unispal.un.org/pdfs/PA_EndingOccupation-Statehood.pdf; and its *National Development Plan 2011-13 Establishing the State, Building our Future* (2011) available at www.apis.ps/up/1332062906.pdf
14 I am drawing here on my own criticism of Fayyad's approach as published in *The Guardian*; 'The Palestinian Authority's State-First Mistake', 28 October 2009. See also a critical Israeli review and analysis of the plan in http://jcpa.org/article/prime-minister-salam-fayyad%E2%80%99s-two-year-path-to-palestinian-statehood-2/
15 For more on this, see Agha and Khalidi, 2017.
16 Theodore Herzl, *Altnueland* (The New Land), Leipzig: Seemann Nachf, 1902.
17 See for instance, 'The Israel victory Project' spearhead by the US right-wing Zionist *Middle East Forum* (www.meforum.org) and Daniel Levy, 'Has Netanyahu Defeated the Palestinians?', *The National Interest*, 24 August 2017.

6 PERMANENT IRRESOLUTION OF THE KURDISH ISSUE

Jordi Tejel

"States get weak and sick but they do not die."

Kurdish Proverb

The origins of the Kurdish question can be traced back to the immediate aftermath of the First World War as the victorious powers proposed dividing up Anatolia into three independent states: an independent Turkey limited to north and central Anatolia, a Kurdish state in south-eastern Anatolia and an Armenian state in north-eastern Anatolia. According to Article 64 of the Treaty of Sèvres (1920), the Kurdish peoples of present-day south-eastern Turkey were to access independence from Turkey in those areas. In theory, the Kurds inhabiting the former Ottoman *vilayet* of Mosul (Northern Iraq) would be also allowed to adhere to such an independent Kurdish state.[1]

Diverse international, regional and local dynamics, such as the Kemalist revolt initiated already in 1919, divisions among the Kurds in Turkey and the increasing tensions between France and Great Britain over territorial claims in the region, rendered the Treaty of Sèvres futile. In 1923, the Treaty of Lausanne acknowledged the territorial sovereignty of the new Turkish state and abandoned any promise of an autonomous Kurdistan as well as any provision to secure 'minority rights' for Kurds within Turkey. In 1925, the League of Nations (LoN) awarded the Kingdom of Iraq control over the former Ottoman province of Mosul. Although the LoN extracted a promise that Kurds would administer the province and that Kurdish would be an official language alongside Arabic, neither of these commitments was fulfilled.[2] Henceforth, the foundations were laid for what we today know as 'the Kurdish Question' – a conflict that has proved to be together with the Palestinian issue the longest-lasting national-related conflicts in the Middle East.

Once considered as a marginal conflict in the region, the Kurdish question has gained momentum in the early twentieth century. In the aftermath of the American invasion of Iraq in 2003 and the subsequent fall of Saddam Hussein's regime, Western journalists, think tanks and scholars, as well as Kurdish media outlets, foresaw the establishment of a Kurdish state in present northern Iraq. Since then, the number of reports and articles speculating on the possible creation of a

Kurdish state has literally exploded.³ Furthermore, as the Iraqi army abandoned its positions following the Islamic State of Iraq and al Shaam's (ISIS) incursion into Mosul in June 2014, Kurdish security forces advanced beyond the Kurdistan Regional Government (KRG)-controlled areas. Subsequently, Masoud Barzani, president of the KRG, made a call for an independence referendum within 'a few months'. Although the referendum has been postponed on different occasions, the post-Saddam Hussein era and the unexpected consequences of the Syrian uprising of 2011 – namely the partial retreat of the Syrian army from Northern Syria in 2012 and the subsequent establishment of a de facto autonomy in the Kurdish regions now known as *Rojava* – have purportedly created a unique opportunity for the Kurds where 'the great losers of the Ottoman Empire could be winners'.⁴

However, despite this unprecedented 'opportunity' – including the holding of an independence referendum in September 2017 – Iraqi Kurds did not appear overtly keen to implement the hypothetical plan for independence immediately due to financial constraints, divisions among Kurdish parties and geostrategic considerations. In parallel, in 2017, the YPG – the military wing of the Democratic Union Party (PYD), a Syrian offshoot of the Kurdistan Workers' Party (PKK) – actively took part in military operations alongside the United States against ISIS around Raqqa, the 'capital' of its self-proclaimed Caliphate from 2014 to 2017. More significantly, the PYD/PKK had become a regional actor able to challenge states such as Turkey, as well as competing Kurdish leaders such as Masoud Barzani. Put differently, the perspectives of either the emergence of a united Kurdish state or sustained intra-Kurdish cooperation against 'state enemies' – Iran, Iraq, Syria and Turkey – seemed to be unlikely, to say the least.⁵

Paradoxically, though the pervasive activities of the diverse Kurdish movements had highlighted the illegitimacy of the successive regimes in each of these countries, the former have not jeopardized the durability of the latter. Indeed, the gains obtained by the Kurdish movement both in Iraq and Syria were directly related to either external military interventions – Gulf War in 1990 and the American invasion of Iraq in 2003 – or the collapse of state control over the entire national territory due to a context of warfare in other areas of the country – Syria after 2011. Notwithstanding these two exceptional breakthroughs, how can the 'permanent' irresolution of the Kurdish issue be accounted for?

Towards an interactionist approach to minority group mobilization

Traditionally, scholars and observers have studied the evolution of the Kurdish issue in the respective countries through the lenses of the dichotomy of *accommodation versus resistance* while neglecting a range of individual and collective strategies that warrant further attention. In this sense, one should avoid the over-determination of oppositional logics and the assumption of situations of competition. Some segments of a given 'minority'[6] might accept their current situation or even take advantage of the existing political system. In connection to this, if the articulation of identities and interests is indeed necessary in order to analyse ethnic movements and some of their features such as political violence,[7] scholars should also consider subjective perceptions of social relations (present experience, collective memories and so forth),[8] which may lead states and non-state actors alike to choose a strategy which might be perceived as 'unbelievable' from the 'outside.' Hence, for the purpose of an initial assessment and in order to better grasp the relations between majorities and minorities in the Middle East (and beyond), researchers should approach this issue from a simultaneously dynamic and interactionist perspective that encapsulates three key principles.

First, majority and minority groups are not *always* and *everywhere* opposed. In that sense, a long-term perspective allows us to identify periods in which minority members participate in the economic and political life of a given society, cooperate with other political forces (both within the government and the opposition) on the one hand, and, on the other hand, periods of extreme state violence against a given minority. As Hamit Bozarslan points out, cooperation of some Kurdish sectors with non-Kurdish actors throughout the twentieth century was not only due to the co-optation of 'traitors' to the Kurdish cause by the subsequent Arab, Iranian and Turkish regimes but also to the traditional aspiration of the mainstream Kurdish movements to combine a permanent search for *particularism* – Kurdishness – and *universalism*. While putting forward their 'national' claims, which constitute indeed their 'ultimate *raison d'être*', Kurdish parties and clubs aimed at placing their struggle 'in their *time* and in their *world*'.[9]

Unsurprisingly, the first Kurdish clubs were thus ideologically close to the Turkish Young Turks movement in the early twentieth century. Likewise, the first modern Kurdish parties established in the interwar era held a modernist agenda similar to that of Mustafa Kemal and Reza Khan in Turkey and Iran, respectively. In the post–Second World War years, new Kurdish elites heralded developmentalist and anti-imperialist discourses that resembled those of progressive Arab leaders such as Gamal Abdel Nasser in Egypt and Abdul Kareem Qassem in Iraq, as well as those of the Communist parties in the Middle East. Finally, in the late 1960s and 1970s, some Kurdish parties embraced further radical ideologies, thereby participating in the rise of left-wing organizations in the region alongside the Palestinian, Turkish and Iranian movements.

This long-lasting quest for universalism would explain why the Islamist political actors were not successful in dominating the Kurdish political space from 1979 onwards as was the case in most Middle Eastern political arenas. Ultimately, it would help us to account for the discrete yet unchecked singular ideological as well as organizational evolution of certain Kurdish political parties such as the PKK and its sister organizations in the early twenty-first century.[10] Whatever the case might be, the aspiration to be *in time* allowed the Kurdish parties to establish bridges with their Arab, Iranian and Turkish counterparts on different occasions and in different ways in order to secure Kurdish rights, on the one hand, and to appear as legitimate actors in the eyes of the rest of the world, on the other hand.

Second, consequently, the relationship between majorities and minorities is a part of a dynamic process in which both *continuity* and *change* must be taken into account. Minority populations are constantly negotiating their individual and collective identities – ethnic and religious boundaries, relations in each social space, etc. – with the state and other social groups. Therefore, ethnic identities can be activated or deactivated within the political field depending on the context, the needs and the subjectivity of the actors involved.

Finally, although regimes and minority groups project an *image* of homogeneity to the outside world, the actual practice or routine performance of state actors and agencies in various arenas, as well as the contradictions minorities undergo, often counter this *image*.[11] Joel Migdal has elaborated a theoretical approach – 'state-in-society' – that can help us to understand these dynamics. The 'state-in-society' perspective views society as a *mélange* of social organizations rather than the dichotomous centre-periphery model. According to Migdal, societies are not static but are constantly *becoming* as a result of permanent struggles over social control. In this model, authority can be delegated to other organizations peacefully, as opposed to organizations vying for authority resulting in conflict. In some cases, segments of the state ally themselves with minority segments in order to overcome the deficiencies of the state or, occasionally, they place themselves in opposition, in defence of particular interests, to certain strategies put forth by the regime itself, producing a 'fragmented tyranny'.[12]

Similarly, in spite of ethnic movements' claims, the groups and communities they seek to represent are not entirely homogenous or cohesive. Thus, ethnic movements must struggle to impose their values on the society as they attempt to exert their influence in different arenas where other actors are already present. Furthermore, while actors within an ethnic movement may define the 'we-group' against their 'enemy', other dissident groups or individuals whom their advocates seek to define as members of the 'we-group' may redefine themselves against it. Thus, ethnic movements are, like states, merely participants in a 'fray of ideological competitors, and its activists must contend with many other collectivities seeking the right to establish their own internal norms and external boundaries'.[13]

Taking these principles into consideration, this chapter aims to probe the relationship between the Iraqi, Syrian and Turkish states with their respective Kurdish minorities beyond the dichotomy of accommodation versus resistance or rebellion, in both comparative and long-term perspectives. Given the space constraints, this chapter will thus limit itself to some illustrative examples and mainstream tendencies in the former Ottoman territories, leaving the Iranian case aside. In the first part, I shall discuss the constitutional arrangements the four states chose to deal with their respective minorities. I argue that the choice of government majority does not necessarily account for the actual relationship between those states and their minority groups over time. Factors, such as political stability and regional dynamics, might affect state–minority relations and lead regimes to 'betray' their official ideologies to secure their durability.

In the second part, I highlight the similarities and differences not only between state policies but also between the strategies of Kurdish groups. A brief historical survey will allow me to identify periods of peaceful coexistence as well as episodes of widespread state violence against the Kurds. Consequently, in the last part, I argue that the dilemma the Kurds face in the Middle East is not a choice between accommodation and rebellion but one of guaranteeing their collective rights within legal systems, while pushing for further de-centralization or even asymmetrical federalism. In that respect, the Kurdish case can be inscribed in a broader trend; the increasing number of ethno-national communities that exercise self-determination without constituting separate states, using instead mechanisms of devolution or other political arrangements.[14] At the same time, for most Kurdish groups, incorporation of federalism and de-centralization principles into a constitution is actually a starting point, not an end game. Real willingness of the central government to implement legal arrangements and peaceful co-existence will thus by and large determine the actual Kurdish attachment to the state framework.

Dealing with minorities

Historically, two diverging constitutional choices have shaped state–society relations in a different way in each country in the postcolonial Middle East: either the choice of government representing the demographic majority (i.e. Syria, Turkey, Egypt, Israel, Iran and Iraq notably), or the choice of 'consensus democracy' (i.e. Lebanon, and Iraq since 2005). In theory, in the former, which was the choice made by the vast majority of Middle Eastern elites, the party or the leader who secures the numerical plurality of votes in electoral processes enjoys the legitimate right to govern and impose upon state and society their own identity and cultural preferences. However, as Elizabeth Picard put it, in the Middle Eastern states, the rationale for this model was somehow different. 'In order to strengthen their new and often fragile power, the rulers held a discourse of unanimity, either in support of a charismatic or traditional leader, or based on a nationalist ideology.'[15] As the diverse projects of 'bourgeois democracy'[16] faded away in the Middle East, authoritarian leaders and parties were also 'prone to deny cultural pluralism, suppress minority claims and even eradicate minority movements in the name of a shared national identity'.[17]

In Turkey, this process started in the 1920s when Mustafa Kemal and his followers sought to create centralized states and came to regard the Kurds as a feudal ethno-class that had to be assimilated for the sake of both state security and social 'progress'. Accordingly, Turkish elites and military officers envisioned diverse symbolic, as well as demographic engineering policies, in order to shape a new national ethos that erased religious and ethnic plurality in the new

Turkish 'nation-state'. Consequently, Kurdish language was banned, and Kurdish topographic names were replaced by Turkish ones. In addition, Kurdish nomadic and semi-nomadic tribes were forcibly resettled in non-Kurdish areas in order to accelerate their ethnic and social assimilation.[18]

In Syria, this course began in 1951 when Colonel Adib Shishakli not only banished all references to confessional affiliations in the official data but also encouraged the stigmatization of minorities in the political debate in Syria. His increasingly chauvinistic notion of Arab nationalism was predicated on the denial that minorities even existed in Syria.[19] At the time of the United Arab Republic (UAR, 1958–61), the short-lived merger between Syria and Egypt, however, the emphasis was placed on the pan-Arab discourse of the state. Consequently, the Kurds became a major scapegoat of Arab nationalism and became part of the *shuubiyyun* or, in other words, people who would not accept to be Arabized. Thereafter, diverse Baathist constitutions incorporated pan-Arabism and Arab socialism principles in the constitution, thereby denying the very existence of national or ethnic groups other than the Arabs.

In Iraq, the relations between the Kurds and the Arabs followed a different pattern. As noted, according to the Treaty of Sèvres (1920), the Kurds inhabiting the former Ottoman vilayet of Mosul would be allowed to adhere to a potential independent Kurdish state located in Eastern Anatolia. Yet, diverse international, regional and local dynamics made the Treaty of Sèvres pointless. In 1922, a joint Anglo–Iraqi statement recognized the right of the Kurds living within the boundaries of Iraq to set up a Kurdish government (*hukumet*). However, the promise made by the British was never implemented and by 1926, the Iraqi government and the British dismissed any possibility of establishing an autonomous region in northern Iraq.[20] Like in Syria, the Baathist party inscribed Arab socialism and the search for Arab unity as the two main ideological principles of the regime into the 1970 Iraqi constitution.

Therefore, in spite of some hints made at particular junctures by state elites in order to recognize the rights of religious and ethnic minorities, national identity in the abovementioned states was built on the false premises of cultural homogeneity insofar as regimes could hardly acknowledge pluralism without de-legitimizing themselves. In this sense, nation-building experience in the Middle East was reminiscent of what Benedict Anderson has called official nationalism, 'a process by which states create fictions of national identity by disseminating the cultural characteristics of the elite to the citizenry, and reciprocally, by proclaiming the ethnicity of the elites as prototypically national'.[21] In the Arab and Turkish leaders' eyes, the nation and the state were the same, and they were both sovereign and indivisible. In so doing, Arab and Turkish nationalism became a compulsory aspect of civic life, whereas the exclusion of 'Kurdishness' became part of the official doctrine of the state.

However, as Anderson points out, official nationalism is a *fiction*, which is more often than not challenged by its own contradictions. Besides the fact that Iraq,

Syria and Turkey have always been plural societies from an ethnic and religious viewpoint, power struggle and strategies to secure the durability of the ruling elites have brought about unexpected outcomes and practices in these countries. On the one hand, Syrian and Iraqi rulers imposed a ruling majority at odds with its demographic and social weight. Thus, Syria has been governed by members of the Alawi sect (11 per cent of the nation's population) since 1970, whereas Iraq was ruled by a limited group of Sunni Arabs through their clannish Tikriti networks from 1968 to 2003. At the same time, Syrian and Iraqi regimes had to tone down their official ideology in order to be socially viable. It was within this framework that Hafez al Assad in Syria, and Saddam Hussein in Iraq, opted for a more pragmatic strategy regarding the Kurds and other groups (e.g. Muslim Brotherhood in Syria and Shia clerics in Iraq), which had been excluded from the official ideology. Consequently, Kurdish religious, tribal and political leaders were at times co-opted by the central governments in order to ensure the balance between different social groups, thereby fostering regional, ethnic and sectarian lines.

Kurdish urban notables and tribal chiefs integrated the political and economic system in Turkey only after two decades of numerous Kurdish rebellions against the authoritarian drive of the Kemalist regime (1923–1937) and the end of the single-party period in 1946. Thus the deep social fatigue among rural populations that had been victims of state repression and the integration of the eastern provinces to the 'national' arena opened the door to a 'period of silence' as well as the establishment of solid bridges with the Turkish political parties.[22] Significantly, in the early 1960s, thousands of Kurds joined the Turkish Workers Party (TIP), thereby making this party hegemonic in several cities and towns in Eastern Anatolia. Although the Kurdish constituency within the Turkish Left rapidly put forward the right to claim their 'Kurdishness', by the end of the 1960s the political agenda of the Kurdish activists did not go beyond administrative and/or cultural autonomy for the Kurds within the borders of the Turkish state.

On the other hand, while the Baathist regimes in Iraq and Syria vowed to fight 'ethnic chauvinism' (meaning 'minority' nationalism) and sectarianism for the sake of the (Arab) nation, the actual practices of the state apparatus contradicted official discourse. As a matter of fact, archival research reveals that the administrative and intelligence services systematically categorized Syrian and Iraqi citizens along ethnic and sectarian lines. In Iraq, for example, the forms given to job applicants assessed the political leanings of citizens as well as their 'nationality' ('Kurd'/'Arab') and religion ('Muslim'/'Christian'). Furthermore, the intelligence apparatus or *mukhabarat* developed special forms for 'traitors' and 'saboteurs' (e.g. Kurdish activists) in which choices of 'nationality' and 'religion' were further expanded.[23] Likewise, in Syria, the *mukhabarat* systematically reported on the ethnic and religious background of citizens being arrested or interrogated.

The collection of exceptional measures implemented against thousands of Kurds in Turkey, whether or not they were directly involved in the armed movements in the interwar era, contributed to the delimitation of a non-physical boundary separating the 'West' from the 'East', the latter being viewed as a specific region possessing a *homogeneity* that did not really exist. The 'East' thus became a territory of refuge for an intrinsically counter-revolutionary popular culture. In this respect, Kurdish identity (language, social structures, attachment to religious brotherhoods) was put forth as a symbol of 'otherness' and politicized by the state itself. Ironically enough, the awareness of living in a particular social and political space nourished Kurdish dissent from the late 1960s onwards.[24]

Minorities' contradiction and mimesis effect

Because of their diverse geographic origin and history, different lifestyle (nomadic/sedentary) and their settlement in various environments, the Kurds did not constitute a homogeneous group in the first half of the twentieth century. On the contrary, the populations designated as Kurds were characterized by their segmented nature. However, minority groups, and in particular nationalist movements, responded to states' discourse with similar *fictions* of national identity. In so doing, a process of *mimesis* between the ruling group (the state) and the opposition took place over time as minority groups borrowed nationalism and other ideological tools for nation-building from their rulers and adapted them in order to dominate their own society.[25] This process of mimesis was, however, open to third-party influences and dynamics.

In Iraq, conflicting visions over citizenship and national identity were nourished by external factors. The 1922 Anglo-Iraqi statement and the LoN provisions had explicitly recognized the Kurds in Iraq and their claims to special rights as a *group* on a specific territory, namely the former vilayet of Mosul. Furthermore, as Mark Mazower puts it, the LoN and the leading powers within it established a system that was a source of tension from its inception because, on the one hand, they accepted the nation-state as the norm of international relations and, on the other, accepted minorities as collective entities.[26] As a matter of fact, from 1919 onwards, diverse Kurdish leaders and forces used 'minority rights' as a master frame for mobilization and claimed their *collective* rights to some kind of self-rule within the boundaries of the ex-Ottoman province. Subsequently, although in terms of minorities' protection, the United Nations Charter represented a definite step backwards from the LoN, the anti-colonialist struggle in vast regions of the Global South throughout the 1950s and 1960s provided the Kurds with a new discourse that legitimated their struggle for national rights and political autonomy.

Like the official state discourse, however, the Kurdish 'national identity fiction' often reflected contradictions within the 'minority group'. Thus, hegemonic ambitions of Kurdish nationalist leaders over the whole Kurdish province in northern Iraq were challenged by local identities, as well as by linguistic and religious cleavages. After the establishment of a Kurdish 'government' in Sulaimaniyya district led by Sheikh Mahmud Barzanji in 1922, Kurdish opposition blocs emerged, not only in Sulaimaniyya but also in Kirkuk where local leaders did not recognize Sheikh Mahmud as the 'King of Kurdistan'.[27] Over the years, these dynamics were repeated in different contexts and regions of northern Iraq. Thus, Mustafa Barzani rose against the Iraqi government in the 1940s but was unable to attract military support from the neighbouring tribes, which became allies of Baghdad. During the Long Revolt (1961–1970), divergent views about war strategies, as well as ideological disagreements, brought about a significant split within the Kurdistan Democratic Party (KDP) in 1964. Subsequently, the dissident branch of the KDP established in 1975 a competing bloc made up of 'progressive forces', the Patriotic Union of Kurdistan (PUK). Even nowadays, the autonomous Kurdish region is divided into two well-established regions, one dominated by the KDP, and the other by the PUK along political, clannish, linguistic and regional lines, despite the apparent unity Kurdish leaders have intended to imprint on the Kurdish Regional Government since 1992.[28]

In Syria, Kurdish claims have been traditionally rooted in cultural rather than territorial domain. During the French Mandate (1920–1946), French representatives did not encourage territorial autonomy, except for a brief period between 1936 and 1939 in Upper Jazira. After the establishment of the first modern Kurdish political party in Syria in 1957, the Kurdish Democratic Party of Syria, Kurdish activists kept loyal to this low profile. Yet, after more than 120,000 Kurds in 1962 were stripped of Syrian citizenship, Kurdish parties added a new political demand, namely the revocation of such decree.[29] However, due to the re-politicization of Kurdish identity from the 1980s onwards, which I shall analyse later in this chapter, new parties started to use the expression 'Syrian Kurdistan' overtly and thus asked for territorial autonomy or at least political decentralization within Syrian borders. Subsequent events in Syria, after the onset of the 2011 civil war, opened the door to further political demands by the majority of Kurdish political parties.

In Turkey, the harsh repression of the Kemalist regime led all Kurdish activists to seek refuge in the neighbouring countries, in particular in Syria and Lebanon. Under the protection of the French authorities, Kurdish intellectuals, who organized themselves around the Khoybun Committee (1927–1943), became 'legitimate' representatives of the Kurdish opposition to the Kemalists. Notwithstanding their capacity to challenge the Kemalist discourse thanks to the relative freedom of action in the Levant under the French mandate, Kurdish intellectuals lacked powerful ideological tools, such as schools, to instil a Kurdish sentiment among the Kurds in Northern Syria. More importantly, they were by and large constrained in their response to Turkish state propaganda. As such, though carrying a message concerning the 'we-group', Kurdish intellectuals were not independent of Turkish categories: the search for an ancient and golden age of the Kurds, the 'purity' of Kurdish language, the 'homogenous character' of Kurdish society, the merciless race of the Kurdish people towards (Western) 'civilization'.

Seemingly, the integration of thousands of Kurds into the Turkish Left from the 1960s onwards marked the discourse (anti-imperialist and secular) and organizational character (centralized and strongly hierarchical) of the Kurdish parties established in the 1970s. Thus, for example, the PKK, established in 1978, sought to reunite or rather lead the divided revolutionary Left in Turkey. Ideologically, the PKK was directly inspired by the latter and, tellingly, some of the founders of the PKK, such as Haki Karer and Kemal Pir, were ethnic Turks.[30] Regardless of the contradictions present in all nationalist discourses, the process of mimesis between the discourse and the repertoire used by ruling groups and the Kurdish opposition has had profound and long-term impact on the relationship between the Turks, the Arabs and the Kurds. Since both sides ('majority' and 'minority') have framed their 'we-groups' as homogeneous and 'naturally' subjects of collective rights in the name of international law and universal values, the acceptation, recognition and incorporation of various ethnic and religious groups into a more inclusive 'national identity' by the ruling group has turned out to be rather complex, at the very least.

Unsurprisingly thus the actual progress made by Kurdish communities in Syria and Iraq was the result of political opportunities (e.g. regional tensions, foreign interventions) and shifting power relations (e.g. between 1958 and 1970 in Iraq, and between 2004 and 2008, and since 2011 in Syria) rather than the outcome of a genuine search for a new social contract. At the same time, a historical overview allows researchers to identify periods of peaceful coexistence, episodes of widespread state violence against the Kurds, of active involvement in national politics as well as political ruptures. Clearly, in times of acute conflicts, including the widespread use of violence, minorities' margin of action is reduced severely due to their lack of organizational resources when compared to central governments. However, throughout the twentieth century minorities proved their ability to mobilize internal and external resources to meet these challenges, as well as to invest in the national arena in order to create a context of relatively peaceful existence, and even to become a main broker in national power relations (e.g. Kurds in Iraq since 2005 and increasingly important in Syria since 2011).[31] Hence, minorities must be analysed from a dynamic perspective, for they are not the passive victims much of the literature on majority/minority relations has put forward.

Finally, the Kurdish case shows that after all, political claims on behalf of minorities have frequently been claims not for separation, but for more liberal politics, and with implications for the majority as well, provided that the Kurds were not obliged to choose between the former and the latter. A popular Kurdish slogan 'democracy for Iraq, autonomy for Kurdistan', first used in Iraq in the 1960s and later on adopted by the Kurds in Syria and Iran, perfectly encapsulates this view.

The long quest for autonomy in Iraq

Despite the participation of some Kurdish representatives in the Iraqi parliament as well as in several Iraqi cabinets throughout the Monarchist Period, it was not until the First Republic (1958–1963), led by Abdel Kareem Qassem, that the Iraqi constitution recognized Kurdish 'national rights'.[32] Threatened both by the Ba'athist party in Iraq and the increasing regional ambitions of Egyptian president Gamal Abdel Nasser, Qassem sought to secure the stability of his government thanks to communist and Kurdish support. Consequently, many Kurds were appointed to high offices, and Mustafa Barzani, leader of the KDP in exile since 1945, was able to come back to Iraq. By the same token, Kurdish activities increased under Qassem. Kurdish publications were freely circulated (*Khabat, Jin, Azadi, Hewa, Rojy Nwi*), there was a special Kurdish section in broadcasting and television services, and many Kurdish intellectuals joined the Iraqi Communist Party, Qassem's main ally, or cooperated with it.[33]

However, relations between Qassem and the Kurds deteriorated rapidly. Neither Qassem nor his government was willing to give the Kurds the administrative self-rule they aspired to. In July 1961, Barzani submitted a memorandum to the government, demanding a substantial degree of autonomy for the Kurdish region. The government, afraid that such plan might induce the Shia to demand a similar status, rejected it, and the relations with the KDP worsened to the extent that a nine-year war started between the central government and the Kurds. Taking advantage of the alliance with Iran (backed by Israel and the United States), Barzani was able to challenge militarily the Iraqi forces and severely weaken the state's stability. Hence, the Ba'athist party in power since 1968 negotiated an autonomy agreement with the Kurds. By 1973, the relations deteriorated once again and the Iraqi government reneged on its commitments; in turn, the Kurds resumed their insurgency. In a dramatic turning point of the conflict, the Shah of Iran signed suddenly a treaty with Baghdad settling the Shatt al Arab border dispute and withdrew his support to the rebels in 1975. Without Iranian complicity, Kurdish resistance collapsed and Barzani was forced into exile, first to Iran and then to the United States, where he died in 1979.

Despite sporadic tactical contacts made by the two camps throughout the 1980s, the 1970–1973 talks were the last true negotiations between the central government and the Kurds on self-government within the Iraqi state. Furthermore, within the context of the Iran–Iraq war, the Ba'athist regime launched a massive coercive campaign against Kurdish rebels. The most famous of these reprisals was the attack on the town of Halabja in March 1988, in which five thousand civilians were killed when Iraqi warplanes dropped mustard gas and other chemical weapons on the inhabitants. Halabja's attack was the peak of a broader military campaign aiming at the annihilation of the Kurdish guerrilla as well as of its local support.[34]

The effective self-government the Kurds have enjoyed in northern Iraq since 1992 was the result of Saddam Hussain's decision to invade Kuwait, triggering a broad international military campaign to drive his forces out. Although the US forces did not help the Kurds to take the three main Kurdish provinces, the American government helped to establish a 'safe haven' and a no-fly zone in northern Iraq after the Gulf War ended in April 1991. In October of that year, Iraqi forces and state employees withdrew unilaterally from Kurdistan, thereby allowing the two main political parties to organize free elections and set up a regional government. Eventually, the US invasion of Iraq in 2003 reinforced Kurdish autonomy and the role of the Kurdish parties within the Iraqi political arena in the aftermath of the war.

As Joost Hiltermann put it, from 2003 onwards, the Kurds have succeeded in 'Kurdifying Iraqi politics to the extent that no decision can be taken without Kurdish input or, more, without the threat of a Kurdish veto.'[35] Significantly, Article 117 of the 2005 Iraqi Constitution recognizes the region of Kurdistan, along with its authorities, as a federal region, thus enshrining the principle of federalism in the country's basic law. Iraqi federalism is, however, asymmetrical. On the one hand, the Iraqi Constitution establishes a federal system based on four levels of government: decentralized capital, regions, governorates and local administrations. Region-formation is deferred to legislation, but the constitution states that one or more governorates have the right to form a region. By defining those general guidelines for the emergence of federalism in Iraq, the constitution rejects both the models of purely ethnic and purely territorial federalism. On the other hand, Article 117 acknowledges the existence of a separate entity for a large number of Iraqi Kurds.

The offensive in 2014 by the Islamic State in Iraq and Syria (ISIS) favoured a political rapprochement between the KRG and the Iraqi government. While Barzani postponed the announced independence referendum, Nouri al-Maliki was replaced by the more consensual figure of Haider al Abadi as Iraqi Prime Minister. Subsequently, the two entities reached a preliminary agreement on sensitive issues such as oil wealth and national budget distribution. Internally, ISIS threat sparked a revival of tensions between the two main Kurdish political parties, the KDP and the Patriotic Union of Kurdistan (PUK), thereby hindering any unitary project for Kurdish independence.

From cultural to political claims in Syria

A dialectic approach based on the evolution of the Syrian state and that of Kurdish communities can provide some explanation for the present Kurdish predicament. At the end of the Mandate, the Syrian state and the elites who succeeded one another until 1963 possessed neither a unanimous ideology nor a sufficiently coercive power base to pose a serious threat to Kurdish identity. State authority was more of an illusion than a reality, especially in the countryside where real sovereignty lay in the hands of two rivals, prominent citizens and landowners 'who did little to encourage any feelings of national identity'.³⁶ In this context, by the early 1950s and according to reports of the French Legation in Damascus:

> The Kurdish settlers, the majority of whom can be found in Jazira, live in harmony with the Syrians. They continue to speak their national language and wear typical Kurdish clothing, but as long as the government does not force the issue of taxes and closes its eyes to the lucrative smuggling of illegal goods […], there is no Kurdish problem to speak of in Syria, where numerous functionaries and high-level officers belong to this community.³⁷

If the rise to power of the Ba'ath led to the imposition of a unanimous ideology on Syrian population, the new regime suffered from internal divisions which prevented it from ever-establishing viable official institutions, or even a myth of national integration, which would have given it some legitimacy. It was not until Hafez al Assad came to power in 1970 that a dominant power structure was finally established. In reality, behind the official unanimous ideology (e.g. socialism and pan-Arabism), significant splits exacerbated by the foundation of the regime's political culture continued to exist at the margins of the Syrian legal political system. While the government in Damascus cultivated the loyalty of its Kurdish 'clients,' the majority of Kurds opted for a strategy of 'dissimulation'.³⁸ This concept, which is similar to the religious term *taqiyya*, means that under certain adverse socio-political conditions, individuals or a given group disguise their differences or distinguishing features in order to challenge the official unanimous ideology at its deepest roots. However, when the conditions improve it, this formerly hidden group ceases to play the game of conformity and insists on being visible and exposing its differences.

Like in the Iraqi case, the international context provided Syria's Kurds with political opportunities from the 1970s onwards. By 1968, tensions between Syria and Iraq manifested themselves primarily in the struggle for Ba'athist ideological legitimacy. Damascus showed unabashed support for those in political opposition to the Baghdad regime. Thus, Jalal Talabani, leader of the PUK, was able to open a permanent office in Damascus. In 1979, Idris Barzani formalized relations between Syria and the KDP. More importantly, during the Iran–Iraq war, Syria worked on reconciliation of the PUK and the KDP, which was accomplished in 1987.

It was, nevertheless, the alliance between the Syrian government and the PKK that brought about further consequences into the Syrian–Kurdish arena. In the 1980s, external pressure compelled Hafez al Assad to take an interest in the Kurdish nationalist movement in Turkey. The conflict between Turkey and Syria was rooted in the transfer of sovereignty from the *sandjak* of Alexandretta in 1939 during the French Mandate that benefited Turkey. Besides this territorial dispute, Turkish dams on the Euphrates threatened Syria's water supply.³⁹ A connection between these two issues emerged when Turkey proposed an agreement to Syria on sharing the Euphrates' waters in exchange for the recognition of its borders. Syria, however, refused to integrate the border question into the negotiations, preferring to exert pressure on Turkey by allowing the PKK to establish bases on its territory, from which Kurdish fighters launched military operations against the Turkish army.[40] Thanks to the cooperation of the Assad regime, northern Syria became a breeding ground for PKK militants during the 1980s and 1990s.[41] Furthermore, six candidates from Kurd Dagh, overtly declaring themselves as representatives of the PKK, ran for office in the Syrian elections in May 1990.

However, resorting to 'parallel diplomacy' led to increased pressure and caused collateral damage to Syria. Thus, while using the Kurdish movement against Iraq and Turkey, Hafez al Assad's regime had to accept the strengthening of cross-border relations between the Syrian Kurds and the Kurds in neighbouring countries. By the same token, Syria relinquished a part of its sovereignty, particularly in its relations with the PKK. In order to attract followers, the PKK, thanks to its relative freedom of action, started sponsoring literacy programmes and quickly succeeded in steering Kurdish culture away from the private sphere towards the public arena. On the other hand, the increasing visibility of the Kurdish ethnic identity led to the establishment of new political parties that, for the first time, asked for political autonomy within the Syrian framework; the Yekîtî, for example, was to play a relevant role in the Qamishli revolt of 2004.[42]

In the aftermath of the Qamishli revolt, Syrian Kurdish parties sought to establish a new balance both with the regime and the Kurdish movement; Syrian regime would be more likely to allow a flexible approach with respect to public expressions of Kurdish identity (language, music, cultural festivals, publications), while the Kurdish movement would not embrace, for the time being, the goal of overturning the government of Bashar al Assad. Although the majority of Kurdish parties opted for the return to the 'peaceful struggle' in 2005, the Syrian uprising of March 2011 opened the door for a new surge of Kurdish mobilization and the actual territorial and military control of the northern enclaves by the PYD's militias.

Searching for a solution to the Kurdish issue in Turkey and beyond

The military coup of 12 September 1980 in Ankara and its subsequent repression affected vast sectors of the Turkish society. According to some reports, 'a total of 650,000 people were detained [...]. Over five hundred people died while under detention as a result of torture; 85,000 people were placed on trial mainly in relation to thought crimes by association; 1,683,000 people were officially listed in police files as suspects ... ; 15,509 people were fired from their jobs for political reasons'.[43] Yet while Turkey witnessed a long 'cycle of demobilisation' (1980–2013), observation of the Kurdish arena in Turkey suggests a different picture. Physical, as well as political repression, led at first to a dramatic drop in activism. Yet despite scarce openings in the political system or the lack of 'political opportunities', from 1984 onwards, the PKK became the dominant dissent movement in Turkey as a whole.

The PKK, which had been established formally in 1978, sought to establish a socialist Kurdish nation-state. The main ideological difference of the PKK, among other newly established groups with regard to previous organizations, was that the former considered employing political violence as the main instrument for creating political influence not only against the Turkish state but also Kurdish 'challengers', namely competing Kurdish organizations and Kurdish 'collaborators'.[44] On 15 August 1984, the PKK launched its military campaign against the Turkish state; several soldiers and officers were killed and wounded near the Turkey–Iraq border. This unexpected action came as a relief among dormant revolutionary groups. In fact, many 'young boys (and some girls) welcomed this new phase of violence as a means of the re-conquest of their symbolic resources and their Kurdish identity and as the starting point of a new and violent, but nevertheless open, process of socialisation'.[45]

Although at first the PKK did not meet with a rapid success among Kurdish populations, by the late 1980s the numbers of PKK guerrillas increased significantly, which allowed it to build its presence in the region and challenge the Turkish state, both ideologically and military. The evolution of the PKK into a mass popular national liberation movement had nevertheless a negative impact on social life in the Kurdish areas. The thirty-year conflict (1978–1999) cost the lives of more than 45,000 people and resulted in the forced evacuation of 3,500 villages and hamlets.[46] Overall, more than three million Kurds moved from Eastern Anatolia to Western Turkey (in particular, Istanbul, Mersin and Izmir) due to general insecurity and lack of economic opportunities in the Kurdish war-torn region. Though the PKK declared several unilateral ceasefires throughout the 1990s, the actual turning point for the armed conflict came as a result of a diplomatic crisis between Syria and Turkey. As mentioned, relations between the PKK and the Syrian government were mutually beneficial, the former having a base in Syria for its activities against the Turkish state while the PKK militants provided Hafez al Assad with a shield against its internal (e.g., potential Kurdish challengers) and external opponents. Yet, the Kurds' role as minority clients with Syria acting as a patron state turned out to be a risky choice for the PKK.

Threatened by the Turkish–Israeli alliance of 1996, isolated internationally and dependent on water supply from the Euphrates, Syria succumbed finally to Turkish pressure to withdraw all support for the PKK. Damascus expelled Abdullah Öcalan, the leader of the PKK, on 9 October 1998. The following January, he began the long journey that took him to Kenya, where he was arrested and transferred to Turkey. The repercussions of these developments were felt deeply in Turkey and Syria; in August 1999 the PKK withdrew its guerrillas from Turkey to Iraqi Kurdistan and declared a permanent ceasefire. In addition, various high-ranking PKK cadres were handed over to Ankara, and former PKK fighters returning to Syria were sentenced to prison. More significantly, the 1999 crisis brought about a radical ideological re-orientation of the PKK. In that sense, the movement conceptualized the solution to the Kurdish question on the basis of development and the deepening of democracy without the need to alter the existing state system. The actual meaning of 'democracy' and the 'solution to the Kurdish national question' evolved rapidly. While in the early 2000s the PKK seemed to abide by and large to the 'democratic package' proposed by the European Union (decentralization and linguistic rights), by 2003 a slight ideological change towards a de-territorialized and post-national paradigm was perceptible already.

The solution to the Kurdish question implied the democratic transformation of the state system in the Middle East into federal and confederal entities. More precisely, the new programme contained proposals to reconstitute the Kurds as a nation without contrasting their own nation-state or being based on a particular territory.[47] Also, the new orientation had organizational consequences, as the PKK decided to split into different sister organizations in order to adapt better its new orientation to local dynamics and issues in Iraq (Party for a Democratic Solution for Kurdistan or PÇDK, 2002), in Syria (Democratic Union Party or PYD, 2003) and in Iran (Free Life Party of Kurdistan or PJAK, 2004). In parallel, following a series of secret negotiations, the Turkish Prime Minister Tayyip Erdoğan announced a peace initiative in May 2009, the Kurdish Opening, which came to be known as the Democratic Initiative – namely the recognition of the Kurdish and other minority rights within the Turkish state system. Despite legal attacks against the pro-Kurdish legal movement represented by the Peace and Democratic Party (BDP), the Democratic Initiative allowed for peace negotiations and eventually a three-year ceasefire (2012–2015).

Although the principles of democratic autonomy were first implemented clandestinely in Turkey, the Arab Spring of 2011 provided unexpected opportunities for the development of the new ideological and organizational orientation of the PYD in Syria. Freed from any significant opposition, the PYD alone promoted the declaration of a local administration followed by the appointment of three governments in the 'cantons' of Jazira, Kobane and Afrin in January 2014. Moreover, on 17 March 2016, the PYD decided to establish a federal administrative system throughout the Kurdish enclaves, in which 'democratic autonomy' and 'democratic confederalism' were to prevail. In theory, the Kurdish cantons sought to strengthen local administrative capacities organized in the form of councils at a very local level, of streets and then neighbourhoods, through districts/villages and towns/cities to regions. In addition, following Abdullah Öcalan's prison writings, the PYD claims that all peoples in the Middle East should abandon the nation-state system to embrace a kind of communal self-organization and other principles such as ecological feminism. In doing so, since the early 2000s, some sectors of the Kurdish movement seem to have evolved largely independently from mainstream political parties in the Middle East, which are still torn between the 'national question' and/or the role of Islam in politics.

Conclusions

It is a commonplace of much research on ethnic conflicts that the ethnic and sectarian categories should not be considered essential; in other words, they are fluid and a product of constant construction by political actors as well as by scholars. Yet, the fluidity of sectarian and ethnic boundaries does not imply that they are void of meaning. Within certain contexts (e.g. war, massive violence, fist dictatorship), they may become salient and determine the collective feeling of belonging by individuals or groups, and, eventually, their political commitment.[48] Therefore, instead of accepting or rejecting the validity of works focused on power, clan, ethnicity and sectarianism as grids of analysis, it seems more appropriate to multiply the sites of observation and levels of analysis (between local, regional and global, between internal and external), so that our perspective on the issues of majority/minority relations can be renewed.

By the same token, although researchers should avoid studying Kurdish minority claims, as the 'natural' outcome of a deep-rooted primordial identity, scholars cannot overlook the fact that the search for recognition of Kurds as a 'national' group within aforementioned states is an old and widespread claim. Thus, the dilemma the Kurds face in Iraq, Syria and Turkey is not a choice between accommodation and rebellion, but one of guaranteeing their collective rights within the legal system while pushing for further de-centralization, or even for an asymmetrical form of federalism. Federalism is perceived both by the Kurds and some scholars as a tool for accommodating conflicting ideas while preserving territorial cohesion and permitting self-government for minority groups. In addition to enhanced autonomy, federalism is supposed to increase personal liberties, recognize group rights, improve governance through increased accountability and local ownership, contribute to nation building and ultimately, enable peaceful co-existence.[49] Yet, there are divergent views about the actual impact of federalism in the long run. Hence, to some researchers and very often to political leaders representing the 'majority', federalism fosters existing divisions through the hardening of identities, eventually fuelling secessionist movements.[50]

Either way, the federal paradox – that federalism contributes to stability in some cases and to disintegration in others – suggests that research on federalism and the political and legal arrangements between minority/majority groups should concern the conditions under which those arrangements operate, in particular, in countries lacking democratic culture. Therefore, in the long run, the emergence of federal or confederal arrangements that would be considered legitimate and effective both by the population and the elite will depend on the interaction of institutional provisions with several contextual elements which simply cannot be produced by a specific agreement. This does not mean that institutional design is irrelevant, but that it might be less important in managing the conflict than stated generally by research. Eventually, the emergence of federalism/confederalism as an instrument of peaceful co-existence between territorial ethnic groups and a given 'majority' needs to go hand in hand with other developments, namely the emergence of trust between the elites and the willingness to solve conflicts peacefully, the commitment to democratic institutions and processes, and the rule of law.

Yet if, as noted, the actual autonomy of the Kurds is related directly to periods of crisis and the subsequent weakness of the central government, one can expect that the willingness of state elites to accept and implement federal or confederal provisions will also depend on the power relations between the 'minority' and the 'majority', as well as on regional dynamics. In that respect, the lack of trust, as well as the authoritarian drift of the Maliki cabinet, undermined potential benefits of federalism in Iraq up to 2014.[51] In addition, the 2005 Constitution is often imprecise or contradictory, in particular regarding the division of competences and sharing of oil revenues, which is likely to exacerbate tensions between the central government and the KRG. In Syria, few, if any, representatives of the mainstream Syrian political actors seem to be eager to accept the principle of federalism or even territorial de-centralization within the future Syrian constitution.[52] Finally, Recep Tayyip Erdoğan's presidential ambitions in Turkey, the rising power of the PYD in northern Syria since 2013 and the lack of a clear Kurdish agenda led the Turkish government to increase its pressure on the main pro-Kurdish party in Turkey and boost the military and financial aid to diverse Syrian rebel groups against the PYD, thereby paving the way for a new phase in the Turkish-Kurdish conflict.

A century after the collapse of the Ottoman Empire and the subsequent materialization of the Kurdish question in the international arena, the resolution of the Kurdish issue remains uncertain. On the one hand, although the idea of an independent and united Kurdistan may remain a powerful political myth that provides legitimacy to Kurdish political parties, old and new challenges might lead the latter to keep on vowing their willingness to present solutions to the minority issue within the existing international borders. In that sense, federalism, confederalism and democratic confederalism are proposals that might allow states in the region to secure their durability and to regain some legitimacy in the eyes of their citizens, minority and majority groups alike. On the other hand, it remains to be seen whether state elites are ready to embrace these forms of governance, which are still perceived as dangerous in the Middle East, but which indeed pertain to 'the *world's time*'.[53]

Notes

1. On the Peace negotiations of 1919 and the claims from different national committees, see Erez Manela, *The Wilsonian Moment – Self-Determination and the International Origins of Anticolonial Nationalism*, Oxford: Oxford University Press, 2007.
2. J.E. Shuckburgh to Mr. Osborne, 'Kurdish situation', 25 January 1923, FO 371/9004/E1019.
3. Robert Lowe and Gareth Stansfield, *The Kurdish Policy Imperative*, Washington, DC: Brookings Institution Press, 2010; Michael M. Gunter, *The Kurdish Ascending – The*

Evolving Solution to the Kurdish Problem in Iraq and Turkey, New York: Palgrave Macmillan, 2011; and Michael M. Gunter and M.A. Ahmed Mohammed, *The Kurdish Spring, Costa,* Mesa: Mazda Publishers, 2013.

4   David Hirst, 'This Could Be the Birth of an Independent Kurdish State', *The Guardian*, 9 January 2013.
5   Some arguments of this paper were first developed in Jordi Tejel, 'Beyond the Dichotomy of Accommodation versus Resistance: The Kurdish Minority in Iraq and Syria in Long-term and Comparative Perspectives, 1920–2015', in Michael M. Gunter, ed., *Kurdish Issues – Essays in Honour of Robert W. Olson*, Costa Mesa: Mazda, 2016, pp. 258–82.
6   'A national minority is not simply a group that is given by the facts of ethnic demography. It is a dynamic political stance, or, more precisely, a family of related yet mutually competing stances, not a static ethno-demographic condition'. Rogers Brubaker, *Nationalism Reframed – Nationhood and the National Question in the New Europe*, Cambridge: Cambridge University Press, 1996, p. 60.
7   Dale F. Eickelman, 'Changing Interpretations of Islamic Movements', in William R. Roff, ed., *Islam and the Political Economy of Meaning*, London: Croom-Helm, 1987, pp. 13–30; Jean Leca, 'La Rationalité de la Violence Politique', in Baudoin Dupret, ed., *Le Phénomène de la Violence Politique – Perspectives Comparatistes et Paradigme Égyptien*, Cairo: CEDEJ, 1994, pp. 17–42.
8   Reinhart Koselleck, *Le Future Passé – Contribution à la Sémantique des Temps Historiques*, Paris: Éditions de l'EHESS, 1990.
9   Hamit Bozarslan, *'Being in time*, the Kurdish Movement and Universal Quests', in Gareth Stansfield and Mohammed Shareef, eds., *The Kurdish Question Revisited*, London: Hurst and Company, 2017, p. 62.
10 Ibid., pp. 72–3.
11 In Migdal's definition, the image of the state is of a dominant, integrated, autonomous entity that controls, in a given territory, all rule-making, either directly through its own agencies or indirectly by sanctioning other authorized organizations to make certain circumscribed rules. Joel S. Migdal, *State in Society – Studying How States and Societies Transform and Constitute One Another*, Cambridge: Cambridge University Press, 2001, p. 16.
12 Charles Tilly, *The Politics of Collective Violence*, Cambridge: Cambridge University Press, 2003.
13 Nicole F. Watts, 'Institutionalising Virtual Kurdistan West – Transnational Networks and Ethnic Contention in International Affairs', in Joel S. Migdal, ed., *Boundaries and Belonging – States and Societies in the Struggle to Shape Identities and Local Practices*, Cambridge: Cambridge University Press, 2008, p. 147.
14 Ephraim Nimni, 'Stateless Nations in a World of Nation-states', in Karl Cordell and Stefan Wolff, eds., *Routledge Handbook of Ethnic Conflict*, London and New York: Routledge, 2011, pp. 55–66.
15 Elizabeth Picard, 'Nation-building and Minority Rights in the Middle East', in Anh Nga Longva and Anne Sofie Roald, eds., *Religious Minorities in the Middle East – Domination, Self-Empowerment, Accommodation*, Leiden and Boston: Brill, 2012, p. 329.
16 Nadine Méouchy and Peter Sluglett, eds., *The British and French Mandates in Comparative Perspectives/Les Mandats Français et Britannique dans une Perspective Comparative*, Leiden: Brill, 2004.
17 Picard, 'Nation-building and Minority Rights', p. 329.

18 Kerem Ökten, 'The Nation's Imprint: Demographic Engineering and the Change of Toponymes in Republican Turkey', *European Journal of Turkish Studies*, 7, 2008, www.ejts.org/document2243.html
19 Joshua Landis, 'Shishakli and the Druzes: Integration and Intransigence', in Thomas Philip and Birgit Schäbler, eds., *The Syrian Land – Processes of Integration and Fragmentation*, Stuttgart: Franz Steiner Verlag, 1998, pp. 369–96.
20 Jordi Tejel, 'Urban Mobilisation in Iraqi Kurdistan during the British Mandate: Sulaimaniya, 1918–1930', *Middle Eastern Studies*, 44, 4, 2008, pp. 537–52.
21 Benedict Anderson cited in Deborah Kaspin, 'Tribes, Regions and Nationalism in Democratic Malawi', in Ian Shapiro and Will Kymlicka, eds., *Ethnicity and Group Rights*, New York and London: New York University Press, 1997, p. 469.
22 Hamit Bozarslan, *Violence in the Middle East – From Political Struggle to Self-Sacrifice*, Princeton, New Jersey: Markus Wiener, 2004, p. 36.
23 NIDS, 'Subject of Crime', PUK 011, Box 045 (070019).
24 Azat Zana Gündogan, 'The Kurdish Political Mobilisation in the 1960s: The Case of the Eastern Meetings', Master's Thesis, Middle East Technical University of Ankara, 2005.
25 Hamit Bozarslan, *La Question Kurde – États et Minorités au Moyen-Orient*, Paris: Presses de Sciences Po, 1997.
26 Mark Mazower, 'Minorities and the League of Nation in Interwar Europe', *Daedalus*, 126, 2, 1997, p. 51.
27 Tejel, 'Urban Mobilisation in Iraqi Kurdistan', pp. 537–52.
28 Martin Van Bruinessen, 'Kurdish Paths to Nation', in Faleh Abdul Jabar and Hosham Dawod, eds., *The Kurds. Nationalism and Politics*, London: Saqi Books, 2006, pp. 21–48.
29 On 23 August 1962, the central government issued a decree (no. 93) authorizing a special census of the population in Jazira, which was conducted in November of the same year. Following the results, 120,000 Kurds were stripped of their Syrian citizenship. The reasoning put forth for this action was that only 60 per cent of the Kurds found in Syria were 'true' Syrians. The others, the government claimed, had illegally infiltrated Syria, coming from Turkey and Iraq.
30 Joost Jongerden and Ahmet Hamdi Akkaya, 'The Kurdistan Workers Party and a New Left in Turkey: Analysis of the Revolutionary Movement in Turkey through the PKK's Memorial Text on Haki Karer', *European Journal of Turkish Studies*, 14, 2012, http://ejts.revues.org/4613.
31 Longva and Roald, *Religious Minorities in the Middle East*, p. 3.
32 Ismet Cheriff Vanly, *Le Kurdistan Irakien – Entité Nationale*, Neuchâtel: Les Éditions de la Baconnière, 1970, p. 150.
33 KSSE, *Kurdistan* 5, 1959, p. 19.
34 Joost Hiltermann, *A Poisonous Affair – America, Iraq and the Gassing of Halabja*, Cambridge: Cambridge University Press, 2007.
35 Joost Hiltermann, 'To Protect or to Project? Iraqi Kurds and Their Future', *MERIP*, 247, 2008, www.merip.org/mer/mer247/protect-or-project.
36 Volker Perthes, *The Political Economy of Syria under Asad*, London: I.B. Tauris, 2002, pp. 91–2.
37 CADN, *Fonds Ankara, Embassy, No. 104*. M. J. Emile, the French Minister in Damascus to his Excellency the Minister of Foreign Affairs, Damascus, 5 December 1951.
38 See Jordi Tejel, 'Les Kurdes de Syrie: De la "Dissimulation" à la "Visibilité"?', *Revue des Mondes Musulmans et de la Méditerranée*, 115–16, 2006, pp. 117–33.
39 The Southeast Anatolia project (GAP), aimed at exploiting the hydraulic resources of the Euphrates' and Tigris' basins. When completed, a total of 22 dams and 19 power plants would have been built on the two river basins. In addition, the GAP would

increase the area under irrigation in Turkey by 40 per cent. However, Syria and Iraq claimed that the GAP project could cost Syria 40 per cent and Iraq 90 per cent of the Euphrates flow. John Bulloch and Adil Darwish, *Water Wars – Coming Conflicts in the Middle East*, London: Rowland, 1993, p. 60.

40 Martin Van Bruinessen, 'Between Guerrilla War and Political Murder: The PKK', *MERIP*, 153, 1988, p. 44.
41 Harriet Montgomery, *The Kurds of Syria – An Existence Denied*, Berlin: EZKS, 2005, p. 134.
42 Media sources reported that on 12 March 2004, during a football match in the town of Qamishli between the local team and Dayr al Zur, the insults between the fans of the two sides escalated into a riot that spilled out into the streets. Rumours of a real massacre quickly circulated and thousands of people demonstrated in the main Kurdish towns, and even in Arab cities with a strong concentration of Kurds, like Aleppo and Damascus. The reaction of the security forces was surprising in its brutality. See Jordi Tejel, *Syria's Kurds – History, Politics and Society*, London: Routledge, 2009, pp. 115–26; and Harriet Allsopp, *The Kurds of Syria – Political Parties and Identity in the Middle East,* London: I.B. Tauris, 2014, pp. 34–7.
43 Ismet G. Imset, 'The PKK: Twenty Years of Separatist Violence in Turkey', *Yayinlari* (Ankara), 1992, p. 60.
44 Uygur Ercan, 'The Global Crisis and the Turkish Economy', Working Papers 2010/3, Turkish Economic Association, 2010. There were other political groups that pledged for armed struggle as the only means to reach their political goals (independence and socialism): Rizgarî (1975), Kawa (a Maoist group, 1975), the KUK or Kurdish National Liberators (1977).
45 Bozarslan, *Violence in the Middle East*, p. 47.
46 Cengiz Gunes, 'Kurdish Political Activism in Turkey: An Overview', in Gunter, *Kurdish Issues* p. 88.
47 See Joost Jongerden and Ahmet Hamdi Akkaya, 'Democratic Confederalism as a Kurdish Spring: the PKK and the Quest for radical democracy', in Gunter and Ahmed, *Kurdish Spring*, pp. 163–85. For a critical assessment of PYD's practices in Rojava, see International Crisis Group, *Flight of Icarus? The PYD's Precarious Rise in Syria*, 151, 2014; and Michiel Leezenberg, 'The Ambiguities of Democratic Autonomy: The Kurdish Movement in Turkey and Rojava', *Southeast European and Black Sea Studies*, 16, 4, 2016, pp. 671–90.
48 Hank Johnston and Bert Klandermans, 'The Cultural Analysis of Social Movements', in Hank Johnston and Bert Klandermans, eds., *Social Movements and Culture*, Minneapolis: University of Minnesota Press, 1995, p. 8.
49 Kristin M. Bakke and Erik Wibbels, 'Diversity, Disparity, and Civil Conflict in Federal States', *World Politics*, 59, 1, 2006, pp. 1–50; and Lisa Anderson, 'The Non-Ethnic Model of Federalism: Some Comparative Perspectives', in Reidar Visser and Gareth Stansfield, eds., *An Iraq of Its Regions – Cornerstones of a Federal Democracy?*, New York: Columbia University Press, 2008, pp. 205–55.
50 Dawn Brancati, 'Decentralisation: Fuelling the Fire or Dampening the Flames of Ethnic Conflict and Secessionism?' *International Organization*, 60, 3, 2006, pp. 651–85; and Valerie Bunce, *Subversive Institutions – The Design and the Destruction of Socialism and the State*, Cambridge: Cambridge University Press, 1999.
51 Toby Dodge, *Iraq – From War to a New Authoritarianism*, London: IISS, 2012, pp. 147–79.
52 Dilxwaz Bahlawi, 'Syrian Kurds Should not Demand Guarantees or Autonomy', *Rudaw*, 13 January 2013, www.rudaw.net/english/news/syria/5653.html.
53 Bozarslan, '*Being in time*', pp. 73–4.

PART THREE

REINVENTIONS AND RETURNS

7 EGYPT'S POST-ARAB SPRING NEO-AUTHORITARIANISM

Bruce K. Rutherford

When Egypt achieved independence in 1922, it had already benefitted from an ambitious state-building programme initiated by Ottoman governor Muhammad Ali over a century before that created the outlines of Egypt's modern state and laid the foundations for the authoritarian regime that guides it.[1] The key features of Egypt's authoritarianism were further defined in the 1950s and 1960s under President Gamal Abdel Nasser. However, Egypt's authoritarianism was not static. Political, economic and international pressures led to adjustments and adaptations under the presidencies of Anwar al Sadat in the 1970s and Hosni Mubarak from the 1980s to the early 2010s. The 2011 uprising of the Arab Spring created another important moment of change.

This chapter begins with a brief discussion of the historical development of Egyptian authoritarianism. The bulk of the chapter then focuses on the changes from Mubarak to the regime of Abdelfattah al Sisi (since 2013) and, particularly, the new elite pact that underlies that regime. This new pact, it is argued, is not grounded in patronage, which was the foundation of elite support for Mubarak. Rather, it is premised on protection of elites from shared threats. The pact has created a new form of authoritarianism that commands a narrower base of elite support and a limited capacity to undertake economic and other reforms.

Muhammad Ali and the foundations of the Egyptian state

Muhammad Ali's nineteenth-century state-building efforts in Egypt were centred on creating a modern and powerful military. Such military strength would ensure his command over domestic rivals and enable him to extend Egypt's regional power throughout the Sudan, the Levant and parts of Arabia. In order to pay for this new military, Muhammad Ali (1769–1849) undertook extensive economic reforms. Ali invested heavily in new irrigation projects and introduced new export crops, such as high-quality long staple cotton that was prized by textile factories in Britain and France. He undertook an extensive industrialization campaign that included shipyards and foundries as well as factories to produce weapons, ammunition, textiles, refined sugar and other products. In order to acquire the capital for these projects, the state took control of most agricultural land and became the sole purchaser of raw materials as well as the sole distributor of goods of all types, enabling it to add taxes and fees at every step in the production and distribution chain. Ali created an extensive bureaucracy to manage this growing economy, which became the foundation for the modern civil service. He also transformed Egypt's education system, creating state-run schools to train military officers, engineers, doctors and administrators.[2]

While some of these reforms were rolled back later in the nineteenth century, the broad outlines of the Egyptian state began to take shape. These were grounded in a central role for the state in raising and allocating capital. The state wielded this power through a large bureaucracy that was empowered to regulate broadly in the economy and society. The state was governed in a tightly centralized fashion with few mechanisms for representation and even fewer checks on executive power. The heart of state power was the military, which was large, well equipped and well organized. Even at this early stage, the military's influence extended beyond security to shape the economy, the education system and society. In order to ensure the loyalty and obedience of the country's vast conscript army, the state also developed a national intelligence apparatus that monitored soldiers and their families.[3]

Britain's occupation of Egypt, which began in 1882, reinforced several of these features. The state's central role in the economy continued, with the creation of a more extensive set of regulations to ensure that the economy focused on producing the raw materials that Britain needed to sustain its industrial revolution.[4] The bureaucracy's size and capabilities grew accordingly. The key change under British rule was to weaken the military, a process that the British had begun in mid-century by defeating the Egyptian navy off the coast of Greece. This policy of maintaining a relatively small military continued under the Egyptian governments formed after independence in 1922. In the mid-1930s, a military academy was opened to youth of the lower middle classes. When the political and economic system reached a state of crisis in the early 1950s, the opposition was led by angry and alienated military officers, from those lower middle classes, whose very isolation from the regime gave them the motivation and credibility to challenge it.

With the Free Officers' 1952 coup against King Farouk, the Nasser era soon marked an important break with the past through the abolition of the monarchy and the implementation of sweeping land reform. However, the path of state-building adopted by Nasser showed significant continuities with the Muhammad Ali era. The state assumed an even more important role in the economy. The regime nationalized virtually all of the country's industries and established large state-owned firms that dominated every sector of the economy. The government created an extensive subsidy system that aimed to provide food, electricity, gasoline, transportation, education, medical care and other services for free or at heavily subsidized prices. The state also developed an even larger and more complex bureaucracy to administer these subsidies and, more generally, to guide the economy and society.[5]

Nasser also dramatically expanded the role of the military, particularly in the early years of his rule. In addition to the country's defence, military officers led the growing domestic security and intelligence agencies and the ministries responsible for censorship and propaganda. They controlled the newly established ruling party and the country's growing bureaucracy, as well as some of the new state-owned enterprises that were the cornerstone of Nasser's economic strategy. Nasser introduced an important innovation: a political order centred on a single party, the Arab Socialist Union (ASU), which was tasked with mobilizing the masses to achieve social transformation. The ASU's less publicized function was to contain the masses and ensure that their political activity was tightly controlled and directed clearly in support of the regime.[6] In addition, the Union assumed the ideological role of explaining Nasserism to the party faithful and spreading the key features of this ideology throughout the Arab world.[7]

Finally, Nasser built a dramatically more capable security apparatus and made it a central feature of the regime's structure. Indeed, Nasser's Egypt became an early example of the *mukhabarat* (intelligence services) state that came to characterize state-building in much of the Arab world. The surveillance capabilities of Egypt's general intelligence service grew to unprecedented levels. Phones, offices and homes were bugged. Mail was regularly checked. Neighbours and colleagues were routinely enlisted as informants. Political opponents were detained indefinitely without charge, frequently tortured and often forced to sign confessions that led to long prison sentences.[8]

These three institutions – the military, the ruling party and the domestic security apparatus – became the central pillars of Egyptian authoritarianism,[9] although their structure and relative power would change in the coming decades. With Nasser's death and Anwar al Sadat's ascension to power in 1970, Nasser's heir faced an immediate challenge from the ASU. He responded by weakening and eventually disbanding it, converting its three ideological trends – left, centre and right – into separate parties. However, the party of the 'centre' – the newly founded National Democratic Party (NDP) – became the hegemonic party and Sadat's new instrument of political control. Under Mubarak, the NDP would develop into an extensive and robust vehicle for distributing money, contracts, jobs, permits and other largesse to the regime's supporters. The party set aside any pretensions of ideological rigour. The NDP was primarily a patronage machine, focused on consolidating a broad coalition of elite support through the provision of material rewards and the promise of more generous rewards in the future.[10]

The military posed an even more formidable challenge to Sadat. Accordingly, he imprisoned the minister of war, Muhammad Fawzy, for high treason in 1971, and began reorganizing the military's senior leadership. Tensions with the generals grew even more pronounced during the October 1973 war with Israel, when senior officers vehemently objected to Sadat's strategy of 'limited war' that failed to take maximum advantage of Egypt's early successes in battle. Sadat's decision to pursue a peace agreement with Israel increased tensions even further. Sadat dealt with this growing challenge by strengthening the internal security apparatus, particularly the Ministry of Interior, to counterbalance the military's power. In addition to more resources and manpower, the Ministry of Interior was given the authority to vet candidates for positions of leadership throughout the ruling party, the economy and the education system. The ministry's military intelligence branch kept tabs on the military and had the authority to disqualify candidates for military promotion.[11] Despite his concerns about the military, Sadat needed to retain its support. To this end, he allowed a steady expansion in the military's economic role. Military factories and other military-linked businesses were permitted to sell their goods and services in the civilian economy. The resulting revenue sustained a comfortable lifestyle for the officer corps.[12]

Mubarak continued this path of strengthening the Ministry of Interior and limiting the military's political role. While retired military officers still held some provincial governorship and other posts, Mubarak appointed former police officers to senior political positions in the cabinet and in the governing council of the ruling party. He also continued Sadat's policy of expanding the ranks of the ministry. From 1974 to 2002, the number of soldiers in the ministry rose from 9 to 21 per cent of state employment, reaching the unprecedented level of 1 million in 2002. By comparison, the military had no more than 460,000 men. The defence budget increased from 3.5 per cent of GDP to almost 6 per cent between 1988 and 2002.[13] Thus, while the core institutions of Egyptian authoritarianism took shape under Nasser, the relative power of these institutions (the military, the ruling party and the domestic security apparatus) changed over time. The 2011 uprising inaugurated another period of change.

The 2011 uprising and Egypt's new authoritarianism

Several scholars of Egyptian politics have observed that the regime of Abdelfattah al Sisi differs from that of Hosni Mubarak. Joshua Stacher noted that al Sisi's regime has weakened the rules and institutional boundaries of the Mubarak era and is '[so] fuzzily defined that Egyptians doubt it is one coherent entity'.[14] Nathan J. Brown and Oren Samet-Marram wrote that al Sisi has tried to create a 'Salazar-type regime' that lacks a clear ideology, minimizes political mobilization and tolerates a high degree of autonomy among the various parts of the state.[15] Shadi Hamid observed that both the extent and nature of repression under al Sisi differ from that of Mubarak and have led to a regime that is 'more vulnerable to violence and insurgency'.[16] Each of these analysts has noticed meaningful changes. However, scholars have not yet developed a clear conceptualization of the significance of these changes and their repercussions for Egypt's political future.

To address these questions, we turn to the literature on comparative authoritarianism and, particularly, the work of Dan Slater.[17] Slater argued that authoritarian regimes can be categorized based on the type of governing coalition that underlies them. He identifies two ideal types. The first is a 'provision pact' that entails an authoritarian regime gaining the support of elites by providing them with resources such as jobs, public funds, state contracts and subsidised raw materials.[18] This type of regime buys the support of its followers with state largesse and sustains their support through the steady flow of additional material benefits. A robust ruling party is generally an important feature of this type of regime. Such party organizes the distribution of patronage to the most loyal supporters of the regime. It also enables the regime to develop a durable relationship with elites that leads them to invest money and effort to build the party in exchange for a promise of future benefits.[19]

The second type is a 'protection pact', which is a 'broad elite coalition unified by shared support for heightened state power and tightened authoritarian controls as institutional bulwarks against continued or renewed mass unrest'.[20] This type of governing coalition is not based on shared ideology, patronage or material interests. Rather, it is founded on a single consideration: a shared sense of threat. Diverse members of the elite who may have conflicting policy and material interests set aside these differences in order to stand behind the regime and confront this shared threat. In order for a protection pact to endure, this threat must have several characteristics: it must be a broad and serious challenge to elites' property, privileges and personal safety; it must be endemic, rather than episodic; and it must be unmanageable by any political means and, thus, the only solution lies in enhancing the state's security apparatus.[21] When a threat of this magnitude exists, the regime enjoys 'crisis legitimacy' that enables it to extract resources from elites (through taxes and other means) and to utilize these resources to expand the security capability and authoritarian controls of the state.[22] The regime has little need of a robust ruling party that dispenses largesse to its supporters, as the distribution of patronage does not underlie the pact. In its fullest form, a successful protection pact entails the military providing reliable coercion, businessmen and the middle classes paying taxes to support it, and religious authorities and secular intellectuals providing public endorsements of its conduct.[23] The key institution for sustaining this type of pact is the military. Domestic police are, of course, also relevant for maintaining order. However, in a robust protection pact, the military – with its extensive equipment, training and personnel – is the essential institution for ensuring public order and sustaining the pact. Thus, one would expect the military's political and economic role to expand under such a pact. In addition, this form of governing coalition is grounded in increasing the security capability of the state and, thus, we would expect to see wider repression of regime opponents under this type of governing coalition. Indeed, the extensive and sustained repression of threats to public order lies at the foundation of the pact.

If Egypt is in the late 2010s and early 2020s undergoing a transition from a provision pact to a protection pact, we would expect to see changes in the three core institutions of Egyptian authoritarianism: the resources and reach of the military will have expanded; the patronage role of the ruling party will have declined; and the level of repression will have increased. The following discussion focuses on these three areas and examines whether in fact there have been significant changes in these areas from the Mubarak regime to the al Sisi regime.

The military's role in politics and the economy

As Hicham Bou Nassif documents, the Mubarak regime appointed retired military officers to several posts in the civilian political system. In the first decade of the Mubarak era (1981–1989), 30 per cent of all provincial governors were retired military officers. In Mubarak's last decade (2000–2011), 44 per cent of provincial governors were from the military.[24] In addition to governorships, retired officers held a wide range of lower-ranking positions such as deputy governor, director of the governor's office, secretary general of the local governorate council, assistant secretary general of this council and other positions. Yezid Sayigh estimates that two thousand posts related to local government were occupied by retired officers at the conclusion of Mubarak's rule.[25]

Soon after the removal of Mohammed Morsi in July 2013, al Sisi appointed twenty-five new provincial governors (out of a total of twenty-seven). Of the twenty-five appointees, eighteen were retired generals.[26] Thus, 67 per cent of provincial governors came from military backgrounds – a figure substantially higher than at any time during the Mubarak era. In addition, twenty-four major generals served as deputy governors, secretaries general or assistant secretaries general.[27] Retired officers were also appointed to numerous other administrative posts throughout government.[28] This pattern of appointing military officers to provincial posts has continued throughout al Sisi's term in office.[29]

There is certainly a patronage component to these appointments. They are a means of rewarding loyal officers – and of incentivizing current officers to exhibit the same loyalty, in the expectation that they will enjoy the same privileges when they leave service. However, these appointments also provide the military with a network of officers that can shape governance at the local level. This network can be relied on to influence a wide range of policies, from the awarding of local contracts, to lower-level patronage appointments, to security measures taken against Islamists and others. While there may not be explicit coordination among retired military officers holding positions in local government, there is a shared worldview, a shared institutional and corporate identity, and a shared sense of obligation to protect the military as an institution. These appointments effectively create an alternative governing hierarchy separate from that of the civilian political system with distinct leadership, patronage networks and objectives.[30]

In addition, several changes to the constitution enhance the military's autonomy from civilian oversight and broaden its capacity to influence political life. Article 201 of the 2014 constitution specifies (for the first time) that the minister of defence must be an active-duty military officer appointed with the approval of the Supreme Council of Armed Forces (SCAF).[31] The constitution further indicates that the military's budget is not subject to review by any civilian entity, including the parliament. The parliament will only see a single number for the entire military budget when it reviews the national budget each year.

The military leadership also revived the National Defence Council (NDC), which provides a legal basis for its involvement in virtually any domestic policy matter. According to the 2014 constitution, the NDC has fourteen members. Only five of these are civilians.[32] The remainder are from the military (seven), the Ministry of Interior (one) and the general intelligence service (one). The NDC holds a broad and vague mandate. Article 203 specifies that it is responsible for examining 'matters pertaining to preserving the security and integrity of the country'. Its jurisdiction can be further broadened by parliamentary legislation. The constitution does not indicate whether only the president can convene the NDC or whether his presence is even required for the NDC to reach a decision. Furthermore, it is the only entity with the authority to review the military budget and the allocation of United States' military aid.

The legal basis for the military to become involved in domestic affairs is further expanded in Article 200, which states that 'the armed forces belong to the people, and their duty is to protect the country and preserve its security and the integrity of its territories'. The clause makes no reference to the military being governed by the constitution or having any obligation to obey or defend it. The clause provides a constitutional basis for the military to intervene in domestic politics whenever it concludes that the security of the country is at stake. The military, alone, is empowered to make this assessment.

The 2014 constitution also addresses the jurisdiction of the military judiciary. The military courts had already assumed broader jurisdiction when the SCAF held executive power (from 11 February 2011 until 30 June 2012). As a result of SCAF decrees, over twelve thousand civilians were tried before military courts during the seventeen months that it held power.[33] More civilians faced military courts during this period than during the entire twenty-nine years of Hosni Mubarak's rule. The 2014 constitution formalizes this expanded power and jurisdiction. More specifically, Article 204 states that the military judiciary holds exclusive jurisdiction over all crimes related to the armed forces and the general intelligence services. In essence, it ensures that soldiers and intelligence officers are insulated from any civilian oversight or prosecution.[34] Article 204 adds that civilians will face trial before military courts if they commit a crime that represents a 'direct assault against military facilities, military barracks and ... military zones'. It further notes that 'the law defines such crimes and determines the other competencies of the military judiciary'. This latter clause has assumed great importance. In October 2014, al Sisi declared that all state-owned facilities were 'strategic installations' and, thus, any crimes committed in or around these facilities could be tried in military courts.[35] Furthermore, because this enhanced power for the military courts has been elevated to constitutional law, the accused has no opportunity to appeal to a civilian judge or to invoke civilian criminal law. Trials proceed entirely based on military law as interpreted by military judges who are appointed by the military leadership and are accountable to them. According to Human Rights Watch, military courts tried at least 15,500 civilians between October 2014 and September 2017.[36]

The resources directed to the military have also grown under al Sisi. Its budget increased 20 per cent in 2014 (al Sisi's first full year in office) and rose another 17 per cent in 2015.[37] The military's acquisition of foreign weaponry grew sharply, reaching $5.3 billion in 2015 – making Egypt the largest weapons importer in the developing world in 2015.[38] The extent of the military's involvement in the Egyptian economy has also expanded. The military has played an important role in the economy for decades. It began establishing factories and other types of enterprises in the 1950s with the goal of supplying the armed forces with food, housing and other basic needs. In the 1970s, many of these military enterprises began to sell their surplus production in the civilian economy, which generated a substantial revenue stream that sustained the lifestyle of the officer corps. Under Sadat and Mubarak, military enterprises also provided lucrative professional opportunities for loyal officers when they retired. After several decades of growth, the military's economic empire includes companies involved in construction, agriculture, fertilizer, food production, steel, cement, security services, land reclamation, oil services, tourism, armaments and ammunition.[39]

These firms have several advantages over their competitors. They may use military conscripts as cheap labour and benefit from subsidized land, fuel and electricity. Labour unrest at military factories can be suppressed quickly and with no legal repercussions on the grounds of protecting national security. The firms' profits are exempt from taxes, according to Article 47 of Egypt's 2005 income tax law. In addition, a 1986 law ensures that imports by the Ministry of Defence and the Ministry of State for military production are exempt from any tariffs or taxation.[40]

These advantages make the military an attractive partner for foreign investors. If a foreign firm establishes a joint venture involving the military, the joint enterprise gains all the advantages mentioned above. In addition, the firm benefits from preferential treatment in bidding for state contracts, privileged access to infrastructure and services, and advance notice of pending projects. It can also rely on Egyptian soldiers to protect its land and buildings from any domestic turmoil.[41] The firm also enjoys immunity from civilian oversight. More specifically, military-related firms are not subject to review by the country's primary anticorruption agency, the Illicit Gains Authority.[42] Rather, the military has its own anticorruption body – the Administrative Monitoring Authority – which has, at best, a checkered history of confronting corruption.[43]

Under the al Sisi regime, the economic role of the military has undergone both quantitative and qualitative changes. The most notable quantitative change arises from al Sisi's emphasis on large infrastructure projects to revive the economy. The largest of these is the Suez Canal Regional Developmental Project, which includes expansion of six Egyptian ports, the construction of six tunnels underneath the canal and the dredging of a parallel canal to allow for two-way traffic. The project's total budget exceeds $55 billion.[44] The military plays the central role in designing, coordinating and supervising the project. Not surprisingly, military-related firms have won many of the key contracts within the plan.[45] The project also includes ancillary construction opportunities such as the establishment of wind farms and solar energy arrays on both sides of the canal. Military-owned firms are involved in manufacturing the towers, gearboxes and fibreglass blades used in the wind turbines as well as panels for the solar arrays.[46]

Other major infrastructure projects involving the military include building a new administrative capital east of Cairo, at an estimated cost of $45 billion; constructing one million units of affordable housing, at an estimated cost of $20 billion; expanding the Toshka project in the Western desert that includes forty-eight new cities, eight airports, fish farms, a railroad and an eight-lane highway; and constructing a nuclear reactor west of Alexandria.[47] In each case, the military serves as coordinator/supervisor of the project and as active participant in its construction either directly or through firms that it owns.[48]

Beyond these quantitative increases in the extent of the military's economic influence, there have also been qualitative changes. The most important lies in a new law that enabled the military to leverage its control of land into economic returns. Under a presidential decree issued in 1997, the military is empowered to manage all undeveloped non-agricultural land. Analysts estimate that this decree enabled the military to control between 87 per cent and 95 per cent of the country's territory.[49] This decree gave the military input into virtually every developmental decision taken by the government as the land that it controls is needed for urban development, manufacturing, tourism, oil and gas production and agriculture. During the Mubarak era, this power was used primarily to generate a flow of revenue to the military by either renting the land to private developers or selling it to them outright. It also provided an opportunity for some corrupt military officials to sell land to developers at below-market rates in exchange for kickbacks. In addition, some retired officers were sold land at below-market rates in order to help them start businesses.[50]

The key change under al Sisi is presidential decree 466, issued in December 2015, which allows the Armed Forces Land Projects Organisation (AFLPO) to establish commercial enterprises that it owns jointly with private firms. This decree enables the military to enter into joint ventures with private enterprises in which its contribution consists of the land that it controls, which it can allocate to a new business enterprise without any cost to itself. The military is then entitled to a share of the revenue generated by this new enterprise.[51] This step enables the army to use its existing land assets in a manner that expands both the size and reach of its already-large economic empire.

This overview indicates that the scope of the military's power has broadened significantly under al Sisi. The military leadership, through the NDC, can intervene in virtually any domestic policy matter. The military has a network of retired officers in provincial leadership post that can support and implement its policy goals, particularly in the security arena. The army can utilize military courts to prosecute virtually any opponent. It also has access to extensive economic resources with no civilian oversight. When taken together, these changes enable the military to function as a separate branch of government above the other branches. In the past, the military could shape policy outcomes through discussion and pressure.[52] Now, it can determine them through direct intervention. Under Mubarak, the military largely stayed out of politics and policy so long as its interests were protected. Under al Sisi, the military leadership has moved directly into the political arena with the economic capacity and legal authority to be a dominant actor.

Ruling party, elections and patronage

In the Mubarak era, the ruling NDP was a central institution for dispensing patronage to the civilian backers of the regime. It was also integral to building a durable coalition of regime supporters. As Jason Brownlee noted, this latter goal required persuading elites to adopt a longer time horizon for the fulfilment of their interests.[53] In essence, a member of the elite had to be willing to accept a short-term setback that might serve a competing group without defecting to the opposition. The NDP facilitated this process by providing credible assurance that, if an individual accepted a short-term loss, the NDP would reward him in the medium and long term. The party's structure and durability ensured that this medium and long-term gain would, in fact, materialize. In a similar vein, the NDP provided an arena for reconciling the interests of conflicting parts of the regime's elite coalition. For example, the conflicting interests of the civil service and the private sector, or of public sector workers and management, could be aired. Deals could then be made to minimize tensions by distributing resources to an aggrieved group, arranging a choice appointment for an individual leader who felt slighted or providing other benefits.[54] The NDP was not an ideological party. Rather, it was a political machine that helped to create and sustain a coalition of civilian elites that would back the regime.

In this political setting, elections served several functions. First, they provided a means for assessing the competence and loyalty of party cadres. The Mubarak regime found particular utility in pitting the NDP candidate in a district against independent candidates (often businessmen or local notables).[55] If the independent did well, he/she would be invited to join (or rejoin) the NDP, thereby ensuring that the NDP was co-opting those individuals who could deliver meaningful support at the local level.[56] Elections were also useful for evaluating the opposition. They enabled the regime to identify the districts where the opposition enjoyed support and then either deny those districts state resources or develop a strategy to entice them into the government's camp. In addition, elections provided a means for signalling the regime's strength. As noted, the NDP was more effective if it could persuade elites that it commanded vast resources and broad mobilization capability – and, therefore, was a powerful ally who could reward its friends and punish its enemies now and in the future. Through large victories, the NDP demonstrated its power and thereby consolidated the elite coalition that underlay the regime. Even if these victories were facilitated by violence and fraud, they still served the political purpose of demonstrating that the NDP could control the political arena, reliably place its supporters in parliament, and assure them the opportunity to profit while enjoying immunity from legal prosecution. However, this system had its limits. In the parliamentary elections of 2010, the party's leadership engaged in electoral abuse on an unprecedented scale in order to gain complete control of parliament and, possibly, lay the groundwork for the ascension of Mubarak's son, Gamal, to the presidency. The scope of this abuse was outrageous even by the standards of Mubarak's Egypt and contributed importantly to the public anger that fuelled the 2011 uprising.[57]

In the wake of Mubarak's ouster in February 2011, the NDP was dissolved by court order. It was declared illegal, and its assets were seized by the state. The SCAF-led government undertook extensive prosecution of the party's senior leadership. Gamal Mubarak, Safwat Sharif, Ahmed Ezz and other senior figures were convicted of corruption in high profile trials that dominated the media for months.[58]

Given the extent of the SCAF-led regime's efforts to dismantle the NDP, it is not surprising that al Sisi has left the NDP in the dustbin. However, he has also chosen not to create an alternative ruling party. His motives for this decision are probably varied. They may include concern that the establishment of a ruling party would enable groups threatening to the military's interests to regain a measure of power; that a ruling party would consume patronage resources that he would prefer to direct to the military; or that a strong party could mobilize the masses against his regime if it were to stumble. Whatever his motivation, al Sisi has given no sign that he plans to reconstruct a single hegemonic party.

As a consequence, the parliamentary elections in October and December 2015 functioned differently than elections under Mubarak. The August 2015 electoral law allocated four hundred and forty-eight seats (79 per cent) to individual candidates and one hundred and twenty seats (21 per cent) to winner-take-all party list.[59] Twenty parties won seats, some of whom grouped themselves into alliances during the election. The largest alliance, a ten-party bloc named For the Love of Egypt (*Fi Hubb Misr*), won all of the seats allotted to party lists. However, as a result of the electoral law, the majority of seats were held by independents. Some of these independents were affiliated with parties, but many were not. Under Mubarak, these independents would have been integrated into the NDP and rewarded for their demonstrated mobilization skills with access to state resources and the opportunity to enrich themselves while enjoying parliamentary immunity from prosecution. For The Love of Egypt did not play this role. The three largest parties in the alliance were unwilling to name a single individual to represent the alliance.[60] The largest party in the alliance (the Free Egyptians) underwent a divisive leadership battle that rendered it largely ineffectual.[61] A smaller group of parties formed a new bloc, the Support Egypt Coalition (*I'tilaf Da'm Misr*), which went on to lead the parliament. There is considerable evidence that the security services played a substantial role in the formation of the Support Egypt coalition and participated in its leadership.[62]

Under al Sisi, the parliament is not the relatively orderly patronage machine of the Mubarak era, guided by a well-oiled ruling party. Rather, under the guidance of former and current security officials, it has become an enthusiastic supporter of steps to enhance the authoritarian structurers of the state. In the name of protecting Egypt from the 'terrorist threat' allegedly created by political Islam, parliament passed legislation that constrained civil society, expanded state control over the media, limited public assembly, reduced due process rights and expanded executive authority over senior judicial appointments.[63] Parliament has made little use of its constitutional power to monitor and constrain the executive. Rather, the speaker of parliament has emphasized the importance of standing behind the president as he claims to protect the country from the challenge posed by terrorism carried out by Islamist groups.[64]

Scope and character of repression

Human rights groups have documented a substantial increase in the level of repression since al Sisi rose to power in July 2013 (formally in June 2014). The regime deployed extraordinarily violence to disperse largely peaceful pro-Brotherhood demonstrations in Rabi'a al Adawiyya Square and Al Nahda square in August 2013. According to Human Rights Watch, 'using armoured personnel carriers, bulldozers, ground forces and snipers, police and army personnel attacked the makeshift protest camp and gunned down protestors, killing at least eight hundred and seventeen people.'[65] The government chose this course of action despite the availability of peaceful alternatives for dispersing the crowd.[66] The number of political detainees also rose sharply. According to Human Rights Watch, Egyptian security forces detained, charged or sentenced at least 41,000 people between July 2013 and April 2014, mostly because of their alleged association with the Muslim Brotherhood.[67] Hundreds of Egyptians have also been sentenced to death, many after trials that fall far short of minimal standards of due process (including mass trials in March and April 2014 that convicted 683 and 529 defendants, respectively). In many cases, convictions were reached after testimony by security officials without any corroborating evidence, and the accused were granted little opportunity to offer a defence.[68] In addition, monitoring of university students and faculty has increased. University presidents, who are appointed by al Sisi, are now empowered to dismiss any faculty member or student deemed to have 'disturbed the educational process'.[69]

The Muslim Brotherhood has endured a particularly harsh crackdown. It was declared 'a terrorist organization' and its assets seized by the government; its political party, the Freedom and Justice Party, was disbanded; and upwards of five hundred civil society organizations with affiliations to the Brotherhood were closed.[70] Its senior leaders were sentenced to life in prison, and many thousands of its activists arrested.

The regime has made several legislative changes that limit the rights of assembly and speech. Law number 107 of 2013 bans protests without a permit from the authorities.[71] Police can now monitor citizens' communication indefinitely without a court order and detain a suspect without trial for up to two years.[72] Law number 136 of 2014 declares roads and bridges to be 'strategic installations' and, thus, any trespassing on them (such as conducting a protest) is illegal. The regime adopted a new NGO law in May 2017 that sharply limited the capacity of civil society groups to criticize the government and expanded the government's control of their budgets and decision-making.[73] Another NGO law, adopted in August 2019, retained most of these restrictions.[74] In addition, the security forces have reportedly engaged in torture on a routine basis against many detainees.[75] Finally, the regime declared a state of emergency in 2017, which further expanded its authority to monitor communications, censor publications, sequester property and detain suspects. This state of emergency also broadened the authority of State Security Emergency Courts to try civilians without normal rights of due process, including the right of appeal.[76] The emergency law was revised in 2020 to grant the military even greater powers to arrest and try citizens.[77]

These developments reflect an intensification of the Egyptian security state and an increase in the scale of repression. However, the regime has also developed new dimensions to the security state that constitute important qualitative changes in the nature of Egyptian authoritarianism. These changes include:

The military's role in domestic security

A presidential decree in October 2014 (Decree 136/2014) empowered the military to protect all 'public and vital facilities' in the country – a function previous held by the police.[78] Al Sisi expanded this power in June 2016 when he authorized the military to manage security on lands up to two kilometres from any public road or highway.[79] Parliament then extended this enhanced power for five additional years until 2021.[80] These measures effectively enable the military to monitor and suppress freedom of speech and assembly in and around any public land or facilities. When one considers that at least 87 per cent of Egyptian territory falls into this category, the scope of this power becomes clear. Furthermore, as mentioned above, the jurisdiction of military courts has increased sharply under al Sisi. In the past, a civilian could appear before a military court only under very specific circumstances or if the president expressly ordered the transfer of his case from the civilian courts to the military courts. Under al Sisi, the military prosecutor can directly charge civilians for any transgression deemed threatening to national security. Furthermore, in the light of Decree 136/2014 that declares all roads, bridges and public sector enterprises to be 'strategic installations', any act in any of these areas that is deemed contrary to the national interest can be prosecuted in a military court. Trials in military courts fall well short of international standards. Judges are appointed by their military superiors and are beholden to them. Their rulings can be overruled by a superior officer who did not attend the trial. In addition, the accused is not guaranteed an attorney or the right to appeal to a civilian court.[81]

The increased use of repression outside of the legal system

Under Mubarak, the regime was capable of great repression. However, if individuals were detained, human rights groups could usually locate them within a few days and visit them within a few weeks. Under al Sisi, the regime has engaged in much wider use of what critics call 'enforced disappearances' of citizens without any legal trail. Amnesty International reports that as many as four hundred Egyptians have been disappeared and tortured by the security forces in a single military-run facility.[82]

The authoritarianism of Mubarak, while often brutal, was also highly legalistic. The regime went to considerable lengths to prosecute an adversary within some legal framework, even if it was a flawed framework such as the security courts or the military courts.[83] It also targeted repression against specific groups and individuals. Under al Sisi, the regime has apparently granted parts of the security apparatus carte blanche to repress citizens without legal constraints. Repression has become broader and more random and, thus, more difficult to confront and contain.

An incomplete protection pact and the fragmentation of politics

The analysis above suggests that al Sisi has attempted to move Egypt from the provision pact of the Mubarak era to a protection pact: the military's power and resources have increased, the patronage-based ruling party has been dismantled, and the degree of repression has risen. It is unlikely that these steps are the product of a single decision or grand strategy by al Sisi. Rather, they reflect a series of individual decisions in response to specific challenges and opportunities that aggregated over time into a significant change in the regime. However, al Sisi faces several formidable impediments to consolidating this type of governing coalition.

The fundamental problem – what Slater would call a 'birth defect' – is the nature of the threat that al Sisi has used. His protection pact is centred on the threat posed by political Islam which, he claims, leads to unremitting terrorism that imperils the country's values and institutions and seeks to plunge Egypt into violence and chaos.[84] In al Sisi's view, all forms of political Islam – from the Muslim Brotherhood to the Islamic State – are equally violent and equally threatening.[85]

According to Slater's research, a durable protection pact requires that elites face a threat to their property, privileges and personal safety that is endemic and unmanageable through political means. The clearest example for Slater is the threat posed by groups seeking redistribution of wealth, such as the communist movements in Indonesia and Malaysia in the 1960s. The extent of this threat unified property owners regardless of their political views. The protection pact became even stronger when this threat of redistribution was reinforced by a communal conflict along ethnic or religious lines. The elites who were targeted faced not only a threat to their wealth but also a challenge to their way of life and to their physical safety. A threat of this scope and scale welded together elites who held sharply differing views over policy and ideology. They set aside these differences in order to survive in the face of an immense challenge.[86]

Political Islam in Egypt falls short of this magnitude of threat in several respects. With regard to the specific points raised by Slater, it lacks the class-based component that could unify urban elites. One of the key actors among Islamist movements, the Muslim Brotherhood, is largely a middle-class organization that supports private property and, thus, poses no threat to the property rights of urban or rural landowners.[87] Political Islam in Egypt also has no ethnic component that could persuade large portions of the elite that their physical safety was immediately and unavoidably threatened. In addition, political Islam in Egypt has several other features that render it ill suited to generating a strong and durable protection pact.

Political Islam is not a unified threat with a single leadership

At least three different types of Islamist opposition movements exist in Egypt: the Muslim Brotherhood, indigenous Islamic radical movements (such as Sinai Province and Jihad), and transnational Islamic radical movements (such as Al Qaeda and the Islamic State). While there may be some ideological similarities among them and occasional cooperation, there are also important differences over goals and tactics and little evidence that the movements engage in coordinated action. For example, the Muslim Brotherhood's leadership condemned attacks carried out by more radical groups and they, in turn, criticized the Brotherhood for its less militant stance.[88]

The extent of the threat posed by political Islam is unclear

The Brotherhood's candidates for elected office garnered a large share of the vote in each election between 2011 and 2013.[89] These electoral results suggest some public support for the general idea of broadening the role of Islam in politics and society, even if subsequent events showed little public backing for how the Brotherhood implemented this idea.[90] Furthermore, the regime has allowed an Islamist party to remain in the political arena – the al Nur party – whose platform shares at least some of the objectives of the Brotherhood.[91] It is difficult to portray political Islam as a monolithic and existential threat to Egyptian society when some of its ideas have received broad public endorsement and the regime allows some of its goals to be advocated within the country's political system.

The type of threat posed by political Islam varies among different parts of the elite

The radical movements under the umbrella of 'political Islam' pose a physical threat to some citizens – particularly, individuals associated with the regime's leadership, the military, the judiciary and the Ministry of Interior. The less radical movements, such as the Muslim Brotherhood, pose an ideological threat to some citizens, particularly Christians and secular Muslims who fear that the persistence of political Islam in the public arena could challenge their way of life. The Brotherhood is an ideological competitor to still others, particularly representatives of 'establishment Islam' such as Al Azhar, who share at least some of its goals (such as expanding the role of Islam in public life) but not its methods. The multiple dimensions of the challenge posed by political Islam, and its different effects on different parts of the elite, render it a far less cohesive threat. In addition, because of the complexity of the threat that it poses, political Islam may aggravate fissures among parts of the elite who feel threatened by it in different ways and to different degrees and, thus, support different responses ranging from repression to co-optation.[92]

These distinctive features of political Islam in Egypt suggest that it is not the clear, cohesive and unmanageable threat required to sustain a protection pact. However, in the months immediately following Morsi's ouster in July 2013, the political climate was sufficiently polarized that al Sisi could persuade much of the elite that it faced an immense threat from political Islam. It is worth recalling the political context that made this claim resonate with many Egyptians. In the span of less than three years (January 2011–July 2013), Egypt had experienced an uprising of unprecedented scale; the removal of a dictator who held office for twenty-nine years; confusing and sometimes inept military leadership under the SCAF; eight national polls (to vote on constitutional amendments, a constitution, both houses of parliament – including run-offs – and a President, including a run-off); the dissolution of parliament by court order; the removal of an elected President by the military; and a sharp decline in economic growth due, in part, to the country's political upheaval. The sense of crisis that arose from these tumultuous events – culminating in Morsi's removal in July 2013 – gave al Sisi the opportunity to create a temporary bond of solidarity among groups with different interests such as businessmen, labour leaders, religious leaders and secular intellectuals. He asserted that the disorder that engulfed the country was the product of a treasonous scheme hatched by the supporters of political Islam and led by the Muslim Brotherhood. Furthermore, only the military could rescue the country from this perilous condition. In this climate, al Sisi and the appointed caretaker President, 'Adli Mansour, were able to take measures that created key features of a protection pact, including the dramatic expansion of the military's power and resources, an electoral law that produced a weak and fragmented parliament without a hegemonic party, and expansion of the repressive capability of the security apparatus. However, the crisis legitimacy of the first few months of the al Sisi regime has dissipated. The threat posed by political Islam has not produced a unified elite that backs al Sisi's protection pact. Instead, the pact is unconsolidated and is likely to remain so.

As a consequence, the tensions among the groups that initially supported the regime have resurfaced, leading to greater elite fragmentation. An early example of this fragmentation arose in the wake of the 2015 parliamentary elections, when several parties that supported the 2013 coup that brought al Sisi to power did not join the pro-government Support Egypt coalition – most notably, the Free Egyptians party, which won the most seats of any party in the election.[93] Secular intellectuals began to distance themselves from the regime when al Sisi agreed to transfer sovereignty over two islands (Tiran and Sanafir) to Saudi Arabia, apparently as a gesture of gratitude for Saudi financial and political support to him.[94] Some parts of the state elite have also grown less supportive of the regime. For example, Al Azhar's leaders have challenged al Sisi's calls to 'renew Islamic discourse' and to revise the divorce law.[95] Even parts of the judiciary have been critical. Several administrative courts attempted to block the transfer of Tiran and Sanafir islands to Saudi Arabia. In addition, the Supreme Constitutional Court struck down parts of the protest law and the emergency law.[96]

Further evidence of growing divisions among the elite can be seen in the clash between the regime and the journalists' syndicate. On 1 May 2016, security officials entered the syndicate's headquarters and arrested two journalists on the grounds that their reporting constituted incitement against the state.[97] The action led to strong condemnation from the president of the syndicate and its governing council, as well as several demonstrations and a sit-in by fellow journalists. The regime responded by placing three members of the syndicate's leadership on trial for harbouring fugitive journalists.[98] It also created a new state body to monitor and regulate the media.[99] These events are significant in at least two respects: they indicate that support for the regime among some journalists is tenuous and, thus, an important component of the elite is unwilling to provide sustained backing to the regime; and, they indicate that the regime considers its position sufficiently precarious that it must engage in highly visible acts of repression in order to deter dissent. Both considerations bode poorly for building strong and durable elite support for the regime.

In essence, Egypt had a brief period of crisis legitimacy that enabled al Sisi to expand the military's power and to strengthen the authoritarian structures of the state. However, the elite cohesion and support that enabled these steps has waned and appears unlikely to return. As a consequence, Egypt's regime is in a structural limbo. It has the institutions of a protection pact without the elite civilian support to sustain it. In order to broaden civilian support, al Sisi would need to revive at least part of the Mubarak-era provision pact by creating a ruling party, expanding the capacity of parliament to distribute patronage and transferring substantially more resources to the ruling party and to parliament. The military is unlikely to accept this diversion of resources. Furthermore, the generals have sufficient autonomy and power to resist any efforts by al Sisi to pursue this path.

As the protection pact grounded on the threat posed by political Islam has weakened, the regime has highlighted other threats in an attempt to shore up elite support. The list of threats invoked by the regime includes Iran, the Islamic State, Qatar, Ethiopia, civil society groups, human rights organizations, foreign aid organizations, private media and the LGBTQ community.[100] To date, these other threats have also not produced the broad and unified elite backing needed to sustain a protection pact.

The historical impact of an incomplete protection pact

Abdelfattah al Sisi's unsuccessful attempt to construct a durable protection pact in Egypt in the mid-to-late 2010s has had several repercussions for the country's politics.

The regime's options for managing mass politics have narrowed

The uprising of 2011 was fuelled by deepening poverty, growing economic inequality, and increased violence by the police.[101] All of these sources of public anger have risen since 2011.[102] Furthermore, Egyptians have a vivid memory of the power of large demonstrations to bring about political change, including the removal of Mubarak in 2011 and of Morsi in 2013. If Egyptians begin to engage in large-scale demonstrations, the regime's options for responding are limited. In general terms, autocratic regimes can deal with mass demonstrations through either co-optation or repression. As noted, al Sisi has reduced the regime's capacity to respond with co-optation through patronage and other incentives. As a consequence, the only means at his disposal is enhanced repression. This repression, in turn, may aggravate one of the underlying sources of public anger – brutality by the security apparatus – and lead to higher levels of violence.

Increased reliance on the military enhances the generals' bargaining leverage

As the protection pact discussed above erodes and civilian elite support for the regime becomes weaker, al Sisi will have little choice but to turn increasingly to the military for support. If the security situation deteriorates, the regime will rely even more heavily on the generals. This increased dependence on the men in uniform will give them greater influence. If the past is any indication, they are likely to use this influence to gain access to greater resources, acquire greater autonomy,[103] and broaden their influence in the policy arena.[104] The military's specific policy preferences are not yet clear. As noted below, it is likely to support an economic reform strategy that preserves its economic power. The military leadership may also hold specific preferences with regard to the degree of regime openness, the breadth of the military's economic role, the extent of the military's direct involvement in state institutions and the power of civilian political institutions (particularly, the parliament). However, there is little information available in the public arena to indicate its positions.

If al Sisi pursues policies that diverge from those supported by the military leadership, a coup is also possible.[105] Nasser, Sadat and Mubarak adopted several strategies to 'coup proof' their regimes. These measures included creating a separate branch of the security services to protect the president, ensuring the president's involvement in senior military appointments, granting the president supervision over key features of the military's budget (particularly, US military assistance) and expanding the Ministry of Interior's role in vetting military promotions.[106] Al Sisi has weakened some of these coup-proofing features by allowing the military to gain greater legal autonomy and to exercise greater control over its budget.[107] These changes are difficult to reverse, as the military leadership now has sufficient power and autonomy to resist any steps by al Sisi to limit its role.

The governing coalition that supports the regime is weak and easily fractured

In the months following Morsi's ouster, al Sisi managed to fuse together a remarkably diverse set of elites, including the religious leadership of al Azhar, civil servants and the security apparatus as well as some secular intellectuals, businesspeople (from both the public sector and private sector), labour leaders and students. These elites held conflicting ideological views and material interests but set these differences aside to coalesce behind al Sisi in order to ensure their safety. As noted, this protection pact had several structural flaws. As the protection pact erodes, the tensions among these groups have become more pronounced. If the regime encounters a period of economic or political strain, members of these competing elites who feel slighted or neglected may quickly reduce their support for al Sisi. As noted, this process has already begun. These disgruntled elites are unlikely to form vibrant opposition groups, in large part because such groups are effectively prohibited. However, they may deny the regime the breadth of civilian support needed to implement unpopular policies or undertake significant reform. Furthermore, if robust civilian support is lacking, the regime will have little choice but to rely more heavily on the military with at least some of the repercussions mentioned earlier.

Economic reform is more difficult

The fragility of the regime's civilian support may make economic reform more difficult. An additional consideration lies in the economic logic for political survival in such an environment. The ruling party was a key institution for the distribution of patronage under Mubarak and for building a cohesive governing coalition of civilian elites behind the regime. Al Sisi has not re-created this institution and shifted some of its patronage resources to the military. If al Sisi hopes to retain significant civilian support, he will need to expand patronage to at least some civilian elites. One of the most significant patronage resources still at his disposal is the provision of jobs in the civil service and the public sector. Thus, he may expand employment in these areas for political reasons or, at a minimum, avoid the largescale restructuring and dismissals needed for meaningful market reform.

In addition, the extent of the regime's reliance on the military has important repercussions for economic reform. Military firms have a host of advantages over their competitors, including lower labour costs, much lower tax rates, advance notice of government contracts and easier access to government permits for business operations. These advantages enable them to win contracts across virtually every economic sector and, as a result, deny private businesses many opportunities to expand.[108] This development does not mean that the private sector will cease to exist. Rather, it means that Egypt's economic trajectory is likely to include a prominent role for military-related firms as well as joint ventures involving private sector firms and the military. Several large infrastructure projects currently underway involve cooperation between private sector companies and the military or military-related firms. These military/private sector joint ventures are, in most cases, private enterprises and will likely be reported in economic statistics as evidence of an expanding private sector. However, they will not build the dynamic and globally competitive private sector that market reformers seek. Rather, this private sector is a *de facto* appendage of the state. Furthermore, as the military's role in the economy grows, it will be able to block reforms that could create a genuinely autonomous private sector.

In addition, the incomplete protection pact currently in place entails a scale of repression that may make economic growth difficult. Al Sisi has argued that an intensification of the security state will lead to greater social order and labour peace which, in turn, will attract investment and facilitate economic growth.[109] However, intensified repression may lead to escalating violence. The regime has created an environment in which persons with grievances have virtually no peaceful avenue through which to seek redress. If the regime responds with unremitting force to the grievances that arise, regime opponents may calculate that they have no choice but to escalate their use of force. The result could be a smouldering low-level conflict between the regime and its opponents that does not reach the level of civil war but creates a constant undercurrent of attack and counterattack that undermines social peace. This level of violence may limit the flow of foreign and domestic investment.

The political and institutional bargains that al Sisi made in order to govern have rendered the Egyptian state less manageable

In the absence of a robust protection pact, al Sisi had to persuade leaders of key institutions to lend their full support to his leadership by granting them greater autonomy – particularly, the military, the Ministry of Interior, the judiciary, al Azhar and some other parts of the bureaucracy.[110] This enhanced autonomy was codified in the constitution as well as in new statutory laws and regulations.[111] These institutions not only have greater statutory power to handle matters related to personnel, policy formulation and policy implementation. They also have substantial funds at their disposal that they can deploy at their discretion.[112] They now command the legal authority and the budgetary capacity to pursue their own policy agendas separate from al Sisi. These agendas may, under many circumstances, align with those of al Sisi or at least allow for cooperation with the president. However, the degree of institutional autonomy enjoyed by the subunits of the Egyptian state will complicate al Sisi's efforts to pursue a coherent policy agenda. He may be able to cajole and pressure the various institutions of the state to follow his lead. However, he lacks the legal authority and financial control to direct them toward a shared goal. Furthermore, this degree of fragmentation of the state raises the possibility for conflict among the various parts of the state, which would further complicate the orderly exercise of power needed to sustain a clear policy agenda.

This fragmentation also extends to the security arena. Some observers have speculated that the increase in enforced disappearances is not a reflection of the regime's strategy but rather an indication of the increased autonomy of some parts of the security apparatus.[113] In essence, parts of the repressive apparatus may have acquired sufficient authority to act on their own without orders from above or accountability to any superiors. Haphazard repression by parts of the security apparatus undermines the regime's efforts to present itself as a strong and effective defender of public safety.[114] It also raises the possibility that parts of the state have become a significant threat to the public.[115] In the current legal and institutional environment, al Sisi has little capacity to rein in this problem unless he dramatically expands the military's role in day-to-day security matters.

Conclusions

In the wake of Mohammad Morsi's removal from power in July 2013, Abdelfattah al Sisi attempted to create a governing civilian coalition grounded in a 'protection pact'. This pact entailed the regime protecting the country's diverse elites from the threat posed by political Islam. However, this threat lacked the breadth and magnitude needed to fuse Egypt's diverse elites into a coherent bloc that would support the expansion of Egypt's security state. As a consequence, Egypt has the institutions of a protection pact – particularly, an expanded role for the military, reduced mechanisms for the distribution of patronage to civilian allies and enhanced repression. However, this pact lacks the broad civilian elite support needed to sustain it. The result is a disintegrating protection pact that leaves the regime with narrowing civilian support, growing dependence on the military, increased reliance on repression to maintain order and reduced capacity to implement a coherent policy agenda.

These shortcomings do not mean that the Sisi regime would collapse easily. On the contrary, it may be able to remain in power simply by virtue of its repressive capability and the absence of a plausible alternative. However, the regime is unlikely to be capable of the economic restructuring that most observers consider essential for the country's medium- and long-term stability. Its increasing reliance on repression may also trigger a violent response from the country's opposition that moves the country more deeply into sustained, low-intensity conflict that further prevents economic growth and saps the regime of the broad legitimacy needed to implement its policy agenda.

Notes

1 I am grateful to Samer Abboud, Eva Bellin, Nathan Brown and Elizabeth Nugent for comments on drafts of this chapter. An earlier version of the chapter appeared in *The Middle East Journal*, 72, 2, Spring 2018, pp. 185–208. It is used here with permission.
2 Panayiotis Jerasimof Vatikiotis, *The History of Modern Egypt – From Muhammad Ali to Mubarak*, Baltimore: Johns Hopkins University Press, 1992, pp. 50–7.
3 Khaled Fahmy, *All the Pasha's Men – Mehmed Ali, His Army and the Making of Modern Egypt*, Cairo: American University in Cairo Press, 2002, pp. 103, 116–17, 122–6, 144–5.

4   Robert L. Tignor, *Modernisation and British Colonial Rule in Egypt, 1882-1914*, Princeton: Princeton University Press, 1966, pp. 232–5.
5   John Waterbury, *The Egypt of Nasser and Sadat – The Political Economy of Two Regimes*, Princeton: Princeton University Press, 1983, pp. 57–64; 228–31; 214–16; and 242–6.
6   Ibid., p. 322.
7   It was formally charged with spreading the conception of Nasserism articulated in the National Charter of 1962.
8   Hazem Kandil, *Soldiers, Spies and Statesmen – Egypt's Road to Revolt*, London: Verso, 2012, p. 44; Owen L. Sirrs, *A History of the Egyptian Intelligence Service – A History of the Mukhabarat, 1910–2009*, London: Routledge, 2010, pp. 29–40.
9   Kandil refers to these three institutions as the 'Power Triangle'. Hazem Kandil, *The Power Triangle – Military, Security and Politics in Regime Change*, Oxford: Oxford University Press, 2016.
10 Maye Kassem, *Egyptian Politics – The Dynamics of Authoritarian Rule*, Boulder: Lynne Rienner Publishers, 2004, pp. 54–85; Kandil, *The Power Triangle*, pp. 313–19. For a thoughtful case study of how the NDP patronage machine operated in a specific district of Cairo (Misr al Qadima), see Mohamed Fahmy Menza, *Patronage Politics in Egypt – The National Democratic Party and the Muslim Brotherhood in Cairo*, New York: Routledge, 2013.
11 Kandil, *Soldiers, Spies and Statesmen*, pp. 168–71.
12 Zeinab Abul-Magd, *Militarizing the Nation – Army, Business and Revolution in Egypt, 1952-2015*, New York: Columbia University Press, 2016.
13 Kandil, *Soldiers, Spies, and Statesmen*, pp. 193–5.
14 Joshua Stacher, 'Egypt Running on Empty', *MERIP Reports*, 8 March 2016.
15 Nathan J. Brown and Oren Samet-Marram, 'Sisi Channels Salazar … Whoever He Was', *The Washington Post*, 3 June 2014.
16 Shadi Hamid, 'Rethinking the US-Egypt Relationship: How Repression Is Undermining Egyptian Stability and What the United States Can Do about It', Testimony for the Tom Lantos Human Rights Commission, 3 November 2015.
17 Dan Slater, *Ordering Power – Contentious Politics and Authoritarian Leviathans in Southeast Asia*, New York: Cambridge University Press, 2010.
18 Ibid., pp. 17, 19.
19 For more detailed discussion of the role of a ruling party in this type of regime, see Milan W. Svolik, *Politics of Authoritarian Rule*, New York: Cambridge University Press, 2012, pp. 163–5.
20 Slater, *Ordering Power*, p. 5.
21 Ibid., p. 13.
22 Ibid., p. 6.
23 Ibid., p. 16.
24 Hicham Bou Nassif, 'Wedded to Mubarak: The Second Careers and Financial Rewards of Egypt's Military Elite, 1981–2011', *Middle East Journal*, 67, 4, Autumn 2013, p. 517.
25 Yezid Sayigh, *Above the State – The Officers' Republic in Egypt*, Beirut: Carnegie Middle East Center, August 2012, p. 14.
26 Yezid Sayigh, 'Reconstructing the Police State in Egypt', *Al Hayat*, 22 August 2013.
27 Shana Marshall, *The Egyptian Armed Forces and the Remaking of an Economic Empire*, Washington, D.C.: Carnegie Endowment for International Peace, 15 April 2015, p. 12.
28 Zeinab Abul-Magd, 'Egypt's Adaptable Officers: Business, Nationalism, and Discontent', in Elke Grawert and Zeinab Abul-Magd, eds., *Businessmen in Arms – How the Military and Other Armed Groups Profit in the MENA Region*, New York: Rowman and Littlefield, 2016, pp. 35–6.

29 'Egypt Names Six Provincial Governors, Mostly Ex-Generals', *Reuters,* 7 September 2016.
30 Sayigh, *Above the State,* pp. 13–15.
31 Constitution of the Arab Republic of Egypt, 2014, available on the World Intellectual Property Organization website at www.wipo.int/wipolex/en/text.jsp?file_ id=347589. For an unofficial translation published by the Egyptian government, see the website of the State Information Service, www.sis.gov.eg/Newvr/Dustor-en001.pdf.
32 Article 203. The civilians include the President of the Republic, the Prime Minister, the Speaker of the House of Representatives, the Minister of Foreign Affairs and the Minister of Finance.
33 Amnesty International, *Year of Rebellion – The State of Human Rights in the Middle East and North Africa,* London: Amnesty International, 2012, p. 13.
34 Significantly, this protection is not extended to Ministry of Interior police.
35 This expansion of the jurisdiction of military courts was originally limited to two years. However, in 2016, the parliament extended it through 2021. Tahrir Institute for Middle East Policy, 'Egypt Parliament Watch: Session One Report – January-September 2016', 9 January 2017, p. 17. Also, Sahar Aziz, 'The Expanding Jurisdiction of Egypt's Military Courts', Carnegie Endowment for International Peace, 12 October 2016.
36 'Egypt', in *World Report, 2018 – Events of 2017,* Washington, D.C.: Human Rights Watch, 2017, p. 158.
37 This calculation is based on budget figures in Egyptian pounds for each calendar year, see Stockholm International Peace Research Institute, 'SIPRI Military Expenditure Database, 1988-2015', 2016, available on the Knoema data company website at https://knoema.com/SIPRI2016/sipri-military-expenditure-database-1988-2015. Al Sisi increased military pensions by 10 per cent by decree in 2014. Abul-Magd, 'Egypt's Adaptable Officers', p. 37. Military pensions were increased another 10 per cent in 2016 by vote of parliament. 'Egypt Raises Military Pensions for the Seventh Time in Three Years', *Middle East Monitor* (UK), 8 July 2016. They were raised again in 2019. 'Egypt to Raise Army Pensions for the 10th Time since 2013 Coup', *The New Arab,* 14 May 2019.
38 Catherine A. Theohary, *Conventional Arms Transfers to Developing Nations, 2008–2015,* Washington, D.C.: Congressional Research Service, 19 December 2016, 49. Also, Nael Shama, 'Egypt's Power Game: Why Cairo Is Boosting Its Military Power', *Jadaliyya,* 6 September 2017.
39 Marshall, *The Egyptian Armed Forces,* pp. 4–6; Sayigh, *Above the State,* pp. 16–17.
40 Ahmed Morsy, 'The Military Crowds Out Civilian Business in Egypt', Carnegie Endowment for International Peace, 24 June 2014.
41 Shana Marshall and Joshua Stacher, 'Egypt's Generals and Transnational Capital', *MERIP Reports,* 262, Spring 2012, pp. 12–18.
42 Marshall, *The Egyptian Armed Forces and the Remaking of an Economic Empire,* p. 6.
43 Sayigh, *Above the State,* p. 12.
44 'Country Report: Egypt', *The Economist* Intelligence Unit, August 2015, p. 32.
45 The firm that won the contract to design the master plan, Dar Al-Handasah Shair and Partners, submitted its bid in partnership with the engineering arm of the Egyptian military. *The Economist* Intelligence Unit, 'Country Report: Egypt', September 2014, p. 27. Also, 'Egypt Awards Ambitious Suez Project to Army-Linked Gulf Firm', *Reuters,* 19 August 2014.
46 Marshall, *The Egyptian Armed Forces and the Remaking of an Economic Empire,* p. 8. *The Economist* Intelligence Unit, 'Country Report: Egypt', September 2015, p. 22. Zeinab Abul-Magd, 'The Military', in Emile Hokayem and Hebatalla Taha, eds., *Egypt after the Spring – Revolt and Reaction,* London: Routledge, 2016, pp. 66–7.

47 Marshall, *The Egyptian Armed Forces and the Remaking of an Economic Empire*, p. 11.
48 For further detail on the extent of the military's economic activity, see Abul-Magd, 'Egypt's Adaptable Officers', p. 36. Also, Abul-Magd, *Militarizing the Nation*; Lina Attalah and Mohamed Hamama, 'The Armed Forces and Business: Economic Expansion in the Last 12 Months', *Mada Masr*, 9 September 2016; and Jessica Noll, 'Egypt's Armed Forces Cement Economic Power', German Institute for International and Security Affairs, SWP Comments No. 5, February 2017.
49 Ahmed Morsy puts the figure at 87 per cent while Laila Sawaf puts it at 95 per cent. Morsy, 'The Military Crowds Out Civilian Business in Egypt'; Laila Sawaf, 'The Armed Forces and Egypt's Land', *Mada Masr*, 26 April 2016.
50 Morsy, 'The Military Crowds Out Civilian Business in Egypt'; Sawaf, 'The Armed Forces and Egypt's Land'. Lina Attalah and Mohamed Hamama, 'The Armed Forces and Business'. Zeinab Abul-Magd, 'Egypt's Adaptable Officers', pp. 27–31.
51 Sawaf, 'The Armed Forces and Egypt's Land'.
52 See Steven A. Cook, *Ruling but Not Governing – The Military and Political Development in Egypt, Algeria, and Turkey*, Baltimore: Johns Hopkins University Press, 2007.
53 Jason Brownlee, *Authoritarianism in an Age of Democratisation*, New York: Cambridge University Press, 2007, pp. 11–12.
54 Ibid., pp. 12–13, 122–56.
55 Lisa Blaydes, *Elections and Distributive Politics in Mubarak's Egypt*, New York: Cambridge University Press, 2011, p. 10.
56 Ibid., pp. 2, 4–5, 9–10.
57 The NDP won 97 per cent of the seats in parliament after a campaign that featured extensive violence, vote buying, and manipulation of the vote count. For further discussion of the 2010 elections, see Human Rights Watch, *Elections in Egypt: State of Permanent Emergency Incompatible with Free and Fair Vote*, New York: Human Rights Watch, December 2010.
58 For further discussion of the events in the months following Mubarak's removal, see M. Cherif Bassiouni, *Chronicles of the Egyptian Revolution and Its Aftermath: 2011-2016*, New York: Cambridge University Press, 2016, pp. 41–102.
59 Parliament has a total of 568 elected seats. A further 28 MPs are appointed by al-Sisi. *The Economist* Intelligence Unit, 'Country Report: Egypt', January 2016, 34. The turnout rate for the elections was 28.3 per cent. Serap Gur, 'The 2015 Parliamentary Elections in Egypt', *Electoral Studies*, 44, 2016, pp. 461–4.
60 *The Economist* Intelligence Unit, 'Country Report: Egypt', January 2016, p. 34. Also, Abdel Monem Said and Sobhy Essaila, 'Egypt's 2015 Parliamentary Elections: Prelude to Stability?' Brandeis University, Crown Center for Middle East Studies, Middle East Brief No. 98, April 2016, p. 4.
61 Heba Afify, 'Infighting among the Free Egyptians', *Mada Masr*, 6 January 2017. 'Sawiris Ultimately Dismissed from Free Egyptians Party', *Al-Masry al-Youm*, 22 February 2017.
62 Bahgat reports that the security services stage-managed the creation of the For the Love of Egypt alliance, the Nation's Future party, and the Support Egypt coalition. Hossam Bahgat, 'Anatomy of an Election', *Mada Masr*, 14 March 2016. At least 47 MPs are retired military or police officers. Former security officers chair the parliamentary committees on African Affairs, Agriculture, Arab Affairs, Defence, and Transportation. Tahrir Institute for Middle East Policy, *Egypt Parliament Watch: Session One Report – January-September 2016*, p. 8.
63 El-Sadany, 'Legalised Authoritarianism', pp. 12–14; Ragab Saad, *All the President's MPs: The Egyptian Parliament's Role in Burying Human Rights and Silencing Dissent*,

Washington, D.C. Project on Middle East Democracy, June 2017. Also, see the periodic reports on the Egyptian Parliament by the Tahrir Institute for Middle East Policy available at timep.org/epw/.

64   Ahmed Hidji, 'Just How Independent Is Egypt's Parliament?' *Al-Monitor,* 9 May 2016. Also, *The Economist* Intelligence Unit, 'Country Report: Egypt', March 2017, pp. 20–1.

65   The UK director of Human Rights Watch described it as, 'perhaps the largest mass killing of protesters on a single day in modern history, worse even than Tiananmen Square'. David Mepham, 'Repression Unbound – Egypt under Sisi', Human Rights Watch, 4 November 2014. Human Rights Watch produced a detailed report on these events which found that 1,150 demonstrators were killed in five separate incidents and that the actions of the security forces ' … likely amounted to crimes against humanity'. See, Human Rights Watch, *All According to Plan – The Rab'a Massacre and Mass Killings of Protesters in Egypt,* New York: Human Rights Watch, August 2014, p. 1.

66   Paul Taylor, 'West Warned Egypt's Sisi to the End: Don't Do It', *Reuters,* 14 August 2013. Also, David D. Kirkpatrick, Peter Baker, and Michael Gordon, 'How American Hopes for a Deal in Egypt Were Undercut', *New York Times,* 17 August 2013.

67   Mepham, 'Repression Unbound – Egypt under Sisi'.

68   Human Rights Watch, 'Egypt: New Leader Faces Rights Crisis', 9 June 2014.

69   Human Rights Watch, 'Egypt: Release Arrested University Students', 14 October 2014. Also, *The Economist* Intelligence Unit, 'Country Report: Egypt', November 2014, p. 19; and Amr Hamzawy, 'Egypt Campus: The Students versus the Regime', Carnegie Endowment for International Peace, 6 March 2017.

70   Rania al Malky, 'The Egyptian Government Is Waging a War on Civil Society', *The Guardian,* 14 October 2014. Also, '434 Muslim Brotherhood NGOs Shut Down', *Daily News Egypt,* 8 July 2015.

71   The law originally specified that any group seeking to hold a protest must acquire permission from the Ministry of Interior. The Supreme Constitutional Court found this clause unconstitutional. The law was amended by parliament in January 2017 to grant the judiciary the final word on whether a protest may occur. 'Protest and Freedom of Assembly in Egypt', Tahrir Institute for Middle East Policy, 18 October 2017.

72   Human Rights Watch, 'Egypt: Counterterrorism Law Erodes Basic Rights', 19 August 2015. Ruth Michaelson, 'Justice Delayed: Egypt's Illegal Use of Pre-Trial Detention', *World Policy Journal,* 33, 2, Summer 2016, pp. 82–9.

73   Human Rights Watch, 'Egypt: Renewed Crackdown on Independent Groups', 15 June 2015. Also, United Kingdom, Foreign and Commonwealth Office, 'Human Rights Priority Country Update Report: July to December 2016 (Egypt)', 8 February 2017.

74   Human Rights Watch, 'Egypt: New NGO Law Renews Draconian Restrictions', 24 July 2019.

75   Human Rights Watch, *'We Do Unreasonable Things Here': Torture and National Security in al Sisi's Egypt,* New York: Human Rights Watch, 5 September 2017.

76   Jenna Amlani, 'A Quick Look at Egypt's New Security Measures', Project on Middle East Democracy, 14 April 2017.

77   Mahmoud Khalid, 'Egypt's Emboldened Military Courts', Carnegie Endowment for International Peace, 23 June 2020.

78   Marshall, *The Egyptian Armed Forces and the Remaking of an Economic Empire,* p. 13.

79   Aziz, 'The Expanding Jurisdiction of Egypt's Military Courts'.

80   Tahrir Institute for Middle East Policy, *Egypt Parliament Watch: Session One Report – January-September 2016,* p. 7.

81 *The Economist* Intelligence Unit, 'Country Report: Egypt', November 2014, p. 21. Bianca C. Isaias, 'Military Tribunals and Due Process in Post-Revolutionary Egypt', *International Lawyer*, 49, 2, Fall 2015, pp. 199–227.
82 'Dozens of Disappeared Civilians Face Ongoing Torture at Military Prison', Amnesty International, 22 May 2014. Also, Amnesty International, *Egypt: Officially, You Do Not Exist: Disappeared and Tortured in the Name of Counter-Terrorism*, London: Amnesty International, 12 July 2016. United Nations General Assembly, Human Rights Council, 'Report of the Working Group on Enforced or Involuntary Disappearances', 28 July 2016, p. 15. A nongovernmental organization based in Cairo, the Egyptian Commission for Rights and Freedoms (ECRF), documented 340 cases of disappearances from August to November 2015, see Amina Ismail and Declan Walsh, 'Hundreds Vanishing in Egypt as Crackdown Widens, Activists Say', *The New York Times*, 26 January 2016. Also, Human Rights Watch, 'Egypt: Dozens Detained Secretly', 20 July 2015.
83 A. Seif El-Islam, 'Exceptional Laws and Exceptional Courts', in Nathalie Bernard-Maugiron and Baudouin Dupret, eds., *Egypt and Its Laws*, New York: Kluwer Law International, 2002, pp. 359–76.
84 See al Sisi's speech to the House of Representatives on 13 February 2016, available at Sisi at www.alborsanews.com/2016/02/13/. Or his speech on the fifth anniversary of the 2011 uprising, 25 January 2016, available at http://alwafd.org/. Also, 'Abd al-Fattah al-Sisi, interview by Dieter Bednarz and Klaus Brinkbäumer, 'Extremists Offend the Image of God', *Spiegel Online* (Germany), 9 February 2015.
85 See the interview with al Sisi in *Spiegel Online*, 9 February 2015.
86 Slater, *Ordering Power*, p. 14.
87 Tarek Masoud, *Counting Islam – Religion, Class, and Elections in Egypt*, New York: Cambridge University Press, 2014, pp. 93–120.
88 For Brotherhood criticism of attacks by radical groups, see 'Muslim Brotherhood Statement on the Terrorist Attack on Mamina Church', www.ikhwanweb.com/, 30 December 2017. The Ikhwan website contains numerous other similar statements. For ISIS criticism of the Brotherhood, see Ban al-'Ani, '*Harb al Fatawi bayn al Ikhwan wa Da'ish, [War of Fatwas between the Brotherhood and ISIS]*, Al Bowaaba, 23 August 2014. The leader of Al Qaeda, Ayman al Dhawahiri, wrote a lengthy condemnation of the Brotherhood in 1999, *Al Hasad al Murr* [The Bitter Harvest], Dar al-Bayariq, 1999. It was reissued in 2006 by Al Fajr Information Centre. See also: Meir Hatina, 'Redeeming Sunni Islam: Al Qaeda's Polemic against the Muslim Brethren', *British Journal of Middle Eastern Studies*, 39, 1, April 2012, pp. 101–13.
89 The Brotherhood-led Democratic Alliance won 10.1 million votes (37.3 per cent) in the 2011/12 elections for the now-defunct People's Assembly (*Majlis al Sha'b*) and 2.9 million votes (45 per cent) in the 2012 elections for the now-defunct Consultative Council (*Majlis al Shura*). The Brotherhood's candidate for president in 2012, Mohamed Morsi, won 5.8 million votes (24.8 per cent) in the first round and 13.2 million votes (51.7 per cent) in the run-off. Results from the website of Egypt's National Election Authority, www.elections.eg/; Mazen Hassan, 'Elections of the People's Assembly, Egypt 2011/12', *Electoral Studies*, 32, 2, June 2013, pp. 370–74; International Foundation for Electoral Systems, 'Election Guide: Arab Republic of Egypt', www.electionguide.org/countries/id/65/.
90 Masoud argues that the Brotherhood's electoral success was also a product of its organizational skill and its record of delivering goods and services to its supporters. Masoud, *Counting Islam*, pp. 207–8.
91 The al-Nur party's electoral program for the 2015 parliamentary elections called for the application of *Shari'a*, more extensive government monitoring of the

moral content of broadcast media, and 'equal dignity' for men and women. These positions are similar to those of the Brotherhood's electoral program in the 2011/12 parliamentary election. See *'Al Watan tanshar Malaamah al Birnamij al Intikhabi li Hizb al Nur'* [*Al Watan* Publishes an Outline of the al-Nur Party's Electoral Program], *al-Watan*, 1 October 2015 and *Birnamij Hizb al Huriyya wa al'Adala* [Programme of the Freedom and Justice Party], 2011.

92 For views supportive of the government's decision to widely repress political Islam, see Ahmad 'Amir, *'Muhammad al Suwaydi, Ra'is I'tilaf Da'm Misr, fi hiwar ma'a al-Ahram'* [Muhammad al Suwaydi, President of the Support Egypt Coalition, in a conversation with *Al Ahram*], *Al Ahram*, 24 December 2017. For views critical of this approach and calling for less repression and more political openness, see the program of the Constitution Party (*Hizb Al Dustur*) published 25 October 2015, available at https://drive.google.com/file/d/0BwPiUJWQSjzOSmNFYjRPVmc4UjQ/view.

93 For a thoughtful discussion of Egypt's secular parties and their varying degrees of support for the regime, see Michele Dunne and Amr Hamzawy, 'Egypt's Secular Political Parties: A Struggle for Identity and Independence', Carnegie Endowment for International Peace, Paper No. 305, 31 March 2017.

94 This decision triggered sharp criticism of Al Sisi from several prominent intellectuals. See Ian Black, 'Egypt's President under Fire over Red Sea Islands Transfer to Saudi Arabia', *The Guardian*, 11 April 2016; Kareem Fahim, 'Egyptians Denounce President Sisi in Biggest Rally in 2 Years', *New York Times*, 15 April 2016; and Timothy E. Kaldas, 'Tiran, Sanafir, and the Island of Executive Power in Egypt', Tahrir Institute for Middle East Policy, 21 April 2016.

95 Nathan Brown and Mariam Ghanem, 'The Battle over Al Azhar', Carnegie Endowment for International Peace, 31 May 2017.

96 *The Economist* Intelligence Unit, 'Country Report: Egypt', March 2017, pp. 21–2. Also, Nathan Brown, 'Judicial Militancy within Red Lines', Carnegie Middle East Center, 2 November 2016; Nathan Brown and Amr Hamzawy, 'An Egyptian Court Just Struck Down Part of a Repressive New Law – Here's What That Means', *The Washington Post, Monkey Cage* (blog), 7 December 2016.

97 *'Al Niyaba taqarrar habas "Badr" wa "al Saqqa" 15 yomaan fi 'Qalb Nitham al Hukm'* [The Prosecutor decides to confine ('Amru) Badr and (Mahmud) Al Saqqa for 15 days in 'the heart of the regime'], *Mada Masr*, 2 May 2016.

98 The three leaders – Gamal Abdul Rahim, Khaled al-Balshy and Yehia Qallash – were convicted and given two-year sentences. Amira El-Fekki, 'Journalist Amr Badr Recounts Press Syndicate Incidents in Defence of Sentenced Leaders', *Daily News Egypt*, 21 November 2016.

99 Mai Shams El-Din, 'Will Egypt's Supreme Media Regulatory Council Become a New Censorship Body?' *Mada Masr*, 9 June 2017.

100 See Amr Khalifa, 'Sisi's Egypt and the Politics of Fear', *Middle East Eye*, 23 October 2017. Declan Walsh, 'Egyptian Concertgoers Wave a Flag, and Land in Jail', *New York Times*, 26 September 2017.

101 For analysis of the grievances that drove the 2011 uprising, see Neil Ketchley, *Egypt in a Time of Revolution – Contentious Politics and the Arab Spring*, New York: Cambridge University Press, 2017. Also, Kira D. Jumet, *Contesting the Repressive State: Why Ordinary Egyptians Protested during the Arab Spring*, New York: Oxford University Press, 2017.

102 Mohamed El Dahshan, 'The Egyptian Economy', in Emile Hokayem and Hebatalla Taha, eds., *Egypt after the Spring – Revolt and Reaction*, London: Routledge, 2016, pp. 201–18; Michele Dunne and Nik Nevin, 'Egypt Now Looks a Lot Like It Did in 2010, Just before 2011 Unrest', *The Wall Street Journal, Washington Wire*

(blog), 16 December 2015; Human Rights Watch, *Egypt: 2019* (New York: Human Rights Watch, 2019); 'Egypt Is Reforming Its Economy, but Poverty Is Rising', *The Economist*, 8 August 2019.

103 In the past, increased military autonomy has meant greater control over personnel, budgetary matters, and procurement decisions.

104 For further discussion of the military's goals, see Stephan Roll, 'Managing Change: How Egypt's Military Leadership Shaped the Transformation', *Mediterranean Politics*, 21, 1, 2016, pp. 23–43. Also, Hicham Bou Nassif, 'Coups and Nascent Democracies: The Military and Egypt's Failed Consolidation', *Democratization*, 24, 1, January 2017, pp. 157–74.

105 Bahgat reports that 26 military officers were tried and convicted for plotting a coup in 2015. Hossam Bahgat, 'A Coup Busted?' *Mada Masr*, 14 October 2015. For further discussion of the possibility of a coup, see Hazem Kandil, 'Sisi's Egypt', *New Left Review*, 102, November/December 2016, pp. 11, 40. Also, Nathan Brown, 'A Dispensable Dictator?' Carnegie Middle East Center, 5 May 2017.

106 Hazem Kandil, *Soldiers, Spies, and Statesmen*, pp. 146, 168–9, 183–5, 191, 197. Also, see James T. Quinlivan, 'Coup-proofing: Its Practice and Consequences in the Middle East', *International Security*, 24, 2, Fall 1999, pp. 131–65.

107 These changes are reflected in Articles 200 through 204 of the 2014 Constitution. The military has achieved greater budgetary control through its dominant position in the National defence Council (NDC), which is the body that supervises the military's budget and the distribution of U.S. military aid.

108 Morsy, 'The Military Crowds Out Civilian Business in Egypt'.

109 For example, see al Sisi's speech to the House of Representatives on 13 February 2016, available at www.alborsanews.com/2016/02/13/.

110 Brown argues that this trend began before al Sisi's ascension to power. Nathan J. Brown, 'Egypt's Wide State Reassembles Itself', *Foreign Policy*, 17 July 2013. See also Nathan Brown and Mai El-Sadany, 'Devils in the Details', Carnegie Middle East Center, 17 January 2017.

111 The relevant articles of the 2014 Constitution are 7, 184–97, and 200–4. Also, Brown, 'Egypt's Wide State Reassembles Itself'.

112 Manek and Hodge estimate that individual ministries have access to many millions of pounds that are outside of the official national budget and beyond the control of the President. Nizar Manek and Jeremy Hodge, 'Opening the Black Box of Egypt's Slush Funds', *Mada Masr*, 28 May 2015. Also, European Union, European Court of Auditors, 'EU Cooperation with Egypt in the Field of Governance', Special Report No. 4, 2013, p. 22.

113 Hisham A. Hellyer, 'The Regimen of Sisi's Non-Regime', Atlantic Council, *MENA Source* (blog), 3 February 2016.

114 Sayigh observes that divisions within the military have become more pronounced under al Sisi. Yezid Sayigh, 'The Return of Egypt's Military Interest Groups', Carnegie Middle East Center, 21 December 2015. Kandil notes that divisions have also emerged within the Ministry of Interior and between the Ministry of Interior and the Ministry of Defence. Hazem Kandil, 'Sisi's Egypt', pp. 7, 17.

115 If this has occurred, Egypt may have moved toward a 'protection racket', rather than a protection pact. In other words, the regime asserts that it will protect the public from threats that it has created. For further discussion of protection rackets, see Charles Tilly, 'War Making and State Making as Organized Crime', in Peter Evans, Dietrich Rueschemeyer and Theda Skocpol, eds., *Bringing the State Back In*, New York: Cambridge University Press, 1985, pp. 170–1.

8 ARMED MILITANCY AND ALTERNATIVE STATEHOOD: AL QAEDA, THE ISLAMIC STATE AND REVOLUTIONARY ISLAMISM

François Burgat

It is often forgotten that the *jihadi* movement that arose in the late twentieth century and early twenty-first century – first with the rise of Al Qaeda in the 1990s then with its successor and rival, the Islamic State (IS or ISIS/ISIL for Islamic State in Iraq/the Levant) in the 2010s – is only the most recent episode in a lengthy process of challenges to the borders of Middle Eastern and North African states drawn during colonization. In this respect, transnational jihadism follows on from two other great registers of political mobilization that challenged these colonial borders. The first questioned the outline of these borders in the context of post-colonial rivalries between the newly formed states. The second challenged their very existence in the name of pan-Arabism. One criterion that differentiates these three registers of mobilization is the level of antagonism that its actors mobilized against the Western authors of these borders. This was latent in the first case, in which Europeans were principally ascribed responsibility for decolonization. It is more explicitly present in the second, in which the transnational rise of so-called 'secular' Arabism challenged the imperial ambitions of the former colonial powers, or of the United States, the new imperial state. With the Al Qaeda generation, this antagonism became the central and primary variable of the revolt against the so-called 'far enemy' (*al adou al ba'eed*) represented by the West.

This chapter discusses how *jihadi* movements fit in this history of challenge to the original state-determined post-colonial *status quo*. The discussion starts by examining how, in the aftermath of the United States' invasion of Iraq in 2003, a major shift occurred in *jihadi* mobilization against the far enemy. At the heart of the Middle East and North Africa, that mobilization found social and political spaces in which to deploy itself. Surfing both on the tribalization of the Iraqi regime[1] and on a swift-moving globalization of resentment, the Islamic State both extended and amplified in the 2010s the dynamic that Al Qaeda had initiated in Afghanistan twenty years earlier. The chapter then delves into the dynamic whereby international jihadism adapted itself to the configuration of the Iraqi-Syrian theatre. Finally, the discussion considers the idea that while this *jihadi* movement was inscribed in letters of blood through attacks on the territory of Western states, the question arises of how this historical manifestation of jihadism is itself understood by the political and intellectual actors of these Western countries. Few among these analysts accept to situate this episode in the historicity of successive Arab reactions to the colonial era. Furthermore, very few of them accept to recognize the eminently political framework of this generation of jihadism. Such are the lessons to be drawn from academic and media discourse. The discussion draws principally on the dominant terms of this discourse in France, which resonates across the wider European and Western stages.

From contesting the post-colonial order to the *jihadi* rift

To contextualize the contemporary rise of jihadism, one needs to outline two great registers of contestation that preceded it historically. A first generation of those militants disillusioned by the colonial order denounced how the borders had been drawn in the early twentieth century. From about the mid-1950s, that generation also denounced the recipients or beneficiaries of the nation-states that had emerged from the decomposition of the Ottoman Empire. Decolonization treaties granted sovereignty to some territories and nations but not to others, these critics argued. This first category of contestation was by far the least homogenous. It included episodes of conventional direct competition between the new governing elites, as in the Algeria-Morocco war of 1963, as well as latter episodes of decolonization – for instance after the British left the Gulf in 1968. One might also include here the activity of 'liberation' movements that were often remote-controlled by inter-state rivalries, as in the case of Algeria's support for the Polisario Front from 1975,[2] or the struggle by *jihadi* groups against the Marxist regime of South-Yemen supported by its rival in the North.[3] Some states resorted to proxy wars to challenge the borders inherited from decolonization, in some cases staking out regional hegemonic ambitions in the process. Armed protests of ethnic groups whose nationalist aspirations had been shun aside during the consecration of statehood also fall in this category. This included the Kurds, torn apart by the colonial divisions between Turkey, Syria, Iraq and Iran; and, across the Sahel as a whole, the Tuareg. At the time, the common denominator of these challengers was that they developed no explicit claims towards the world of the former colonizer, nor towards the West in general – other than the politics of memory. Indeed, they often sought out its support.

The early 1960s witnessed the development of new modes of challenge to the post-colonial borders. These partially superimposed themselves upon the first register of armed militancy. The very principle of division into nation-states then found itself challenged ideologically and fought militarily in the name of a first transnational ideology that mobilized Arab ethno-cultural identity, Arabism. In its different versions, whether Nasserist or Ba'athist, this pan-Arab ideology enabled fleeting *rapprochement* between the states of the region. More often than not, however, it provided cover for conventional regional rivalries. Such Arabism was most formally carried forward by the secular republics, in particular Syria, Iraq, Egypt, Algeria and Libya. Routinely, it was the ideological prop of their struggle for power with the conservative monarchies – in particular Saudi Arabia, Jordan, Morocco and the Gulf countries. As such, pan-Arabism often gained the support of these monarchies' domestic opposition. These movements, some of them armed, were also, however, more conventionally themselves pretexts for rivalries between the pan-Arabist state actors – such as the one between Nasserists and Ba'athists, or between Iraqi and Syrian Ba'athists. This second register of militancy, while not being indifferent to Western presence in the region, was not exclusively focused against it.

From the end of the 1970s, secular Arabism saw its capacity to mobilize eaten away at by the rise of its rival and soon-to-be-successor, Islamism. This transition was more continuity than rupture. With the rise of Islamism, identity-based political mobilization in some sense came to outstrip the register of ethnic and cultural belonging and to lean upon a more globalizing religious identity.[4] During the 1980s, Islamist mobilization gradually rose on every Arab political stage. Such congregation had multiple registers of action; social, political and religious. It culminated in a new and radical Islamist self-assertion, which could be seen clearly from the turn of the 1990s. By force of arms, this challenged further the foundations of the state order inherited from decolonization. This transnational *jihadi* movement wielded an elitist and anti-democratic rhetoric aiming to propose a unified Sunni alternative to the state-based 'dispersion' of a regional order – one that had remained largely dependent on the old European colonial world in the face of US imperialism. Importantly, transnational jihadism could now designate the 'far enemy' (the Western states), rather than the local Arab states, as its principal foe.

For all its complexity and this intricate historical sequence, the *jihadi* movement has nonetheless been depicted in reductionist ways. For most Western analysts, it has remained a marginal expression of 'Islamism' writ large, which runs, as the phrase has it, 'from the Taliban to Erbakan'. Throughout the 1990s in the Middle East and North Africa, we witnessed indeed the rise of an outsider's gaze on 'the Islamist trend' characterizing indistinctly what were eminently diverse forms of Islamism. From the 1990s onwards, some Islamist parties achieved significant progress in joining formal political processes. Parties that were more or less direct (and more or less exclusive) emanations from the Jama'at al Ikhwan al Muslimeen (Muslim Brotherhood) trend entered parliaments in Jordan, Algeria, Palestine, Lebanon, Kuwait and Morocco. Elsewhere, it took up ministerial posts (Yemen) and even led a government (Sudan).

Within these national frameworks, the fleeting openings of the end of the 1980s swiftly showed their limits. More or less everywhere, the main contribution of elections was to make the brittleness of these regimes' popular base more explicit. In the Maghreb and in Egypt in particular, the leaderships became aware, or convinced themselves, that it would be impossible to stand up to their main opponents in the electoral sphere. They chose to lower the stakes of elections – going so far as to 'defuse' the political system.[5] More consequentially, the governments chose to embark on a course of active repression of their most legalist opponents, and, when possible, to militarize that repression. Even in Saudi Arabia or in Jordan, where versions of coexistence or cooperation had prevailed for a time, pro-active repression gradually came to address obvious failures of representation.[6] Putting an end to cosmetic, 'for-the-Yankees-to-see' political openings, governments elected to shift competition with their opposition to the security field only. Throughout this period, as it was birthed at the tail end of the Soviet invasion of Afghanistan (1979–1989), Al Qaeda crystallized at the crossroads of this dual dynamic of transnational radicalization and what can be termed a 'regionalization of exasperation' in the Arab world. This was indeed exasperation at the impasse produced by the failure of the Arab state. As authoritarianism prevailed in almost all the states of the region, with blind support from the West, tentacular institutions of repression replaced embryonic agencies of representation.

In January 1992, in Algeria, the second round of parliamentary elections was on the brink of consecrating the victory of al Jabha al Islamiya lil Inqadh (Islamic Salvation Front or FIS from its French acronym Front Islamique du Salut), providing it with a parliamentary majority and a launchpad to legitimate national governance. The elections were cancelled. With active approval from Western governments, notably France, the regime then launched a violent and manipulative campaign of armed eradication against the election winners. The methods used were not without recalling those of the Chilean junta that had been brought to power in September 1973 at the expense of Salvador Allende's democratic government, thanks to the highly active support from the United States' Central Intelligence Agency (CIA). In a sense, such international cooperation in repression[7] became the ideological matrix of a regional and international lockdown of the political sphere – one that became generalized over the course of the 1990s, and, again, one that presided over the rise of Al Qaeda.

For their part, Arab autocrats exploited an extremely one-sided interpretation of the 'Algerian crisis' to legitimate the reinforcement of their repressive apparatus in the eyes of a Western public opinion that was ill-informed of the scale of the manipulation of violence conducted by Algeria's security services.[8] They portrayed this as their 'struggle against fundamentalism' to fight off 'the *jihadis*' who had returned triumphant from Afghanistan, and who were one-sidedly ascribed wholesale culpability for the close to 200,000 dead of the Algerian civil war. In the eyes of many, including democrats in the West and in the Arab world, this was sufficient to justify the regimes' about-turn with respect to democracy and the outbursts of repression which – in Tunisia,[9] Libya, Algeria or Egypt – brought to a close the brief parenthesis of the 1990s political openings. In the wake of the 11 September 2001 attacks led by Al Qaeda on the United States, Algeria's military-led government rode the outrage wave and launched a public relations narrative portraying it as 'democrats' confronting 'international Islamist terrorism'. Beyond this tactical Arab state level, the denial of representation of political Islam affected a second set of more internationalized issues. This was notably the case of the Arab–Israeli conflict, in which the balance of power had become more asymmetrical than ever. Though the Palestine Liberation Organisation (PLO) had recognized the state of Israel in November 1988, Israel had gone on to enact a policy of Bantustanization of the Occupied Palestinian Territories, strangling their economy and walling-in Palestinian society.[10] This degenerated sequence replaced the state pledges that had been the basis for the truce leading to the 1993 Oslo Peace Accords. For the Islamist political actors, and many others, the management of the Israeli–Arab conflict especially emphasized the negative role played by the American and European countries, and specifically their ambivalence with respect to international law norms and United Nations resolutions. The Islamists then argued the inanity of wielding any legalist strategy in dealing with Israel and its Western supporters.

The third feature of this prevailing unilateralism further operated on a global scale. The militarization of US foreign policy came to echo the normalization of repression and torture at the national level of Arab states. The fall of the Soviet Union had put an end to an East-West rivalry whose positive aspect had been that it kept in check the interventionist inclinations of both sides. In 1990–1991, the Second Gulf War opened a decade in which the United States, now a sole superpower freed from the constraint of its Soviet rival, increasingly openly isolated itself from international institutions and opinion. Because it had tried to seize Kuwait's oil wells, Saddam Hussein's Iraq became the target of a lengthy air and ground campaign, which – having destroyed Iraq's military potential and set its economic infrastructure back several decades – had the primary consequence of extending US guardianship over oil in the Middle East. In the same period, the UN-led coalition left the regime's security capabilities intact, and, with it, the local version of the prevailing regional authoritarianism. The United Nations then imposed an economic embargo whose civilian victims were to be counted in the hundreds of thousands.[11] The disarmament of the only regional power able to resist Israel militarily gave the United States a pretext to set up a military presence in the Gulf, where it had been invited to by Saudi Arabia to protect it from the territorial ambitions of its Iraqi neighbour. This enormous US military intervention in the Arabian Peninsula – again, actively sought by Gulf leaders – was to play a key role in the emergence of Al Qaeda.

Security cooperation became institutionalized between the three scales of the political order: national, regional and global; the leaders of the US-led new world order, their Israeli ally and their Arab state client states. A new conflict configuration and regulation was introduced. Wielding the pretext of a 'struggle against terrorism', US, European, Israeli and Arab security services built up and enforced a shared new ideological rhetoric depoliticizing and criminalizing any and all resistance (armed or otherwise) to their national, regional or global authoritarianisms. In March 1996, such internationalized cooperation in repression by Arab autocracies with the unconditional support of the US superpower and its Israeli and European allies was made explicit at the occasion of a global anti-terrorism summit in the Egyptian seaside resort of Sharm al Sheikh. Despite their diversity, Russian, European and Arab states united to designate a common enemy: Islamist terrorism. They portrayed it as having arisen not from an exacerbated historical socio-political reaction to their authoritarian practices but solely from the impromptu emergence of a radical ideology. To the Muslim 'fundamentalists' who were designated as the main targets of this campaign, *the transnational securitization of the repression of any expression of protest that used Islamic vocabulary encouraged the reactive development of an identical transnationalization of resistance* to these deep global dysfunctions. With the birth of Al Qaeda, this reactive transnationalization was initially more regional (in Egypt or Saudi Arabia) than it was truly global. However, the movement had nonetheless already scaled up, and Al Qaeda's revolutionary approach was to now make the United States its main target.

The life histories of Al Qaeda's leaders all reflect a shift from challenging their own local authoritarianisms towards transnational jihadism.[12] Osama Bin Laden came from a family from Yemen's Hadhramaut region that had immigrated to Saudi Arabia, and he was shaped by his opposition to the Saud.[13] In turn, his successor, Ayman al Dhawahiri, a physician from the Cairo bourgeoisie, was the product of reaction to the repressive drift of the Nasserist system, and Anwar Sadat's submission to the regional *pax Americana* in the footsteps of Saudi Arabia. As well, Abdullah Azzam, Al Qaeda's original number three man (he was killed in 1989), had emerged from the long tunnel of Palestinian resistance to Israeli occupation. On 23 August 1996, a few months after the Sharm al Sheikh summit, Bin Laden issued his first call 'to chase the Americans from the Arabic peninsula'.[14] Suicide attacks then followed on the US embassies in Nairobi and Dar-Es-Salaam in August 1998, on the *USS Cole* vessel in the Aden harbour in October 2000 and on the World Trade Centre's Twin Towers and the Pentagon in New York and Washington in September 2001. During the funerals of the seventeen victims of the attack on the *U.S.S. Cole*, the rhetoric of US President Bill Clinton laid the keystone, as it were, of Western blindness towards the reactions to which its policies had given rise, and which it had one-sidedly characterized as 'terrorism'. The *U.S.S. Cole* destroyer had been taking part in a murderous embargo that had been recognized as having caused several hundreds of thousands of deaths among Iraq's children. According to Clinton, however, America's new enemies were hostile; they hated American citizens' love of freedom.

The Islamic State and the confessionalization of resentment

In Iraq, both the rise of Al Qaeda and the Islamic State can be directly linked to the reaction generated by the imbalance of power created by the United States between the Shia and Sunni communities in the wake of the 2003 overthrow of Saddam Hussein's Ba'athist regime. Under Prime Minister Nouri al Maliki (May 2006 to September 2014) – former deputy head of the Committee for De-Ba'athification – the Iraqi government swiftly proved itself incapable of ensuring credible representation of Sunnis; the once-privileged allies of the fallen Ba'athist regime. At the expense of building up a state based on the rule of law, the new authorities allowed abuses by Shi'a militias to multiply while enjoying the political and operational support of neighbouring Iran. Initially, the Sunni opposition responded peacefully before militarily escalating its reaction to its ostracization. The insurgency was promptly labelled terrorist and dealt with accordingly by the government's forces and militias. Politically, the Sunnis were also abandoned by the United States well before Washington's exit from Iraq in 2010. Gradually, the new insurgent groups in the country merged with other radical groups, some of which were composed of veterans from the Afghanistan war. This was notably the case of Abu Mus'ab al Zarqawi and his Jama'at al Tawhid wal Jihad (Group of Unity and Jihad). Al Zarkawi's group, which had been set up in 1999, spearheaded the rebellion against the United States occupation in the spring and summer of 2003. It then reached out, a year later, to Bin Laden offering to become Al Qaeda in the Land of the Two Rivers (i.e., Mesopotamia). Upon the death of al Zarqawi in 2006, what had become by then Al Qaeda in Iraq gradually turned inward, setting the stage for the eventual rise of a locally led yet globally oriented Iraqi entity, Al Dawla al Islamiya (the Islamic State).[15] In 2011, the post-Arab Spring, anti-Assad rebellion offered the opportunity to transnationalize further the brewing movement. What was then coalescing as the Islamic State, and which in Syria was known as Jabhat al Nusra (the Front of Victory) led by Abu Mohammad al Jolani, chose to use the territory of Syria as the counterpoint to its regional strategy, and as the territory in which to re-energize an organization that was then losing momentum in Iraq.

What subsequently emerged in 2013 as the Islamic State in Iraq and Syria/Levant (ISIS/L) had a paradoxical convergence of interests with the Syrian regime – temporarily at least, until ISIS' victorious capture of the Iraqi city of Mosul in June 2014 and its leader Abu Bakr al Baghdadi's proclamation of the restoration of the Caliphate led by the Islamic State (IS). For a long while, ISIS fighters concentrated their efforts merely on reinforcing their hold on areas that had already been liberated from the Syrian regime, thereby limiting their operational cooperation with the other armed groups. It was highly significant that ISIS sites and convoys were strangely spared by the bombs of the regime air force and its Russian sponsor – unlike the fighters of the Free Syrian Army (FSA) and the civilian population in

FSA-controlled areas. The Syrian regime's interests were to encourage the rise of a radical opposition, given its useful function as a terrorism bogeyman. From the perspective of ISIS, the interests were less obvious. Yet since the group's agenda was to enable the Syrian portion of its transnational state-in-formation to endure, toppling the regime in Damascus was far from being a strategic priority for it. Statehood emerged as a malleable category of martiality. This would bring about the formation of a coalition against ISIS, gathering together most of the Sunni rebels and the remnants of the Alawi regime – with the added intervention of US drones.[16] This was in line with the scenario that the *jihadi* fighters had already faced in the Iraqi theatre. There, from 2007, the Islamic State of Iraq had to face a front made of the US military, the troops of Nouri al Maliki's government and the Sunni militias of the Sahwa movement.

That the initial dynamic of ISIS radicalization was linked to the Syrian regime's strategy of survival is arresting. It speaks revealingly of the criss-crossing of the statehood and counter-statehood projects, which had come to characterize the Middle East and North Africa by the second decade of the twenty-first century. This was also to give, by any means necessary, sufficient visibility to that component of the opposition to the regime to discredit the opposition as a whole. Its challenge was to make the truncated representation that it had forged with meticulous care since the onset of the crisis plausible. This portrayed an aggression launched by Sunni commandos financed by the West and its Israeli or conservative Arab allies, to punish Syria for its resistance to the Israeli-American regional order. The revolt therefore had to be sectarianized. To this end, several stratagems were deployed. At the top of the list was the violent repression traditionally used by the state, whose primary characteristic was that it was out of any proportion to the threat constituted by a protest movement, which had initially been peaceful, and indeed actively tried to remain so in the face of state violence. Such new violence was then highly selectively meted out towards Sunnis. In parallel, as early as May 2011, and to crucial effect, the Syrian regime freed militants from its prisons, knowing full well that they would head to bolster the ranks of the Salafi component of an opposition that was in the process of becoming militarized. Next, it spared the nascent *jihadi* component of the rebellion the aerial bombing that it inflicted on the remainder of its players. The regime itself called on Shi'a militias (from Lebanon, Iran and Iraq in particular) that inscribed their role in the conflict within an explicitly sectarian logic. In time, the *jihadi* variable of the Syrian crisis became indeed a bogeyman waved by all those who sought to discredit the opposition. Any consideration of its role cannot, however, fail to take into account that for a long time the number of foreign *jihadis* fighting on the regime side was larger than that of the foreign fighters present in opposition ranks. In 2013, for instance, nearly 10,000 Hezbollah fighters tipped the balance of the battle of Qusayr in favour of the regime, prompting vocal religious celebrations around the tomb of the Shi'a saint Sayeeda Zainab in Damascus.

The efficacy of the Syrian regime's strategy resulted in large part from the inability of its opponents to frustrate it. The fact that the radical option became increasingly credible fed upon the assessment that there was no alternative to it, since the international community considered that there was no acceptable partner with which to replace the regime. The weakening of potential opponents to the *jihadi* camp therefore resulted from the double standards of the Western camp's humanism. Because they had no rational criteria with which to judge the import of political Islam in the region, the European and American friends of Syria came to ostracize – and therefore asphyxiate – many brigades that were considered 'insufficiently secular'. These then very directly took part in increasing the ranks of those 'disillusioned' by the Western coalition. A good number of opponents to the regime then wandered, in 2013–2015, between divided groups, bereft of weapons and financing. They ended up turning towards those brigades that were endowed with a far more substantial logistical base, notably, in Iraq.

In June 2014, the rout of the Iraqi army in the face of Abu Bakr al Baghdadi's Islamic State had been a game-changer. The Syrian opposition had failed to mobilize a Western intervention to support it. This suddenly became possible by virtue of a 'Pearl Harbor factor' that was brewing next door. Assassinations of American journalists in response to the first US bombings of ISIS position brought momentum to the conflict. The West's entry into the war did not, however, take place in support of the Arab Spring protests nor was it directed against the Syrian regime. Western interventionism was explicitly against the Islamic State; an entity which had largely emerged as the product of the permanent repressive capacity that the West had itself granted regimes in the region for nearly forty years. Incidentally, for the Western camp, the enemy of the past 30 years, Iran, thereby became a *de facto* ally in this new campaign. Even more so than the Global War on Terror launched against Al Qaeda ten years earlier, the Western response to the Islamic State fell short of the standards of technical rationality and exigency required of a reasoned foreign policy designed to serve tangible objectives. Similarly, even more so than in the past, this new foreign campaign entered directly into the calculations of domestic politics, and the 'electioneering' inherent to these. It is fairly easily shown that, in each Western national political arena, Western management of the Syrian crisis in particular, and of the question of terrorism in general, became unstoppably a local issue. The Syrian regime's proven manipulations alone could never have conferred on the new *jihadi* movement of the Islamic State the scale that it had grown to had the movement not enjoyed its own historicity and its own militant base, in Afghanistan then in Iraq. Depending on the contexts in which it had taken root since the 1980s, contemporary jihadism had taken on different shades and outlined different strategic sub-priorities. Globally, however, its ambitions have remained the same. They were primarily concerned with countering those actors (whether state or sub-state) standing in the way of the jihadis from putting into practice the political and social expression of their specific understanding of the Sunni Muslim faith. These groups were also opposed to Western interventionism in the Muslim regions, and to Shiite communities, notably in Iraq and Lebanon.

Though it shared many commonalities with Al Qaeda, the Islamic State was different from the organization from which it grew – primarily as regards the basis on which it mobilized support. The process by which the Islamic State became institutionally autonomous with respect to Al Qaeda was initially the expression of a dispute as regards the question of sectarianism. Starting with al Zarqawi, who had multiplied attacks against the Shiites in the mid-2000s, the leaders of the Islamic State realigned themselves in order to take into account the confessional specificities of the Iraqi theatre. In Iraq, they therefore abandoned the priority that the founders of Al Qaeda had, in their time, ascribed to the far enemy. The Islamic State chose instead to focus on the near enemy or enemies. In particular, this meant focusing on the Shi'a; first the Iraqi Shi'a and later the Iranian and Syrian ones. This stood in stark contrast with how Al Qaeda had behaved in the Afghanistan setting circa late 1980s and early 1990s awarding far less importance to the issue of sectarian divide than what IS was now doing amidst the 'ethnic and sectarian mosaic' of the Middle East and North Africa. The aggressive isolation of Sunni sectarian belonging (from which Al Qaeda's leadership came to dissociate itself) in some sense responded to the proven sectarian dimension of the Iraqi and Syrian states themselves. Sectarianism also became explicit through the direct encounter with Christian minorities, which were physically absent from the Afghan theatre.

The second defining characteristic of the Islamic State may be understood as a shift in scale. Compared to Al Qaeda, the new group's ability to mobilize, even more explicitly so once it renamed itself 'Islamic State', marked a consequential qualitative change. First, the group's militants successfully took up the challenge of acquiring a territorial base – the condition of any pretence to statehood – and doing so on a scale larger than what Osama Bin Laden had acquired in the mountains of Afghanistan. Notably controlling the cities of Mosul in Iraq and Raqqa in Syrian for three and a half years (2014–2017), as well as several other territories in these two countries and in Libya, the Islamic State managed to extract itself from the limits of the extreme periphery of societies to which they had long been confined. For the first time, a radical armed group demonstrably gave itself an operational territorial basis and lasting military, administrative and financial means comparable to those of a state – sustaining them for three consecutive years against a largescale international military campaign led by international and regional powers supported by local militias and armed groups. In order to take control of Iraq's second city in June 2014 and to rout Iraqi government troops almost without a fight, Islamic State fighters had to capitalize on the trust of at least part of the population. Above all, they did so by demonstrating a growing ability to relay the demands – including the separatist ones – of their potential constituency. In Iraq, this was a significant component of the Sunni population, which, as noted, had been ostracized by the central government in Baghdad since 2003. In Syria, it was some of their Syrian co-religionists – though a smaller proportion of them – since, in Syria, the Islamic State could lay no claim to a monopoly of representation of the Sunni opposition. Elsewhere in the Middle East, but also in North Africa and the Sahel, IS capitalized on the exclusion, in Mali, of the Tuareg population; in Yemen, of 'the Southerners'; in Nigeria, of 'the Northerners'; in Libya, on the defeated in the revolution of February 2011.

On the international stage this time, and on the scale of the Sunni community as a whole, the novelty brought by the Islamic State was its ability to appear as a state actor in a manner unprecedented in contemporary history. The non-state actor projected an image of an entity freed from any allegiance, whether to the West or to the Shi'a Iran. Its territorial basis enabled it to express such independence more credibly than Al Qaeda had in Afghanistan. It was this 'statehood reality' that gave the Islamic State power and appeal. The primarily Arab transnationalization out of Afghanistan, which Al Qaeda had overseen in the wake of the 9/11, attacks had been forced onto the group as a result of the Global War on Terror. Yet that wave gradually expanded, taking Al Qaeda to many regions around the world – in time birthing the notion of 'regional franchises' by the mid-to-late 2000s. Eventually, such 'franchising' was taken a step forward by the Islamic State (itself the result of the Iraq 'franchise' of Al Qaeda). Without having been formally recruited, or merely embraced by the Islamic State, the disillusioned and excluded from over eighty countries around the world came to internalize that imaginary of exclusion, which was beaming broadcast from the Middle East. In Europe and the United States, these soon-to-be-known as 'foreign fighters' spontaneously provided the demand for the supply of *jihad* to the Islamic State and onto its bases in Iraq and Syria. Several factors opened the door to such new modes of globalization. In particular, the organization's transformation from *tandheem* (planning) to *nidhaam* (system or regime), as Abu Musa'b al Suri (Mustapha Setmariam Nasser) had advocated in his 2004 book *Da'wat al Muqawama al Islamiyya al 'Alamiyya* (The Global Islamic Resistance Call). Next, IS' development of its networks from direct territorial expansion (as Al Qaeda had moved from Afghanistan to Iraq) to a system of more or less institutionalized regional franchises (such as Al Qaeda in the Islamic Maghreb, AQIM, and Al Qaeda in the Arabian Peninsula, AQAP). Finally, the organization could count on several group's collective allegiance – and later even spontaneous individual allegiance through the self-recruitment practices of foreign disciples acting on their own initiative.

A revolution can conceal another. Moreover, an uprising can parasite an earlier one, and confiscate its visibility if not its meaning. This was, in many ways, the case of the encounter between the Syrian national revolt and another protest dynamic that was simultaneously national, regional and global, namely the one sparked by the radical component of the Iraqi Sunni political field when it joined with the remnants of the losers from the fall of Saddam Hussein's regime. In Syria, the jihadis who chose to join the ranks of their fellowmen come from Iraq were the product of the 'bidding' call the Iraqi group had put out. These new militants were also the product of a series of Syrian-specific variables. As far as the Syrian nationals among them were concerned, they could also be considered as outcasts from the institutionalization of a national opposition that had been unable to mount effective unity, and which was gradually cut loose by its main foreign patrons. As for the foreigners in the Islamic State, these appear more broadly as the disillusioned/excluded of the political stage in the rest of the world. These 'angry Sunnis' or 'jihadis without borders' primarily came from the Arab world. In particular, they came from Tunisia, Libya, Morocco and Egypt, where the openings of the Arab Spring had been left unfinished or cut short brutally with Western assent – leaving behind significant spaces for political contestation and significant frustrations. They also came from a number of theatres in Asia. The Chechen victims of Russia and, in lesser numbers, the Uighur victims of China brought to Syria their dreams of revenge on their respective repressive states. Finally, these militants also came from the United States and, more often still, from Western Europe and from France in particular.

These fighters from the four corners of the globe gave in to the temptation of *hijra* (migration) to a territory where they hoped to freely live all the requirements of their religiosity. Their struggle to establish this ideal 'Sunnistan' seemed all the more inevitable to them that no state in the region had historically accepted such a role. Instead, all of these states, from Egypt to Jordan, periodically expelled European Muslims who travelled to these lands in search of religious identity. The flight to Syria of these North American and European citizens pointed as well the failure of so-called 'integration' policies in a wide range of Western countries. Such was the case in France where the system that radicalized a group of individuals (some 2,000) was not, as is often argued, economic or social. Nor was it even religious. Rather, the trigger to the radicalization of these individuals was primarily political. The malaise of very many Muslims, both young and not-so-young, does not merely take us back to the very real difficulties that youth from the hard-scrabble housing projects of the urban periphery encounter in entering the labour market – much less to their purported 'misinterpretation' of Islamic doctrine. And this includes those who distance themselves radically from such age-old ways of 'breaking with society'.

The analysis that this malaise requires is a rather ordinarily political one. The table at which the French model of coexistence is served is terribly wobbly. It is so because the Muslim 'leg' of the table is kept too short to play its levelling role with any efficacy. On the one hand, the political representation of Muslims is far from being satisfactory. But neither is their day-to-day ability to share with their compatriots, in the French media, their desires, their pains, their impatience and, where relevant, their moods. On a daily basis, Muslims in France come up against other interlocutors' arrogant and hegemonic control over public speech. In a first stage, potential future jihadis endure as an intolerable humiliation the fact of watching themselves represented by pre-fabricated Muslim elites in which they do not recognize themselves in the slightest. The Islam preached by these 'Muftis of the Republic' is deemed 'moderate' only from exactly the point it stops playing its designated role – namely, to air some or all of the political and social frustrations of Muslims in France faced with the deep dysfunctions of a system which they feel rejects them.

Jihadism of a few, or selfishness of many?

In France, the socio-political blind spots of the country's policies towards its Muslim citizens have been reflected – if not perpetuated – by academia taking on the question of 'radicalization' and 'violent extremism'. As Mohammad-Mahmoud Ould Mohamedou put it,

> In France, where you can no longer totally be 'a free man' (the country is under open-ended state of emergency since November 2015), ... the contemporary transnationalization of political violence is, according to local media, summed-up in the straightforward opposition between two local intellectual schools of thought: ... In this corner, an argument about 'the Islamization of radicalism', and, on the other side, an alternative view on 'the radicalization of Islam'. Pick your favourite (or disliked), fit the facts (or rationalize them), draft a policy (ever so quickly) and move on to relate any new development (however dissonant) to it.[17]

The French dualism denounced by Mohamedou and others tends towards reducing the variables of *jihadi* commitment to individual processes. Such construct therefore limits, indeed conceals, the fundamental variable of the interactions between these individual processes and the social and political dynamics of the environments in which they develop.

To those who defend the primacy of the religious variable, individual enrolment in the transnational networks of Salafi-jihadism constitutes an almost autonomous explanatory matrix. Within this universe of systematized action and thought, men and ideas are purported to circulate in a vacuum with no significant interaction with the current social and political dynamics in the societies they originate from. It is in this sense that, according to this approach, which is more or less based on received wisdom, the only parties responsible for anti-Western violence must be those ... who commit it. That approach follows in the footsteps of the 'simplicity' of the American neo-conservative thesis associated with Bernard Lewis in particular.[18] Since the dynamics of paths towards violence cannot be political, argues Lewis and others, they must therefore be purely ideological or, in this case, religious. Importantly, the policies of states targeted by violence are therefore exonerated from any part in producing such violence – a violence whose roots are deemed to be as strictly one-sided as they are purely ideological. With the greatest meticulousness, Gilles Kepel thus charts intellectual and territorial genealogies that connect Muslim conservatism to political violence, precisely locating these in space. Here, from Sayyid Qutb to Ayman al Zawahiri and from Abdessalam Faraj to Abu Musa'b al-Suri, the *jihadi* revolt is presented as having been conceived, theorized and initiated by but a few individuals. This tendency leads to a highly reductive individualization of dynamics that are, in fact, largely collective ones. To this is added a 'spatialization of trajectories' with radicalization purported to have passed through a particular individual or militant then through another and to another country. Jihadism transitions, in Kepel's account, through a given neighbourhood in a given (e.g., Belgian) town – and even (due to lack of soundproofing surely) from the fourth to the third floor of a French prison ... And it is transmitted through a technological medium (the Internet, social media, Al Jazeera and so on). When those who more-or-less-consciously minimize accounting for the political causes of radicalization take into account its human and technological *carriers,* then, the result can only be to limit the understanding of the issue as a whole. The carriers, mediators and ancillaries of a protest movement are turned into its ... causes – and so the 'how' overrides the 'why'.

Beyond its methodological shortcuts, this approach, which eschews the questions of stateness or lack thereof at the core of political Islam, focuses near-exclusively on the religious variable and suffers from the same culturalist and one-sided bias that plagued the Global War on Terror. In the wake of the US response to the 9/11 attacks, this perspective had proved unable to explore any register except that of 'hard power', from the carpet-bombing of Afghanistan to the human rights violations of the Patriot Act on US soil and onwards. Briefly, a cultural component to the US response appeared to constitute an alternative to this one-sided dominion of brute force. A publicized 'Dialogue of Civilisations' proved to be a mere monologue of culturalist injunctions aimed at reforming only one of the relevant cultures, namely the culture of the West's Muslim interlocutor. It remained easier to reform 'the Other' than to mount a clear-headed reflection concerning the true distribution of responsibilities. The eventual results of this imbalance in strategic thinking were revealing. By 2018, seventeen years after the events of 9/11, the few thousand jihadis of 2001 had increased tenfold and settled around the world.

The second thesis prevalent in the West in the early twenty-first century to account for political Islam was that of the 'Islamization of radicalism'. That view, identified in France with the work of Olivier Roy,[19] centres on the psychosocial variables of *jihadi* commitment. The political content of *jihadi* commitment is analysed as fashion in the market of radicalism. It is considered 'nihilist' and pathological, and the invoked ideologies involved are interchangeable. In order to function, Roy's paradigm requires, however, positing a break between *jihadis* and their *milieu* that is not only generational but absolute, i.e., a rupture from all other Muslims, in France and elsewhere. These few 'radicalized' jihadis are thereby purported to have cut off all ties with their family environment – an environment which, furthermore, is assumed to reject them entirely. These individuals are presumed to be free of any belief system, any commitment and any conviction liable that might be liable to tie them to their co-religionists. Given that their family and community environments are said to reject them, there is no path to explaining their development by examining the denials of all kinds that this environment may have collectively fallen victim to. In *Jihad and Death*, Roy emphasizes the argument that the disciples of the *jihadi* break are purportedly not the direct victims of violence against Muslims.[20] In no way, therefore, could their commitment be correlated to Western policies, both within European societies where this rebellion takes root or in the Middle East, and especially in the Syrian, Iraqi, Palestinian and Afghan contexts. Nor, therefore, would there be any reason to correlate the *jihadi* trend with what Roy dismisses as an 'old Third-Worldist broken record'. This, he portrays with disdain, is 'postcolonial suffering, youth identification with the Palestinian cause, their rejection of Western interventions in the Middle East or their exclusion from a racist and Islamophobic France'. Nor, he argues equally abruptly, does jihadism has anything to do with colonization since young jihadis 'did not live through it'.[21]

Insistence on the relatively high number of converts (around 25 per cent) in the ranks of Western *jihadis* has long served to support this thesis. These youth could not be said to have any relationship to the question of colonial or community suffering. Such suffering could not therefore be 'scientifically' ascribed any significant standing in the inventory of the variables that lead to radicalization. As time went on, however, more precise socio-economic data regarding converts emerged. These data all but nullified the thesis that, taking as its evidence the existence of radicalized converts, hoped to gloss over (or simply deny) the role played by processes of colonial and community exclusion. Not only did the testimonies collected – in one study by David Thomson, for instance – confirm that most converts came from the same socially deprived environments as their neo-co-religionists from Muslim backgrounds, they also showed that these converts suffered from being ostracized in a way that was highly similar, if not identical. For most of these actors, such ostracization was not only social but also, if not religious (i.e., Muslim), then at least ethnic (i.e., Arab, African, Brown, Black) – and, in every case, identity-based. 'Among converts', Thomson asserts, there exists 'a significant specific variable: They themselves come from other minorities. Jihadi converts are more often called Kevin than they are called Jean-Eudes. In general, when they are called Jean-Edouard, Jean-Michel or Willy, they are of Caribbean background. A very sizeable proportion are raised in Christian homes of Sub-Saharan background, but also Portuguese or, to a lesser degree, East Asian (Korean or Vietnamese) ones. France's overseas territories are also very strongly represented among jihadi converts', Thomson continues. 'Their ranks even feature a few members from the Roma community. These are primarily drawn from the working classes. For them too, jihadism provides an identity shield. It transforms humiliated egos – the internalising of social inferiority – into a cathartic feeling, by professing to draw a line under nationality and technical inequalities, even while it poses as the sole bearer and guarantor of Islamic Truth.'[22]

These two approaches of contemporary radical Islamism squaring with statehood have dominated Western analysis. They differ on the importance awarded to the religious variable. One of them posits it as key; the other rejects its centrality. On one issue, however, they concur: *the two schools largely isolate the jihadi trend from the socio-political processes that produce it.* To caricature, they both feature the same flaw which, despite their divergences, groups them nonetheless in identical denial: they both minimize, understate or even altogether ignore the impact of the persistence of the old North-South relations of domination on the players concerned – both in the Eastern political theatre and within Western societies. Both of them identify the itineraries, the auxiliaries and the modes in which hostility arising from the Muslim world with respect to the West is expressed. Yet they evacuate the political heart of the matter and its deep historical roots. Both approaches occupy the space in which the question 'how?' is answered, but both abandon the other, more essential question, namely the 'why?' As a result, they provide limited insight as to how the statehood project of radical Islamists has evolved over the past century.

Conclusions

The *jihadi* expression of global tensions in the early twentieth century, as illustrated by the back-to-back stories of Al Qaeda and the Islamic State, is the visible part of a political and historical iceberg denouncing failures of statehood in the Middle East and North Africa, foreign interventionism and haphazardly putting forth an alternative project of governance. That iceberg is also the growing disavowal of Europe and the United States by a large part of the rest of the world's population, deeply incensed by continuous imperialism directly inspired by its colonial basis in the region, and feeding 'extremism' and 'radicalism' far more than official narratives – and some in academe as discussed – acknowledge.

That widespread discontent is certainly less radical and less sectarian than the *jihadi* fringe itself, which indulges violence in the pursuit of its local and global projects. It is also, of course, far more important for the discussion at hand since the question of statehood speaks to wider societal dynamics and involves a plurality of groups, whether organized or not. The contemporary reductionism interpretation of 'terrorism', and even more so the response to it, must therefore go searching for its political roots where, hidden from view, they grow all too easily. In the Middle East and North Africa, this elusive search has been located at the heart of the colonial suffering and post-colonial dispossession of the countless direct and indirect victims of the foreign policies of Western societies and the repression of their states, and of both mechanisms' to stigmatize and exclude whole swaths of citizens away from a viable statehood project.

Notes

1   See Chapter Four, 'A State in Search of a Nation: The Case of Iraq' by Faleh Abdul Jabar.
2   Jeremy Keenan, *The Dark Sahara – America's War on Terror in Africa*, Chicago: University of Chicago Press, 2009.

3   Fred Halliday, *Revolution and Foreign Policy – The Case of South-Yemen 1967-1987*, Cambridge: Cambridge University Press, 1990.
4   François Burgat, *Face to Face with Political Islam*, London: I.B. Tauris, 2003.
5   Mohamed Tozy, 'La Mosquée: Lieu de Culte, de Culture et de Politique', in Camille and Yves Lacoste, eds., *L'État du Maghreb*, Paris: La Découverte, 1991.
6   See Pascal Ménoret, *Graveyards of Clerics – Everyday Activism in Saudi Arabia*, Redwood City, California: Stanford University Press, 2020.
7   See Marie-Monique Robin, *Escadrons de la Mort, l'École Française*, Paris: La Découverte, 2008.
8   See Lounis Aggoun and Jean-Baptiste Rivoire, *Francalgérie, Crimes et Mensonges d'État – Histoire Secrète, de la Guerre d'indépendance à la 'troisième Guerre' d'Algérie*, Paris: La Découverte, 2005.
9   Béatrice Hibou, *The Force of Obedience – The Political Economy of Repression in Tunisia*, London: Polity, 2011.
10 See Penny Green and Amelia Smith, 'Evicting Palestine', *State Crime Journal*, 5, 1, 2016, pp. 81–108; and Rashid Khalidi, *Iron Cage – The Story of the Palestinian Struggle for Statehood*, Boston: Beacon Press, 2007.
11 See Joy Gordon, *Invisible War – The United States and the Iraq Sanctions*, Cambridge: Cambridge University Press, 2012.
12 See Abdel Bari Atwan, *The Secret History of Al Qaeda*, Berkeley: University of California Press, 2008.
13 Peter L. Bergen, *The Osama Bin Laden I Know – An Oral History of Al Qaeda's Leader*, New York: Free Press, 2006; and Steve Coll, *The Bin Ladens – An Arabian Family in the American Century*, New York: Penguin, 2009.
14 Bruce Lawrence, *Messages to the World – The Statements of Osama Bin Laden*, London: Verso, 2005, p. 23.
15 See Mohammad-Mahmoud Ould Mohamedou, *A Theory of ISIS – Political Violence and the Transformation of the Global Order*, London: Pluto Press, 2018.
16 François Burgat and Romain Caillet, 'Une Guérilla Islamiste ? Typologie Idéologique de la Révolte Armée', in François Burgat and Bruno Paoli, eds., *Pas de Printemps pour la Syrie – Acteurs et Enjeux de la Crise, 2011–2013*, Paris: La Découverte, 2013, pp. 55–83.
17 Mohammad-Mahmoud Ould Mohamedou, 'St.-Germainising ISIS', *Le Temps*, 5 June 2016. Also see François Burgat, *Comprendre l'Islam Politique – Une Trajectoire de Recherche sur l'Alterité Islamiste, 1973-2016*, Paris: La Découverte, 2016.
18 For a discussion of Lewis' problematic views, as notably articulated in *What Went Wrong – The Clash between Islam and Modernity in the Middle East*, New York: Harper, 2003, see Adam Sabra, 'What Is Wrong with What Went Wrong?', *Middle East Research and Information Project (MERIP)*, 15 August 2003.
19 Olivier Roy, *En Quête de l'Orient Perdu*, Paris: Le Seuil, 2014.
20 Olivier Roy, *Jihad and Death – The Global Appeal of Islamic State*, London: Hurst and Company, 2016.
21 Ibid., p. 19. Roy writes: 'From that standpoint, François Burgat's "suffering" experienced by Muslims who were formerly colonized, or as victims of racism or any other form of discrimination, US bombardments, drones, Orientalism and so on would imply that the revolt is led primarily by victims. But the relationship between radicals and victims is more imaginary than real. Those who perpetrate attacks in Europe are not residents of the Gaza Strip, or Libyans, or Afghans. They are not necessarily the poorest, the most humiliated or the least integrated'.
22 David Thomson, *Les Revenants*, Paris: Le Seuil, 2016, p. 283.

9 AUTHORITARIANISM, WEAKNESS AND THE NEW GREAT GAME

Bertrand Badie

Historically, the century-long Middle Eastern and North African state-building sequence has played out amidst a dominant statehood process previously determined in Europe. The Westphalian State has long been associated with international politics of power – a set composed of interstate competition, balance of power and war. The traditional international order which emerged in Europe after the Thirty Years' War was constituted by a juxtaposition of sovereign territorial entities, which were supposed to survive through permanent mobilization of the main power resources. Military capacity was considered as the most credible attribute of a state in this international race. In such a perspective, power politics have always had three main implications: the state should be driven to accumulate more and more power resources, a state's coexistence with other states depended on a sophisticated balance of power and war appeared as the normal and inevitable result of such an accumulation. A hypothesis initially articulated by Charles Tilly in 1982 sought to account for this sequence: the state needs war for achieving its own building and war is erected as a normal and even banal practice in the international arena since war emerges as the common result of a power competition.[1]

However influential, the Westphalian matrix is not necessarily relevant in post-colonial situations such as in the Middle East and North Africa.[2] The post-colonial state emerged in a characteristically different context. Firstly, the post-colonial state generally appeared as a weak structure, that is to say provided with a weak capacity of penetration and mobilization, a low level of efficiency and legitimacy and a precarious and fragile accumulation of power resources. Secondly, the international relevance of the post-colonial state is much more bound to its weakness than to its power capacity. Thirdly, the post-colonial state is growing and developing in a context where power is clearly located outside, more precisely in what is considered as the 'centre' of the international system. Tilly's hypothesis is in fact relevant only where power is commonly shared, not where it is a rare resource. For this simple reason, it would be a dangerous preconception to consider that the post-colonial Middle Eastern and North African state needs war to reach full development, as it was mainly the case throughout European history.

Traditional power politics, the cornerstone of international relations theory, must be contrasted therefore with 'weakness politics.' The latter can be considered as much more appropriate analytically when we take the post-colonial state into account. In other words, *weakness* itself would be here more clarifying and explaining than *power*. For weakness sheds helpful light on the structure, the behaviour and the foreign policies of the post-colonial state and overall it is that aspect that seems to be the major cause of contemporary wars. Tilly's model is then reversed: war is no more caused by power, but by three main kinds of weaknesses impacting the state and its capacities, namely the nation, the social contract and the constitutive social bounds that are woven in society. Weakness politics, as we can term them, come then to appear as a substitute to power politics, and will be considered here as the primary explaining dynamic of the post-colonial situation in the Middle East and North Africa – this configuration took shape as well in sub-Saharan Africa in such a drastic way that it strongly impacted the common rules of the international system and had a feedback on the rest of the world.[3]

Weakness politics and authoritarianism

Weakness accounts primarily for the collapsing process of several post-colonial states, but it also explains their tendency to sink into endless wars. Many cases fall in this category: the Yemen in the 1960s and again in the 2010s, Libya in the 2010s and Somalia since the 1990s. These states, as well as many other Southern states, failed to achieve their regular functions, while their collapsing opened the way to lasting wars in such a manner that a 'war society' could frequently settle in place of the state.[4] Here, war comes out clearly as a first kind of competition of political weaknesses. Significantly, state weakness may also result in an authoritarian thrust: the low level of efficiency and legitimacy triggered many coup d'états after the decolonization wave which took place from the 1930s onwards (there were, for instance, no less than eleven coups in Iraq between 1936 and 1968).[5] The so-called praetorian societies, such as Iraq and Syria, were actually considered in most of the social sciences literature a consequence of low-level political institutionalization.[6]

Moreover, a strongly authoritarian state commonly results in an increasingly weaker social contract. Authoritarianism fuels vertical social relations rather than horizontal ones, boosts clientelism and prevents the constitution of organized civil societies.[7] Fragmented societies commonly face authoritarian states made of competing ethnic or religious communities, and this has been the dominant experience in the Middle and North Africa since the early twentieth century. In lieu, however, of mere state weakness – resulting from that historical sequence in the region – an additional configuration promotes a second kind of political pathology, which here can be termed *nation weakness*. Such weakness risks paving the way to civil wars, as was the case in Iraq (divided into three fighting communities, Shiites, Sunnis and Kurds), or in Syria. If a divided and divisive context of this sort does not always necessarily lead to actual war, it nonetheless invariably fuels authoritarianism – in addition to often creating conditions for minority dictatorship, like the case of the Alawis in Syria, and the Zaydis or the Sunnis in Yemen.

A third kind of weakness is to be found in the very nature of the social bond. A society in which resources are rare dismantles solidarity and creates the conditions of a social verticality and a permanent competition among people in accordance with the concept of 'state of nature', as it was classically described by Thomas Hobbes.[8] The societies which are located at the bottom of the ladder by the United Nations Development Programme (UNDP), such as Yemen, are frequently experiencing war. More generally, it is of note that, according to twenty the Human Development Index (HDI), fifteen countries have experienced war since the 1990s (Afghanistan, Burundi, Chad, Central African Republic, Guinea Bissau, Eritrea, Ethiopia, Ivory Coast, Liberia, Mali, Mozambique, Sierra Leone, South Sudan and Yemen). This kind of weakness appears close to the Durkheimian vision of a society of anomie, in which too weak social relations impede an efficient social division of labour.

Weakness politics must be considered both as a major pathology of the post-colonial era – as vividly observed in the Middle East and North Africa – as well as a dynamic of its own, which is continuously fuelling competition among states (again, per an inversion of Charles Tilly's model). These politics create a kind of 'insecurity regional system', which can be overcome only through social treatment, including a strong effort of political and social engineering. These weakness politics are first of foremost affected by a deficit of politics and of policies, which result in chronic violence – something comparable with the dynamics of coercion and violence that Tilly observed subsequently in the competition for power[9] – such as the one observed historically in the Middle East and North Africa.

The parameters of intervention

Conceived and practiced as such, weakness politics open the way to a novel understanding of the configuration of the international arena, and give special meaning to intervention – a key dimension and manifestation that has chronically impacted the state-building process of Middle Eastern and North African states.[10] Under the Westphalian system, intervention was looked upon principally as a (temporary) suspension of the sovereignty principle, which was at that time the cornerstone of the international order, both legally and politically. In the Westphalian context, sovereignty was more specifically a step developed out of earlier principles: imperial arguments (when the Holy Roman Germanic and then the Habsburg empires intervened in the domestic affairs of European kingdoms), dynastic arguments (wars of succession) and religious arguments (the Crusades and the European wars of religion). The issue of sovereignty subsequently played amidst dynastic conservatism and political stability during the Concert of Powers in Europe after the Vienna Congress (1815), when French King Louis XVIII was urged to send 'one hundred thousand sons of St-Louis' to Cadiz, Spain to fight the Spanish liberal revolution, or when Austrian Foreign Minister Klemens Von Metternich intervened in Piedmont and Naples, Italy against the liberal and nationalist movements there in the 1820s. The legitimization of this kind of intervention was then constructed in terms of 'stability and peace': a domestic movement should be handled by the informal international community as it jeopardized the international order; sovereignty was, for the first time, contained by a stronger principle which related to a potential global order.[11] This is probably the starting point and the founding principle of the long history of Western interventionism in the Middle East and North Africa (and in other Southern countries), which spanned the period from the nineteenth century to the twenty-first one.

The post-Westphalian sequence was partly conceived on the same 'international order' basis: that configuration came up with a 'collective responsibility' principle for maintaining peace and stability in the world. That principle could lead to using force for 'restoring peace and security' where they are deemed to be in threat. In time, this orientation would appear as the major point of Chapter VII of the United Nations Charter. However, important differences should be taken into account in the contemporary context. Firstly, the 'threatened peace' is no more considered as a regional one but rather as an international one affecting countries that are not located inside the same regional complex of security. Secondly, intervention is by now targeting sovereign states rather than backing a threatened conservative order as it was previously the case. Thirdly, the intervening powers have from now on face weakness politics, which are hardly compatible with their own tradition of power politics.

The first difference led to amend the legitimization of this new wave of interventions as 'international order' had to be substituted to 'regional order'. The intervening powers had then to claim and even conjure up a 'global responsibility' or a 'special responsibility'. The first one is universal and creates a new category of powers designated as 'hegemons' or 'stabilizers'.[12] The concept of 'responsibility' was then coined as symmetric to sovereignty,[13] even if the latter's real meaning has never been clear (Who has responsibility? Decided by whom? According to which criteria? Who is able to monitor?). If responsibility is not conceived as 'global', it is rather frequently defined as 'special'. The argument has mostly been used by intervening powers in the Middle East and North Africa, or in Africa generally, as a *historical legacy*. Commonly bound to the colonial past, this old imperial argument is then recycled, rehearsing a colonial past with a view to justifying new practices.[14]

The second difference paved the way to the adventure of the famous new concept of 'failing state' or 'collapsing state'.[15] The argument was ingeniously displayed: sovereignty is really violated only if the concerned state is *still sovereign*. If the state is no more able to achieve its main sovereign functions (e.g. Libya in 2011), it cannot be considered any more as … sovereign, and intervention should not be then conceived as being in conflict with international law. Let us keep in mind that this new vision of the collapsed state was elaborated before the 1992–3 US intervention in Somalia and the Restore Hope operation. In point of fact, this perspective opened the way to a subjective vision of sovereignty which is no more an attribute of any state but an assessment made by the strongest states on the real rights of the weakest ones. Weakness is thus captured as an argument by the traditional power politics. For instance, the US-backed Saudi intervention in Yemen in March 2015 was considered as legitimate – even legal – mainly because the Yemeni State headed by Abd Rabbo Mansour Hadi was collapsing.[16]

Such a theoretical arrangement gives a crucial importance to the third difference, namely the contrast between *power politics* and *weakness politics*, resulting in a new context fraught with uncertainties. Firstly, it is not at all clear whether power and military forces coming from abroad are able to overcome a situation created by local weakness politics in the Middle East and North Africa. Secondly, using traditional power and military instruments adds to the existing conflict an additional war, which is strictly an interstate one. This graft brings back the nationalist reference and reconstructs the intervening army as a potential enemy, even if the target is limited to containing violence and keeping peace. This was the case experienced by American military operation in Somalia in 1992–3. Several instances can be found, notably in Iraq after 2003, supporting Robert Pape's thesis that suicide attacks became more frequent in reaction to foreign intervention.[17] Thirdly, this situation sets a crucial question which has never been really taken into account: Is a foreign power able to appropriate the (domestic) war of the others? Seen in this way, the 'perennial' conflicts of the Middle East and North Africa emerge as more often than not linked 'organically' to the problematic practice of interventionism (e.g. Egypt in 1956, Iraq in 1991, Iraq in 2003, Libya in 2011 and Syria in 2014).

In contradistinction, Western countries fought each other for many centuries in their own arena. They did not experience the foreign interventionism they have historically projected, and continue to subject others to. The Western culture of war comes from a long experience during which Europe was the self-contained battlefield of the world. Nowadays, the Old Continent has become a marginal battlefield in the international system, while the new international conflicts spring from a vast area spreading from Western Sahel to the Congo Basin to the South and Pamir Mountains at the East, with the Middle East and North Africa located squarely at the centre of this arc. The social nature of the conflictual issues which are at stake is hardly compatible with the military targets that are shaped by the intervening powers: the Clausewitzian vision of war is thus challenged and even possibly removed from 'the great game.'[18]

These layered complexities explain why the post-Westphalian interventions rarely achieve their goals. Specifically, some of them resulted in clear *military* defeats as was the case in Somalia in 1992–1993, Afghanistan and Iraq since 2003. Most other interventions resulted in a *political* defeat, as was the case in Libya since 2011 and Yemen since 2014. Even worse, many foreign interventions reinvigorated local fighters (as was the case in Iraq, Libya or Afghanistan in the 2010s), so much so that the combatting parties are generally expecting a foreign intervention and even try to provoke it (as the Islamic State's strategy in the Levant showed when the group publicly executed American journalist James Foley in August 2014). Earlier, the leader of Al Qaeda in Iraq, Abu Mus'ab al Zarqawi, had welcomed the 2003 American intervention in Iraq as 'divine grace.'

The further complexity of this new situation can be appreciated through the sophisticated process by which the so-called 'international community' defined its role and met this challenge. Interventionism has always been assessed in a balanced way. Grotius himself considered, at the beginning of the seventeenth century, that punishing a prince of another kingdom was sometimes necessary but would also dangerously affect his own people: this risk was considered as high enough for making the intervention as exceptional as possible.[19] Two centuries later, John Stuart Mill took opposite arguments into consideration: on behalf of his liberal considerations, he strove to distinguish between the respect of sovereignty which led him to contain all kinds of intervention and humanitarian considerations, which should urge neighbouring states to intervene in a conflict. His conclusion was to restrict intervention to but a few cases which should be proportional to the risk incurred by the population.[20] With regular concerns about 'impact on civilians' and 'collateral damage' in contemporary armed conflicts in the Middle East and North Africa, this proportionality aspect emerges as a constant feature, albeit an ambiguous and oft-instrumentalized one.

Nothing really new happened in the post-Westphalian context as regards interventionism. The debate is still structured around the traditional opposition between humanitarian goals and the sovereignty principle. The 'right to interference' (*droit d'ingérence*), as it was debated, in December 1988, by the United Nations General Assembly (UNGA), is still based on the failing capacity of the sovereign to protect his citizens, while the report on 'the responsibility to protect' (R2P), which was elaborated in 2001 by the International Commission on Intervention and State Sovereignty (ICCS) commission, chaired by Gareth Evans and Mohamed Sahnoun, restricted the practice by referring to the same set of criteria (proportionality, exception and use of prevention).[21] In the same balanced way, the UNGA specified, as early as 1970, in Resolution 2725, that all kinds of interference were banned against a state which would respect international law, democratic principles and human rights. With such reading, the UNGA was offering a restrictive formulation of intervention.

Yet if intervention is officially banned, everything has been actually conceived to render it possible as an attribute of power politics. UNSC resolutions opened the way for power interventions (e.g. Resolution 678 in November 1990 on Kuwait, Resolution 1973 in March 2011 on Libya), and *a posteriori* UNSC resolutions legitimized on several occasions a unilateral intervention (Resolution 1386 in December 2001 on Afghanistan; Resolution 1483, Resolution 1511 and Resolution 1546 on Iraq in, respectively, May 2003, October 2003 and June 2004). Additionally, tacit agreements were repeatedly given informally on a 'tutorship' role played by a given regional power, as it was the case with Saudi Arabia in Bahrain in March 2011 at the height of the Arab Spring, and later in Yemen in March 2015, or with Iran during the Shah era in the Dhofar in 1973–1975,[22] and indeed with the Syrian intervention in Lebanon in 1976. Such interventionism has three consequences impacting the traditional conception of the state. First, a potential intervention is a source of fragility for all political systems in which it is supposed to be promoted, acutely so for those in the making. As such, importantly, intervention appears as a sword of Damocles hanging over all countries of the Middle East and North Africa (including when they embrace the practice). Intervention is a marker of these states' fragility and their unachieved legitimacy. In that respect, and combined with their weakness, intervention is at once a source of a growing dependence on old and former colonial powers and a new factor of authoritarianism – with Iraq post-2003 as a vivid illustration. Whether the Western powers choose to depose Saddam Hussain in Iraq in 2003, abandon Hosni Mubarak in Egypt in 2011, remove Muammar Gaddafi in Libya in 2011, protect Hamad bin Isa al Khalifa in Bahrain in 2011 or keep Bashar al Assad in power in Syria in 2016, their actions partake of the same interventionist logic dominating the politics of the region for the past century. Under the same logic, for instance, the US military had been mobilized in June 1958 to save the pro-Western Lebanese President, Camille Chamoun. Time and again, sovereignty in the Middle East and North Africa has systemically and systematically resulted from an articulation of weakness politics, orchestrated from above and from afar.

To be certain, many politically threatened leaders around the world had called on their protective power, notably in Africa, where France has intervened some forty-five times since 1960. Yet, when it comes to the Middle East and North Africa, such regularly replayed pattern is clearly a factor of external direct unceasing influence but also of domestic authoritarianism. Western intervention in the region has comforted the protected dictator in the idea that fraud and illegal operations are permitted and could be pursued in impunity (until such time, that is, that the protector comes to regard the matter otherwise).[23] Yet for all its despot-protective aspect, intervention ultimately weakens the legitimacy of the leader and deepens the gap between the ruler and the society. Contributing to a normalization of the use of force in politics, it establishes the conviction that the real sovereignty is abroad. Such a scheme clearly moves the national sovereignty from inside to outside and shakes the main international law principles up. For these reasons, sovereignty appears, more than ever, as a form of organized political and security hypocrisy.[24] Even if they are not considered 'failed' or 'collapsed', all those entities which are concerned appear clearly as 'artificial states', in which there are no real political deliberations and where political decisions are taken elsewhere. Per this model, US President George W. Bush set up the political and institutional calendar of Iraq in a speech delivered on 24 May 2004 without regard for the Iraqi Coalition Provisional Authority (an entity he had himself created). A few months later, said calendar and structure were 'confirmed' from London by British Prime Minister Tony Blair on 20 September.

Finally, this type of 'power' intervention so prevalent in the state-building history of the Middle East and North Africa has yielded a vicious circle per which any breach of the sovereignty rule strengthens and makes common the use of political violence, which then in turn renders banal any kind of authoritarian practices. The graft of new international practices on weak states pushes them into the configuration of 'succession war societies': Iraq *after* Saddam Hussein, Libya *after* Muammar Gaddafi and Yemen *after* Ali Abdallah Salah are the prototypes of these intervened-upon war societies reeling from the aftermath of a fallen authoritarian system. They become societies with lasting conflicts, in which political, economic, social functions are from thereon achieved by war, warriors and warlords,[25] creating 'grey zones' inside the international arena as well as unrecognized political powers, and many kinds of informal and deviant transnational relations.

The new Great Game

For all its deeper history, intervention is nowadays a new parameter of international relations. Foreign interventionism has impacted the nations of the Middle East and North Africa lastingly, and it continues to shape their state-building process. More importantly, intervention is no longer a marginal action as it was during the bipolar system of the Cold War, and even earlier since the beginning of the nineteenth century.[26] As the battlefield of the world has now moved from the North to the South, intervention into neighbouring areas and external conflicts has become the primary way by which old powers participate in conflicts. Whether active or passive, this participation shapes the new military strategy of the main state actors of the world. and it is, arguably, the single most consequential determinant of the geopolitics of the Middle Eastern and North African states. However, this strategy remains obscure and sometimes contradictory as it has to answer three perilous questions: Who is supposed to intervene? How? For which purpose? The answers to these questions are conditioned by the state of the international system, by the nature of regional security and by the history and trajectory of the Middle Eastern and North African states themselves.

The international system and international law could have organized intervention as the 1945 United Nations Charter had done, establishing legal provisions for achieving a multi-national action on behalf of the international community in order to restore peace and a collective security (Article 27 and Article 43 of the UN Charter). However, the Cold War durably neutralized these provisions, and particularly the United Nations Military Staff Committee (Article

47), which was provided for this purpose but which was promptly deprived of any real capacity. The United Nations was no longer able to have a real army, while military instruments remained under the control of each state; that is to say mainly under the control of great powers. Henceforth, as the states of the Maghreb and the Mashreq were going through the throes of decolonization, they were doing so amidst a post-1945 world arguably made of gendarmes deprived of a gendarmerie. The international system failed to give legitimacy, legality and organization to intervention and thus inevitably boosted the resurgence of power competition. It was therefore merely a matter of time before the newly emancipated states of the region met anew with the military might they had thought they were escaping lastingly – and indeed had fought during the decolonization wars.

A gendarme without gendarmerie is indeed precisely who is managing the international order, according priority to his own interest without necessarily having regard for legality. In the Middle East in particular, the American superpower increasingly played a hegemonic role by conceiving of its own interventions either as a global strategy (e.g. the Global War on Terror) or as a regional option for protecting its own security. Starting in the 1990s and accelerating in the 2000s after the 11 September 2001 attacks, the Neo-Cons largely used the first option as an instrument for a global 'regime change' strategy, particularly in, 2004, what they called the 'Greater Middle East.' Before and after, they resorted to the second regional option as merely an adjustment variable for protecting their own national interests in the Middle East and other parts of the world. This then is the main feature of the contemporary intervention, namely *adding a global stake to a domestic crisis*, and the Middle Eastern and North African state-in-the-making was directly impacted by such strategy and practice. A local conflict is turned into a 'glocal' conflict in which a unique solution is no more possible, as the international new parameters are different and independent from the real origins of the conflict. Along the Westphalian wars, there was clearly a continuum in the dynamic of the conflict, all the participating actors being committed to the same rationality. An intervention from abroad creates several levels of rationality which is completely blurring the game and makes all the more difficult the conflict-solving process. For instance, in the case of the Western interventions in Northern Syria or Northern Iraq throughout the 2010s, the Islamic State (IS) was pointed as the main enemy, while Iran was locally opposed to IS but globally opposed to the Western coalition. Saudi Arabia was allied to the Western world but was locally close to radical Islamist movements. The United States and Russia would be logically allied against the Islamic State, but were in fact international rivals. Turkey and the Western countries were common members of NATO, but in a situation of local competition in the Near East. Such conflicts of rationalities appear as common in all kinds of intervention decided from abroad. The contentions which are at stake do not spring from the same game according to whether the actor is a local one or an international power, and this has long stood in the way of viable statehood in the Middle East and North Africa.

As a result of this new-old Great Game, the conflicts change in nature, function and dimension, while the local actors are marginalized and dependent on powerful external forces. A case in point was the intervention in Libya in 2011, which experienced major transformations. As it was handled by the Western permanent members of the UN Security Council, it was promptly turned into a NATO initiative which clearly modified the real meaning of the 1973 UNSC resolution. The intervention was incorporated within the NATO agenda. The priorities inevitably changed in a way that placed the local actors under the dependence of the intervening powers or, on the contrary, run the risk of boosting their autonomy up to creating a second and more radical conflict. The same logic prompted the three Western powers to change the agenda and even to exceed the UNSC mandate by putting the regime change and the toppling of Gaddafi as the real final goals of the operation, as it was clearly claimed in the conference held on 15 April 2011 by UK Prime Minister David Cameron, US President Barack Obama and French President Nicolas Sarkozy. The second option prevailed and is probably at the origin of the subsequent inextricable and lasting Libyan war. On the contrary, the NATO intervention in Afghanistan under the International Security Assistance Force (ISAF) flag placed the Hamid Karzai Afghan government under Western dependence, limited its legitimacy and its popular support. Inevitably, and per the larger historical pattern in the region, the intervention weakened the new government's governance capacity and eventually fuelled its authoritarianism and its corruption.

As a result of this evolution, intervention has acquired in the early twenty-first century a central position in enabling the old (colonial and imperial) power foreign policies. It is through intervention that Russia has in the 2010s pursued the restoration of its earlier capacity and role as superpower in the international arena. Intervention in Ukraine and especially Syria (as well as forays in Libya in 2020) has been instrumentalized for this purpose. The same practice was at the core of the Neo-Cons strategy during the George W. Bush presidency, while its rejection was among the major attributes of Barack H. Obama's foreign policy. Indeed, Obama was self-critical of his own initiative in Libya.[27] President Sarkozy and his successor François Hollande both singled out Europe by resorting frequently to intervention, particularly when the British foreign policy started standing away from it (in August 2013, the British parliament voted against authorizing military action in Syria).

Intervention has become a shaper of local conflicts, and equally of inter-power rivalry. Yet none of the interventions that took place has been conclusive. A typology would distinguish four kinds of results: extending the original conflict, consolidating the *status quo ante*, displacing the conflict, and stopping or blocking an initiative for change. The first 'extension' case is probably the most frequent and corresponds to the operations led in Iraq or in Libya, which opened to new battlefields which spilled over national borders lines spreading to neighbouring countries (Syria and Sahel, respectively) – just as the US intervention in Vietnam had overflown into Cambodia and Laos. The 'consolidation' type is to be found in Somalia (1993) and in Afghanistan (1979 and 2001). In both cases, a great power intervention could bring new life and nationalist legitimacy to embattled local actors who suddenly appear as resisting foreign invasion (whether driven by ideology, culture or religion). Afghan mujahideen facing USSR army circa 1979, Taliban opposed to NATO in 2001 or Somali fighters battling American GIs in 2004 all benefitted from this configuration. In Somalia, the Islamic Court Union (ICU) precisely received such support when it called for jihad against the Ethiopian intervention in 2006. The third type of intervention is akin to letting a cat loose amongst pigeons. The disruptive nature of contemporary intervention, as witnessed in the Middle East and North Africa, is importantly driven by the fluidity of the new wars. The Westphalian wars were essentially related to a national territory, which was supposed to be defended, while territory is nowadays a precarious instrument that can be abandoned for relaunching the conflict elsewhere. Many cases illustrate such mobility, notably in the Levant, in Afghanistan and in the Sahel. The 2013–14 French interventions in Mali (Serval and Barkhane) opened a very large area of instability which gained ground when regular armies swept in as violence entrepreneurs. Earlier since 2001, NATO's intervention in Afghanistan had boosted the same kind of extension towards Pakistan, through Waziristan in 2004 and Buner district, near Islamabad, in 2006 (as a consequence of the Medusa operation). In Syria and Iraq, the same dynamic was in full effect during the 2010s and into the 2020s.

The last type of intervention refers to apparent military prowess which actually functions as window-dressing. The military capacity of the intervening old powers creates, in an initial moment of intervention, the illusion of a victory: Saddam Hussein was defeated in three weeks when the United States invaded Iraq in March 2003. The radical Islamists who had occupied Northern Mali were pushed back towards the Algerian desert within weeks by the French army in January 2013. Muammar Gaddafi's forces in Libya were prevented from entering the city of Benghazi, which they were poised to devastate, in a mere few days, and Gaddafi was forced to flee before being captured within months. The Aden airport in Yemen was taken back by the Saudi military from the rebellious Houthi militias in few hours just after the Saudis had set up their Decisive Storm (*'Asifat al Hazm*) operation in March 2015. However, none of these military operations could result in a political victory – just as the French army won the battle of Algiers in 1957 against the Algerian Front de Liberation National (FLN) but lost the war. Either the military defeat was converted by the rebels into a political success, as it was clearly the case of the Algerian war, or, more frequently, the ability to transform a military success into a political benefit for the powerful was not possible. In that respect, war has lost its Clausewitzian meaning. A military victory does not have a real political extension: instead of being a political instrument, war has become a way of comforting authority or consolidating legitimacy. War appears as a kind of socialization and a mode of spreading (new) values. As a fruitful opportunity, internationalized local conflicts are wished for by violence entrepreneurs who do their best to attract foreign actors into the game, especially if these actors are imperial and culturally different from the affected people. The classical war zero-sum game does not work anymore: the apparent victory of the most powerful does not imply the defeat of the weakest one, but the losses and the costs endured by the strongest remain just the same.

This new configuration has a strong impact on the political systems in the Middle East and North Africa which are affected by the intervention process. Three main consequences can be noted. Firstly, intervention creates a new arena of interactions within the political system in which it takes place. This arena is characterized by regression of sovereignty and an appropriation of the main functions which are commonly attributed to the local state. The state is then weakened, and it loses parts of its attributes, principally legitimacy and social anchoring. This was the case for the successive Iraqi governments, those of Iyad Alawi (2004–5) and Haidar Al Abadi (2014–18) notably, and for the Hamid Karzai (2001–14) and then Ashraf Ghani (b. 2014) presidencies in Afghanistan. Western – essentially American – interferences for managing the relationship between Syrian or Iraqi partners have had the same impact, worsening the conditions of a functional nation-building process. This 'semi-sovereignty' reduces the sovereign choices of the affected state and submits them to the intervening power, thus making more difficult a national agreement and then a national contract. Such *constrained sovereignty and limited statehood* emerge then as a historical hybrid system determining the political pathologies generated by regular Western military intervention in the Middle East and North Africa. Further, confined sovereignty becomes a way of reconfiguring nascent or reconstructed political systems through politically modulated elections, as seen in Iraq, Afghanistan and Mali (Libya would have been in line with this post-intervention election process, but the attempt failed). In Afghanistan, Hamid Karzai was elected president in October 2004 as the candidate clearly backed by the intervening power. He was supported by the Neo-Cons, and his election was marred by widespread fraud. The first Iraqi parliamentary election took place in January 2005; it was largely boycotted by the Sunni community with a turnout of 2 per cent in the Sunni province of Al Anbar. In Mali, the date of the national election itself was decided by the French president. Intervention is commonly associated with truncated elections, which delay or impede national reconstruction.

Conclusions

Intervention, elusive statehood and authoritarianism interact in a vicious circle in early-twenty-first century Middle East and North Africa. These three elements can be analysed as both the causes and the consequences of the same interweaved political phenomenon. Intervention weakens state capacity, lowers its legitimacy, delays the national social contract, exacerbates community tensions and then enables authoritarian practices. The elusive nature of the Middle Eastern and North

African state fosters and prompts intervention, which in turn becomes appealing for local rulers who look upon it as a way to fortify the authoritarian orientation of their policy. Authoritarianism encourages the use of force and the yearning for a 'strongman powerful protector,' while it delays the institutionalization of the state and cancels out its democratic order. In the final analysis, intervention can be considered as a most problematic feature of the authoritarian nature of the regimes in the region, as well as a consequence of the weakness of the state apparati. Both of these characteristics encourage the international clientelization of these states and downgrade the role of the local actors while they do not give priority to national integration. For all these reasons, intervention has stood and continues to stand in the way of the establishment of viable and lasting Middle Eastern and North African states properly and legitimately integrated into the international system.

Notes

1 Charles Tilly, 'War Making and State Making as Organised Crime', in Peter Evans, Dietrich Rueschemeyer and Theda Skocpol, eds., *Bringing the State Back In*, New York: Cambridge University Press, 1985, pp. 170–1. The original version was published in February 1982 as a working paper (no. 256) for the Center for Research on Social Organization at the University of Michigan.
2 Mohammad-Mahmoud Ould Mohamedou, 'In Search of the Non-Western State: Historicising and De-Westphalianising Statehood', in Bertrand Badie, Dirk Berg-Schlosser and Leonardo Morlino, eds., *The SAGE Handbook of Political Science – A Global Perspective*, London: Sage, 2020, pp. 1335–48.
3 On weakness politics, see Badie Bertrand, 'Toward a Theory of Weakness Politics: Does Weakness rule the World?', *Global Society*, 32, 2, 2018, pp. 139–48.
4 On war societies, see Bertrand Badie, *Nous ne Sommes Plus Seuls au Monde*, Paris: La Découverte, 2016.
5 See Mohammad-Mahmoud Ould Mohamedou, *Iraq and the Second Gulf War – State-Building and Regime Security*, San Francisco: Austin and Winfield, 1998, p. 98.
6 This perspective was first elaborated by Samuel Huntington in *Political Order in Changing Society*, New Haven: Yale University Press, 1968.
7 As it was pointed out by Edward Banfield. See his *Moral Basis of a Backward Society*, Glencoe, Illinois: The Free Press, 1958.
8 Thomas Hobbes, *Leviathan*, Oxford: Oxford University Press, 2012 [1651].
9 Charles Tilly, *Capital, Coercion and European States AD 990-1992*, New York: Wiley, 1993.
10 See, for instance, Jeremy Salt, *The Unmaking of the Middle East – A History of Western Disorder in Arab Lands*, Berkeley, California: University of California Press, 2009.
11 See Francis Deng et al., *Sovereignty as Responsibility – Conflict Management in Africa*, Washington, DC: Brookings Institution Press, 1996.
12 Charles Kindleberger, *The World in Depression, 1929–1939*, Berkeley, California: University of California Press, 1973.
13 John Stuart Mill, *A Few Words on Non-intervention*, 1859. Also see, Michael W. Doyle, *The Question of Intervention – John Stuart Mill and the Responsibility to Protect*, New Haven, Connecticut: Yale University Press, 2015.

14 See Derek Gregory, *The Colonial Present – Afghanistan, Palestine, Iraq*, New York: Wiley, 2004.
15 William Zartman, *Collapsed States – The Disintegration and Restoration of Legitimate Authority*, Denver, Colorado: Lynne Rienner Publishers, 1995.
16 See Helen Lackner, *Yemen in Crisis – Autocracy, Neoliberalism and the Disintegration of a State*, London: Saqi Books, 2017.
17 Robert Pape, *Dying to Win – The Strategic Logic of Suicide Terrorism*, New York: Random House, 2006. Also see the follow-up work Robert Paper and James K. Feldman, eds. *Cutting the Fuse – The Explosion of Global Suicide Terrorism and How to Stop It*, Chicago: University of Chicago Press, 2010.
18 Carl Von Clausewitz, *On War*, New York: Random House, 1943 [1832].
19 Hugo Grotius, *On the Law of War and Peace*, Cambridge: Cambridge University Press, 2012 [1625].
20 Mill, *A Few Words on Non-intervention*.
21 Report of the International Commission on Intervention and State Sovereignty (ICISS), *The Responsibility to Protect*, Ottawa: International Development Centre, 2001.
22 See James Worrall, *State-Building and Counter-Insurgency in Oman – Political, Military, and Diplomatic Relations at the End of Empire*, London: Bloomsbury, 2018.
23 See Brian Klaas, *The Despot's Accomplice – How the West Is Aiding and Abetting the Decline of Democracy*, Oxford: Oxford University Press, 2016.
24 To borrow the metaphor from Steven Krasner, *Sovereignty – Organised Hypocrisy*, Princeton, New Jersey: Princeton University Press, 2000.
25 On warlords, see, Notably, William Reno, *Warlords Politics and African States*, Boulder, Colorado: Lynne Rienner, 1999; and Romain Malejacq, 'Warlords, Intervention and State Consolidation: A Typology of Political Orders in Failed and Failing States', *Security Studies*, 25, 1, 2016, pp. 85–110.
26 See Davide Rodogno, *Against Massacre – Humanitarian Interventions in the Ottoman Empire, 1815–1914*, Princeton, New Jersey: Princeton University Press, 2011.
27 See Jeffrey Goldberg, 'The Obama Doctrine', *The Atlantic*, April 2016.

10 LONGING FOR THE STATE, MISTRUSTING THE STATE

Ghassan Salamé

Whether or not we do it consciously, we generally talk about the state – in the Middle and North Africa, and elsewhere – while having in the back of our minds the legal structure that has gradually emerged throughout centuries in the European historical experience. Such explicit or implicit discourse references a given European trajectory, which Joseph Strayer had captured in 1970 in a seminal work.[1] Strayer had argued that the state is a concept that emerged in Europe towards the early second millennium, and ever since underwent subsequent stages of progression and regression until it cemented in its current form in the sixteenth century. According to this line of thinking, the state is a stand-alone, man-made construct that governs intra-community relations and protects them against the fear that emanates from the state of *omnium contra omnes* (all against all), which Thomas Hobbes later addressed in detail.[2] The emergence of the state allows every person with no family or religious affiliation to lead a full life, argued Hobbes, since human resources have been centralized to the interest of the state in a manner that pushed all other social structures aside. In its essence, the state is a conception that principally grows in the hearts and minds of the citizenry. If they attain no such belief in its being, it shall not be. Understood this way, the state becomes part of other constructs such as religion, which presume the existence of transcendent entities that positively contribute to steering realities, or such as limited liability companies, which are man-constructed entities that equally imply an imagined, self-standing entity independent from the will of its human authors. Thus emerges *the sense of longing for the state*: it is the yearning for an external force powered by self-propulsion; a force that manages to free itself from the influence of the human groups that gave rise to it, and which can protect individuals within its geographic realm from each other or against the aggression of others, and is as well able to help them with the conduct of their daily affairs. Norbert Elias had – somewhat excessively – highlighted the European origin of this structure.[3] He linked it to a social perspective that centred around ending the constant infighting between lords of different regions. He highlighted the shift to 'civilization' of those subordinate *courtiers* (brokers) coming under a single state authority that upended them after a drawn-out conflict. That force of statehood led these actors to giving in to its will and its might, so that individuals end up trading their liberty in exchange for the state's providing them with security. Regardless of how correct this Eurocentric conception is, the fact remains that that specific model of statehood has spread globally. It did so along with the European colonial expansion around the world as a construct that elevated loyalties above primordial tribalism, as a vertically structured and long-lasting entity that embodies a legal and administrative entity that monopolizes coercive power, including wealth distribution, as Max Weber offered.[4] In this sense, the state remains one of the least rejected or averted colonial residue. When one walks by United Nations buildings in New York, Geneva or Vienna and sees about two hundred flags waving, one can subliminally think that these flags really do symbolize two hundred political and administrative entities that could all be seen categorically as one thing: 'the state'. Such statehood construct in the collective conveys an understanding of a single notional entity that combines three elements – agreeable among sociologists and lawyers, but not necessarily verifiable by historians – namely a central government that monopolizes the use of power and taxation, a group of individuals that consider themselves one people and a viable geographic realm on the world map.

Being such *a conceptualized and perceived entity*, the state is also accompanied by a similarly abstract notion of sovereignty. Sovereignty is so conventional that Stephen Krasner dubbed it 'organized hypocrisy'.[5] The notion of sovereignty stands indeed at the core of the discord that drives global politics, yesterday and today. The nations of the Middle East and North Africa, and many others, borrowed the concept of the 'sovereign state' in the European sense, bringing along other constructs such as international law. The latter is framing, consequential and operational as it organizes relations between these 'sovereign' states, and it also determines the work of (intra-state) international organizations which are institutional frameworks for cooperation. However, such rules only applied to the relations between sovereign states, which were mainly European until the early twentieth century, with about thirty states at most. The dramatic global transformations of the twentieth century practically bridged the deep gap between a limited number of sovereign states, on one side, and numerous previously subordinated countries and regions on the other. The First World War led to the fragmentation of two vast and old empires, the Ottoman and the Austrian, giving birth to a large number of new entities. With the Second World War, anti-colonial national liberation movements were able to further enable a much larger wave of independent entities. A third wave later came with the downfall of the Berlin Wall and the eastern bloc in 1989, after which a couple dozen entities emerged as new sovereigns. In less than a decade, the number of sovereign entities multiplied, breaking the European exclusive club of sovereign states, while various regions from the Old World strived to prove their sovereignty to the centre until the latter were almost completely side-lined. To a large extent, these new states, notably in the Arab world, were vast territories whose authorities had no full control over; and the nations remained as well subject to contestation between great powers.

Besides its own idiosyncratic trajectory,[6] the history of the Middle East and North Africa from the nineteenth to the twenty-first century illustrates the fact that the concept of the state was globalized away from its European origin. This modern-day regional experience also shows how the notion of sovereignty has shifted from a stabilizing and organizing governance tool in Europe to an instrument in the hands of people(s) seeking to gain independence from colonial centres. The different imperialism theories put forth some decades ago do not often duly account for such a development but rather tend to perceive legitimate independence as *fait accompli* built around incidents with no contextualized and agential significance of their own.[7] Such interpretations do not take fully into account the very important repercussions of constitutional transformations on societies; economic approaches to historical analysis – however important – cannot serve as a sole interpretative framework for statehood. If material interests can clearly account for the emergence of particular political, legal and administrative structures, such structures equally determine in turn how wealth distribution is to be analysed. This was the core of the theoretical revisionism articulated in Theda Skocpol's writing on this matter in the 1980s,[8] as did too Francis Fukuyama, who eventually realized that history did not really end in 1989 in spite of his earlier claim.[9]

As dozens of new entities rose across the Middle East and North Africa and elsewhere in the twentieth century, 'sovereignty' shifted from being a reinforcing element promoting the West's control of others to being a protective shield against it. The West then stood unable to refute the emancipating and empowering idea of sovereignty because the South drew it away from the West. Ruling elites around the world – of whom many, notably in the Arab world, had received Western education (in Iraq, in Jordan, in Egypt, in Morocco) and understood its legal reasoning and rationale – did not hesitate to use sovereignty to assert their control over physical realms they declared to be theirs. Those Middle Eastern and North African elites came to understand the markers of statehood in a threefold manner. Firstly, *sovereignty has a crucial domestic dimension* as it encapsulates both public authority (i.e., government) and the use of force in one entity, that is, the state – two functions meant to be uncontested by any other domestic actor. The supremacy of the state allows it to revisit how any of its components operate, but the state itself shall not answer to any other frame of reference. Secondly, those postcolonial elites accepted – and not necessarily begrudgingly – the fact that *the state is Westphalian in essence*; that is, every state has the right to choose its religious identity and political system without religious or worldly interference from any other party.[10] Thirdly, these actors factored-in readily *the inevitable international dimension of the state*. A state that has met the criteria of physical existence in a certain geographic realm, ruling over a certain population and has a functional authority in control should also be recognized by its peers as a legitimate entity.

This they saw both as a bulwark against interventionism, and as a way for them to be treated in accordance with the principle of legal reciprocity. It is imperative not to underestimate those three dimensions – especially the last – in the regional thinking about statehood since the middle of the twentieth century. Even though globalization dynamics have played an increasingly undermining role as regards sovereignty during the last three decades, the major powers' recognition of the sovereignty of the small states does not necessarily reflect the former's goodwill or compliance with international law. Rather, it is the result of pragmatic calculations that posit a 'stable' world order based on state sovereignty – or even equal standing among states – as being in their interest even if it implies organized hypocrisy (given the immense gaps between the capabilities of those allegedly equal states).

Such an ideal sovereign-state model never saw the light of day in the Middle East and North Africa. However, the fact that sovereignty was incomplete in the countries of this region does not alter the fact that *states did emerge and borders have been demarcated*, and that all of this is not historically meaningless. Notwithstanding how perfunctorily postcolonial emerging Arab states could represent their people, and regardless of how their control over their respective territory may be less than full, and how much they continuously underwent internal debates and questions about their very being, they still came to exist *per se*. These imagined constructs manifest themselves in several tangible ways: the state wages wars, confiscates property, provides services, levies taxes, delegates representatives to vote on its behalf in international fora and has a flag, a national anthem, museums, police forces, a military and an administrative apparatus. This is why it is the question of state-building in the Middle East and North Africa remains so central and why indeed it is fundamental to *keep the state in* – as a centre of decision-making and influence that managed to gain autonomy not just versus the forces that build it but also vis-à-vis the economic interests and social dynamics that operate in it.[11]

In reality, the idea of the modern state experienced globalization at a time witnessing the downfall of the West as a dominant power steering the world. Today, the White Man finds himself at a time in history when his political and economic influence as well as demographic power, are all declining *vis-à-vis* the rest of the world. Within a century, the White Man's control of land went down from 80 per cent to less than 30 per cent of the globe and has also seen during the same period a reduction in half in terms of population. The White Man's interventionism has been similarly increasingly constrained by the emerging states' newfound waving of international law and sovereignty. On the other side, the White Man looks at its former colonial subjects with a mixed feeling of longing to the past and being 'appalled at the behaviour' of postcolonial ruling elites that were given sovereign governance but misused it either due to ignorance, recklessness or greed, and, as he views it, drove their countries down in many cases to a path of open civil wars, failed states or oppression pockets.[12] Accordingly, the debate and the issue continue to play out today divisively. On the one hand, the emerging states claim that their sovereignty should not be undermined, especially by former colonial powers which controlled them and their wealth for too long, and which should, today, spare them condescending, paternalistic and self-interested advice. As 'adults', these emerging states, such as the nations of the Middle East and North Africa, express the view that they are free to enjoy their sovereignty in however manner they see fit. On the other hand, the answer from the old Western states is that state sovereignty – which, the West imparts, explicitly or implicitly, *it* invented – is not absolute. Though, as noted, sovereignty may well play as a domestic prerogative, feature Westphalian codes and is articulated internationally, it still has an additional key dimension that cannot be overlooked, namely security. Failing to satisfy the security responsibility, it is argued, sovereignty can be limited. Since the end of the Cold War and even more so in the post-11 September era, this Western disposition was made abundantly clear to the Middle East and North Africa. Notions such as 'failed states', the 'responsibility to protect' and 'humanitarian intervention' have been introduced forcefully – both conceptually and practically. These parameters of modern-day global politics allow the West to remind emerging states that their maximalist interpretation of sovereignty is one that is limited.

It is important to look at this modern element of sovereignty as a combination of duties and responsibilities, though one often instrumentalized politically.[13] Such additional aspect of sovereignty might be used to legitimize Western interventions in the affairs of emerging states through these states' armies, corporations or non-governmental organizations (especially those advocating for the transnational protection of human rights). This accusation of Western manipulation and hypocrisy is, for instance, often repeated in international fora by Russian, Chinese as well as several African and Arab governments. The West, however, should not be reduced to a handful of imperialist agents looking for pretexts to interfere in world politics. It would indeed be a mistake to make such an accusation in haste. Not everyone who expresses interest in or solidarity with repressed peoples or vulnerable minorities is a neo-imperialist in humanist disguise. The manner in which the Middle Eastern and North African states have practiced their sovereignty is equally part of the problem; and we have witnessed calls – from the midst of the region – for foreign interventions in regional affairs to put a leash on local repression. It is certainly legitimate to reject the principle of foreign intervention in the face of policies such as those of the Neo-Conservatives who seek the downfall of the regimes they dislike, as well as in the face of the neo-liberals who acquiesced with colour revolutions in Eastern Europe. However, blind adherence to national sovereignty that regards every foreign interest in the affairs of the Arab and Muslim world merely as a pretext to interfere and violate sovereignty is akin to the local repressive authorities exercising their tyranny and repression. No matter how much we try to fixate sovereignty, the rapidly changing information and technology revolution will render the classical absolute application of sovereignty impossible, in particular because the ways cyberspace operates run against the logic of geography and borders – and accordingly sovereignty.

To be sure, Western manoeuvres around classical sovereignty have in recent years manifested themselves in the economic and commercial realms too. The West stood zealously for globalization as a post–Cold War ideology, which – as Susan Strange contended – led to a 'retreat of the state'.[14] Yet this evolved subsequently as the impersonal market forces realized that globalization – being a hyper-dynamic mechanism – could work to the benefit of other states. Isolationist populism, trade protectionism and ideological chauvinism have been recently on the rise in the West; all with a common denominator of anti-globalization, which was manifested in the 2016 election of Donald J. Trump as President of the United States, and the 'no' votes in the United Kingdom and Italy, as well as the rise of neo-nationalism across the world. Such shift of roles and policies is not insignificant, but it remains incomplete. Neither China is able to yet focus its attention on the trade and financial aspects of globalization and turn a blind eye to its conceptual and political aspects, nor could the West conclude at a stable, long-term position towards the dynamism of globalization. The nations of the Middle East and North Africa are pursuing their statehood projects amidst this arduous context. They have to interact with Western elites that have, as noted, globalized the concept of sovereignty and are now witnessing its evolution away from their control. This turn of events has also fuelled tension between North and South, beyond the colonial legacy – the issue becoming now one of competition (witness the advance since the 2010s of major commercial ventures by Qatar or the United Arab Emirates in the heart of Western capital cities). The West actively promoted free trade in the 1980s and the 1990s, and this has ultimately benefited the emerging economies – and also led the Western countries' capital to invest in foreign countries where it created jobs away from the home country of the capital. The enthusiasm of those Western elites for free movement and exchange of information, ideas, goods and capital led to an equal pressure to make the movement of people also free, including labour migration to the West or as refugees escaping bloody calamities in their own countries. Yet in the face of such movements, notably after 2014 and in the wake of the conflict in Syria, Europeans and American felt the urge to consolidate their borders in the face of what right-wing forces started depicting as a 'human invasion' from the impoverished global south. In particular, Donald Trump won the 2016 election riding an anti-Muslim and anti-Latino migrant platform. It is ironic that what Trump called for in 2016 replicated advice by Samuel Huntington in his 2004 book *Who are we?*, in which he called for an immediate end to the immigration of Catholic Hispanics to the United States; an idea that was widely ridiculed (including by *Foreign Affairs* which perceived his book as hallucinations of a man who in his old age had become hysterical).[15]

In various Western countries today, we witness an angry uprising against ruling elites who are perceived as having failed their peoples in return for promoting their personal interests around the world without regard for its patriotic duties, and without solidarity with those who have been harmed by globalization. If there is any common denominator between various neo-nationalisms – which echo the societal frustrations in the Middle East and North Africa – that we see on the rise in Vladimir Putin's Russia, Donald Trump's America, Viktor Orbán's Hungary, Jaroslaw Kaczynski's Poland or Jair Bolsonaro's Brazil, it is that elites are accused of having betrayed patriotic principles, favoured their interests over identity and chose to promote cosmopolitan global elite relations over domestic national solidarity. This neo-nationalist wave has not peaked yet; it is deeply rooted in the history of a number of Western countries and has been expanding to many others. This wave is negatively impacting the statehood project in the Middle East and North Africa, as it is reinforcing the existing authoritarianism and weakening struggling democratizing initiatives. In addition, the world finds itself today in the midst of a heated debate on sovereignty that is causing a major rift among Western and non-Western elites, and this further impacts the future of fledging state-building projects. On one side, some are trying to save the globalization ideology by setting limits for such an absolute concept, which would make sovereignty relatively confined. Advocates of this position argue that humanity has higher common interests across state borders, such as environmental protection, biodiversity, linguistic diversity, climate change and the protection of human rights. On the other side, another group calls for a return to the classical definition of sovereignty because the consequences of globalization for the West have much surpassed its benefits compared to the past, and because going back to political isolationism, economic protectionism and tightened borders against 'dark-skin immigrants' from the global south is a lot safer for the White Man than his desperate unrealistic attempts to maintain his intellectual and physical hegemony over the world order. One can nowadays smell a sense of fear and desperation in the now-vivid, post-COVID-19 Western neo-nationalism which believes that the West has been 'too kind' to the Global South by 'giving it' laws, institutions and concepts such as the state that the 'other' – Arabs, Africans, Turks, Persians Chinese, Russians, Indians or the dark-skinned in general – have used as ammunition against it.

What does such a global situation entail for the Middle East and Africa and its elusive statehood project? The gravest mistake the region made in that regard was to confuse sovereignty and ownership. This mix-up finds its roots in the historical heritage of the region as much as it was born of contemporary practice. On reading the masterly writings of Ibn Khaldun, one feels that he actually regards the state as an inferior entity. To him, the state is a tool of governing, through solidarity ('*asabiya*), people who have managed to erect a rulership of their own. Thus, the state will wither down when this solidarity declines. Early Middle Eastern and North African historians rarely used the word 'state' without attributing it to the 'house' that established it. They also rarely mentioned states without wondering about their origins or reasons for downfall, in contradistinction with the European model which presumes that the state will endure while power (flowing into it and out of it) will transition. Arab dictionaries are replete with examples of the 'fragility' and 'mortality' of the state. The root verb of the Arabic word for the term 'state' indicates alternation, change and shift. For example, if the root verb of 'state' (*al dawla*) were to be used in conjunction with 'time' (*al zaman*), this would convey a notion of reconfiguration. If 'state' is associated with a person, it means the subject in question 'belongs' to it. If the term is used to describe the condition of clothing, it means that it has been worn out; thus, necessitating its substitution by new clothing. In his poem 'Lament for the Fall of Andalusia' (1267), Abu al Baqa al Rundi famously uses a derivative of the root verb of the word 'state' to illustrate such frailty:

> Everything declines after reaching perfection,
> Therefore, let no man be beguiled by the sweetness of a pleasant life,
> As you have observed, these are the decrees that are inconstant,
> He whom a single moment has been made happy, has been harmed by many other moments.

Such a classical Arab outlook on the notion of the state is as arresting as it is consequential. Belief in *an ingrained vulnerability of the state* remained a feature of politics in region – to be witnessed time and again. It was, for instance, exacerbated by the Marxist ideas that were imported and applied in the twentieth century (notably in the Yemen in the 1960s and 1970s but also in the Levant and in parts of the Algerian and Moroccan respective polities). Above all else, Middle Easterners and North Africans understood from Marxism that the state is a tool in the hands of the capitalist bourgeoisie which legitimizes their control of the lower classes. Similarly, they understood from Antonio Gramsci that there can be no state without a domination project to carry it forward.[16] The subsequent communist or proto-communist experiences in the twentieth century then came to further humiliate state representatives; reducing them to bureaucrats in the service of the omnipotent single party – such as the Ba'ath party in Syria and Iraq or the FLN in Algeria – which in itself was supposed to be a means for the working class to govern. Thus, the wretched state was further degraded. We must, therefore, put aside our interest in the state *per se*, and rather seek to understand who or what is using the state as means to consolidate hegemony and ideological dominance.

Indeed, anthropological studies did not save the state from this 'inferior' perception. Like me, you might enjoy reading Peter Evans' interesting work on the making of the state, where he argues that state-making is essentially a criminal scheme that deviated from its original purposes.[17] However, Evans later exaggerated the contribution of anthropology in deconstructing the Weberian narrative on the making of the modern state. Much like other concepts, the state, as it were, emerged in a certain historical and cultural context before becoming then subject to globalization, which altered its original features due to the interaction with other cultures and thus injecting it with tangible modifications. This was carefully considered by Jean-François Bayart and others.[18] Evans argued that state-making cannot be exported as a commodity, say like canned goods, because it comes in a variety of types, forms and shapes. He remarks that this variation of states, either predatory (such as the state in the former Zaire or Democratic Republic of Congo), developmental (such as in Asia) or intermediate (such as Brazil), does not mean that embedding the idea of the state in different environments would necessarily lead to a variation in types of state. Thus, we must also study the reasons for such variation by analysing the structure of each state as well as its external connections so that we can explain how or why it has embarked on such a unique trajectory.

In the Middle East and North Africa, pån-Arabist ideas played an important role in deepening such 'inferiority' of the state. In the early 1980s, it was felt that after three decades since independence, it was time to evaluate that state that had been claiming rule over its local societies. At the time, I took part in two research projects on the subject; one Arab led by Saad Eddin Ibrahim and one European led by Giacomo Luciani.[19] I recall at the time how hard-headed pan-nationalists were questioning our 'hidden agendas' in promoting despicable nationalism only because we were interested in doing research on the state. They had their reasons to loathe existing states which they viewed as fragments of a larger, single delusional entity to which they had been longing for until they subscribed to a childish belief that one may scrub out existing states by only ignoring their being. As a result, in both projects, we could not dare to talk about the 'state' without adding the 'nation' (*umma*) to the title; as if we had implicitly accepted that the state – our original research subject – could not be understood except if embedded into the greater context of the nation – and as if the latter was not itself also a by-product of imagination, as Ernest Gellner argued in his seminal work.[20]

This inevitably curtailed our curiosity to understand how dominant and ruling groups in the Middle East and North Africa really embedded the concept of the state, and why there exists much variation in the way different Arab states approach the concept of the state. In reality, we all relied excessively on views that consider the state an 'inferior entity' whereas our own old and contemporary heritage almost blocked us from deeply examining its current state of affairs. We were distracted by the 'timeless message' which one state claimed to carry, or by the working class whose protection was allegedly the mission of another state, or by the masses which were claimed to be able to make a state as they pleased, or indeed by Islam which we were told consumed another state's whole existence, let alone dynasties who named states after themselves as if they were their property. This all led to a synchronization between our heritage of reducing the state to a mere tool and what we conceived in terms of other experiences and ambitious slogans, which undermined our pursuit to understand the efficacy of the state and its relationship with society. This historical state of affairs also undermined our ability to understand the potential for the state to gain autonomy vis-à-vis its founders or post-independence rulers and to become an impersonal entity that is here to stay; unaffected by how rulers or dynasties may come or go, unlike what the poet described in his Andalusian lamentation. Today, we find ourselves longing for a state whose fate is not doomed by its origins. A state not used as means of government for a specific regime but rather one that is free of patrimonial chains and of the authority of its leaders. A state that makes its politicians rotate in power and not see it as a reward for their personal ambition.

As the nations of the Middle East and North Africa forged ahead in the late twentieth century and early twenty-first century, things went down a different path. Rulers increasingly felt possessive of their duty to govern. They came to regard the state as part of their own private property, a tool to be used to up their influence, solidify their power and multiply their wealth. Such neo-patrimonial regimes did not distinguish between the state and the regime, nor between their duty to govern and their willingness to control government.[21] As a result, the basic differences between public and private property diminished, leading notably to privatization policies enacted largely to the benefit of the rulers' relatives and friends. The state itself came, in some instances (e.g. Muammar Gaddafi's Libya), to be seen as a personal property. Such aberration manifested itself vividly when one ruler – Syria's Hafez al Assad – passed on the state to one of his sons as if it were a transferrable commodity within the family. Instead of evolving from family solidarity ('*asabiya*) to institutional autonomy, the state-building project had now regressed to a dynastic mindset. Yet another feature of this path is the identification of the ruler with the state, an aspect which reached its peak when some rulers declared 'it is either me or chaos' or 'it is me or civil war', thus implicitly threatening to sacrifice the state if people were to seek to change the regime. With the events of the 2011 Arab Spring, most of the Middle Eastern and North African countries often found themselves between submission to the rulers in place or collapse in the quagmire of protracted civil war. The region would not have been in this position had it paid attention to the fact that existing regimes had succeeded to place their legitimacy above that of the state, using vague slogans aimed at avoiding accountability for their failure to deliver on their foremost task: building a modern state that works in service of society.

A state used by a dynasty as a tool of governing or annexed to a republican regime as means of control can only generate disbelief and disinterest. One can only long for a state that has been able to gradually impose its logic, not only on people but also on those who run its affairs. This is the 'state as an idea' not the 'state as an instrument'; one that is run by a set of bureaucrats who enjoy protection against the domineering and vacillations of the ruling class. It is the rational state that uses its reason as a leash on fervent emotions that sometimes take on people. It is a state that is fixated around several institutions which are largely immune to the fluctuations of politics and politicians, most important of which being the justice institutions which were early signals of the emergence of the modern state. It is the neutral, non-partisan state whose only 'greater mission' is the security and welfare of its people. This may be a tall order, but not all Arab states have equally failed in building states. On the contrary, there are some interesting experiences. The more the state is autonomous versus its builders and free from claims of being part of 'greater missions or goals', the more promising a path it can be seen to embark on. Some Arab states have sought to be developmental and productive states (e.g. Iraq in the 1970s), while others tended to remain rentier and distributive states (e.g. the Gulf countries). There are states that remain governed by a bond of '*asabiya* and others that opened up, to use Ibn Khaldun's metaphor, to other groups in a way that transformed their perception of population from subjects to citizens. There are states that rapidly turned into wealth-pillage machines and others who sought to nationalize such wealth. The Arab region paints a diverse picture that almost reflects different forms of recently emerging states across the world.

Nonetheless, the gap remains significant between the overall situation of these states and the generic model discussed above. If we compare the situation in Arab states to that historical and conceptual model, we find problems when applying at least one or more of the different key elements that altogether constitute the model. The governance approach in Arab states has long been mixing up the state with the regime, so much so that the state would sometimes be a subordinate of the regime. Thus, the people remained connected to inherited loyalties and therefore have not come to hold a higher sense of belonging to the state – a sentiment and affiliation which are in turn needed for the state to deliver. Other reasons have contributed to such a gap. The first reason is the general failure of existing Arab states to transform from the sense of affiliation to tribal and sectarian structures domestically, and to transnational pan-Arab and religious belonging into belonging to the nation-state, which is essential to the building of modern states. State-partitioning, reunification or annexation maps keep coming to the forefront especially in recent years – just as they did a century ago with the Sykes-Picot agreement – with, for instance, calls for dividing Yemen or indulging tribal and regional divisions in Libya, all of which actively preventing the emergence of the state. These non-exhaustive examples indicate the illness the Middle East and North Africa region is suffering from, namely the repressed readiness to translate complex political crises into new geopolitical projects. Though the European colonial demarcation of Africa was no more rational than that in the Middle East and North Africa, Sub-Saharan Africans have been more rational than Middle Easterners and North Africans in not revisiting the borders of their states whenever a crisis flared up. Similarly, earlier, Latin American nations accepted the territorial demarcations imposed on them by the European powers during the nineteenth century. Decades after independence, it is in the interest of the Middle East and North Africa to dismiss such an obsession with borders and to understand that the type of governments running these state entities deserves at least as much attention as is given to concerns over geography and borders. Had the region paid due attention to the nature of authority in the local systems, it would have been able to realize the absence – or at best hollowness – of a foundational social contract in most of these states. A social contract would allow groups and individuals to secure that sense of belonging, without which it would be challenging to build a stable and effective state. The concept of citizenship will remain irrelevant as long as the Middle Eastern and North African citizen does not feel secure or supported except within or through their traditional loyalties. Therefore, it is arguably a mistake to think of state–society relations as a zero-sum equation. It is equally an error to subscribe to the belief that a strong state requires a weak society, except if we were to think – mistakenly then – that the power of the state is measured by how prone it is to the use of force. In reality, more stable states are effective and capable along with organized and vibrant communities.

A further reason for the state–society gap is the prevalent tendency to justify the enormous pressures the region's fragile states are under as a result of the information technology revolution. If this ever-dynamic and changing telecommunications revolution has indeed been spreading uncertainty in consolidated democracies, it will certainly not spare closed societies no matter how resistant to historical and global change they can be. Access to mobile phones, internet coverage and satellite television has given every citizen an inexhaustible source of (true or fake) information, wise or unwise views, as well as unprecedented belief in one's ability to affect the ongoing events, which was almost non-existent in the past. How will the Middle Eastern and North African regimes approach such a development that is moving faster – and producing quicker consequences – than the industrial revolution in European countries? This is an open question today and tomorrow. However, the impact of this revolution on sovereignty is an irrefutable reality. Historical transformation of this magnitude has no regard to states' borders, cannot be stopped by censorship and has opened new horizons to new forms of communication, interaction, solidarity and dissonance.

Finally, if state-building is vulnerable when the intra-society relations are in turn fragile, it is a process made even more difficult when it comes to democratic transformation. The Libyan case might be particular on the matter, but it is one of the most indicative models in the region. In Libya, it has, so far, proven almost impossible to build a democracy in the absence of a state that is whole. Yet state-building is in turn also impossible in the absence of a strong bond among the people of the nation-state. Libya, however, also teaches us that the millions of Libyans inhabiting the country cannot be asked to wait until a national bond is built, which may later result in building an effective state that would in turn enable popular participation as a basis to democracy. Libyans thus have no other option but to accept to expedite all these stages: build a national bond, an effective status apparatus and a democratic system altogether at the same time. Libyans may not be ready for this triangular process any more than the Iraqis or the Yemenis. In Iraq, Saddam Hussein leaned on the support of a certain group that gained control of a Stalinist-like party, which in turn subjugated state institutions through which it engineered a type of intra-society relations in line with the interests of the ruler, thus effectively turning the state into a tool of governing. The United States then came in 2003 preaching democracy colonially. The ruler in question was toppled, the sense of '*asabiya* he relied on dampened, his Ba'ath party dissolved, the state disintegrated, the fabric of society was torn apart, and Iraqis found themselves before a vacuum of a fallen state and a torn society.

Over the past century, the countries of the Middle East and North Africa have wasted precious time claiming myriad reasons for why they did not build a modern and effective state that is autonomous vis-à-vis both those who built it and those who vie for power in it. This would have been a state whose legitimacy derives from what it achieves for the people and not for alleged greater missions it hides behind; a legitimate state able to project its autonomy and stability to the benefit of its people, per a constructive engagement with the other actors of the international system whole world. One hundred years after the fall of the Ottoman Empire and having gone through decades of nationalism-driven conflicts, these states are paying the heavy price of such indolence.

Notes

1   Joseph R. Strayer, *On the Medieval Origins of the Modern State*, Princeton, New Jersey: Princeton University Press, 1970.
2   Thomas Hobbes, *Leviathan or The Matter, Forme and Power of a Commonwealth Ecclesiasticall and Civil*, 1651.
3   Norbert Elias, *The Civilising Process – Sociogenetic and Psychogenetic Investigations*, Oxford: Blackwell Publishers, 1994 [1939].
4   Max Weber, 'Politics as a Vocation', (*Politik als Beruf*) lecture in Munich, 28 January 1919.
5   Stephen D. Krasner, *Sovereignty – Organised Hypocrisy*, Princeton, New Jersey: Princeton University Press, 1999.
6   See Chapter One, Chapter Two and Chapter Three in this volume.
7   The classic statement of imperialism' was put forth by Johan Galtung in 'A Structural Theory of Imperialism', *Journal of Peace Research*, 8, 2, 1971, pp. 81–117.
8   Theda Skocpol, 'Bringing the State Back In: Strategies of Analysis in Current Research', in Peter B. Evans, Dietrich Rueschemeyer and Theda Skocpol, eds., *Bringing the State Back In*, Cambridge: Cambridge University Press, 1985, pp. 3–38.
9   See Timothy Stanley and Alexander Lee, 'It's Still Not the End of History', *The Atlantic*, 1 September 2014: and Louis Menand, 'Francis Fukuyama Postpones the End of History', *The New Yorker*, 27 August 2018. Also see Francis Fukuyama, *State-Building – Governance and World Order in the 21st Century*, Ithaca, New York: Cornell University Press, 2004.
10 For a different perspective, see Mohammad-Mahmoud Ould Mohamedou, 'In Search of the Non-Western State: Historicising and De-Westphalianising Statehood', in Bertrand Badie, Dirk Berg-Schlosser and Leonardo Morlino, eds., *The SAGE Handbook of Political Science – A Global Perspective*, London: Sage, 2020, pp. 1335–48.
11 On this point, see Eric A. Nordlinger, *On the Autonomy of the Democratic State*, Cambridge, Massachusetts: Harvard University Press, 1982.
12 For a discussion, see, for instance, William Cunningham Bissell, 'Engaging Colonial Nostalgia', *Cultural Anthropology*, 20, 2, 2005, pp. 215–48.
13 See, for instance, Brian Klaas, *The Despot's Accomplice – How the West is Aiding and Abetting the Decline of Democracy*, London: Hurst and Company, 2016.
14 Susan Strange, *The Retreat of the State – The Diffusion of Power in the World Economy*, Cambridge: Cambridge University Press, 1996.

15 Samuel Huntington, *Who Are We? The Challenges to America's National Identity*, New York: Simon and Schuster, 2004; Alan Wolfe, 'Native Son: Samuel Huntington Defends the Homeland', *Foreign Affairs*, May/June 2004, pp. 120–5. Also see Carlos Lozada, 'Samuel Huntington, a Prophet for the Trump Era', *The Washington Post*, 18 July 2017. In an earlier work, *American Politics – The Promise of Disharmony* (Belknap Press, 1983), the late Harvard University professor had forecasted such nationalistic and divided evolution in the United States.
16 For a discussion, see, for instance, Raymond A. Hinnebusch, 'Order and Change in the Middle East: A Neo-Gramscian Twist on the International Society Approach', in Barry Buzan and Ana Gonzalez-Pelaez, eds., *International Society and the Middle East*, London: Palgrave MacMillan, 2009, pp. 201–25.
17 Peter Evans, *Embedded Autonomy – States and Industrial Transformation*, Princeton, New Jersey: Princeton University Press, 1995; and Peter Evans and Patrick Heller, 'Human Development, State Transformation and the Politics of the Developmental State', in Stephan Leibfried, Evelyne Huber, Matthew Lange, Jonah D. Levy and John D. Stephens, eds., *The Oxford Handbook of Transformations of the State*, Oxford: Oxford University Press, 2015, pp. 691–713. The 'state as criminal scheme' thesis was first articulated by Charles Tilly. Charles Tilly, 'War Making and State Making as Organised Crime', in Peter Evans, Dietrich Rueschemeyer and Theda Skocpol, eds., *Bringing the State Back In*, New York: Cambridge University Press, 1985, pp. 170–1.
18 See Jean-François Bayart, *La Greffe de l'État*, Paris: Karthala, 1996.
19 The project led by Giacomo Luciani under the auspices of the Roma-based Istituto Affari Internazionali (IAI) produced a four-volume on 'Nation, State and Integration in the Arab World': Ghassan Salamé, ed., *The Foundations of the Arab State*, London: Croom-Helm, 1987; Hazem Beblawi and Giacomo Luciani, *The Rentier State*, London: Croom-Helm, 1987; Adeed Dawisha and I. William Zartman, *Beyond Coercion – The Durability of the Arab State*, London: Croom-Helm, 1988; and Giacomo Luciani and Ghassan Salamé, *The Politics of Arab Integration*, London: Croom-Helm, 1998. A fifth book was subsequently released collecting essays from the four volumes: Giacomo Luciani, ed., *The Arab State*, London: Routledge, 1990.
20 Ernest Gellner, *Nations and Nationalism*, Ithaca, New York: Cornell University Press, 1983. Also see his *Muslim Society*, Cambridge: Cambridge University Press, 1981.
21 See Hisham Sharabi, *Neopatriarchy – A Theory of Distorted Change in Arab Society*, Oxford: Oxford University Press, 1993.

CHRONOLOGY, 1901–2021

1901
28 May: The Shah of Persia awards a British subject, William Knox d'Arcy, the concession for oil rights in nearly all of Persia, in exchange for 16 per cent of his company's profits.

1902
15 January: Forces loyal to Abdulaziz ibn Saud seize control of the township of Riyadh in the eastern part of Arabia, beginning a thirty-year conquest of the Arabian Peninsula.

1903
19 April: On Easter Sunday, Jews in the Russian city of Kishinev are murdered in a pogrom. The massacre is the triggering event for the second *aliya* (immigration wave of Jews to Palestine). Thirty-five thousand Jewish refugees settle in Palestine over the next eleven years.
17 August: An army of several thousand Berber fighters in Morocco unsuccessfully attacks a French colonial garrison at Taghit in French-occupied Algeria, withdrawing after a multi-day siege and thousands of casualties.

1904
June: Imam Yahya of the al Qasimi dynasty, recognized as caliph by Zaydi Muslims, takes power in North Yemen, an Ottoman territory.
3 October: France and Spain sign a treaty assigning each power zones of influence within Morocco, then under the rule of Sultan Abdelaziz Ben Hassan.

1905
December: A mass protest movement erupts in Persia, demanding a constitution to limit the Shah's political powers.

1906
13 June: In the Egyptian village of Denshawai, British officers clash with local peasants, leading to the death of a local woman and a British officer. Thirty-two

villagers are convicted of murder and four are publicly hung, while no British officers are punished, infuriating Egyptian public opinion.

5 August: In response to mass anti-government protests that have continued unabated for eight months, the Qajar Shah of Persia, Muzzafar al Din, issues a decree providing for the creation of a National Assembly to draft a constitution for the country.

30 December: In Persia, Muzzafar al Din confirms a new constitution for his country, which defines the rights of citizens and the powers of the legislature and makes Twelver Shi'ism the official religion of the state.

1907

January: In Persia, Muzzafar al Din dies and is succeeded by Mohammed Ali Mirza.

August: Russia and Great Britain sign a treaty dividing Persia into respective zones of influence – Russian in the north, British in the south.

7 August: After nine Europeans are murdered by a mob in Casablanca, France bombards and occupies the city, beginning its twenty-seven-year war of conquest in Morocco. In Marrakesh, Sultan Abdelaziz's brother Abd al Hafid is proclaimed Sultan, and leads the anti-French struggle.

22 October: The first nationalist party in the Arab world, Al Hizb al Watani, is formally established in Egypt (it had been founded as a political movement in 1895).

1908

23 June: Civil war begins in Persia as the Shah dissolves parliament and declares martial law. Government troops attack the country's parliament building.

24 July: After a three-week uprising led by military officers in the Committee of Union and Progress (CUP) organization (also known as the 'Young Turks'), Ottoman Sultan Abdulhamid II announces the restoration of the 1876 Ottoman Constitution. In the brief constitutional period that follows, elections, newspapers and political activity flourish throughout the empire. The Young Turks take power in Istanbul.

1909

26 March: Russia invades Persia in support of the Shah's government as the civil war intensifies.

April: In the Ottoman Empire, a countercoup fails to overthrow the CUP, which moves to depose the Sultan. The struggle touches off pogroms against the Armenian population in Adana province; tens of thousands are massacred.

12–13 July: Rebel forces capture Tehran, and force Mohammed Ali Mirza Shah to abdicate in favour of his son, Sultan Ahmad Mirza, and restore the constitution and parliament in Persia.

14 November: Arab students in Paris set up Al Fatat (The Youth), an underground political society advocating for autonomy for the Ottoman Empire's Arab provinces.

1910
20 February: Egypt's Prime Minister Boutros Ghali, who presided over the trial of the Denshawai villagers, is assassinated by a twenty-five-year-old nationalist, Ibrahim Nasif al Wardani.
August: Ottoman expeditionary forces crush an uprising in the Jabal Druze region of modern-day Syria.

1911
October: British forces invade and occupy southern Persia seeking to secure protection of the d'Arcy oil concession.
4 October: Italy invades the Ottoman provinces of Tripolitania and Cyrenaica in modern-day Libya.
7–8 November: After a dispute over the Jellaz cemetery, anti-French riots take place in Tunis, the capital of the French Protectorate of Tunisia. Martial law is imposed, and will remain in place for ten years.
20 November: Russian forces invade and occupy northern Persia and force Iranian prime minister Samsam al Saltanah to dissolve parliament.

1912
30 March: Morocco's Sultan Abdel Hafid is forced to sign the Treaty of Fez, which turns Morocco into a French protectorate, and abdicate.
13 August: Yusuf, the younger brother of deposed Sultan Abdelaziz, becomes sultan of Morocco under the French protectorate.
October: Greece, Bulgaria, Montenegro and Serbia, all having achieved their independence from the Ottoman Empire in the previous decades, go to war with the empire to pursue nationalist territorial claims.
17 October: In Switzerland, the Ottoman Empire signs the Treaty of Lausanne with Italy, recognizing the latter's sovereignty over Libya a year after Italy's invasion of that country.
28 November: Taking advantage of the Ottoman military collapse, notables in Albania proclaim their country's independence from the Ottoman Empire.
3 December: The Ottoman Empire signs an armistice with Bulgaria, Montenegro and Serbia.

1913
23 January: Determined to continue the war in the Balkans, three Young Turks CUP leaders, Enver Pasha, Talaat Pasha and Jamal Pasha, seize power in a coup in Istanbul and overturn the armistice of 3 December.
May: In Oman, the *imam* of the Ibadi Muslims leads a rebellion against the British-backed sultan, seizing control of most of Oman's hinterlands.

30 May: The Treaty of London ends the First Balkan War. The Ottoman Empire loses almost all of its European territory.

18–23 June: An Arab National Congress is held in Paris, calling for autonomy for the Ottoman Empire's Arab regions.

29 June: The Second Balkan War begins as Bulgaria attacks Greece and Serbia. The conflict among the First Balkan War's victors allows the Ottoman Empire to recover some of its European territory.

30 September: The Treaty of Constantinople ends the Second Balkan War. In one year, the Ottoman Empire has lost 85 per cent of its European territory.

1914

2 November: A month after the beginning of the First World War, the Ottoman Empire enters the conflict, fighting alongside Germany and Austria-Hungary, and against France, Great Britain and Russia.

November: In Persia, the parliament reconvenes for the first time in three years and declares the country's neutrality in the First World War. Ottoman forces invade northern Persia the same month.

17 December: With the beginning of war between Great Britain and the Ottoman Empire, Britain officially declares Egypt to be a British protectorate, thirty-two years after its initial occupation by British troops. The British depose Egypt's Khedive Abbas II and replace him with his uncle, Hussein Kamil, who bears the title of sultan.

1915

February: Hundreds of thousands of British and French troops land on the Gallipoli peninsula near Istanbul, beginning an attempt to take the Ottoman capital. After nearly a year of fighting, they are forced to withdraw.

24 April: The CUP government rounds up prominent Armenian citizens in Istanbul for execution or deportation. Over the next several years, between 800,000 and 1.5 million Armenian citizens of the Ottoman Empire, as well as hundreds of thousands of Greeks and Assyrians, perish in massacres and forced deportation marches carried out by the Ottoman state and its local proxies. The non-Muslim population of Anatolia, which was about 20 per cent of the total population before the war, is nearly liquidated.

Autumn: The great famine begins in Lebanon and Syria. From 1915 to 1918, hundreds of thousands die of hunger under the impact of a British and French naval blockade of the Syrian coastline, Ottoman state-ordered conscriptions and food confiscations, a series of poor harvests and a locust plague.

1916

3 November: Following the Ottoman renouncement of sovereignty over Qatar, Abdullah bin Jassim Al Thani signs a treaty of protection with Great Britain.

16 March: British forces in Sudan invade the neighbouring Sultanate of Darfur. The entire territory is conquered in the next six months, and folded into British-Egyptian Sudan.
16 May: Great Britain and France ratify a secret agreement on the post-war distribution of Ottoman lands, known as the Sykes-Picot Agreement. The agreement assigns southern Iraq and Palestine to a British sphere of influence, and Lebanon, Syria and Mosul to a French zone. The Russian Empire gives its assent.
10 June: Hussein bin Ali, the Sharif of Mecca, officially launches the Great Arab Revolt against the Ottoman Empire. With British support, his son, Emir Faysal, leads thousands of tribesmen irregular fighters into battle against Ottoman armies in greater Syria.

1917
11 March: British troops occupy Baghdad as part of their war effort against the Ottoman Empire.
26 March: British forces invade Palestine from the southwest. Arab forces loyal to Sharif Hussein of Mecca, under the command of his son Faysal, fight their way north.
9 October: Ahmed Fuad Pasha becomes Sultan of Egypt after the death of his brother, Hussein Kamil.
2 November: The British Foreign Secretary, Arthur Balfour, writes to Lord Rothschild that 'His Majesty's Government views with favour the establishment in Palestine of a National Home for the Jewish people, and will use their best endeavours to facilitate the achievement of this object.' The 'Balfour Declaration' becomes the political basis for the Zionist movement to create a Jewish state in Palestine after the First World War.
November: Following the Bolshevik Revolution, the Russian government withdraws from the war and reveals the existence of the Sykes-Picot Agreement.
30 December: British troops enter Jerusalem.

1918
25 October: Sharifian Arab forces take over the Levantine city of Aleppo in the name of Emir Faysal, completing their conquest of the Ottoman Empire's Arab territories. Faysal sets up a kingdom in Syria's interior, with Damascus as its capital. French forces occupy the Syrian coastline and Cilicia. Anti-French insurgents rise up against the French and their local allies.
30 October: The Armistice of Mudros (Greece) ends the fighting between the Ottoman Empire and the Allied Powers.
November: Imam Yahya of the al Qasimi dynasty, recognized as caliph by Zaydi Muslims, declares North Yemen's independence from the Ottoman Empire. South Yemen, or Aden, is controlled by Great Britain.
3 November: British forces occupy Mosul and force Ottoman troops to evacuate. The British administer the Ottoman provinces of Mosul, Baghdad and Basra as a single administrative unit, soon to become the new state of Iraq.

13 November: British, Italian and French forces occupy Istanbul.

November: A delegation (*wafd*) of seven prominent Egyptians presents the British high commissioner in Cairo with a request for independence. After they are rebuffed, they begin touring the country with their demands, and create a political party, the Wafd Party.

1919

9 March: Great Britain deports the leaders of the Egyptian nationalist Wafd Party to Malta, triggering a nationwide uprising. Protests, strikes, sabotage and attacks on British personnel break out across the country. The British kill hundreds of Egyptians in suppressing the uprising, and unrest persists for several months.

Mid-March: Italy begins landing troops in southern Anatolia.

May: In the territory under Emir Faysal control in Syria, elections are held for a Syrian Arab Congress to be seated in Damascus.

14 May: Greece invades western Anatolia to assert territorial claims under the Treaty of Sèvres (France), capturing the port city of Izmir.

19 May: Mustafa Kemal, an Ottoman military leader of the Battle of Gallipoli, arrives in Samsun on the Black Sea and begins organizing resistance to the Allied partition of Anatolia.

25 May: Forces loyal to Abdulaziz Ibn Saud ambush a Hejazi army under the command of Abdullah, the son of Sharif Hussein of Mecca. The Sharifian forces are routed, and Ibn Saud's conquest of the Arabian peninsula continues.

4–11 September: At a congress in the city of Sivas, a Turkish resistance movement to the post-war settlement coalesces under the leadership of Mustafa Kemal.

October: Great Britain announces its intention to withdraw its troops from Syria, in favour of the French. Armed resistance to the French presence in Syria mounts, led by insurgent leaders Saleh al Ali and Ibrahim Hananu.

19 December: The *S.S. Ruslan* arrives in Jaffa, Palestine, with 671 Jewish refugees from Russia on board. It is a harbinger of the third *aliya*, which will bring 30,000 Jewish refugees to Palestine from Eastern Europe in the next four years.

1920

8 March: The Syrian Arab Congress declares Syria independent, and Emir Faysal its king. A draft constitution for the country is prepared.

19–26 April: In a post-war peace conference at San Remo, Italy, the victorious European powers agree to distribute Ottoman Arab territories to Great Britain and France as 'mandates' under the new League of Nations system. Syria is assigned to France; Palestine and Iraq to Great Britain.

23 April: As the Turkish War of Independence rages, the Turkish National Assembly in Ankara elects Mustafa Kemal as president.

June: Triggered by a new tax levy, a major rebellion against British rule begins among the tribes of Iraq's Euphrates river valley. The uprising lasts for five months. Thousands of Iraqis are killed.

July: The French parliament rejects demands for independence issued by Tunisia's nationalist Destour Party.

24 July: French forces invade Emir Faysal's Syrian domain. Faysal flees the country, and French forces defeat Syrian resistance in battle at Maysalun. Armed rebellions against French rule continue in northern Syria and the Alawite territory.

10 August: The Treaty of Sèvres (France) divides most Ottoman territory, including Anatolia, between British, French, Greek and Italian zones of influence and control. The independence of a large Armenian state in eastern Anatolia is recognized, and provisions are made for a Kurdish referendum on independence.

1 September: France declares the state of Greater Lebanon, encompassing a territory much larger than the Ottoman-era autonomous region of Mount Lebanon. In what is present-day Syria, distinct states are also created in Damascus, Aleppo, Alexandretta, Druze territory and Alawite territory.

13 September: Turkish forces invade the territory assigned to Armenia under the Treaty of Sèvres.

25 September: The British-brokered Treaty of al Sib ends the seven-year conflict in Oman. Oman's sultan recognizes the autonomy of the country's interior and the spiritual authority of the Ibadi Imam.

4 December: The French territory of Mauritania is annexed to l'Afrique Occidentale Française (AOF), a colonial administrative structure headquartered in Dakar, Senegal.

1921

21 January: The Turkish National Assembly adopts a provisional constitution.

21 February: With British encouragement, Colonel Reza Khan seizes power in Iran, ending the rule of the Qajar dynasty.

12–22 March: Winston Churchill chairs the Cairo Conference, which resolves to award the throne of Iraq to Emir Faysal of Mecca, who had ruled Syria for eighteen months until the French invasion, and to make his brother Abdallah governor of Transjordan, after the latter marches north from the Hejaz to invade Syria.

May 30: Abdelkrim al Khattabi, a Berber leader in Morocco's Rif mountain region, goes to war against French and Spanish forces in the country. The 'Rif War' lasts for five years and ends in French and Spanish victory after thousands of deaths and extensive use of chemical warfare.

23 August: A year after the French expel him from his rule in Damascus, the British install Faysal of Mecca as king of Iraq. Faysal's government, which includes prominent Arab nationalists and former Ottoman military officers, sets about building a modern state dominated by Iraq's Sunni Arab elites.

20 October: France signs a separate peace treaty with the new Turkish National Assembly, taking France out of the war. Under the treaty, France abandons its claims to Cilicia, but momentarily secures its hold over northern Syria. Tens of thousands of Armenians evacuate Cilicia.

1922

28 February: Britain grants Egypt formal independence but retains control over Egypt's foreign policy and the use of the country for military purposes. Sultan Ahmed Fuad becomes Fuad I, king of Egypt.
September: Turkish forces recapture the western port city of Izmir from Greek forces. Most of the city is destroyed in a fire which kills thousands of its residents.
22 September: Great Britain creates a separate administration in Transjordan, the Palestine Mandate territory east of the Jordan River, and forbids Jewish settlement there. Abdallah, the son of Sharif Hussein of Mecca, is governor.
10 October: With British troops still occupying the country, Iraq's new King Faysal signs a treaty with Britain confirming the British League of Nations Mandate over his country.
11 October: The Armistice of Mudanya, signed by Turkey, Greece and Great Britain, ends the fighting in the Turkish war of independence, provides for the Greek withdrawal from Anatolia, and promises a renegotiation of the Treaty of Sèvres.
2 December: In the Uqair Convention, Great Britain forces Ibn Saud to recognize the defined borders of Iraq and Kuwait.

1923

30 January: With international encouragement, Greece and Turkey sign an agreement to forcibly exchange their respective Muslim and Greek Orthodox Christian populations. As many as two million people will be deported between the two countries under the agreement.
19 April: Egypt adopts a constitution enshrining a liberal constitutional monarchy.
24 May: In Sudan, Ali Abd al-Latif, a Muslim former army officer from the Dinka tribe, forms the White Flag movement to advocate for Sudanese unification and independence from Egypt and Great Britain.
24 July: In Lausanne, representatives of the Turkish National Assembly sign a treaty with the European powers, replacing the 1920 Treaty of Sèvres and bringing the Turkish War of Independence to an end. Turkey renounces its claims to former Ottoman territories outside of Anatolia, but its modern-day borders are essentially established.
23 October: The Turkish National Assembly formally proclaims the creation of the Turkish Republic. Six days later, Mustafa Kemal (later to take the name Ataturk, father of the Turks) is elected president by the Assembly. He goes on to rule Turkey unopposed for fifteen years, and undertake transformational social, religious, economic and linguistic reforms with the goal of creating a secular national state.

1924

January–December: The fourth *aliya* brings 50,000 Jewish immigrants to Palestine from Poland.
January: Egypt holds free parliamentary elections; the Wafd Party wins 90 per cent of the seats.

3 March: The Turkish National Assembly abolishes the Caliphate, leaving the Sunni Muslim world without a Caliph for the first time in centuries. The Turkish government also bans all Kurdish schools, organizations, publications and religious fraternities.

20 April: The Turkish National Assembly adopts a constitution establishing Turkey as a Republic.

4 July: Ali Abd al-Latif, the leader of the Sudanese nationalist White Flag movement, is arrested by British authorities.

19 November: Sir Lee Stack, the British Governor-General of Sudan, is assassinated in Cairo.

27 November: Sudanese army units loyal to the White Flag movement rise up in Khartoum against British rule. British forces put down the uprising.

1925

8 February: In southeastern Turkey, Shaykh Sa'id launches a large-scale Kurdish uprising against the Turkish government, the first of several that will occur over the century. By May, Turkish forces have captured Shaykh Sa'id and suppressed the rebellion after thousands of deaths.

March: Iraq grants a seventy-five-year oil concession to the British-owned Iraq Petroleum Company (IPC).

21 March: Iraq adopts a national constitution, which grants the king wide-ranging powers.

19–20 July: Druze insurgents in southern Syria led by Sultan Pasha al Atrash shoot down a French surveillance plane and occupy the city of Salkhad. The revolt quickly spreads to the Hawran region, Lebanon, the Damascus countryside, Hama and the Qalamoun mountains. This revolt, referred to as the Great Syrian Revolt or the Druze revolt, lasts for two years, claims thousands of lives and imposes a heavy cost on the French occupation of Syria and Lebanon.

18–19 October: After rebels enter Damascus's old city, French forces bombard the city with artillery for two days, killing thousands and destroying large parts of the city. The destruction is met with international outrage.

23 December: Forces loyal to Abdulaziz ibn Saud capture the port city of Jeddah on the Red Sea, completing Ibn Saud's conquest of the Kingdom of Hejaz and most of the Arabian Peninsula.

1926

February–March: The Turkish National Assembly abolishes *shari'a* law and replaces it with European civil and penal codes for nearly all cases.

25 April: Having ruled Iran for five years and suppressed several tribal rebellions, Colonel Reza Khan is officially crowned Shah of Iran. He becomes the founder of the Pahlavi dynasty. Reza Shah embarks on a programme of modernization, centralization and secularization in Iran, swelling the ranks of its military and bureaucracy.

23 May: As the Great Syrian Revolt rages in southern Syria and Lebanon, France promulgates a constitution for the Lebanese Republic.

6 June: After an eight-year-long dispute and two years of tense negotiations, Turkey officially renounces its claims to Mosul in a treaty signed in Ankara with the United Kingdom and Iraq.

1927

20 May: Britain recognizes Ibn Saud as ruler of the Nejd and the Hejaz in the Treaty of Jeddah.

5 November: The Ikhwan, a military-religious movement dedicated to the principles of Wahhabism and previously loyal to King Abdulaziz Ibn Saud, launch a raid on Busayya, Iraq, against the king's wishes. It is the beginning of the Ikhwan rebellion against Ibn Saud.

17 November: Sultan Yusuf of Morocco dies; Sultan Muhammad V accedes to the throne of Morocco, still under French protectorate.

1928

March: A schoolteacher named Hassan al Banna and six employees of the Suez Canal Company in Ismailia, Egypt, form the Muslim Brotherhood. Within a decade, the organization will have five hundred branches and tens of thousands of members, and go on to become one of the largest and most influential Islamist organizations in the world.

April: Chastened by the Great Syrian Revolt, the French High Commission in Syria allows elections for a national Constituent Assembly which returns a pro-independence majority dominated by the country's landowning class. Over the next eight years, the French will repeatedly dissolve Syria's parliament and block its attempts to pass a constitution.

1929

February: Kurdish nationalists led by Ihsan Nuri Pasha launch a rebellion in the Mount Ararat region of Turkey, with Iranian support. The Turkish government suppresses the rebellion by 1931.

August: After a dispute in Jerusalem, Arab Palestinians and Jews clash in the cities of Jerusalem, Safad and Hebron: 116 Arabs and 133 Jews are killed.

1930

10 January: The Ikhwan rebellion against Abdulaziz Ibn Saud in Arabia ends as its last leaders surrender to British forces.

1931

16 September: Italian occupying forces execute Shaykh Omar al Mukhtar, who fought against Italian rule in Libya for twenty years. The Libyan uprising is soon crushed. Tens of thousands of Libyans have died in the conflict, including many who were relocated to concentration camps.

1932

23 September: Abdulaziz Ibn Saud unifies the territory under his rule into the Kingdom of Saudi Arabia.

3 October: Iraq officially becomes an independent country under the rule of King Faysal. Per the terms of a bilateral treaty agreed in 1930, Britain maintains the right to two large airbases in Iraq, the right to use Iraq's communications infrastructure and the exclusive right to train and supply the Iraqi military.

1933

30 January: Adolf Hitler becomes chancellor of Germany. Over the next three years, 170,000 Jews from Germany arrive in Palestine, doubling the territory's Jewish population.

7 August: The Iraqi military begins an assault on Assyrian Christian communities in northern Iraq, centred around the town of Simele. Thousands of Christians are killed, and thousands more flee to Syria. Previously, the British administration in Iraq had used Assyrian refugees as an auxiliary security force.

8 September: Having ruled Iraq for twelve years, and before that Syria for eighteen months, Faysal bin Hussein dies in Bern, Switzerland. His son Ghazi succeeds him as king of Iraq.

1934

2 March: Tunisian nationalists found the Neo-Destour Party, Al Hizb al Hurr al Dusturi al Jadeed, led by Mahmoud Materi, Salah Ben Youssef and Habib Bourguiba.

5 December: Turkish women are granted the right to vote.

1936

January: Nationalists organize a nationwide strike in Syria, leading to major unrest in its cities. Eventually, France agrees to negotiations on a treaty of independence with representatives from Syria's National Bloc party, which largely represents its urban notable class.

15 April: The Great Palestinian Revolt is launched. Violence breaks out between Arab and Jewish and Palestinian communities. Four days later, Arab Palestinian leadership declares a general strike. The British move to suppress the uprising, killing approximately 1,000 Arabs in the next six months.

28 April: At age 16, Farouk I becomes king of Egypt after the death of his father, Fuad.

August: Egypt and Britain sign a new treaty of friendship, which reduces Great Britain's economic privileges in Egypt but still grants it extensive military rights in the country.

September: France and Syria sign a treaty of independence. As France's parliament never ratifies the treaty, it is stillborn and eventually overtaken by the events of the Second World War.

Autumn: In Lebanon, pharmacist Pierre Gemayel founds the Phalanges, Al Kataeb, a youth movement and political party modelled after the Italian fascist party.

29 October: With support from the British and King Ghazi, General Bakr Sidqi overthrows the nationalist government of Prime Minister Yasin al Hashimi in Baghdad. It is the first military coup in the Arab world since the fall of the Ottoman Empire. Sidqi is murdered by rival military officers within the year.

November: Although France remains in control of the country, national elections in Syria lead to the formation of a nationalist government in Damascus, with Jamil Mardam as president. The former states of the Alawites and the Druze are placed under the Damascus government's authority.

1937

March: In Turkey's Derism region, Sayyid Riza leads a Kurdish uprising against the central government. The conflict will continue until December 1938 killing tens of thousands.

11 March: In Algeria, the anti-colonial leader Messali Hadj founds the Parti du Peuple Algérien (PPA).

July: Arab Palestinians revolt again after the British Peel Commission proposes partitioning Palestine into Arab and Jewish states. The British respond with a campaign of collective punishment. The revolt continues for nearly two years.

July: In Syria's northeastern Jazira region, resistance to the Syrian government's nationalizing policy leads to armed conflict between an alliance of local Christians and Kurds and the central government in Damascus. French authorities resolve the conflict by placing the Jazira under direct French rule.

November: After a year of violent political conflict, the Alexandretta region becomes independent from Syria as the Republic of Hatay, still under French Mandate. The new republic's parliament quickly moves to adopt the Turkish language, flag, legal code and currency. Large numbers of Armenians and Alawite and Christian Arabic-speakers evacuate the province.

1938

3 March: In Dhahran, Saudi Arabia, an oil drill owned by the Arabian American Oil Company (Aramco) discovers the largest petroleum deposits in the world.

9 April: Over ten thousand supporters of the Neo-Destour Party demonstrate against French rule in Tunis, Tunisia. French troops fire on the demonstrators, killing over 100. The killings are a seminal moment in the Tunisian national movement.

10 November: Turkey's president and founder of the republic, Mustafa Kemal Ataturk, dies. His former prime minister Ismet Inonu succeeds him as president.

21 December: Britain forces the dissolution of the Legislative Council in Kuwait, at that time a British protectorate. Kuwait does not create a permanent legislature until 1962.

1939

4 April: Iraq's King Ghazi dies in a mysterious car accident, aged twenty-six. His four-year-old son, Faysal II, assumes the throne, with his uncle Abd al Ilah acting as regent.

23 May: The British government issues a White Paper on Palestine, which sharply limits Jewish immigration and land purchases, disavows any intention of creating a Jewish state in Palestine, and promises Palestine independence in ten years. Jewish armed groups in Palestine prepare to fight against the British presence in Palestine. Thousands of Jews start emigrating to Palestine to flee the German Nazi-perpetrated genocide over the next six years.

June: The Alexandretta region, previously included in France's Syria Mandate, is officially absorbed by Turkey as the Province of Hatay.

July: France dissolves the Syrian parliament, suspends its constitution and returns the Alawite and Druze regions to direct French rule.

1 September: The Second World War begins with the German invasion of Poland. Industrial production in the Middle East increases 50 per cent over the course of the war, as Britain and the United States use it as a base for their operations in Europe and North Africa.

1941

1 April: Iraqi army officers overthrow Iraq's pro-British government and install the pro-Axis Rashid Ali al Kaylani as Prime Minister. British forces invade Iraq to prevent Nazi Germany from gaining a foothold there.

1 June: Prime Minister Rashid Ali al Kaylani and his supporters flee as British forces enter Baghdad to restore Iraq's pro-British government. Hundreds of Iraqi Jews are slaughtered in a pogrom, thereafter known as the *farhud*, while British troops stand by.

8 June to 14 July: British and Free French forces invade Syria and Lebanon, ousting its pro-Vichy High Commission and promising the two countries full independence.

25 August: British, Soviet and American troops invade and occupy much of Iran after Reza Shah refuses to cooperate with the Allied war effort. They will remain in the country until 1946.

16 September: Reza Shah abdicates the Iranian throne in favour of his son, Mohammed Reza Pahlavi.

1942

4 February: British tanks surround the palace of Egyptian king Farouk forcing him to appoint an anti-Axis cabinet.

October: The British stop a German armoured invasion of Egypt at al Alamayn.

November: German troops occupy Tunisia after the United States and Great Britain invade north Africa.

8 November: Allied troops drive Vichy French forces out of Morocco.

11 November: Free French forces take power in Algeria after the Allies expel Vichy French forces.

1943
23 January: British troops drive the Italians out of Tripoli, Libya, ending the Italian occupation of Libya. Tripolitania and Cyrenaica on the Mediterranean coast come under British administration; the Fezzan region in modern-day Libya's south is administered by France.
10 February: Algerian Muslim leader Ferhat Abbas presents the French administration with a Manifesto of the Algerian People, demanding equality between Muslims and French colonists in Algeria.
15 May: The Free French take control of Tunisia after German forces are driven out by Allied troops.
July: In Syria, nationalists win elections held under Free French/British rule. Shukri Quwatli becomes president of the country.
October: In British- and Free French-occupied Lebanon, President Bishara al Khoury and Prime Minister Riad al Sulh reach an agreement, the National Pact, that allows Christian and Sunni Muslim elites to share power in Lebanon (rather than seeking to join Lebanon to either Western or Arab powers). Under the agreement, Lebanon's president must always be a Maronite Christian; its prime minister, a Sunni Muslim; and the speaker of the parliament a Shia Muslim. The struggle for independence from France begins in earnest.
11 November: The French arrest Lebanese President Khoury and Prime Minister Sulh and suspend the Lebanese constitution. After eleven days of protests bring Lebanon to a standstill, the French reverse themselves and reinstate the Lebanese government.
10 December: In Morocco, the Istiqlal (Independence) party is founded to struggle against French rule.

1944
1 February: The Irgun, a Zionist armed group under the command of Polish emigré Menachim Begin, declares a revolt against the British in Palestine, with the aim of creating a Jewish state in all of Palestine and Transjordan.
6 November: Lord Moyne, British Minister of State for the Middle East, is assassinated by Jewish militants in Cairo.

1945
14 February: US President Franklin Roosevelt meets with King Abdulaziz Ibn Saud aboard the *U.S.S. Quincy* in the Suez Canal, initiating the US–Saudi alliance.
22 March: The League of Arab States is founded in Cairo.
May: French forces violently suppress a nationalist uprising in Damascus and Aleppo, killing hundreds. Britain forces France to back down and agree to a timetable for withdrawal from Syria.
8 May: On the day of Nazi Germany defeat, French colonial forces and settlers in Algeria murder thousands of Algerians marching for independence in the cities of Sétif and Guelma.

24 August: Soviet troops invade Iran's Mazandaran province in support of a left-wing rebellion.
September: Iranian troops suppress the rebellion in Mazandaran province.
1 November: The Haganah, the official armed militia of the Jewish Agency for Palestine, launches an insurgency against the British in Palestine in cooperation with the Irgun.
21 November: The Democratic Party of Azerbaijan establishes an autonomous government in the Iranian province of Azerbaijan province under Soviet protection.
15 December: With Soviet backing, Kurdish rebels in northwest Iran declare the Kurdish Republic of Mahabad.

1946
22 March: Transjordan formally gains its independence from British Mandate, under the rule of King Abdallah, the son of Sharif Hussein of Mecca and the brother of Faysal, the late King of Iraq.
17 April: The last French troops leave Syria. President Shukri Quwatli declares Syria fully independent.
22 April: The Sudan Administrative Conference recommends ending Britain's 'closed door' policy in South Sudan, which had set up a parallel economic, educational and administrative system in the South, and administering North and South Sudan together. British authorities adopt the conference's recommendations against South Sudanese protests.
9 May: Under US and UN pressure, the Soviet Union withdraws from Iranian Azerbaijan.
22 July: The Irgun conducts a terrorist attack on the King David Hotel in Jerusalem, killing ninety-one people.
31 August: French troops leave Lebanon.
10 December: The Iranian government invades its Azerbaijan province to crush the rebellion there.
14 December: The Iranian government occupies Mahabad, Iran, crushing the year-old Kurdish rebellion there.

1947
7 April: The Ba'ath Party is founded in Damascus under the leadership of Michel Aflaq, Salah al Din Bitar and Zaki al Arsuzi.
1 September: France passes the Organic Statute of Algeria, providing for the creation of an Algerian Assembly in which Europeans and Muslims with full French citizenship are represented in one house, and the vast majority of Algerian Muslims are represented in another.
29 November: After being asked to consider the question of Palestine by the British, the UN General Assembly adopts a plan to partition the territory between an Arab Palestinian state and a Jewish state. The plan is accepted by the Zionist leadership and rejected by the Palestinians and the Arab states.

1948
16 January: The terms of a secret new treaty between Iraq and Britain, the Portsmouth Treaty, are made public, sparking mass protests in Iraq. Hundreds of protestors are killed by police. Although the Iraqi government resigns and the new government publicly repudiates the treaty, the protests continue for months, with the Iraqi Communist Party playing a leading role, challenging the rule of the Iraqi monarchy and its landowning allies.
17 February: Imam Yahya, the ruler of North Yemen, is assassinated along with his prime minister and two of his sons. A former governor of Hodeida tries to take power, but Yahya's son, Sayf al Islam Ahmad, proclaims himself the new imam and suppresses the rebellion.
March: In Palestine's civil war, the Haganah begins Plan Dalet, a strategy to secure a contiguous territory for a Jewish state by occupying and destroying selected Arab population centres.
9 April: The Irgun commits a massacre in the Arab Palestinian village of Deir Yassin near Jerusalem, killing over 100 people. News of the killings prompt Arab Palestinians to flee their homes.
14 May: The British Mandate in Palestine comes to an official end amidst civil war between Arab Palestinians and Jews. Jewish forces declare the independence of the State of Israel. The next day, Egypt, Syria, Lebanon, Iraq and Transjordan intervene in Palestine to prevent the creation of a Jewish state. The first inter-state Arab-Israeli begins.
28 December: The Prime Minister of Egypt, Mahmud al Nuqrashi, is assassinated by a member of the Muslim Brotherhood after he moves to suppress the organization.

1949
29 January: The British administration allows Libya's Jews to emigrate from the country. Facing a climate of hostility after the 1948 war, nearly the entire Jewish population, 30,000 people, leaves Libya in the next two years.
4 February: An assassin tries and fails to kill Iran's Mohammad Reza Shah. In the aftermath, Iran bans the pro-Soviet Tudeh party, and the Iranian parliament grants the Shah the right to dissolve parliament.
12 February: Hassan al Banna, the founder of the Muslim Brotherhood, is assassinated.
24 February to 20 June: Israel signs armistice agreements with (in order) Egypt, Lebanon, Transjordan and Syria, ending the first Arab-Israeli war. Israel controls 78 per cent of the territory of Mandate Palestine. Egypt occupies Gaza, and Transjordan occupies the West Bank. At least 700,000 Arab Palestinians are forced out and housed as refugees in neighbouring Arab states.
30 March: Colonel Husni al Za'im seizes power in Syria in a military coup. The CIA plays an assisting role in the coup.
14 August: Colonel Sami al Hunnawi seizes power in Syria in a military coup. Husni al Za'im and his prime minister are executed.

19 December: Colonel Adib al Shishakli seizes power in Syria in a military coup. Sami al Hunnawi goes into exile in Lebanon, where a relative of the prime minister he executed assassinates him a year later.

1950
14 May: Turkey's opposition Democratic Party wins an overwhelming victory in Turkey's first free parliamentary elections since the foundation of the Republic.

1951
8 February: France attempts to convert Morocco and Tunisia from protectorates into members of the French Union, a reorganization of the French Empire. Under the new arrangement, Moroccans and Tunisians would enjoy some of the rights of French citizens, and be represented in a federal assembly. Morocco's and Tunisia's sovereigns refuse to participate in the scheme.
March: After years of growing state and social hostility towards Jews in Iraq in the wake of the first Arab–Israeli war, the Iraqi government passes a law allowing Jews to emigrate if they give up Iraqi nationality. 130,000 Jews – nearly the entire population – emigrate within a year, often having their possessions confiscated by the state in the process.
7 March: Iranian Prime Minister Ali Razmara is assassinated.
29 April: The Iranian parliament selects Mohammad Mossadeq of the National Front as its new prime minister. Mossadeq moves to nationalize the Anglo-Iranian Oil Company. The Iranian economy plunges after Britain imposes a blockade in response.
20 July: Jordan's King Abdallah is assassinated by a Palestinian gunman in Jerusalem. His son Talal succeeds him as king.
9 October: Egyptian Prime Minister Mustafa al Nahhas unilaterally abrogates Egypt's treaty with Britain, which entitles Britain to station military forces in the Suez Canal Zone until 1956. Britain insists that the treaty is still in force.
24 December: Libya becomes independent from Britain and France as a unified state under the rule of Muhammad Idris, a leader of the Sanusi Sufi order and a long-standing figure in the resistance against the Italians, who now becomes king. Britain retains the right to station troops in Libya.

1952
1 January: Jordan's new constitution goes into effect.
18 January: Amid widespread protests in Tunisia, French authorities arrest the leaders of the nationalist Neo-Destour party. Tunisian nationalists launch a guerrilla war against French rule that lasts three years.
25 January: British forces stationed in the Suez Canal Zone attack an Egyptian police barracks in Isma'iliyya, killing fifty.
26 January: Anti-British riots break out in Cairo, Egypt. The city's central business district is burned down. Twenty people are killed.

18 February: Turkey joins the anti-Soviet North Atlantic Treaty Organization (NATO), along with its old rival, Greece.
March: The seven emirates of Abu Dhabi, Ajman, Dubai, Fujayrah, Sharjah, Umm al Qaywayn and Ras al Khaymah on the eastern coast of the Arabian Peninsula form a Trucial Council. Under treaties dating to the nineteenth century, Britain controls the foreign policies of the seven emirates, Bahrain and Qatar, while allowing local rulers to manage domestic affairs.
23 July: A group of Egyptian military officers calling themselves the Free Officers seize power in Egypt in a coup d'état. Among them are future Egyptian presidents Gamal abd al Nasser and Anwar Sadat. King Farouk abdicates in favour of his infant son.
11 August: King Talal of Jordan is declared mentally unfit to rule after barely more than a year in power. His son Hussein succeeds him as king. He will rule Jordan until 1999. The Iranian parliament grants Prime Minister Mohammad Mossadeq emergency powers, which he uses to attack the Shah's power base.
September: The new Egyptian regime issues the Agrarian Reform Law, which limits land ownership to 200 *feddans*, and redistributes the confiscated surplus.
18 September: Lebanon's President Bishara al Khoury resigns after a popular mobilization and general strike force him to abandon his plans to serve a second term.
November: Opposition parties in Baghdad organize weeks of massive anti-government protests, known as the *intifada*. The Iraqi army eventually crushes the protests.
5–8 December: Riots take place against French rule in Casablanca, Morocco.

1953

29 July: Great Britain signs a twenty-year treaty of friendship and alliance with Libya, granting it the right to station troops in Libya.
16 August: Mohammed Reza Shah flees Iran after unsuccessfully trying to oust Prime Minister Mossadegh.
19 August: Iran's Prime Minister Mossadegh is overthrown in a CIA and British-backed coup d'état. The Shah returns to power and makes General Fazallah Zahedi prime minister.
20 August: The French exile Sultan Mohammad V of Morocco to Madagascar.
9 October: Saudi Arabia's King Abdulaziz creates the Council of Ministers, marking increased institutionalization and a departure from the system of personal rule in Saudi Arabia.
9 November: Saudi Arabia's founder, King Abdulaziz dies and is succeeded by his son Saud. King Saud's brother Faysal is named crown prince.

1954

January: Adib al Shishakli brutally suppresses protests against his rule in the Jabal Druze region in Syria, killing many civilians.
27 February: After four years of dictatorial rule, Syrian President Adib al Shishakli is overthrown in a popular revolt, and flees to Brazil.

September–October: In a two-round election, the Ba'ath Party wins the second-largest number of seats in Syria's parliament.

9 September: The United States and Libya sign a treaty granting the United States the right to station military forces in Libya, especially at the Wheelus Air Base in Tripoli.

October: In Oman, forces loyal to the Ibadi imam renew their rebellion against Oman's sultan, Sa'id bin Taimur, seeking to create an independent state in Oman's interior. Saudi Arabia backs the rebels.

19 October: Great Britain signs an agreement with Egypt to evacuate its last troops from the Suez Canal zone by 20 June 1956.

November: Gamal abd al Nasser has his Free Officer rival, General Muhammed Naguib, placed under arrest. Abd al Nasser replaces Naguib as Egypt's prime minister. Egypt's most influential post-independence leader, he will introduce wide-ranging social reforms and pursue a foreign policy of pan-Arab unity and Third World power.

1 November: In Algeria, the Front de Libération National (FLN) launches an armed revolt against French rule. The Algerian War of Independence will last for eight years and lost the lives of a quarter million people.

1955

24 February: Iraq, Iran, Pakistan and Turkey form the Baghdad Pact, a pro-Western military alliance directed against the spread of Soviet influence.

21 April: French Prime Minister Edgar Faure and Tunisian nationalist leader Habib Bourguiba sign an autonomy agreement in Paris, bringing a three-year war in Tunisia to an end.

August: Shukri al Quwatli is elected president of Syria.

September: Egyptian Prime Minister Gamal abd al Nasser concludes a deal to buy arms from Communist Czechoslovakia, alarming Western powers.

6-7 September: Anti-Greek pogroms in Istanbul kill dozens and destroy massive amounts of property. The emigration of Turkey's already small Greek population accelerates.

18 August: As Sudan moves towards independence, South Sudanese army units at Torit mutiny against their new North Sudanese commanders. A low-level insurgency begins in South Sudan as southern soldiers desert, rather than surrender their weapons or accept northern command.

16 November: Sultan Mohammad V returns to Morocco after being exiled by the French to Madagascar.

December: Jordan sees three new prime ministers in one month amidst fierce popular demonstrations against the country's proposed membership in the pro-western Baghdad Pact.

1956

1 January: Sudan becomes independent from Great Britain and Egypt under a transitional constitution, with Ismail al Azhari as prime minister.

28 January: Habib Bourguiba's rival for control of the Tunisian nationalist movement, Salah Ben Youssef, flees to Libya as Bourguiba secures control over Tunisia's security forces.
2 March: Morocco gains its independence from France after forty-four years as a French protectorate.
20 March: Under pressure from the intensifying independence war in Algeria, France grants Tunisia complete independence. Nationalist leader Habib Bourguiba is elected prime minister and quickly moves to consolidate complete power. He will rule the country until November 1987.
23 June: Egypt's new constitution grants women the right to vote for the first time. Gamal abd al Nasser officially becomes president.
26 July: Egyptian President Gamal abd al Nasser nationalizes the Suez Canal after the United States and Britain withdraw funding for his Aswan High Dam project.
30 September: In Algiers, members of the FLN set off bombs in European areas of the city. French paratroopers descend on the city to root out the FLN. The Battle of Algiers begins, and lasts for over a year.
October: Syrian authorities foil an American-British coup plot. The threat to Syria's sovereignty pushes its government closer to Moscow.
8 October: The internationalized city of Tangier is integrated into Morocco.
29 October: Israel invades Egypt's Sinai Peninsula. Britain and France use the conflict as a pretext to occupy the Suez Canal. It is later revealed that the three countries planned the invasion together. Britain and France withdraw under American and Russian pressure, marking the end of Britain's world power status. Israel occupies the Sinai until March 1957.
22 November: President Nasser issues a decree denying Egyptian nationality to 'persons known as Zionists.' Over half of Egypt's 45,000 remaining Jews leave over the next nine months. By 1970, only 300 Jews will be left in Egypt, down from 80,000 in 1948.

1957
March: Jordan's nationalist government, under the leadership of Prime Minister Suleiman Nabulsi, formally ends the Anglo-Jordanian military treaty. Britain agrees to withdraw its troops from the country.
April: Jordan's King Hussein dismisses his nationalist prime minister Suleiman Nabulsi, suppresses a military revolt, declares martial law and dissolves all political parties. The United States orders naval ships to the Eastern Mediterranean to support the king.
17 July: With American assistance, British troops arrive in Jordan to provide temporary support to Jordan's embattled King Hussein.
24 July: Britain deploys troops to Oman to support Sultan bin Taimur against the *imami* rebellion.
25 July: Tunisia abolishes its monarchy and is declared a republic.
August: Sultan Mohammad V of Morocco takes the title of king.

6 August: Syria signs an economic and technical aid agreement with the Soviet Union. Not long after, Syrian authorities uncover and foil another American coup plot.

13 October: Egyptian troops land in Latakia, Syria, in a show of solidarity against threats to Syria's sovereignty from Western powers.

1958

1 February: Syria and Egypt unite to form the United Arab Republic (UAR), under the leadership of Egyptian president Gamal abd al Nasser. Nasser bans most existing political parties in Syria and implements a limited programme of land redistribution in the country.

14 February: In response to the formation of the United Arab Republic in Egypt and Syria, the cousins King Husayn of Jordan and King Faysal II of Iraq announce that they are uniting their kingdoms in an Arab Federation opposed to the UAR.

May–November: In Morocco, Crown Prince Hassan leads the armed forces to repress a rebellion in the Rif Mountains.

8 May: The editor of Beirut's *Telegraph* newspaper, Nasib al Matani, is assassinated amidst growing tensions in Lebanon over President Camille Chamoun's attempts to hold on to power past the end of his term, and his opponents' support of Nasser's United Arab Republic. Open street fighting breaks out in Lebanon's cities after al Matani's assassination.

13 May: Angered by the failure of the French government to put down the Algerian revolution, European colonists in Algeria storm the French governor-general's office in Algiers.

14 July: Brigadier General Abd al Karim Qasim seizes power in Iraq in a military coup. Qasim rebels after being ordered to Jordan to support the regime of King Hussein. King Faysal II, his uncle Abd al Ilah, and most of the royal family are executed. Qasim moves quickly to introduce wide-ranging agrarian reforms, nationalize the oil industry, and establish close ties with the Soviet Union.

15 July: Fearing a domino effect, the United States lands 15,000 troops in Lebanon to preserve the rule of President Camille Chamoun against threats from Nasserist forces. British troops are also deployed to Jordan.

31 August: The Lebanese crisis is resolved with the election of army commander Fuad Shahib as president.

17 November: General Ibrahim Aboud overthrows the Azhari government in Sudan, establishing a military regime.

1959

March: With encouragement from the Nasser regime in Egypt, pro-Ba'athist Iraqi military officers based in Mosul try to overthrow the Qasim regime, which had refused to join Nasser's United Arab Republic. Communist partisans massacre supporters of the Ba'ath party in Mosul in retaliation.

June: Tunisia's Prime Minister Habib Bourguiba promulgates a constitution that invests the presidency with expansive powers. Bourguiba is then elected to the presidency.

1960

January: Oman's Sultan Sa'id bin Taimur crushes the *imami* rebellion, reuniting the country's coast and interior.

27 May: The Turkish military, led by Lieutenant General Jemal Gursel, overthrows the Democratic Party government in Istanbul, the first of several military coups that will characterize Turkish politics in the coming decades. Turkey's prime minister is arrested and eventually executed.

July–August: Under US pressure to liberalize his regime, the Shah of Iran allows the National Front Party, the party of former Prime Minister Mossadegh, to participate in parliamentary elections.

September: The Organization of Petroleum Exporting Countries (OPEC) is formed in Baghdad. Its charter members are Saudi Arabia, Iran, Iraq, Kuwait and Venezuela.

1 September: The Shah of Iran nullifies the results of parliamentary elections.

28 November: Mauritania proclaims itself independent from France. Mokhtar Ould Daddah becomes president and consolidates power in a one-party state.

1961

January: Fresh parliamentary elections are held in Iran after the Shah nullified the previous results.

26 February: King Mohammad V of Morocco dies; his son Hassan becomes King Hassan II of Morocco.

9 May: The Shah of Iran dissolves parliament in the face of a growing protest movement.

19 June: Kuwait, a British protectorate since 1899, becomes independent under the rule of Amir Abdullah Al Salim of the al Sabah dynasty, which has ruled the area since 1756. Kuwait thereafter joins the League of Arab States in spite of Iraq's territorial claims over Kuwait.

July: Britain deploys military forces in the Persian Gulf to deter a threatened Iraqi invasion of Kuwait.

9 July: Turkish voters approve a new constitution following a military coup the previous year.

19–23 July: After Tunisia tries to force France to evacuate its base at Bizerte, Tunisian and French forces clash, leaving over 600 Tunisian troops dead.

September: Kurds in northern Iraq begin an uprising against the Iraqi central government, under the leadership of Mustafa Barzani.

28 September: A right-wing military coup in Syria ends Syria's union with Egypt. The United Arab Republic is dissolved. After parliamentary elections in December, Nazim al Qudsi becomes president.

1962

18 March: The French government declares a ceasefire in Algeria after successful negotiations with the FLN in Evian on a treaty of independence.

1 July: Algerian voters overwhelmingly vote to confirm the Evian Agreements and make Algeria independent from France, ending 132 years of French rule in Algeria.

5 July: Algeria becomes fully independent of France.

18 September: North Yemen's Imam Ahmad dies, and is succeeded by his son Muhammad Badr.

26 September: North Yemen's civil war begins. Imam Muhammad Badr is overthrown in a military coup led by Colonel Abdullah Sallal, who proclaims the Yemen Arab Republic. Egypt deploys tens of thousands of troops to North Yemen to support the coup and the Soviet Union backs the new government, while Jordan, Saudi Arabia and the United States back Yemeni troops still loyal to Imam Badr. The civil war continues for nearly eight years.

11 November: A new constitution in Kuwait provides for the direct election of a national assembly, the first such parliament in an Arab Gulf monarchy. Elections are held the following year.

7 December: Morocco's first constitution is adopted, granting the king executive powers in a system with a bicameral legislature and an independent judiciary.

1963

January: The Shah of Iran announces the White Revolution, a series of reforms intended to modernize the country. The programme includes an extensive land redistribution campaign and large investments in healthcare, education and industrialization.

8 February: Ba'athist military officers seize power in Baghdad. President Abd al Karim Qasim is executed. Colonel Abd al-Salam Arif becomes president.

8 March: Military officers loyal to the Ba'ath party stage a coup in Damascus. Three Alawite officers of peasant background – Mohammad Umran, Salah Jadid and Hafez al Asad – seize power. The new government embarks on an ambitious programme of reforms to benefit Syria's peasant classes, including expansive land reform. Large numbers of rural and religious minority Syrians enter the ranks of the military and the civilian administration.

5-6 June: Iranian secret police arrest Ayatollah Ruhollah Khomeini, a leading religious figure, after he publicly opposes the Shah. 100 people are killed by police in the mass demonstrations that follow. Khomeini is exiled.

8 September: Voters in Algeria approve the country's new constitution. FLN leader Ahmed Ben Bella becomes the country's first president. Political violence continues in Algeria, especially between socialist rebels and government forces.

9 September: The Anya Nya rebel movement in southern Sudan launches attacks on government forces, beginning the first Sudanese civil war.

15 October: As a result of negotiations in the wake of the Bizerte clashes, the last French troops leave Tunisia.
18 November: In Iraq, President Abd al Salam Arif leads a purge of the Ba'ath party from the government, nine months after coming to power with Ba'ath party's support.

1964

April: In Hama, Syria's fourth-largest city, a brief Muslim Brotherhood-led uprising against the new Ba'athist government is quickly crushed.
28 May: The Palestine Liberation Organization (PLO) is founded in Cairo.
October: In Sudan, the government of General Ibrahim Aboud is overthrown in a popular revolution, and an Islamist-led civilian government is established amidst Sudan's ongoing north–south civil war.
2 November: Saudi Arabia's King Saud is deposed by his brother, Crown Prince Faysal, who becomes king.

1965

21 January: Iran's Prime Minister, Ali Mansur, is assassinated.
22 March: Student and worker uprising in Casablanca, Morocco.
7 June: Facing a growing protest movement, King Hassan II of Morocco suspends the constitution and parliament and declares a state of emergency.
9 June: In southern Oman, the Dhofar Liberation Front (later the Popular Front for the Liberation of the Occupied Arab Gulf, and later the People's Front for the Liberation of Oman) launches a rebellion against Sultan bin Taimur. The rebellion will continue for ten years. Sultan bin Taimur is supported by Great Britain, Saudi Arabia, Jordan and Iran. The rebels are supported by the Soviet Union and South Yemen.
19 June: Colonel Houari Boumediene overthrows Algeria's President Ahmed Ben Bella in a military coup. Boumediene will rule the country until his death in December 1978.

1966

23 February: Salah Jadid and Hafez al Assad consolidate their power in a coup in Damascus. Ba'ath party founder Michel Aflaq goes into exile.
16 April: Iraq's President Abd al Salam Arif dies in a helicopter crash. He is succeeded by his brother, Army Chief of Staff Abd al Rahman Arif.
8 September: An attempted military coup in Syria fails to dislodge Jadid and Assad.

1967

May: Israel reportedly builds its first two nuclear bombs. It will eventually amass an arsenal of several hundred.
5 June: As tensions mount in the region, Israel launches a pre-emptive strike on the Egyptian air force, touching off the Six-Day War. Israel captures Gaza and the Sinai Peninsula from Egypt, the Golan Heights from Syria and the West Bank and East Jerusalem from Jordan.

31 August: Egypt and Saudi Arabia sign an agreement to end their intervention in North Yemen's civil war. All Egyptian troops withdraw from Yemen by 1968.

5 November: North Yemen's president and former coup leader Abdullah Sallal is overthrown in a military coup led by Abdel Rahman Iryani.

November: Britain moves its main naval base in the Arabian Peninsula region from Aden to Bahrain.

29 November: Britain evacuates Aden and the Protectorate of South Arabia, which gains independence as the People's Republic of Yemen. The new nation is initially divided between the Egyptian-backed nationalist Front for the Liberation of Occupied South Yemen and the leftist National Liberation Front. The latter quickly takes power.

1968

January: Britain announces that it will withdraw its forces from the Persian Gulf.

27 February: Bahrain and Qatar join the other seven Trucial States on the Trucial Council, in anticipation of a possible Gulf federation after the expected British withdrawal from the region.

17 July: Ba'athist military officers seize power in Baghdad, overthrowing the regime of Abd al-Rahman Arif.

1969

4 February: Yasser Arafat, the leader of the Fatah Palestinian guerrilla movement, is elected chairman of the Palestine Liberation Organization (PLO).

March: Egypt begins a war of attrition with Israel over the Suez Canal. A million Egyptians are driven from their homes by the fighting.

25 May: Colonel Jaafar al-Numeiri seizes power in Sudan in a military coup. Styling his movement after the Free Officers movement in Egypt, he suspends the constitution and nationalizes Sudan's industries.

22 June: South Yemen's President Qahtan Muhammad Shaabi is overthrown in a Marxist military coup. South Yemen reorients strategically towards the Soviet Union.

1 September: In Libya, 27-year-old Colonel Muammar Gaddafi overthrows King Idris I, seizing power in a military coup. He moves to nationalize Libya's oil industry and expel British and American military forces from the country.

2 November: After six months of clashes between the Lebanese Army and Palestinian militias, Lebanon signs the Cairo Agreement with the Palestine Liberation Organization, which gives the PLO broad rights to operate in Lebanon and launch attacks on Israel from Lebanese territory.

1970

March: After eight years of conflict, the first Iraqi-Kurdish war ends with an agreement that grants Iraq's Kurds limited autonomy. Saddam Hussein, vice chairman of Iraq's Revolutionary Command Council, negotiates the agreement.

March: The government of Colonel Jaafar al Numeiri in Sudan bombs Aba Island in the Nile River, the stronghold of the Islamist Ansar movement. 3,000 people are killed.
14 April: North Yemen's civil war ends with a peace agreement negotiated in Jeddah, Saudi Arabia.
May: Iran's government renounces its claim to Shi'ite-majority Bahrain. After the 1979 revolution, the Islamic Republic of Iran will not recognize this renunciation.
30 May: Iraq's new Ba'athist rulers publish Land Law 117, which extensively redistributes agricultural land from Iraq's old elites to its peasant classes.
23 July: In Oman, Sultan Sa'id bin Taimur is overthrown by his son, Qaboos bin Sa'id, who becomes sultan. Sultan Qaboos reverses his father's approach and pursues a modernization programme in the country.
31 July: Morocco adopts its second constitution; the state of emergency comes to an end.
7 August 1970: The War of Attrition between Egypt and Israel, which had started in 1967, ends.
September: Civil war breaks in Jordan as King Hussein orders his army into combat with Palestinian militant organizations based in Palestinian refugee camps. Syrian tanks briefly cross the Jordanian border to support the Palestinians, but Israeli and American threats force them to turn back. Hussein defeats the Palestinians at the cost of thousands of lives, and the PLO relocates to Beirut. The events come to be known as Black September.
28 September: Eighteen years after his Free Officers' Coup, and fourteen years after becoming Egypt's unchallenged president, Gamal abd al Nasser dies in Cairo.
November: Defence Minister Hafez al Assad seizes complete power in Syria, in what becomes known in Syria as the Corrective Movement. He initiates a programme of economic liberalization called the *infitah* (opening).
30 November: South Yemen's President Salim Rubayyi Ali renames the country the People's Democratic Republic of Yemen.

1971
22 February: Hafez al Assad officially assumes the presidency of Syria. He will hold the office until his death in June 2000.
12 March: Amidst escalating political violence in Turkey, the military forces prime minister Suleyman Demirel to resign.
10 July: A failed coup attempt in Morocco leads to suspension of the constitution.
15 August: Bahrain achieves formal independence from Britain under the leadership of Shaykh Isa bin Salman al Khalifah. Bahrain and Britain sign a treaty of friendship. In declaring independence, Bahrain removes itself from a planned federation of Gulf states, later to become the United Arab Emirates. The British naval base in Bahrain is transferred to US control.
3 September: Qatar declares its independence from Great Britain, removing itself from a planned federation of Gulf states, later to become the United Arab Emirates.

November: Ahead of the independence of the United Arab Emirates, Iran occupies the islands of Greater and Lesser Tunb and Abu Musa, beginning a territorial dispute between Iran and the United Arab Emirates.
2 December: After independence from Britain, Abu Dhabi, Ajman, Dubai, Fujayrah, Sharjah and Umm al Qaywayn come together as the United Arab Emirates (UAE). Sheikh Zayed Bin-Sultan Al Nuhayyan presides over the federation. The UAE joins the League of Arab States.

1972
February: The emirate of Ras al Khaymah joins the United Arab Emirates after initially withdrawing from the planned federation over its refusal to support its territorial claims against Iran. The United Arab Emirates creates a Federal National Council, a forty-member consultative body appointed by the rulers of the seven emirates.
22 February: In Qatar, Prime Minister Khalifa bin Hamad al Thani seizes power from his cousin, the Emir Ahmed bin Ali al Thani, in a palace coup. Khalifa becomes Emir.
1 March: Morocco's third constitution is promulgated.
27 March: The warring parties in Sudan's north-south civil war sign the Addis Abba Agreement, which grants South Sudan autonomy. Sudan's first civil war, which killed half a million people, has come to an end.
19 April: Qatar's new emir, Khalifa bin Hamad al Thani, issues a provisional constitution.
1 June: Iraq nationalizes the Iraq Petroleum Company. As a result, Iraq's state oil revenues are fifty-two times higher in 1980 than in 1968.
July: Egyptian President Anwar Sadat expels over 20,000 Soviet military advisors from Egypt, signalling a major westward shift in his foreign policy.
16 August: A second failed coup attempt takes place in Morocco.

1973
April: In Libya, Muammar Gaddafi announces a 'cultural revolution' (*thawra sha'biya*) suspending all current laws and setting up thousands of 'people's committees' (*jamahiriya*) to reform and purge Libyan society of 'social diseases' and foreign influences.
6 October: On the Jewish Day of Atonement (*yom kippur*), Egypt and Syria launch a combined attack on Israel, pushing deep into the Golan Heights and the Sinai Peninsula. After weeks of heavy fighting and casualties, and with large emergency arms shipments from the United States, Israel pushes the Egyptian and Syrian forces back, but Israeli military confidence is shaken.
19 October: In solidarity with the Egyptian and Syrian war effort, Saudi Arabia suspends all oil shipments to the United States, and the OPEC announces drastic production cuts. Global oil prices soar.
7 December: Bahrain elects its first National Assembly under a constitution that goes into force on 6 December.

1974
11 March: Negotiations between Kurdish leader Mustafa Barzani and the Iraqi central government break down; the second Iraqi Kurdish War begins, with the Kurds receiving support from Iran, Israel and the United States.
April: Egyptian President Anwar Sadat announces a programme of economic liberalization, the *infitah* (opening).
13 June: North Yemeni President Abdel Rahman Iryani, who seized power in a military coup in 1967, is overthrown in a military coup led by Lieutenant Colonel Ibrahim Muhammad Hamadi.
July: Turkey invades northern Cyprus after a military coup on the island brings to power a group committed to unifying Cyprus with Greece. The US responds to the invasion by imposing an arms embargo on its NATO ally Turkey.
22 November: The United Nations General Assembly grants the Palestine Liberation Organization observer status, a month after the League of Arab States recognizes the PLO as the 'sole and legitimate representative' of the Palestinian people, implicitly renouncing other Arab claims to Palestinian territory in favour of Palestinian independence.

1975
2 March: In Iran, Shah Mohammed Reza Pahlavi dissolves the two-party political system and bans opposition political parties.
6 March: Iraq and Iran sign the Algiers Accord, fixing the boundary between the two countries on the Persian Gulf. Iran agrees to cut off support to Mustafa Barzani's Kurdish insurgency in Iraq, which quickly collapses. The Iraqi government forcibly relocates some 250,000 Kurds to southern Iraq over the next five years.
25 March: Saudi Arabia's King Faysal is assassinated by his nephew. His brother Khalid succeeds him as king.
13 April: Christian Phalangist militiamen massacre twenty-seven Palestinians on a bus in Beirut, in retaliation for a shooting at a church earlier in the day. The attacks trigger nationwide violence which spirals into the Lebanese Civil War. The conflict – which will kill over 100,000 people and cause the flight of a million – will last until October 1990, involving invasions by Syria (1976) and Israel (1978, 1982), and intervention by the United States (1982). Initially, the conflict pits the Christian-dominated Lebanese government and the Phalange militias against the Palestinians and the National Front, a loose coalition of Sunnis, Shiites, Druzes and Christians led by the Druze leader Kamal Jumblatt.
26 August: In Bahrain, Shaykh Isa bin Salman al Khalifah dissolves his country's National Assembly and begins ruling by decree.

1976
March: The Lebanese Army splinters, largely along religious lines, amidst Lebanon's ongoing civil war.

11 March: A cessation of hostilities agreement ends nearly eleven years of fighting between the government of Oman and the People's Front for the Liberation of Oman, after the government, supported by troops from Iran and Jordan, inflicts large defeats on the rebels.
31 May: Syria invades Lebanon to stop a Palestinian-Druze advance on Christian strongholds in that country's civil war.
July: 700 people are killed in Khartoum as the government of President Jaafar al Numeiri puts down an Islamist coup attempt.
29 August: Kuwait's emir Sabah al Salim al Sabah dissolves parliament and suspends the constitution.
19 November: Voters in Algeria confirm a new constitution, which makes Islam Algeria's official religion, the FLN the only legal political party and socialism the state economic ideology. Houari Boumediene, Algeria's military ruler in 1965, becomes the country's president.

1977

January: Bread riots take place in Cairo after the Egyptian government abruptly announces heavy subsidy cuts to basic goods. President Anwar Sadat deploys the army to crush the riots, killing 150 people. The subsidies are soon restored.
2 March: In Libya, Muammar Gaddafi announces the creation of the Great Socialist People's Libyan Arab Jamahiriya (state of the masses), and shifts power from the people's committees to new revolutionary committees.
May: Former Irgun commander Menachem Begin's Likud Party wins in Israel's general elections. The new government moves to encourage a programme of Jewish settlement in Palestinian territories occupied in the 1967 war.
10 October: North Yemeni president and former coup leader Ibrahim Hamadi is assassinated. Lieutenant-Colonel Ahmed Hussein al Ghashmi succeeds him as chairman of a three-member presidential council.
20 November: Egyptian President Anwar Sadat travels to Jerusalem to address the Israeli Knesset, in a sign of rapid rapprochement between the two adversaries.

1978

January: Libyan forces invade Chad from the north in support of the Frolinat opposition group, touching off a series of clashes between the two countries that will continue for nine years.
26–28 January: 200 striking union workers are killed by police during a general strike in Tunis.
14 March: Israel launches an invasion of southern Lebanon to strike Palestinian bases.
24 June: North Yemeni President Ahmed Hussein al Ghashmi is assassinated in Sana'a.
26 June: South Yemen's President Salim Ali Rubayyi is overthrown and executed by supporters of the National Liberation Front. He is succeeded as president by Abdel Fattah Ismail.

10 July: President Mokhtar Ould Daddah of Mauritania is overthrown in a military coup. Colonel Mustapha Ould Salek becomes president.

17 July: North Yemen's Constituent People's Assembly chooses Lieutenant-Colonel Ali Abdullah Saleh as president. Saleh will serve as North Yemen's president until 2012, and as president of a united Yemen from May 1990.

17 September: Israeli and Egyptian negotiators at Camp David in the United States agree on outlines of a peace agreement, and a framework agreement for establishing an interim regime for the West Bank and Gaza.

7 September: The Iranian revolution begins as 100,000 protestors take to the streets of Iran to protest the Shah's rule. Police kill 250 protestors in suppressing the demonstrations. Martial law is imposed.

27 November: The Kurdistan Workers' Party (PKK) is founded, with Abdullah Öcalan as chairman. The PKK begins mounting attacks on Turkish government forces.

27 December: Algeria's President Houari Boumediene dies, and is replaced as president by Colonel Chadli Bendjedid.

1979

16 January: The Shah of Iran flees the country. His government continues to struggle against insurgents and opposition parties.

1 February: Ayatollah Ruhollah Khomeini returns to Iran from exile in France.

11 February: Amidst fierce clashes in Tehran, Iran, the Shah's prime minister resigns, and Ayatollah Khomeini's favoured candidate forms a government.

26 March: In Washington, Egyptian President Anwar Sadat and Israeli Prime Minister Menachem Begin sign a formal peace treaty, the first between Israel and an Arab state. Egypt is subsequently suspended from the League of Arab States.

1 April: Ayatollah Khomeini proclaims the Islamic Republic of Iran after voters approve the abolition of the monarchy in a national referendum.

6 April: In Mauritania, the government of Mustapha Ould Salek is overthrown in a military coup. Colonel Mohamed Khouna Haidalla becomes prime minister, and Colonel Mohamed Mahmoud Ould Louly becomes president.

May: In Iran, Ayatollah Khomeini creates the Revolutionary Guards, an armed force independent of the Iranian military.

16 June: In Aleppo, Syria, gunmen slaughter dozens of Alawite Muslim cadets at an artillery college, as the Muslim Brotherhood's insurgency against the Assad regime intensifies.

16 July: Saddam Hussein becomes president of Iraq after President Ahmed Hasan al Bakr resigns.

22 July: At a meeting of the Ba'ath Party Regional Congress, Iraqi President Saddam Hussein accuses twenty-two party members of treason, and has them publicly arrested, and, on 8 August, executed.

16 August: Kurdish rebels in northwestern Iran launch a rebellion against the central government, and go on to capture several key cities.

4 November: Iranian students storm the American embassy, taking 52 Americans hostage. The hostage crisis will continue for 444 days.
20 November: Religious extremists led by Juhayman al Otaybi seize the Grand Mosque of Mecca. Saudi, Pakistani and French special forces take back the mosque on 4 December. A total of 127 people are killed during the siege.
26 November: The Saudi National Guard crushes an uprising in Saudi Arabia's Shiite-majority Eastern Province. Dozens of protestors are killed.
2–3 December: Iranian voters approve a constitution which gives the Islamic clerical establishment the power to supervise and overrule other government institutions, a principle known as *vilayat-i faqih* (governance of the jurist).

1980

25 January: Abolhasan Bani Sadr is elected as the first president of the Islamic Republic of Iran. His short presidency (4 February–22 June 1980) is characterized by a failed effort to restrain Iran's clerical establishment after the 1979 revolution.
26–27 January: A Libya-backed militant group, the Tunisian Armed Resistance, attacks Gafsa, Tunisia with alleged Libyan support. 48 people are killed in the attack. Tunisia expels Libya's ambassador, and France and the United States ramp up military assistance to Tunisia.
February: Iraqi women get the right to vote.
21 April: South Yemen's President Abdel Fattah Ismail is forced to resign. He is succeeded by Ali Nasser Mohammed.
26 June: Hafez al Assad survives an assassination attempt by Muslim Brotherhood supporters. The next day, Syrian troops massacre approximately 500 Brotherhood supporters imprisoned in Palmyra.
6–20 August: The Libyan government suppresses a military revolt in Tobruk. Several hundred people are killed.
12 September: The Turkish military overthrows the civilian government. A National Security Council led by General Kenan Evren and Admiral Bulent Ulusu seizes power, imposes martial law, bans all political parties and carries out extensive purges of the government.
22 September: Five days after abrogating the Algiers Accord, Iraq invades Iran. Over the next eight years, the Iran–Iraq War will kill close to one million people. Iraq receives backing from the United States and Saudi Arabia for its war effort.
November: Saudi Arabia completes its gradual nationalization of the Arabian American Oil Company.

1981

22 February: Kuwait's Amir Jaber al Ahmad al Sabah restores his country's constitution. Elections for parliament follow.
25 May: Saudi Arabia, Bahrain, Kuwait, Qatar, Oman and the United Arab Emirates set up the Gulf Cooperation Council (GCC).

7 June: Israeli warplanes destroy the Iraqi nuclear reactor at Osirak in a surprise raid.

20 June: The Mujahedin-e Khalq, a left-wing revolutionary organization in Iran, launches protests against Ayatollah Khomeini's rule.

21 June: Iranian President Abolhasan Bani Sadr is impeached, and later flees to Paris, forming a government-in-exile.

30 August: In Iran, a member of the Mujahedin-e Khalq assassinates Iran's President, Mohammad Ali Rajai, and Prime Minister, Mohammad Javad Bahonar. The revolutionary Iranian regime launches an unprecedented crackdown on dissent, including mass arrests and executions.

2 October: Ayatollah Ali Khamenei becomes president of Iran.

6 October: At a military parade marking the eighth anniversary of the 1973 war on Israel, gunmen affiliated with Egyptian Islamic Jihad assassinate Egyptian President Anwar Sadat. He is succeeded by his vice-president, former air force commander Hosni Mubarak, who imposes a state of emergency that will remain in place for nearly thirty-one years.

14 December: Israel begins to administer the Golan Heights as part of its own territory. No other country recognizes this region, which was part of Syrian territory before Israel occupied it in 1967, as a part of Israel.

19 December: After Bahraini authorities disrupt a planned uprising by the Shiite Islamist group based in Iran, Bahrain's Sunni ruler, Shaykh Isa bin Salman al Khalifa, signs a mutual defence accord with Saudi Arabia.

1982

2 February: Muslim Brotherhood supporters seize control in the old city of Hama, Syria. Syrian troops besiege and attack the town. Over the next three weeks, thousands of civilians are killed (estimates vary from 2,000 to 40,000) and much of the city is destroyed. The Muslim Brotherhood insurgency in Syria is crushed.

6 June: After an assassination attempt on Israel's ambassador to Great Britain, Israel launches an invasion of Lebanon, fighting alongside Lebanon's Christian-dominated government and Phalange militias in the country's ongoing civil war. By 14 June, Israeli forces lay siege to Beirut.

14 June: Saudi Arabia's King Khalid dies of a heart attack. His brother, Crown Prince Fahd, succeeds him as king.

20 August: American marines arrive in Lebanon as part of a multinational peacekeeping force (also including French and Italian troops) in support of Beirut's fragile ceasefire.

23 August: As part of a ceasefire agreement, the PLO evacuates Israel-besieged Beirut and moves its headquarters to Tunis. Bashir Gemayel, the scion of the Phalangist party and commander of the Lebanese Forces alliance, is elected president of Lebanon with US and Israeli backing.

14 September: Lebanon's American and Israeli-backed president-elect, Bashir Gemayel, is killed by a bomb planted by Habib Shartouni, a Maronite Christian and member of the Syrian Social Nationalist Party. Israel moves to occupy West Beirut.

16 September: During thirty-eight hours, Phalangist militiamen massacre 3,500 Palestinian refugees in the Sabra and Shatila camps in West Beirut, while Israeli military forces, who had approved the Phalanges demand to enter and clear up the camps, guard the entrance to the camps.
23 September: Amine Gemayel, the brother of the assassinated president-elect Bashir Gemayel, becomes president of Lebanon. Lebanon's civil war continues.
7 November: Turkish voters approve Turkey's first new constitution since the September 1980 coup. General Kenan Evren, who led the coup, becomes president.

1983
17 May: Israel and Lebanon sign a peace agreement, spelling out terms for Israeli withdrawal from Lebanon.
5 June: Sudanese President Jaafar al Numeiri forcibly divides Sudan's restive southern region into three provinces. Southern army commanders organize the Sudanese People's Liberation Army (SPLA) in response, and begin fighting to overthrow the Khartoum government.
September: Sudanese President Jaafar al Numeiri, once known as a secular socialist, imposes Islamic *shari'a* law nationwide. The burgeoning insurrection in Christian and traditionalist South Sudan explodes into a new Sudanese civil war.
23 October: A week after the *U.S.S. New Jersey* shells Druze and Shiite militia positions in Lebanon, simultaneous attacks target French and American marine barracks in Beirut killing 307 people. The Shiite Islamist organization Hezbollah is later identified as the attacker.
13 December: In Turkey, Turgut Ozal of the Motherland Party takes over as prime minister after his party wins elections in November, returning Turkey to civilian rule three years after its third military coup.

1984
3 January: Over 100 people are killed in bread price riots in Tunisia.
7 February: US President Reagan orders American marines to withdraw from Beirut.
March–April: Syria narrowly avoids civil conflict as President Hafez al Assad confronts a power challenge from his brother Rif'at al Assad. Rif'at enters voluntary exile in June.
5 March: The Lebanese government repudiates its peace agreement with Israel.
15 August: In southeastern Turkey, the PKK (Kurdistan Workers' Party) launches attacks on government forces in five provinces, beginning a long-running rebellion against the Turkish central government. By the end of the 1990s, tens of thousands of people will have been killed, thousands of villages destroyed, and around two million displaced.
12 December: In Mauritania, Colonel Maaouiya Ould Sid Ahmed Taya overthrows the government of Mohamed Khouna Haidalla while the latter is out of the country. Ould Taya will rule until August 2005.

1985

16 February: Hezbollah, a Shiite Islamist party and militia based in South Lebanon, announces its existence and pledges resistance against the Israeli occupation of Lebanon. Over the course of the Lebanese Civil War, Hezbollah becomes one of the most powerful militias in Lebanon.

6 April: Sudanese President Jaafar al Numeiri is overthrown in a military coup amidst rising social unrest and an escalating north-south civil war.

June: Israel withdraws its forces to a large 'security zone' in southern Lebanon, which it will occupy for the next fifteen years, partly through a local Christian militia it supports, the South Lebanon Army (SLA).

1 October: A week after Palestinian guerrillas hijack an Israeli yacht near Larnaca, Cyprus, killing three Israeli tourists, the Israeli army attacks the PLO's headquarters in Hammam Chott, near Tunis, Tunisia, killing 71 people.

1986

13 January: After South Yemen's former president Abdel Fattah Ismail returns from exile, President Ali Nasser Mohammed orders his bodyguard to open fire on Ismail's supporters. The attack is the beginning of the 'January events,' two weeks of clashes in which five thousand people are killed. President Ali Nasser Mohammed flees the country. Prime Minister Bakr Attas is chosen as president.

26 February: Egyptian paramilitary conscripts riot in Giza, Assiut and other locations. The military crushes the uprising, killing thousands of Central Security Forces personnel.

April: In Sudan, the Islamist Umma Party, led by Sadiq al Mahdi, triumphs in general elections.

April: Qatari troops occupy Bahrain's Fasht al Dibal Island, which Qatar claims as its own territory. Qatar withdraws in June after mediation by Saudi Arabia.

15 April: The United States bombs Tripoli, Libya, in retaliation for the bombing of a night club in Berlin frequented by US servicemen. Over 100 people are killed.

3 July: Kuwait's Amir Jaber al Ahmad al Sabah suspends Kuwait's constitution and dissolves parliament, ten years after his predecessor did the same and five years after parliament's restoration.

November: The King Fahd causeway, which links the island nation of Bahrain to Saudi Arabia, opens.

1987

22 May: The Lebanese parliament votes overwhelmingly to annul the Cairo Agreement of 1969, which gave the PLO the right to operate from Lebanese territory.

June: An attempted coup in the emirate of Sharjah is foiled by the resistance of the other six emirates of the UAE.

7 November: In Tunisia, Prime Minister Zine El Abidine Ben Ali declares Habib Bourguiba, president since 1959, mentally unfit to rule. Ben Ali succeeds him as president, an office he will hold until January 2011.

9 December: An Israeli military vehicle kills four Palestinians. Protests erupt across the Israel-occupied Gaza Strip and West Bank, and are met with violence from Israeli forces. Strikes and demonstrations spread rapidly. The first Palestinian *intifada* has begun, and will eventually prompt Israel to negotiate with the PLO for the first time.

1988

March: As the Iran–Iraq war draws to a close, Iraqi forces launch the Anfal campaign against Kurdish insurgents in northern Iraq who had been fighting alongside Iran. Over the next six months, thousands of villages are destroyed and tens of thousands of Kurds are killed.

16 March: Iraqi forces attack the Kurdish village of Halabja with chemical weapons. 5,000 people are killed.

11 August: The terrorist group Al Qaeda is officially formed in a meeting in Peshawar, Pakistan. Its leadership includes Osama bin Laden, Ayman al Zawahiri (of Egyptian Islamic Jihad), Abdullah 'Azzam and Sayyed Imam al Sharif.

18 August: The Islamic Resistance Movement (Arabic acronym Hamas), a Muslim Brotherhood-affiliated organization in the Gaza Strip, adopts its founding charter, which calls for *jihad* to restore Islamic rule over all of Palestine.

20 August: A truce comes into effect between Iran and Iraq, in accordance with UN Security Council Resolution 598, ending nearly eight years of war, the longest conventional war of the twentieth century.

5–11 October: Widespread protests and riots break out across Algeria in the face of economic collapse and youth discontent. The military suppresses the protests with force, killing approximately 500 people.

15 November: PLO Chairman Yasser Arafat declares Palestine 'independent,' and the Palestine National Council adopts UN Security Council Resolution 242 of 1967, which called on all parties to recognize Israel's existence. Thereafter, the US enters into a dialogue with the PLO for the first time.

1989

January: The Soviet Union loosens controls on emigration, leading to an exodus of about a million Soviet Jews who move to Israel in the coming years.

14 March: Lebanese army commander and interim prime minister Michel Aoun launches a 'war of liberation' against Syrian forces in Lebanon. The campaign ends in disaster.

22 May: Egypt is readmitted to the League of Arab States, ten years after it was suspended for its peace treaty with Israel.

3 June: Iran's Supreme Leader, Ayatollah Ruhollah Khomeini, dies. President Ali Khamenei is appointed as new supreme leader.

30 June: General Omar al Bashir seizes power in a military coup in Sudan, as the north-south civil war continues to rage. He is backed by the National Islamic Front and the powerful Islamist leader Hassan al Turabi.

2 July: Algeria's government lifts the ban on new political parties and allows for multiparty elections.

28 July: Ali Akbar Hashemi Rafsanjani is elected Iran's new president.

22 October: Lebanese parliamentarians sign the Ta'if Agreement at a conference in Ta'if, Saudi Arabia. The agreement reapportions the representation of each religious group in Lebanon's parliament, and amends the Lebanese constitution to devolve certain powers from the president to the cabinet.

8 November: Following riots in several Jordanian cities over price increases, Jordan holds its first general election since 1967. Candidates representing the Muslim Brotherhood's political party enter parliament.

1990

30 January: Fighting breaks out between the two principle Maronite Christian forces in Lebanon's civil war – the forces of Michel Aoun and the Lebanese Forces. Fighting also rages between the two principle Shiite militias in the country, Amal and Hezbollah.

22 May: As the Eastern Bloc unravels, North Yemen and conflict-ridden, Soviet-backed South Yemen are united as the Republic of Yemen, with Ali Abdallah Saleh as President and Bakr Attas as Prime Minister. Yemen is united as an independent state for the first time in history.

2 August: Following a dispute over Iraqi debt payments accrued during the Iran–Iraq war and drilling in the Rumaila oil field at the Iraq–Kuwait border, Iraq invades, occupies and annexes Kuwait as its '19th province'.

6 August: The UN Security Council responds to the invasion of Kuwait by imposing a financial and trade embargo on Iraq. These comprehensive economic sanctions will be expanded and remain in place until 2003.

12 October: Egyptian Islamic Jihad assassinates the speaker of Egypt's parliament, Rifa'at el-Mahgoub. Over the next seven years, Egyptian security forces battle a low-intensity Islamic insurgency that targets government officials, tourists and Egyptian Christians.

13 October: Syrian forces shell the presidential palace in Lebanon, forcing General Michel Aoun to flee. He receives asylum in France. After fifteen years, the Lebanese Civil War has come to an end. Syria is firmly in control of the country.

1991

17 January: The Persian Gulf War (Operation Desert Storm) begins as an international coalition led by the United States launches airstrikes against Iraq to force Iraqi forces out of Kuwait. Thousands of Iraqis are killed and much of Iraq's civil infrastructure is destroyed. Iraq retaliates by firing Scud missiles into Israel and setting Kuwaiti oilfields on fire.

28 February: After a four-day ground conflict, a ceasefire takes effect between the coalition forces and Iraq, which withdraws completely from Kuwait. Iraq has suffered devastating human and material losses in the war.
March–April: Uprisings begin against Saddam Hussein in northern and southern Iraq, led by Kurdish militias and Shiite Muslim army commanders respectively. The uprisings collapse under a counterassault from forces loyal to Saddam. As much as ten per cent of the country's population is displaced in the resulting retaliation and bombing campaigns against rebel centres.
March: Facing harassment from Kuwaiti security forces over the PLO's support for Saddam Hussein, nearly the entire Palestinian population of Kuwait evacuates or is deported from the country.
3 April: The United Nations Security Council passes Resolution 687, keeping economic sanctions on Iraq in place, and requiring Iraq to give up its weapons of mass destruction programmes under international monitoring.
April: The United States, the United Kingdom and France begin Operation Provide Comfort, a military operation to protect Kurds in northern Iraq from attack by Saddam Hussein's forces. The operation includes a no-fly zone in northern Iraq, which is enforced until 2003. A second no-fly zone is added in southern Iraq in August 1992.
April: Most of the militias which fought in Lebanon's civil war are disarmed and disbanded. Hezbollah and the South Lebanon Army are prominent exceptions.
April: International terrorist Osama bin Laden moves his operation to Sudan at the invitation of Hassan al Turabi, an ally of ruling General Omar al Bashir.
15–16 May: Voters in the newly-united Republic of Yemen approve a new constitution.
30 October–1 November: The US and the Soviet Union sponsor a peace conference in Madrid that unprecedentedly brings together Israel, Lebanon, Syria, Jordan and the Palestinians.
26 December: In Algeria's first multiparty elections, the Islamic Salvation Front (FIS) defeats the ruling FLN party in the first round, and is set to win an outright majority in the second round.

1992
14 January: The Algerian military forces President Chadli Bendjedid to resign, and a junta of military officers led by Mohamed Boudiaf seizes power. The military declares a state of emergency and cancels the scheduled second-round parliamentary elections, which the Islamic Salvation Front was on its way to winning. The Algerian Civil War begins, pitting government forces against the Armed Islamic Group (GIA) and other militias. Over 150,000 people will be killed over the next ten years.
31 March: The UN Security Council votes to place economic and military sanctions on Libya, over its refusal to hand over citizens suspected of involvement in the December 1988 Lockerbie airliner bombing.

19 May: Elections held in Iraq's northern Kurdish-majority region – outside of the Iraqi central government's control – establish the first government of the Kurdish Regional Government. The parliament is evenly divided between the Kurdish Democratic Party and the Patriotic Union of Kurdistan.

29 June: Mohamed Boudiaf, the military ruler of Algeria, is assassinated by his bodyguard, Lambarek Boumaarafi, during a televised public speech in the city of Annaba.

21 August: Moroccan voters approve a new constitution which expands parliament's powers.

5 October: Under international pressure after the 1991 Gulf War, Kuwait holds elections for parliament for the first time since the emir dissolved it in 1986. The elections bring an opposition coalition to power.

1993

13 September: In Washington, Israel and the PLO sign the Oslo Accords. The agreement calls for Israel to progressively turn over occupied land in the West Bank and Gaza to administration by a Palestinian National Authority (PNA) run by the PLO, ending in the creation of a Palestinian state within five years. Despite the agreement, Jewish settlement on occupied Palestinian land will continue throughout the 1990s.

October: The Libyan government puts down a military revolt in Misrata.

December: Saudi Arabia's King Fahd inaugurates a sixty-member Consultative Council (*majlis al shura*) whose membership is chosen by the king.

1994

1 May: In northern Iraq, outside the Iraqi central government's control since 1991, fighting breaks out between the Kurdish Democratic Party (KDP) and the Patriotic Union of Kurdistan (PUK). This Kurdish civil war will continue for four years.

5 May: After Yemen's President Ali Abdallah Saleh, a northerner, clashes with Vice-President Baid, a southerner, the armed forces of the country's two regions begin fighting.

10 July: North Yemeni troops crush the southern rebellion, restoring President Saleh's control over the whole country.

26 October: Jordan and Israel sign a peace treaty, the second of its kind between Israel and an Arab state.

10 November: Four years after its invasion and failed annexation of Kuwait, Iraq recognizes Kuwait's borders as demarcated by the United Nations.

5 December: Bahraini authorities arrest Shaykh Ali Salman, a Shiite cleric, for calling for a restoration of the National Assembly disbanded by Bahrain's Sunni ruler in 1975. The arrested shaykh's supporters launch a protest movement in response.

1995

31 April: US President Bill Clinton orders a trade embargo against Iran over its alleged sponsorship of terrorism, pursuit of nuclear weapons, and opposition to the Israeli–Palestinian peace process.

27 June: In Qatar, Emir Khalifa is overthrown by his son, Hamad, who becomes emir.

1 September: Libya's Muammar Gaddafi orders the expulsion of the 30,000 Palestinians living in Libya, as a protest against the Israeli–Palestinian peace process.

4 November: In Tel Aviv, a Jewish extremist, Yigal Amir, assassinates Israeli Prime Minister Yitzhak Rabin.

16 November: Algeria's military leaders hold the country's first free multiparty presidential election after negotiations with imprisoned FIS leadership fail. Algeria's military ruler Liamine Zeroual becomes president.

December: A report by the UN's Food and Agriculture Organization (FAO) reports that 576,000 Iraqi children have died because of the international sanctions placed on the country five years before.

1996

20 February: A failed coup attempt takes place in Qatar, led by Hamad bin Jassem bin Hamad al-Thani, the emir's cousin.

29 May: Benjamin Netanyahu of the opposition Likud party is elected Prime Minister of Israel.

May: Under increasing international pressure, Sudan expels Osama bin Laden from the country. The leader of Al Qaeda relocates in Afghanistan.

25 June: 19 people are killed and 300 wounded in an attack by Al Qaeda on a US military complex near Dhahran, Saudi Arabia.

28 June: In Turkey, Necmettin Erbakan, leader of the Islamist Welfare Party, forms a coalition government, the first Turkish government with Islamist leanings since the founding of the Republic.

28–29 June: Libyan troops kill over 1,200 prisoners at Abu Salim prison in Tripoli.

August: In Derna and Benghazi, Libya, government troops clash with Islamist militias. 200 people are killed.

31 August: In northern Iraq, the Kurdish Democratic Party joins forces with the Iraqi army to conquer Erbil, the Kurdish regional capital. The US responds with airstrikes on Iraqi forces in southern Iraq.

13 September: Morocco's constitution is revised to create a bicameral legislature.

1 November: The Al Jazeera satellite television network begins broadcasting from Qatar. Its reporting on Middle East issues will become a longstanding grievance for states in the region.

1997

23 May: In Iran, reformist candidate Mohammad Khatami wins the presidential election with seventy per cent of the vote, marking a defeat for the country's hardline elites.

June: In a 'soft coup,' the Turkish military pressures Islamist-leaning Prime Minister Necmettin Erbakan of the Welfare Party to resign. Six months later, the Welfare Party is officially banned.

16 October: Oman holds elections for its Consultative Council, the first elections in which women are allowed to vote and stand for office.

17 November: A cell belonging to the Egyptian militant group Al Gama'a al Islamiyya kills 68 tourists and Egyptians in the Temple of Hatshepsut in Luxor. Egypt's Islamist insurgency, which has claimed 1,300 lives, comes to an end soon after as the unity of militant groups splinters amid state crackdown.

1998

14 March: An opposition-led government is created in Morocco for the first time in the country's history, under the leadership of Prime Minister Abderrahmane Youssoufi of the Socialist Union of Popular Forces.

20 August: 13 days after Al Qaeda bombs US embassies in Kenya and Tanzania, the United States bombs a medicine factory in Sudan, alleging that it is manufacturing chemical weapons for the terrorist group, and targets Al Qaeda camps in Afghanistan.

September: The two warring Kurdish parties in northern Iraq, the KDP and the PUK, sign a peace agreement in Washington after four years of conflict.

20 October: After Turkey masses troops on Syria's border, Syria agrees to expel the PKK leader Abdullah Öcalan and cease support for the PKK.

16 December: After Iraqi President Saddam Hussein suspends cooperation with the weapons inspections demanded by the United Nations, the United States and United Kingdom launch four days of airstrikes on Iraq. Weapons inspections are not resumed until 2002.

1999

7 February: Jordan's King Hussein dies after ruling the country for forty-six years. His eldest son Abdallah becomes king.

17 February: After a 21-year insurgency, Turkish police capture Abdallah Öcalan, the leader of the PKK, in Nairobi, Kenya. He is taken to Turkey, tried and sentenced to death. The sentence is eventually not executed.

6 March: Bahrain's ruler, Shaykh Isa bin Salman al Khalifah, dies of a heart attack. He ruled the nation for thirty-eight years, twenty-eight years as the leader of an independent state. His oldest son Shaykh Hamad succeeds him.

8 March: Qatar holds elections for the 29-member Central Municipal Council, the first democratic elections since the coup of 1972.

15 April: In Algeria, former foreign minister Abdelaziz Bouteflika wins a presidential election boycotted by all other parties.
23 July: King Hassan II of Morocco dies having led Morocco since 1961. He is succeeded by his son, Mohammed VI.
16 September: Voters in Algeria approve the Civil Concord Law, granting amnesty to thousands of rebels in Algeria's civil war. The law is the result of secret negotiations between the Algerian government and the FIS. The Armed Islamic Group (GIA) continues to fight.
11 December: Sudanese President Omar al Bashir declares a state of emergency and dissolves parliament, which is led by his ally-turned-opponent Hassan al Turabi.

2000
February: Reformist candidates sweep Iran's parliamentary elections. Reformists now control both Iran's parliament and presidency.
25 May: Under Prime Minister Ehud Barak, in power for a year, Israel withdraws from southern Lebanon, which it has occupied since 1982. Hezbollah quickly fills the void.
10 June: Hafez al Assad dies at age 70, having ruled Syria since 1970 – longer than any other ruler in modern Syrian history.
July: Peace talks between Israel and the Palestinians break down at Camp David.
17 July: Hafez al Assad's son, Bashar, becomes president of Syria. The minimum age requirement for the presidency is lowered by the parliament from 40 to 34, Bashar's age.
September: Likud Party leader Ariel Sharon – who had been deemed by the Israeli Kahan Commission to bear personal responsibility (for 'not taking appropriate measures to prevent bloodshed') during the Sabra and Shatila massacre in 1982 – makes an official visit to the Temple Mount in Jerusalem, revered by Muslims as *Al Haram al Sharif*, the Al Aqsa Mosque. Riots break out in Jerusalem marking the beginnings of the second Palestinian *intifada*. In January, Sharon is elected prime minister.

2001
14–15 February: As Bahrain's new ruler, Shaykh Hamad bin Isa al Khalifah, continues the nation's political opening, voters overwhelmingly approve a referendum that would create a constitutional monarchy in Bahrain, with an elected lower house and an independent judiciary.
April–May: More than 120 protesters are killed in clashes with police in Algeria's Kabylie region, where the majority of the population are non-Arab Berbers (Amazigh). One of the two main Algerian Berber political party withdraws from the government in protest (the second one was not in government).
September: The Damascus Spring comes to an end as the Syrian government imprisons leading civil society activists and re-imposes political controls.

11 September: Al Qaeda terrorists hijack four American passenger planes simultaneously. Two are flown into New York's World Trade Center towers, destroying both. A third is flown into the Pentagon in Washington, D.C., and a fourth crashes in a field in Pennsylvania. Nearly 3,000 people are killed.

2002

8 February: In Algeria, Antar Zouabri, the leader of the Armed Islamic Group, is killed by government forces. The ten-year Algerian civil war is largely over.
March: Algeria recognizes the Amazigh Berber language as a national language alongside Arabic.
27 March: Amidst escalating violence in Israel and the occupied territories, a suicide bombing kills 29 people celebrating the Jewish holiday Passover at the Park Hotel in Netanya, Israel. Two days later, the Israeli military occupy Palestinian cities in the West Bank.
11 April: Al Qaeda bombs a synagogue in Djerba, Tunisia, killing 21 people, including 14 German tourists.
18 June: Israel begins building a wall to separate Israel and Israeli settlements in the West Bank from Palestinian population centres.
September: Iran begins building its first nuclear reactor at Bushehr, with help from Russian technicians.
3 November: Turkey's Islamist-leaning Justice and Development Party (AKP) wins an outright majority in parliamentary elections.
9–16 May: In local elections in Bahrain, women gain the right to vote for the first time. Islamist candidates win more than half of local council seats.
7 October: The US Congress passes the Sudan Peace Act, bringing considerable pressure to bear on the Sudanese government to end the civil war.
24 October: Bahrain has its first parliamentary elections in thirty years. Islamists call for a boycott.

2003

February: Two rebel groups in the Darfur region of Sudan launch an uprising against the Sudanese central government. The government responds with a counterinsurgency campaign, killing some 300,000 people and displacing three million.
11 March: Recep Tayyip Erdoğan becomes Turkey's prime minister after the AKP majority in the Turkish parliament changes the constitution to allow him to serve in spite of his earlier conviction for inciting religious strife. Erdoğan will go on to govern Turkey, first as prime minister and then as president, as of this writing. The AKP government initially presides over a period of strong economic growth and increased political openness, especially for Turkey's Kurdish minority.
20 March: The United States and the United Kingdom invade Iraq to overthrow the government of Saddam Hussein, citing allegations of Iraq's ties to terrorism, production and stockpiling of chemical and biological weapons and advanced nuclear weapons program as justification. These justifications are later proven

unfounded. The Iraq War will last nearly nine years, involve sustained sectarian conflict and kill hundreds of thousands of Iraqis and thousands of American soldiers.

9 April: US forces occupy Baghdad.

29 April: Voters in Qatar approve a new constitution, under which Qatar will have a forty-five-member parliament with thirty elected members and fifteen chosen by the emir.

30 April: The US removes nearly all of its troops from Saudi Arabia, twelve years after they were sent there to protect Saudi Arabia from potential Iraqi attacks.

12 May: In Riyadh, Saudi Arabia, thirty-nine people are killed in an attack on a residential complex, housing American and British nationals.

16 May: In Casablanca, Morocco, twelve suicide bombers kill forty-three people at a Spanish-owned restaurant, a Jewish community centre, a tourist hotel and an Italian restaurant near the Belgian consulate.

8–9 June: Heavy fighting takes place in Mauritania's capital as rebel soldiers try and fail to overthrow President Ould Taya.

13–16 June: In Tehran, Iran, thousands of people demonstrate against the country's clerical establishment in student-run protests.

29 August: Amidst a rising insurgency against US forces in Iraq, a double car-bombing at the Shiite Muslim Imam Ali Mosque in Najaf kills 95 people, including Ayatollah Mohammad Baqir al Hakim, the leader of a major Shiite political party.

12 September: The UN Security Council lifts sanctions on Libya.

24 September: More than 300 Saudi male and female intellectuals deliver a petition to Crown Prince Abdallah, calling for political reform.

8 November: In Riyadh, Saudi Arabia, seventeen people are killed in a bomb attack on a residential complex housing foreign diplomats.

4 October: Oman holds elections for its Consultative Council, the first elections with universal adult suffrage. Previously, electors were chosen from among the country's elites.

19 December: Libya announces its intention to dismantle its chemical, biological and nuclear weapons programmes.

2004

20 February: Conservatives sweep Iran's parliamentary elections after Iran's clerical establishment disqualifies thousands of reformist candidates ahead of the vote.

4 April–1 May: After four American contractors are lynched in Fallujah, Iraq, US forces engage in a three-week battle to restore coalition control in the city. The effort ends in failure.

April–June: A wave of terrorist attacks in Saudi Arabia kill dozens, including many foreigners. Saudi Arabian security forces kill local Al Qaeda in the Arabian Peninsula leader Abdul Aziz al Muqrin in June.

18 June: In northern Yemen, Shaykh Hussein Badr al Din al Houthi, a Zaydi Muslim leader, launches a rebellion against the central government.

10 September: In Yemen, government troops kill Shaykh Hussein Badr al Din al Houthi, bringing the Zaydi uprising to an end for the time being.

27 October: Abu Musab al Zarqawi, a Palestinian-Jordanian insurgent leader in Iraq famous for video recorded beheadings, pledges allegiance to Al Qaeda, and renames his organization Al Qaeda in the Land of the Two Rivers (Mesopotamia, Al Qaeda in Iraq).

2 November: The leader of the UAE, Shaykh Zayed bin Sultan al Nahyan, dies. He is succeeded by his son, Shaykh Khalifa.

7 November–23 December: US forces again attack Fallujah, Iraq, successfully retaking it from Iraqi insurgents but largely destroying the city in the process.

11 November: Palestinian National Authority President Yasser Arafat dies in Paris after a long illness.

November: In a deal with the European Union, Iran promises to suspend most of its uranium enrichment.

15 December: In Morocco, a truth commission investigating the 'years of lead' under King Hassan II begins hearing public testimony from victims. The truth commission is the first of its kind in the Arab world.

2005

9 January: The Sudanese People's Liberation Army (SPLA) and the Sudanese government sign a peace agreement, ending twenty-one years of war, granting South Sudan autonomy, and allowing for a referendum on South Sudanese independence. The war has killed over two million people.

30 January: Iraq holds its first free elections, voting for a National Assembly. The United Iraqi Alliance, backed by the Shiite religious leader Grand Ayatollah Ali al Sistani, wins nearly half of the seats, easily beating its principal rivals.

February–April: Saudi Arabia holds its first-ever nationwide municipal elections. Women are not allowed to vote.

8 February: Israel and the new Palestinian Authority President Mahmoud Abbas announce a truce at a meeting in Sharm al Shaykh, Egypt, officially bringing the Second Intifada to an end after four years and more than 4,000 deaths.

14 February: Rafiq Hariri, Lebanon's first post-war prime minister and a major figure in the anti-Syria opposition in Lebanon, is assassinated in Beirut in an explosion that kills twenty-one other people. The killings trigger large protests against Syria, which is widely blamed for the assassination.

March: A protest movement begins in Bahrain, demanding a fully elected parliament.

14 March: Hundreds of thousands of Lebanese demonstrate against the Syrian occupation of Lebanon in the largest political demonstrations in the country's history, a week after pro-Syria gatherings organized by Hezbollah. The demonstrations come to be known as the Cedar Revolution.

26 April: Syrian forces leave Lebanon, ending their twenty-nine-year-long presence in the country.

16 May: In Kuwait, women gain the right to vote.

9 June: Qatar's new constitution comes into effect, introducing some liberalization reforms.

24 June: Mahmoud Ahmadinejad, Tehran's hardline mayor, is elected as Iran's president.

1 August: Crown Prince Abdallah becomes king of Saudi Arabia after the death of King Fahd.

3 August: A group of military officers led by Mohamed Ould Abdelaziz seizes power in a coup in Mauritania, ending the twenty-year rule of President Ould Taya. The plotters promise to bring democracy to Mauritania.

15 August: Israel withdraws from the Gaza Strip.

7 September: Under American pressure, Egypt holds its first-ever multi-party presidential elections. Hosni Mubarak wins 88% of the vote, lending credence to the widespread perception of the elections as fraudulent.

24 September: After Iran resumes uranium conversion, the International Atomic Energy Agency (IAEA) declares that Iran is in violation of the nuclear Non-Proliferation Treaty.

29 September: Algerian voters approve amnesty for most government officials involved in killings after the 1992 military coup.

October: Official negotiations begin over Turkey's entrance into the European Union. The AKP government in Turkey and its predecessors preside over reforms on a range of issues from cultural rights to the death penalty to bring Turkey in line with EU standards.

15 October: Iraqis approve a new constitution, the second in the country's history, in a national referendum.

November–December: Candidates associated with the Muslim Brotherhood win twenty per cent of the seats in Egyptian parliamentary elections. President Mubarak's National Democratic Party wins seventy-one per cent of the seats.

9 November: In Amman, Jordan, Al Qaeda in Iraq suicide bombers kill sixty people in attacks at three separate hotels.

2006

15 January: Kuwait's Amir Jaber al Ahmed al Sabah dies after ruling for twenty-nine years. In the resulting political crisis, Crown Prince Saad is forced to resign and Prime Minister Sabah al Ahmad al Sabah, the late emir's younger brother, takes the throne on 29 January.

25 January: Hamas triumphs in Palestinian parliamentary elections, defeating Yasser Arafat's Fatah party. Because of Hamas' refusal to accept Israel's existence and renounce violence, Israel, the US and European powers cut off aid to the Palestinian Authority.

22 February: The Golden Mosque in Samarra, Iraq, one of the holiest sites in Shia Islam, is destroyed in a bomb attack by Sunni extremists. Sunni Iraqis across the country are attacked in retaliation.

20 May: Nouri al Maliki, the leader of the Shiite Islamist Da'wa Party, becomes Iraq's new prime minister with American backing. He will hold the post for eight years.

21 May: Kuwait's new ruler, Sabah al Ahmad al Sabah, dissolves parliament and calls for new elections, ushering in a seven-year period of political chaos which sees a dozen governments and six dissolutions of parliament.

12 July: Israel launches a thirty-three-day invasion of Lebanon after Hezbollah kills three Israeli soldiers and kidnaps two along the border. Hezbollah resistance proves much stronger than expected, and the group launches thousands of missiles deep into Israeli territory. The conflict ends on 14 August.

15 October: Iraqi insurgent leaders linked to Al Qaeda announce the formation of the Islamic State in Iraq.

23 December: Eight months after the IAEA votes to report Iran to the UN Security Council for its nuclear activities, the Security Council imposes sanctions on Iran.

2007

3 January: Islamist militants and security forces engage in gun battles in Tunis. Twelve people are killed.

10 January: US President George W. Bush announces a 'troop surge' in Iraq to bring violence in the country under control, coinciding with a new alliance with Sunni tribal leaders disaffected by Al Qaeda's violence.

19 January: In Turkey, the prominent Turkish-Armenian journalist Hrant Dink is assassinated, sparking widespread condemnation and protest marches in Turkey and abroad.

March: The Algerian military launches an offensive against Islamist militants in the country. Islamist groups will bomb high-profile targets in Algiers and elsewhere in Algeria repeatedly throughout 2007.

25 March: Sidi Ould Cheikh Abdallahi wins the first democratic presidential election in Mauritania since independence.

20 May: The Al Qaeda-linked Sunni militant group Fatah al Islam ambushes Lebanese soldiers near Tripoli, killing twenty-seven. The attack leads to a four-month conflict between Fatah al Islam and the Lebanese Army, which besieges Fatah al Islam's stronghold in the Nahr al Bared Palestinian refugee camp.

June: Fighting breaks out between Hamas and Fatah in Gaza. A week of fighting leaves 100 dead, and Hamas takes complete control of the Gaza Strip. Egypt and Israel move to impose a blockade on the Gaza Strip.

28 August: Following another resounding AKP victory in the previous month's parliamentary elections, Abdullah Gül becomes president of Turkey.

6 September: Israeli warplanes destroy an alleged nuclear reactor under construction in Syria, near Dayr az-Zor.

21 October: Turkish voters approve a motion to have presidents elected directly, rather than selected by parliament.

2008

6 August: Mauritania's president Sidi Ould Cheikh Abdallahi is overthrown in a coup after he tries to dismiss senior army commanders. General Mohamed Ould Abdel Aziz assumes power.

8–9 July: Iran tests-fires the Shahab-3 missile, which it claims is capable of striking Israel.

30 July: Turkey's constitutional court penalises, but does not ban, the ruling Islamist-leaning AK Party for violating the principles of secularism.

14 December: US President George W. Bush signs a status of forces agreement with the Iraqi government. Under the agreement's terms, US troops will leave Iraq's major cites by 30 June 2009, and all US troops will leave the country by the end of 2011.

27 December: Israel invades the Gaza Strip in Operation Cast Lead, the first in a series of wars in the Gaza Strip. Over 1,100 Palestinians and thirteen Israelis are killed.

2009

January: Al Qaeda's branches in Saudi Arabia and Yemen merge to form Al Qaeda in the Arabian Peninsula. It will become one of the terrorist group's most effective affiliates.

10 February: The Likud party wins Israel's general elections, and Benjamin Netanyahu again becomes prime minister, beginning the longest single term as prime minister in Israel's history.

4 March: The International Criminal Court (ICC) issues an arrest warrant for Sudanese President Omar al Bashir for war crimes and crimes against humanity in Darfur.

12 June: Iranian President Mahmoud Ahmadinejad wins re-election by a wide margin. Supporters of his Reformist opponent, Mir Houssein Mousavi, claim vote-rigging and launch major protests in a movement known as the Green Revolution. Dozens of people are killed and over a thousand arrested in the protests.

August: Tens of thousands of people are displaced by renewed fighting between Yemeni government forces and Houthi rebels in the northern Saada province.

December: Turkey's AKP government, as part of its Kurdish initiative, increases Kurdish language rights and reduces the Turkish military presence in Kurdish-majority regions in the southeast.

2010

31 May: The Israeli military forcibly board a flotilla of ships carrying supplies to the blockaded Gaza Strip. The Israeli army kills ten Turkish activists in the ensuing fight. Turkey recalls its ambassador from Tel Aviv and expels Israel's ambassador to Ankara.

19 August: The last US combat troops leave Iraq.

12 September: As the AK Party enters its ninth year in power, Turkish voters approve constitutional amendments to increase parliament's control over the army and judiciary.

September: The Yemeni government battles a southern separatist movement in Shabwa province.

23–30 October: Bahrain holds parliamentary elections, in which the opposition party al Wefaq wins eighteen out of forty seats. Ahead of the vote, Bahraini authorities arrest twenty Shiite opposition leaders.

31 October: Al Qaeda in Iraq attacks a church in Baghdad killing nearly sixty worshipers. Nearly two-thirds of Iraq's Christians have already left the country; the massacre prompts another wave of emigration.

November: Riots in Jordan after pro-government candidates sweep parliamentary elections boycotted by the Islamic Action Front (IAF), the Muslim Brotherhood's political party. The IAF continues to boycott parliamentary elections in Jordan.

5 December: Wikileaks publishes secret American diplomatic cables.

17 December: In Sidi Bouzid, Tunisia, a twenty-six-year-old fruit seller named Mohamed Bouazizi sets himself on fire in front of the municipal office after police confiscate his fruit cart. The self-immolation sparks huge protests in Tunisia, which will spread and lead to revolutions, regime change and/or civil war in six Arab states. The events are known as the Arab Spring.

2011

9 January: South Sudan votes to secede from North Sudan and become an independent country.

14 January: After a month of mass protests, Tunisian President Ben Ali flees Tunisia by plane as he loses control of the country. He had ruled Tunisia since 2007.

25 January: Millions of Egyptians take to the streets to demand the end of President Hosni Mubarak's thirty-year reign, most prominently in Cairo's Tahrir Square, where hundreds of thousands of protestors begin a long sit-in.

27 January: Massive street protests break out in Yemen's capital, Sana'a. Already facing insurgencies in the north and south, the protest movement poses a serious threat to the thirty-two-year rule of President Ali Abdallah Saleh. His government attempts to suppress the protests with lethal force. Yemen descends quickly into large-scale political violence.

11 February: After eighteen days of street battles and million-strong protests, a hastily formed Supreme Council of the Armed Forces (SCAF) announces that Egyptian President Hosni Mubarak has resigned, and that free elections will be held soon. The news is met with jubilation in Egypt, but largescale protests will continue to challenge the authority of SCAF and successive Egyptian governments for the next three years.

14 February: Mass protests break out in Bahrain. Tens of thousands of Iranians demonstrate in Tehran against the Iranian regime.

15 February: Protests erupt in Benghazi, Libya. Many people are killed by Libyan security forces.
20 February: Protests in Rabat and other cities in Morocco call for political reform and a new constitution.
20 February: Anti-Gaddafi rebels seize control of Benghazi, Libya's second-largest city.
24 February: Facing a major wave of protests, Algeria lifts its state of emergency, in place since the 1992 military coup.
28 February: Protests rock Oman, and one protestor is shot dead by police. Sultan Qaboos promises jobs and more powers for the country's democratically elected Consultative Council.
March: Saudi security forces occupy the city of al Qatif and arrest hundreds after a wave of protests in the Shiite-majority Eastern Province.
15 March: In Syria, anti-regime protests begin in the southern city of Dara'a after security forces detain and torture several teenagers for spraying anti-regime graffiti on a wall. Syrian security forces kill scores of protestors, but the protest movement quickly spreads to Homs, Hama, Dayr az-Zour, the Damascus suburbs and other marginalized regions of Syria. The disturbances mark the beginning of Syria's civil war, which will kill over half a million people and drive thirteen million people from their homes over the next eight years (out of a pre-war population of 23 million).
14 March: Saudi Arabian troops invade Bahrain across the King Fahd causeway, crushing the popular uprising there.
19 March: As violence escalates in Libya, the United States, France and Great Britain begin bombing the Libyan government under a UN Security Council mandate to protect civilians in the country from government attack.
1–2 June: In Syria, over 100 regime soldiers are massacred in Jisr al Shughour, a sign of the Syrian opposition's increasing militarization.
3 June: Yemeni President Ali Abdallah Saleh is injured in a bombing attack on the mosque of the presidential compound.
1 July: Morocco approves a new constitution in a nationwide referendum. The new constitution expands the powers of the elected government, and recognizes Tamazight as an official language and Amazigh identity as a component of Moroccan national identity.
29 July: Defecting Syrian army officers announce the creation of the Free Syrian Army, an armed opposition movement aiming to bring down the regime and protect civilians from regime attacks.
August: Following the AKP's third general election victory in Turkey, Turkey's president Gül appoints new top military leaders after their predecessors resign *en masse*. For the first time, the Turkish military is run by leaders appointed by a civilian government.

18 August: US President Barack Obama calls for Syrian President Bashar al Assad to leave power, imposes harsh economic sanctions on Syria and asks other countries to do the same.
21 August: Libyan rebels seize control of the capital of Tripoli. Muammar Gaddafi, the country's ruler since 1969, flees.
October 2011–February 2012: Fierce fighting in Homs, Syria. Rebel forces install themselves in key neighbourhoods of the city.
October: Oman holds its first elections to a Consultative Council with expanded powers, promised by the sultan after Arab Spring unrest.
20 October: In Libya, a NATO airstrike hits Muammar Gaddafi's convoy as he tries to flee Sirte. Gaddafi tries to escape on foot, but is captured and lynched by a mob.
November–January 2012: In Egypt's first free parliamentary elections in decades, Islamist parties win a stunning victory. The Muslim Brotherhood's Freedom and Justice Party wins forty-seven per cent of seats in the lower house; the Salafist al Nour Party wins twenty-four per cent.
17 November: Protestors in Kuwait storm parliament building, demanding the resignation of Kuwait's prime minister.
23 November: After eleven months of unrest, Yemeni President Ali Abdallah Saleh agrees to hand power over to his vice president, Mansour Hadi, in a Gulf Cooperation Council-mediated settlement.
25 November: The moderate Islamist Justice and Development Party wins parliamentary elections in Morocco. Abdelilah Benkirane becomes prime minister.
December: After parliamentary elections in October, human right activist and long-time exiled opponent to the Ben Ali regime Moncef Marzouki is elected president of Tunisia by a constituent assembly, while the leader of the Islamist Ennahda Party becomes prime minister.
31 December: The last US troops leave Iraq, nearly nine years after the American invasion.

2012

January: The US begins a massive arms airlift to Syrian rebels, in cooperation with Turkey, Saudi Arabia and Qatar. The Syrian government, in turn, receives increasingly large amounts of support from its allies Russia and Iran.
23 January: A month after it carries out its first suicide attacks, Al Qaeda's official Syria affiliate Jabhat al Nusra announces its existence and declares war on the Syrian regime.
25 February: In Yemen, former President Ali Abdallah Saleh's vice-president, Mansour Hadi, is inaugurated as president after winning an election in which he was the only candidate.
May–June: In Egypt's two-round presidential election widely regarded as free, Mohammad Morsi, the Muslim Brotherhood's candidate, wins a narrow victory. On 30 June, he becomes Egypt's first freely elected president.

20 June: Kuwait's constitutional court dissolves the Islamist-majority parliament elected in February, after Kuwait's amir clashes with the legislature over proposals to make all legislation comply with Islamic law.
1 July: The European Union begins a boycott of Iranian oil exports, increasing the economic stress on Iran.
July: Rebel forces attack Aleppo, Syria's largest city, and seize control of large areas. Aleppo is divided between government and rebel-controlled areas. Four and a half years of urban warfare will follow.
18 July: A suicide bomber kills Syrian President Assad's top aides, including his brother-in-law and defence minister, as rebel forces make serious gains in Damascus' outskirts.
August: An elected government takes power in Libya, but struggles to unify the country or control the many powerful militia groups that have emerged since the 2011 revolution.
11 September: Islamist militants storm the American consulate in Benghazi, Libya, killing the US ambassador and three other Americans.
7 October: Kuwait's emir dissolves parliament. 5,000 protestors clash with security forces outside the parliament building.
14 November: Israel launches an air war against the Gaza Strip. 165 Palestinians and four Israelis are killed in the week-long conflict.
November: The United Arab Emirates ban online mockery of its government amid a crackdown on democracy and human rights activists.

2013
16 January: Al Murabitun, an Al Qaeda-related group, seizes control of a gas facility in In Amenas, Algeria, holding hostage 685 Algerian workers and 107 foreigners. 67 people are killed. Algerian special forces storm the plant after a four-day siege.
6 February: In Tunisia, opposition figure Chokri Belaid is assassinated, triggering mass protests that prompt Prime Minister Jebali to resign.
19 February: Saudi Arabia's King Abdallah appoints thirty women to the nation's ninety-member Consultative Council. It is the first time that women have held any political office in Saudi Arabia.
March: Raqqa, Syria, falls to rebel forces, including Jabhat al Nusra. It is the first provincial capital to fall to rebel forces in Syria's civil war.
8–9 April: Leaders of the Al Qaeda-linked Islamic State in Iraq announce the merger of their organization with Jabhat al Nusra into the Islamic State in Iraq and Syria/Shaam (ISIS/L, Levant). Jabhat al Nusra publicly rejects the merger, and its followers are divided between the two organizations. ISIS consolidates its control over Raqqa City.
23 April: Iraqi security forces kill fifty protestors, mostly Sunnis, at Hawijah. Government counteroffensives against Sunni insurgents force 500,000 people in Iraq's Anbar province – a third of the population – to flee their homes.

May–June: Protests in Istanbul, Turkey, over plans to develop one of the city's last green spaces, turn into mass anti-government demonstrations in Istanbul's Taksim Square and in several cities. The Turkish government cracks down on the protests harshly.

14 June: Reformist candidate Hassan Rouhani wins Iran's presidential election.

25 June: Qatar's emir, Shaykh Hamad bin Khalifa al Thani, abdicates in favour of his son, Shaykh Tamim bin Hamad al Thani.

30 June: On the first anniversary of Egyptian President Mohammad Morsi's inauguration, millions of Egyptians take to the streets to demand a recall vote.

3 July: After three days of mass protests, General Abdel Fatah al Sisi, Egypt's army chief, ousts President Mohammad Morsi in a military coup. Supporters of the ousted president begin a sit-in at al Nahda and Raba'a al Adawiya squares in Cairo.

25 July: In Tunisia, opposition leader Mohamed Brahmi is assassinated, prompting mass protests and a general strike.

14 August: Egyptian security forces attack and forcibly disperse pro-Muslim Brotherhood protest camps at al Nahda Square and Raba'a al Adawiya Square in Cairo, killing over 1,000 Brotherhood supporters and civilians in the worst political violence in Egypt's modern history. Over the next five years, General Sisi will lead a crackdown on civil society in Egypt, arresting over 60,000 people, trying thousands of civilians in military courts and severely restricting freedom of the press.

21 August: Over 1,000 people are killed in chemical weapons attacks in the Damascus suburbs, in spite of US President Obama's warning that such use of banned munitions would constitute a 'red line' that could trigger direct US intervention.

14 September: The US and Russia reach an agreement to destroy Syria's chemical weapons stockpile without US military intervention. Previously, the British parliament had voted against joining a US military intervention in Syria.

5 October: Gunmen kill six Egyptian soldiers near Ismailiyya. In the wake of Egypt's July military coup, an Islamist insurgency emerges to oppose the new regime, particularly in the country's marginalized Sinai region, which sees heavy fighting.

15 December: Civil war erupts in South Sudan between President Salva Kiir (formerly of the SPLA) and Vice-President Riek Machar (formerly of the SPLA-Nasir). The conflict kills tens of thousands of people and turns millions of South Sudanese people into refugees.

2014

26 January: Tunisia agrees to its first new constitution since the 2010–2011 revolution.

5 March: Saudi Arabia, the UAE and Bahrain suspend diplomatic ties with Qatar accusing it of supporting the Muslim Brotherhood, which they consider a terrorist organization.

May: Syrian regime retakes most of Homs city.

16 May: Libyan general Khalifa Haftar launches military attacks on Islamist militias in Benghazi, declares the elected Libyan government illegitimate and tries to seize the Libyan parliament building. Libya descends into civil war.

26–28 May: Abdel-Fatah al Sisi wins Egypt's presidential election with ninety per cent of the vote.

10 June: The Islamic State in Iraq and Syria (ISIS) seizes control of Mosul, Iraq's second-largest city. It will occupy it until 10 July 2017.

8 July: Israel launches a fifty-day ground and air war against Hamas and other Palestinian militant groups in the Gaza Strip. It is the third war in Gaza in six years. 2,200 Palestinians and 73 Israelis are killed. 500,000 people are displaced and 20,000 homes in the Gaza Strip are destroyed.

3 August: ISIS conquers most of Sinjar and Nineveh provinces in Iraq. The region is home to hundreds of thousands of Yazidis, Christians, Kaka'is and Shi'ite Turkmen, which ISIS targets for murder, abduction and plunder. In particular, thousands of Yazidis are executed and enslaved. Hundreds of thousands of people flee ISIS' advance.

7 August: In Iraq, as ISIS drives towards Erbil and Baghdad, the United States begins bombing the group.

10 August: After eleven years as prime minister, Recep Tayyip Erdoğan wins Turkey's first direct elections for president.

18 August: Protests take place in Sana'a and other Yemeni cities after the leader of Yemen's Houthi movement, Abdulmalek al Houthi, calls for mass demonstrations to bring down the government.

September: Houthi rebels seize control of Sana'a, Yemen's capital.

17 September: ISIS begins a major offensive to capture Kobani, Syria.

22 September: The United States and its Arab allies begin airstrikes against ISIS and Jabhat al Nusra forces in Syria.

3 October: Fighters loyal to the Islamic State seize the port city of Derna, Libya.

16 November: Saudi Arabia, the UAE and Bahrain return their ambassadors to Qatar after eight months of suspended ties.

4 November: The Sinai-based militant group Ansar Beit al Maqdis declares its allegiance to the Islamic State and reorganizes itself as ISIS' Wilayat Sinai (Sinai Province).

21 December: Beji Caid Essebsi, the leader of Tunisia's secularist bloc, becomes president after parliamentary elections in October.

2015

22 January: Saudi Arabia's King Abdallah dies. He is succeeded by his half-brother Salman.

27 January: ISIS forces are driven out of Kobani city by the Kurdish People's Protection Units (YPG) and the Free Syrian Army.

6 February: Houthi rebels installed in Sana'a, Yemen's capital, dissolve parliament, take over the government and force President Hadi to flee to Aden, Yemen.

16 February: After the Islamic State posts a video of twenty-one Egyptian Christians being beheaded in Libya, Egypt intervenes in Libya's civil war, bombing IS targets in Derna and Sirte, the first of several bombing raids it will undertake in the coming years.

15 March: The Islamic State kills 137 people in attacks on Shiite mosques in Sana'a, Yemen.

18 March: Three ISIS militants conduct an attack on the Bardo museum in Tunis, Tunisia, killing 23 people.

26 March: Saudi Arabia launches an air war (Operation Decisive Storm) on Yemen and imposes a naval blockade on the country. The goal is to stop the Houthi advance, which Saudi Arabia claims is backed by Iran, and restore President Hadi to power. The United States provides crucial military support. The intervention kills thousands of civilians and creates a humanitarian catastrophe. Within Yemen, Houthi rebels, various army factions, southern separatists, Al Qaeda and the Islamic State do battle.

22 May: The Islamic State bombs two Shiite mosques in Saudi Arabia's Eastern Province, killing twenty-five people.

7 June: The leftist pro-Kurdish People's Democratic Party (HDP) wins enough of the vote in Turkey's parliamentary elections to enter parliament, depriving President Erdogan's AK Party of a majority for the first time in thirteen years.

26 June: Twenty-six people are killed in an Islamic State suicide attack on a Shiite mosque in Kuwait City, the deadliest attack in Kuwait's history. In Sousse, Tunisia, an Islamic State fighter, Seifeddine Rezgui, attacks a tourist resort in Tunisia, killing 39 people, 30 of whom are British nationals.

14 July: Iran reaches a deal with the US, the UK, France, Germany, Russia, China and the EU to limit its nuclear activities and grant UN inspectors access in exchange for sanctions relief.

30 September: Russia begins large-scale military operations in Syria to aid the Syrian government, bombing ISIS and rebel forces in the country. The campaign will decisively change the tide of the war in the Syrian government's favour.

10 October: In Ankara, Turkey, suicide bombers kill over 100 people at a rally calling for an end to the Turkish government's war in the country's Kurdish-majority regions. The Turkish government accuses the Islamic State; Turkish activists accuse the government.

11 October: The creation of the Syrian Democratic Forces, an umbrella coalition dominated by Kurdish groups, is announced in Hasakeh, Syria. The SDF will become a key partner of the United States in its anti-ISIS campaign.

31 October: Sinai-based militants loyal to the Islamic State shoot down a Russian passenger jet over the Sinai Peninsula, killing all 224 people on board.

1 November: In fresh parliamentary elections in Turkey, the AKP regains its majority.

13 November: In paris, ISIS operatives conduct a series of terrorist attacks killing 130 people.

24 November: Turkey shoots down a Russian military jet flying over Syria. Russia imposes economic sanctions on Turkey, cutting it off from its second-largest trading partner.

29 November: Turkey agrees to restrict the flow of refugees into Europe, in exchange for 3 billion Euros from the European Union.

2016

2 January: Saudi Arabia executes the Shiite religious leader Shaykh Nimr al-Nimr on 'terrorism' charges, drawing international condemnation and sparking violent protests in Iran and Saudi Arabia's Eastern province.

7 February: Algeria amends its constitution to limit presidents to serving two five-year terms, and recognizes Tamazight as an official language of the state. The ailing President Abdelaziz Bouteflika is serving his fourth term since April 1999.

17 February: A group called the Kurdistan Freedom Hawks kills 38 people in a bomb attack on a military convoy in Ankara, Turkey, marking an escalation in violence between the Turkish government and Kurdish separatists.

April: Egypt announces plans to transfer two islands in the Red Sea to Saudi Arabia, which has heavily subsidized the new Sisi regime. The announcement sparks widespread protests and outrage among the Egyptian public.

28 June: A shooting and suicide bomber attack on Istanbul's Ataturk airport kills 42. Turkey blames the Islamic State.

30 June: Oman holds its first-ever direct elections for the country's Consultative Council.

15 July: A faction of Turkey's military tries and fails to overthrow President Erdoğan. Erdoğan and his allies place blame for the coup on the network of the exiled Turkish spiritual leader Fethullah Gulen, a former ally of Erdoğan. In the months that follow, Erdoğan's government purges more than 160,000 civil servants, arrests 50,000 people, seizes the assets of 1,000 businesses and shuts down scores of newspapers, radio stations and television channels.

9 August: Turkish President Erdoğan visits Russian President Vladimir Putin in St. Petersburg, as both countries work to restore ties after Turkey shot down a Russian jet in November 2015.

24 August: Turkish troops invade northern Syria and create a large buffer zone between the Kurdish strongholds of Afrin and Kobane.

31 October: Michel Aoun is elected President of Lebanon with backing from Hezbollah and Syria, ending a twenty-nine-month political impasse. Aoun's election reflects a rapprochement among Lebanon's rival Christian factions.

26 November: After Kuwait's emir dissolves parliament in October, opposition groups win nearly half of the seats in parliament in new elections.

11 December: The Islamic State bombs a chapel in Cairo, Egypt, killing twenty-nine people.

22 December: After four and a half years of urban warfare, Syrian regime forces restore government control over all of Aleppo city in a brutal air and ground campaign.

2017
11 May: Aidarous al Zoubeidi forms the Southern Transitional Council, a South Yemeni separatist movement which will become a major player in Yemen's ongoing civil war.
June: As the war in Yemen between Houthi rebels and an international coalition led by Saudi Arabia continues, a cholera outbreak begins that will kill over 2,000 by November, a sign of Yemen's rapidly deteriorating health infrastructure.
5 June: With apparent support from US President Donald Trump, Saudi Arabia, the UAE, Bahrain, Egypt, Yemen, Libya and Jordan cut or downgrade their diplomatic ties with Qatar, over the nation's alleged support of terrorism and closeness to Iran. Saudi Arabia launches an air, land and sea blockade of Qatar. Turkey and Iran deliver food supplies to Qatar in response.
7 June: The Islamic State carries out attacks on the Iranian parliament and the shrine of Ayatollah Khomeini, the first major Islamic State attacks inside Iran. 12 people are killed.
5 July: The Libyan National Army of General Khalifa Haftar declares that it has seized control of Benghazi after three years of battles with Islamist militias in the city, including the Islamic State.
10 July: After a nine-month battle involving the Iraqi army, Iran-backed militias, Kurdish *peshmerga* forces and US air support, the Iraqi government declares Mosul 'liberated' from ISIS. Much of the city lies in ruins.
12 July: Iran and Oman announce their intention to intensify their bilateral relationship.
October: In Syria, Raqqa city, 'capital' of the Islamic State, falls to US-backed Kurdish forces.
November: Saudi Arabia's Crown Prince Mohammed bin Salman carries out a purge of the country's political and business leadership, in an attempt to consolidate power. The young prince promises far-reaching reforms.
24 November: Militants kill 305 people in an attack on a mosque in Bir al-Abed in Egypt's Sinai Peninsula, the largest terrorist attack in Egypt's modern history. No group claims responsibility.
4 December: Ali Abdullah Saleh, president of Yemen from July 1978 to February 2012 and a backer of the Houthi rebels, is killed in fighting in the capital Sana'a.

2018
30 January: With backing from the United Arab Emirates, southern separatists seize Yemen's port city of Aden, the seat of Yemen's internationally recognized government.

18 March: After a two-month military campaign, Turkish military forces conquer the Kurdish-held city of Afrin in northern Syria.

7 April: On the one-year anniversary of the US bombing of Syrian airbases, forty-two people are killed in chemical weapons attacks in the Damascus suburbs.

16 April: The United States strikes Syrian military targets in response to claims of regime chemical weapons use.

8 May: President Donald Trump withdraws the United States from the Iranian nuclear deal of July 2015.

26–28 May: Abdel Fatah al Sisi wins re-election as Egypt's president after a campaign in which multiple opponents of the president were imprisoned.

June: The Syrian regime completes its reconquest of Dara'a province in the country's south. Aside from the Kurdish-controlled areas, Idlib province is the rebels' last remaining major stronghold in Syria.

19 July: The Israeli parliament passes a law which strips Arabic of its status as a national language of Israel and declares that 'the Jewish people have an exclusive right to national self-determination' in the country.

22 September: Arab separatists attack a military parade in Ahvaz, Iran, killing twenty-five people.

2 October: Jamal Khashoggi, a prominent Saudi dissident and *Washington Post* journalist, is murdered and dismembered inside the Saudi Consulate in Istanbul, by a Saudi hit squad despatched by Saudi Arabia Crown Prince Mohammed Bin Salman.

6 December: Qatar becomes the first nation to leave OPEC, eighteen months after the Saudi-led blockade of the Gulf nation began.

19 December: Anti-government protests and riots begin in Atbara, Sudan, and quickly spread throughout the country.

2019

10 February: Algeria's ailing President Bouteflika announces he will stand for a fifth term. The announcement sparks a nationwide protest movement.

25 March: The United States declares that it recognizes the occupied Syrian Golan Heights as part of Israel.

2 April: In Algeria, after nearly two months of massive protests, the military forces President Abdelaziz Bouteflika to resign after twenty years in office. Anti-regime protests continue.

4 April: General Khalifa Haftar's Libyan National Army launches a campaign to take the capital, Tripoli.

11 April: After months of protests, Sudan's military forces President Omar al Bashir from power. Bashir had ruled Sudan since June 1989.

7 August: Fighting erupts in Aden, Yemen, between government forces and UAE-backed southern separatists, nominal allies against Yemen's Houthi movement.

21 August: Abdalla Hamdok is sworn in as Sudan's prime minister as part of a power-sharing agreement between the military and the civilian protest movement.

14 September: Yemen's Houthi movement launches successful drone attacks on two of Saudi Arabia's largest oilfields. The attack prompts Saudi Arabia to begin peace talks with the Houthis.

1 October: Largescale anti-government protests begin in Iraq, the largest since the 2003 invasion. In the months that follow, hundreds of protestors are killed.

9 October: Following a withdrawal of American troops, Turkey launches an incursion into northern Syria, aiming to crush the territorial base of the Kurdish-dominated Syrian Democratic Forces and its associated political entity, Rojava.

17 October: Largescale protests occur in Lebanon after the government proposes a raft of tax hikes. The protests spread throughout the country and morph into a broad-based movement demanding the overthrow of Lebanon's ruling elite.

26 October: In Idlib, Syria, the United States kills Abu Bakr al Baghdadi, the leader of the Islamic State.

5 November: Yemen's Saudi-backed Yemeni President Hadi signs a power-sharing agreement with the UAE-backed southern Yemini separatist movement. The government's civil war with the Houthi movement continues.

15 November: Mass protests break out in Iran after the government introduces fuel price hikes. Over three hundred people will be killed by Iranian security forces in the clashes that follow.

12 December: Algeria holds presidential elections despite widespread popular opposition. Former prime minister Abdelmajid Tebboune is elected.

19 December: The Syrian government and Russia begin a campaign to take back Idlib, the last rebel stronghold in the country. Nearly a million people are displaced in the bombardments that follow.

2020

3 January: The United States assassinates General Qasem Soleimani, the leader of Iran's Quds Force and one of the most powerful figures in the Iranian regime, in a drone strike at Baghdad International Airport. A leader of Iraq's Popular Mobilization Forces and eight others are also killed.

8 January: Iran fires missiles at military bases in Iraq used by US forces and accidentally shoots down a Ukrainian civilian jetliner as it takes off from Tehran. The downing of the plane and subsequent coverup spark major protests across the country.

10 January: Sultan Qaboos bin Said dies after ruling Oman for nearly forty years. He is succeeded by his cousin Haitham bin Tariq.

28 January: US President Donald Trump announces 'the deal of the century,' his proposal for resolving the Israeli–Palestinian conflict. The proposal, which would see the annexation of large parts of the West Bank to Israel and the creation of a demilitarized Palestinian state completely within Israel's borders, is welcomed by Israeli Prime Minister Benjamin Netanyahu, and rejected across the board by the divided Palestinian leadership. The same day, Netanyahu is indicted on corruption charges, the first time in Israeli history a sitting prime minister has been indicted.

1 March: Yemen's Houthi movement seizes control of al Hazm city, in a major blow to Yemen's internationally recognized government and the Saudi-led coalition.

March: A global outbreak of the novel coronavirus (COVID-19) threatens the Middle East and North Africa. Many governments impose curfews, quarantines and strict border controls to stop the spread of the virus, while countries already weakened by civil war and economic sanctions brace themselves for a staggering death toll. Iran is one of the hardest-hit countries in the world.

4 August: A largescale explosion takes place in the port of Beirut in Lebanon causing 180 deaths. The explosion, caused by the storage of confiscated ammonium nitrate, triggers a seismic event of a 3.3 magnitude. The state of emergency is declared in the country, and, two days later, the Lebanese government resigns in the face of massive protests across the nation.

13 August: The United Arab Emirates and Israel sign a peace agreement normalizing their diplomatic relations. Israel agrees to suspend plans for annexing parts of the West Bank.

10 December: Morocco and Israel agree to a rapprochement with a view to open full diplomatic relations and formalize economic ties.

2021

20 January: US President Joe Biden revokes the 'Muslim Ban' that had been introduced by President Trump in January 2017.

7–21 May: Israel deploys forces preventing Palestinians from attending the Ramadan *tarawih* evening prayers at the Al Aqsa Mosque in Jerusalem. Widespread riots take place in the Occupied Territories and in Israel. Israel conducts aerial bombings over Gaza and the West Bank. Hamas launches rocket attacks against Israel. A total of 231 Palestinians and 12 Israelis are killed.

25 July: Tunisian President Kais Saied dismisses Prime Minister Hichem Mechichi and suspends the activities of the parliament, assuming emergency powers.

GLOSSARY

aliya	immigration of Jewish populations to Palestine in the 1880s and 1900s
'asabiya	social solidarity, cohesion, consciousness
ashraaf	noblemen
ayatollah	high-ranking Muslim Shiite cleric
awlad al 'arab	children of the Arabs
'aysh	bread (in the Mashreq)
ba'ath	renaissance
bay'a	oath of allegiance to a leader
bilad al makhzen	territories/social spaces under state control and rule
bilad al siba	territories/social spaces escaping state control and rule
caliph	head of Muslim community; used in the succession after the Prophet
dawla	state
dawla madaniyya	civil state; civil society
da'wa	Islamic proselytizing
dhimmi	non-Muslim subject of state governed by Sharia law; afforded status
effendi	lord, master
emir/amir	leader, commander, ruler
fitna	first major antagonism amongst Muslims at beginning of post-Prophet Islam
fatwa	Islamic decree issued on a specific issue
haram al Sharif	Al Aqsa Mosque in Jerusalem; third holy site in Islam after Mecca and Medina
harratha	agriculturalists
hijra	Prophet Mohammad's migration from Mecca to Medina on 16–19 July 622
hukm	rule
hukuma	government (Arabic)
hukumet	government (Turkish)
huriyya	freedom

ijma'	consensus
imam (Sunna)	worship leader or scholar; no clergy status
imam (Shi'a)	political and religious leader of the community; central role and status
infitah	opening; policies pursued under the Anwar Sadat presidency in Egypt, and Hafez al Assad in Syria
insaniyya	humanity
intifada	uprising; initially associated with Palestinian campaign in 1987
kafir, kuffar	unbeliever, non-believer
karama	dignity
khobz	bread (in the Maghreb)
jihad	struggle
maghreb	North Africa
mahala	quarters
mahkum	ruled
mashreq	Middle East
milla	religious community; from 'millet system' under Ottoman empire
mufti	Muslim legal scholar
mujahid, mujahideen	Muslim holy warrior(s)
mukhabarat	intelligence services; also referred to as *istikhbarat*
murtaad	apostate
naksa	setback; Palestinian reference to June 1967 defeat
naqba	catastrophe; Palestinian reference to May 1948 events
nidham	regime, plural *andhima*; system
pasdaran	Iranian revolutionary guard corps
peshmerga	Kurdish military forces in Iraq
salaf	ancestor
sandjak	administrative division under the Ottoman Empire
shaam	Levant region of the Mashreq
shari'a	Islamic religious law from the Quran and the Prophet's sayings
sharif	nobility title usually associated with descendants of the Prophet
shaykh	elder, leader, governor; connoting age, wisdom and leadership
shia	second largest denomination of Islam (approximately 10 per cent of Muslims)
shura	deliberation, council
sufism	Islamic mysticism or asceticism
sulta	power

sunna	largest denomination of Islam (approximately 90 per cent of Muslims)
tandheem	planning
taifiya	sectarianism
takfir	excommunication, accusation of apostasy
tanzimat	reforms launched under the Ottoman Empire in the period 1839–1876
tariqaat	ways, orders of a religious nature
qadi	judge
'ulama	Islamic scholars, plural (sing. *'alim*)
umma	Islamic nation or collective community
vilayet	administrative province under the Ottoman Empire
vilayet-e faqih	guardianship of Islamic jurist, Shiite system of governance
wafd	delegation
watan	country, homeland
za'im, zu'ama	leader(s)

BIBLIOGRAPHY

Abi-Mershed, Osama, ed. *Social Currents in North Africa*. London: Hurst and Company, 2018.
Abrahamian, Evand. *Iran between Two Revolutions*. Princeton, NJ: Princeton University Press, 1982.
Abul-Magd, Zeinab. *Militarising the Nation – Army, Business and Revolution in Egypt, 1952-2015*. New York: Columbia University Press, 2016.
Aggoun, Lounis and Jean-Baptiste Rivoire. *Francalgérie, Crimes et Mensonges d'État – Histoire Secrète, de la Guerre d'indépendance à la 'troisième Guerre' d'Algérie*. Paris: La Découverte, 2005.
Akcali, Emel, ed. *Neoliberal Governmentality and the Future of the State in the Middle East*. London: Palgrave, 2016.
Al-Khateeb, Firas. *Lost Islamic History – Reclaiming Muslim Civilisation from the Past*. London: Hurst and Company, 2017.
Al-Rasheed, Madawi. *A History of Saudi Arabia*. Cambridge: Cambridge University Press, 2002.
Al-Rodhan, Nayef R. F., Graeme P. Herd and Lisa Watanabe. *Critical Turning Points in the Middle East, 1915-2015*. New York: Palgrave MacMillan, 2011.
Álvarez-Ossorio, Ignacio, ed. *La Primavera Árabe Revisitada – Reconfiguración del Autoritarismo y Recomposición del Islamismo*. Pamplona: Thomson Reuters Aranzadi, 2015.
Amar, Paul. *The Security Archipelago – Human-Security States, Sexuality Politics and the End of Neoliberalism*. Durham: Duke University Press, 2013.
An-na'im, Abdullahi. *Islam and the Secular State – Negotiating the Future of Shari'a*. Cambridge, Massachusetts: Harvard University Press, 2008.
An-na'im, Abdullahi. 'Sharia and the State in the 21st Century.' Video presentation for the conference 'Religion et État: Sécularisation et Citoyenneté en Islam', http://iqbal.hypotheses.org/1010.
Anderson, Benedict. *Imagined Communities*. New York: Verso, 1991.
Anderson, Lisa. *The State and Social Transformation in Tunisia and Libya, 1830-1980*. Princeton, NJ: Princeton University Press, 1986.
Anderson, Lisa. 'The State and Its Competitors', *International Journal of Middle East Studies*, 50, 2, 2018, pp. 317–22.
Ansary, Tamim. *Destiny Disrupted – A History of the World through Islamic Eyes*. New York: PublicAffairs, 2009.
Atiya, Ghassan R. *Iraq, 1908-1921 – A Sociopolitical Study*. Beirut: Arab Institute for Research and Publication, 1973.
Atwan, Abdel Bari. *The Secret History of Al Qaeda*. Berkeley: University of California Press, 2008.

Ayari, Michaël Béchir. *Le Prix de l'Engagement en Régime Autoritaire – Gauchistes et Islamistes dans la Tunisie de Bourguiba et Ben Ali, 1957-2011*. Paris: Karthala, 2016.

Ayoob, Mohammed. *The Third World Security Predicament – State-Making, Regional Conflict and the International System*. Boulder, Colorado: Lynne Rienner, 1995.

Ayubi, Nazih N. M. *Bureaucracy and Politics in Contemporary Egypt*. London: Ithaca Press, 1980.

Ayubi, Nazih N. M. *Over-Stating the Arab State – Politics and Society in the Middle East*. London: I.B. Tauris, 1995.

Badie, Bertrand. *The Imported State – The Westernisation of Political Order*. Cambridge: Cambridge University Press, 2000.

Badie, Bertrand. *Nous ne Sommes Plus Seuls au Monde*. Paris: La Découverte, 2016.

Bamyeh, Mohammed A. 'Anarchist Method, Liberal Intention, Authoritarian Lesson: The Arab Spring between Three Enlightenments', *Constellation*, 20, 2, 2013, pp. 188–202.

Baram, Amatzia. *Saddam Husayn and Islam, 1968-2003 – Ba'thi Iraq from Secularism to Faith*. Baltimore, MD: The Johns Hopkins Press, 2014.

Barkawi, Tarak and Keith Stanski, eds. *Orientalism and War*. London: Hurst and Company, 2012.

Barr, James. *A Line in the Sand – Britain, France and the Struggle That Shaped the Middle East*. London: Simon and Schuster, 2011.

Bassiouni, Cherif M. *Chronicles of the Egyptian Revolution and Its Aftermath: 2011-2016*. New York: Cambridge University Press, 2016.

Batatu, Hanna. *The Old Social Classes and the Revolutionary Movements of Iraq – A Study of Iraq's Old Landed and Commercial Classes and Its Communist, Baathists and Free Officers*. Princeton, NJ: Princeton University Press, 1979.

Batatu, Hanna. *Syria's Peasantry, the Descendants of Its Lesser Rural Notables and Their Politics*. Princeton, NJ: Princeton University Press, 1999.

Bayart, Jean-François. *The State in Africa – The Politics of the Belly*. London and New York: Longman, 1993.

Bayart, Jean-François. *La Greffe de l'État*. Paris: Karthala, 1996.

Bayat, Asef. *Life as Politics – How Ordinary People Change the Middle East*. Stanford, CA: Stanford University Press, 2008.

Beblawi, Hazem and Giacomo Luciani, eds. *The Rentier State*. London: Croom-Helm, 1987.

Beck, Ulrich. 'Toward a New Critical Theory with a Cosmopolitan Intent', *Constellations*, 10, 4, 2003, pp. 453–68.

Beinin, Joel. *Was the Red Flag Flying There? – Marxist Politics and the Arab-Israeli Conflict in Egypt and Israel, 1948-1965*. Berkeley, CA: University of California Press, 1990.

Bellin, Eva. 'The Robustness of Authoritarianism in the Middle East: Exceptionalism in Comparative Perspective', *Comparative Politics*, 36, 2, 2004, pp. 139–58.

Ben-Dor, Gabriel. 'Stateness and Ideology in Contemporary Middle East Politics', *Jerusalem Journal of International Relations*, 9, 3, 1987, pp. 20–37.

Bengio, Ofra. *The Kurds of Iraq – Building a State within a State*. Boulder, Colorado: Lynne Reinner, 2012.

Bergen, Peter L. *The Osama Bin Laden I Know – An Oral History of Al Qaeda's Leader*. New York: Free Press, 2006.

Bevilacqua, Alexander. *The Republic of Arabic Letters – Islam and the European Enlightenment*. Cambridge, MA: Harvard University Press, 2018.

Birdal, Mehmet Sinan. *The Holy Roman Empire and the Ottomans – From Global Imperial Power to Absolutist States*. London: I.B. Tauris, 2011.

Blaydes, Lisa. *Elections and Distributive Politics in Mubarak's Egypt*. New York: Cambridge University Press, 2011.

Blumi, Isa. *Chaos in Yemen – Societal Collapse and the New Authoritarianism*. London: Routledge, 2011.

Bou Nassif, Hicham. 'Coups and Nascent Democracies: The Military and Egypt's Failed Consolidation', *Democratization*, 24, 1, 2017, pp. 157–74.

Bozarslan, Hamit. '*Being in time*, the Kurdish Movement and Universal Quests', in Gareth Stansfield and Mohammed Shareef, eds., *The Kurdish Question Revisited*. London: Hurst and Company, 2017, pp. 61–76.

Brenner, Björn. *Gaza under Hamas – From Islamic Democracy to Islamist Governance*. London: I.B. Tauris, 2017.

Brooke, John L. Julia C. Strauss and Greg Anderson, eds. *State Formations – Global Histories and Cultures of Statehood*. Cambridge: Cambridge University Press, 2018.

Browers, Michaelle L. *Democracy and Civil Society in Arab Political Thought – Transcultural Possibilities*. Syracuse: Syracuse University Press, 2006.

Brownlee, Jason. *Authoritarianism in an Age of Democratisation*. New York: Cambridge University Press, 2007.

Brands, Hal and Jeremi Suri, eds. *The Power of the Past – History and Statecraft*. Washington, DC: Brookings Institution Press, 2016.

Brubaker, Rogers. *Nationalism Reframed – Nationhood and the National Question in the New Europe*. Cambridge: Cambridge University Press, 1996.

Bsheer, Rosie. *Archive Wars – The Politics of History in Saudi Arabia*. Redwood City, CA: Stanford University Press, 2020.

Butenschøn, Nils A., and Roel Meijer, ed. *The Middle East in Transition – The Centrality of Citizenship*. Cheltenham, UK: Edward Elgar Publishing, 2018.

Burgat, François. *Face to Face with Political Islam*. London: I.B. Tauris, 2003.

Burgat, François. *Comprendre l'Islam Politique – Une Trajectoire de Recherche sur l'Altérité Islamiste, 1973-2016*. Paris: La Découverte, 2016.

Burgat, François and Bruno Paoli, eds. *Pas de Printemps pour la Syrie – Acteurs et Enjeux de la Crise, 2011-2013*. Paris: La Découverte, 2013, pp. 55–83.

Calvert, John. *Sayyid Qutb and the Origins of Radical Islamism*. New York: Columbia University Press, 1994.

Camau, Michel. 'L'État Tunisien: De la Tutelle au Désengagement – Portée et Limite d'une Trajectoire', *Monde Arabe Maghreb-Machrek*, 103, 1984, pp. 8–38.

Campos, Michelle. *Ottoman Brothers – Muslims, Christians and Jews in Early Twentieth-Century Palestine*. Stanford, CA: Stanford University Press, 2010.

Caplan, Neil. *The Israel-Palestine Conflict – Contested Histories*. Chichester, West Sussex: Wiley-Blackwell, 2010.

Cassarino, Jean-Pierre. 'Reversing the Hierarchy of Priorities in EU-Mediterranean Relations', in Joel Peters, ed., *The European Union and the Arab Spring – Promoting Democracy and Human Rights in the Middle East*. Lanham, Lexington: Lexington Books, 2012, pp. 1–15.

Chalcraft, John. *Popular Politics in the Making of the Modern Middle East*. Cambridge: Cambridge University Press, 2016.

Challand, Benoît. 'Citizenship and Violence in the Arab Worlds – A Historical Sketch', in Juergen Mackert and Bryan S. Turner, eds., *The Transformation of Citizenship – Struggle, Resistance and Violence, Volume Three*. London: Routledge, 2017.

Chamberlin, Paul Thomas. *The Global Offensive – The United States, the Palestine Liberation Organization and the Making of the Post-Cold War Order*. Oxford: Oxford University Press, 2016.

Chandler, David. *International State-Building – The Rise of Post-Liberal Governance*. London: Routledge, 2010.

Clarke, Killian. ''Aysh, Huriyya, Karama Insaniyya: Framing and the 2011 Egyptian Uprising', *European Political Science*, 12, 2, 2013, pp. 197-214.

Coady, C. A. J., Ned Dobos and Sagar Sanyal, eds. *Challenges for Humanitarian Intervention – Ethical Demand and Political Reality*. Oxford: Oxford University Press, 2018.

Cole, Juan and Moojan Momen. 'Mafia, Mob and Shi'ism in Iraq: The Rebellion of Ottoman Karbala, 1824-1843', *Past and Present*, 112, 1986, pp. 112-43.

Coll, Steve. *The Bin Ladens – An Arabian Family in the American Century*. New York: Penguin, 2009.

Cook, Steven A. *Ruling but Not Governing – The Military and Political Development in Egypt, Algeria, and Turkey*. Baltimore: Johns Hopkins University Press, 2007.

Cronin, Stephanie. *Armies and State-Building in the Modern Middle East – Politics, Nationalism and Military Reform*. London: I.B. Tauris, 2014.

Dabashi, Hamid. *Authority in Islam – From the Rise of Muhammad to the Establishment of the Umayyads*. New Brunswick and London: Transaction Publishers, 1989.

Davies, Brian L. *The Russo-Turkish War, 1768-1774 – Catherine II and the Ottoman Empire*. London: Bloomsbury, 2016.

Dawisha, Adeed and William Zartman, eds. *Beyond Coercion – The Durability of the Arab State*. London: Croom-Helm, 1988.

Dawisha, Adeed. *Arab Nationalism in the 20th Century – From Triumph to Despair*. Princeton, NJ: Princeton University Press, 2003.

Deeb, Lara. *An Enchanted Modern – Gender and Public Piety in Shi'i Lebanon*. Princeton, NJ: Princeton University Press, 2005.

Defay, Alexandre. *Géopolitique du Proche-Orient*. Paris: Presses Universitaires de France, 2003.

Deng, Francis et al. *Sovereignty as Responsibility – Conflict Management in Africa*. Washington, DC: Brookings Institution Press, 1996.

Deringil, Selim. *The Well-Protected Domains – Ideology and the Legitimation of Power in the Ottoman Empire, 1876-1909*. London: I.B. Tauris, 1998.

Dodge, Toby. *Inventing Iraq – The Failure of Nation-Building and a History Denied*. London: Hurst and Company, 2012.

Doumani, Beshara. *Rediscovering Palestine – Merchants and Peasants in Jabal Nablus, 1700-1900*. Berkeley, CA: University of California Press, 1995.

Eickelman, Dale F. 'Changing Interpretations of Islamic Movements', in William R. Roff, ed., *Islam and the Political Economy of Meaning*. London: Croom-Helm, 1987, pp. 13-30.

Eickelman, Dale F. *The Middle East and Central Asia – An Anthropological Approach*. Upper Saddle River, NJ: Prentice-Hall, 2002.

Egnell, Robert and Peter Haldén, eds. *New Agendas in State-Building – Hybridity, Contingency and History*. London: Routledge, 2013.

El-Ariss, Tarek. *Leaks, Hacks and Scandals – Arab Culture in the Digital Age*. Princeton, NJ: Princeton University Press, 2018.

Emiliani, Marcella. *L'idea di Occidente tra '800 e '900 – Medio Oriente e Islam*. Bologna: Rubbetius Editore, 2003.

Esposito, John L. *Islam and Politics*. Syracuse, NY: Syracuse University Press, 1984.

Evans, Peter, Dietrich Rueschemeyer and Theda Skocpol, eds. *Bringing the State Back In*. Cambridge: Cambridge University Press, 1985.

Fahmy, Khaled. *All The Pasha's Men – Mehmed Ali, His Army and the Making of Modern Egypt*. Cairo: American University in Cairo Press, 2002.

Fawaz, Leila. *Occasion for War – Civil Conflict in Lebanon and Damascus in 1860*. Berkeley, CA: University of California Press, 1995.

Fine, Ben, Costas Lapavitsas and Jonathan Pincus, eds. *Development Policy in the Twenty-First Century – Beyond the Post-Washington Consensus*. London: Routledge, 2001.
Fukuyama, Francis. *State-Building – Governance and World Order in the 21st Century*. Ithaca, NY: Cornell University Press, 2004.
Garnier, Emmanuel. *L'Empire des Sables – La France au Sahel, 1860-1960*. Paris: Perrin, 2018.
Gellner, Ernest. *Muslim Society*. Cambridge: Cambridge University Press, 1981.
Gellner, Ernest. *Nations and Nationalism*. Ithaca, NY: Cornell University Press, 1983.
Gelvin, James. *The Israel-Palestine Conflict – One Hundred Years of War*. Cambridge: Cambridge University Press, 2014.
Gerber, Haim. *Remembering and Imagining Palestine – Identity and Nationalism from the Crusades to the Present*. Basingstoke: Palgrave, 2008.
Ghalioun, Burhan. *Le Malaise Arabe – L'État Contre la Nation*. Alger: ENAG Éditions, 1991.
Ghalioun, Burhan. 'Islam, Modernité et Laïcité: Les Sociétés Arabes Contemporaines', *Confluences Méditerranée*, 33, 2000, pp. 25–34.
Ghattas, Kim. *Black Wave – Saudi Arabia, Iran and the Forty-Year Rivalry That Unraveled Culture, Religion and Collective Memory in the Middle East*. New York: Henry Holt and Co., 2020.
Ghazal, Amal and Jens Hanssen, eds. *Oxford Handbook of Contemporary Middle Eastern and North African History*. Oxford: Oxford University Press, 2016.
Gilley, Bruce. 'The Case for Colonialism', *Third World Quarterly*, 2017, pp. 1–17.
Green, Penny and Amelia Smith. 'Evicting Palestine', *State Crime Journal*, 5, 1, 2016, pp. 81–108.
Guazzone, Laura and Daniela Pioppi, eds. *The Arab State and Neo-Liberal Globalisation – The Restructuring of State Power in the Middle East*. Reading: Ithaca Press, 2009.
Gunter, Michael M. *The Kurdish Ascending – The Evolving Solution to the Kurdish Problem in Iraq and Turkey*. New York: Palgrave Macmillan, 2011.
Gunter, Michael M. and M.A. Ahmed Mohammed. *The Kurdish Spring*. Costa Mesa: Mazda Publishers, 2013.
Haim, Sylvia. *Arab Nationalism – An Anthology*. Berkeley, California: University of California Press, 1962.
Halliday, Fred. *Revolution and Foreign Policy – The Case of South-Yemen 1967-1987*. Cambridge: Cambridge University Press, 1990.
Halliday, Fred. *The Middle East in International Relations – Power, Politics and Ideology*. Cambridge: Cambridge University Press, 2005.
Hammoudi, Abdellah. *Master and Disciples – The Cultural Foundations of Moroccan Authoritarianism*. Chicago: Chicago University Press, 1997.
Hanieh, Adam. *Lineages of Revolt*. London: Haymarket, 2013.
Hardy, Roger. *The Poisoned Well – Empire and Its Legacy in the Middle East*. London: Hurst and Company, 2018.
Hasani, Abd al Razzaq al. *Tarikh al Wizarat al 'Iraqiyya* (The History of Iraqi Cabinets). Sidon, Lebanon: Matba'at al Irfan, 1953–1967.
Hatina, Meir. 'Redeeming Sunni Islam: Al Qaeda's Polemic against the Muslim Brethren', *British Journal of Middle Eastern Studies*, 39, 1, 2012, pp. 101–13.
Hehir, Aidan and Neil Robinson, eds. *State-Building – Theory and Practice*. London: Routledge, 2007.
Heydemann, Steven, ed. *War, Institutions and Social Change in the Middle East*. Berkeley, CA: University of California Press, 2000.
Hibou, Béatrice. *The Force of Obedience – The Political Economy of Repression in Tunisia*. London: Polity, 2011.

Hinnebusch, Raymond A. *Authoritarian Power and State Formation in Ba'thist Syria – Army, Party and Peasant.* Boulder, CO: Westview Press, 1990.

Hinnebusch, Raymond A. 'Order and Change in the Middle East: A Neo-Gramscian Twist on the International Society Approach', in Barry Buzan and Ana Gonzalez-Pelaez, eds., *International Society and the Middle East.* London: Palgrave MacMillan, 2009, pp. 201–25.

Hokayem, Emile and Hebatalla Taha, eds. *Egypt after the Spring – Revolt and Reaction.* London: Routledge, 2016.

Hopwood, Derek, et al., eds. *Iraq – Power and Society.* Oxford: St. Antony's College, 1993.

Horne, Alistair. *A Savage War of Peace – Algeria, 1954-1962.* New York: New York Review of Books, 1977.

Hourani, Albert. *Arabic Thought in the Liberal Age, 1798-1939.* Cambridge: Cambridge University Press, 1962.

Hourani, Albert. *A History of the Arab Peoples.* New York: MJF Books, 1991.

Hund, Wolf and Alana Lentin, eds. *Racism and Sociology.* Vienna: Lit Verlag, 2014.

Huntington, Samuel. *American Politics – The Promise of Disharmony.* Cambridge, MA: Belknap Press, 1983.

Huntington, Samuel. *The Clash of Civilisations and the Remaking of the World Order.* New York: Simon and Schuster, 1996.

Huntington, Samuel. *Who Are We? The Challenges to America's National Identity.* New York: Simon and Schuster, 2004.

Hutchinson, John and Anthony D. Smith. *Ethnicity.* Oxford: Oxford University Press, 1996.

Ismael, Tareq Y. and Jacqueline S. Ismael. *Government and Politics of the Contemporary Middle East – Continuity and Change.* London: Routledge, 2011.

Ismail, Salwa. *Political Life in Cairo's Quarters – Encountering the Everyday State.* Minneapolis: Minnesota University Press, 2006.

Jabar, Faleh Abdul. 'Sheikhs, Clerics, Tribes, Ideologues and Urban Dwellers in the South of Iraq: The Potential for Rebellion', in Toby Dodge and Steven Simon, eds., *Iraq at the Crossroads – State and Society in the Shadow of Regime Change.* Oxford: Oxford University Press, 2003, pp. 115–30.

Jabar, Faleh Abdul. *The Shi'ite Movement in Iraq.* London: Saqi, 2003.

Jabar, Faleh Abdul and Hosham Dawod, eds. *The Kurds – Nationalism and Politics.* London: Saqi Books, 2006.

Jakes, Aaron. 'Boom, Bugs, Bust: Egypt's Ecology of Interest, 1882–1914', *Antipode*, 49, 4, 2017, pp. 1035–59.

Joseph, Suad. *Gender and Citizenship in the Middle East.* Syracuse: Syracuse University Press, 2000.

Jumet, Kira D. *Contesting the Repressive State – Why Ordinary Egyptians Protested during the Arab Spring.* New York: Oxford University Press, 2017.

Kamrava, Mehran. *The Modern Middle East – A Political History Since the First World War.* Berkeley, CA: University of California Press, 2015.

Kamrava, Mehran. *Inside the Arab State.* London: Hurst and Company, 2018.

Kandil, Hazem. *Soldiers, Spies and Statesmen – Egypt's Road to Revolt.* London: Verso, 2012.

Kandil, Hazem. *The Power Triangle – Military, Security and Politics in Regime Change.* Oxford: Oxford University Press, 2016.

Karsh, Efraim. *Empires of the Sand – The Struggle for Mastery in the Middle East.* Cambridge, MA: Harvard University Press, 2001.

Kartas, Moncef. 'The Tunisian-Libyan Border Space of the Jefara: Informality as Resistance to Post-Colonial State-Formation', unpublished paper, presented at the Middle East Law State and Society, Yale University, 2016.

Kassem, Maye. *Egyptian Politics – The Dynamics of Authoritarian Rule.* Boulder, CO: Lynne Rienner Publishers, 2004.

Keenan, Jeremy. *The Dark Sahara – America's War on Terror in Africa.* Chicago: University of Chicago Press, 2009.

Kersten, Carool. *The Caliphate and Islamic Statehood – Formation, Fragmentation and Modern Interpretations.* Berlin: Gerlach Press, 2015.

Ketchley, Neil. *Egypt in a Time of Revolution – Contentious Politics and the Arab Spring.* New York: Cambridge University Press, 2017.

Khadduri, Majid. *Republican Iraq – A Study in Iraqi Politics since the 1958 Revolution.* London: Oxford University Press, 1969.

Khalidi, Ahmad Samih. 'The Palestinian National Movement from Self-rule to Statehood', in Joel Peters and David Newman, eds., *The Routledge Handbook on the Israeli-Palestinian Conflict.* London: Routledge, 2013, pp. 20–30.

Khalidi, Ahmad Samih. *The Hundred Years' War on Palestine – A History of Settler Colonial Conquest and Resistance, 1917–2017.* New York: Metropolitan Books, 2020.

Khalidi, Rashid, Lisa Anderson, Muhammad Muslih and Reeva S. Simon. *The Origins of Arab Nationalism.* New York: Columbia University Press, 1991.

Khosrokhavar, Farhad. *The New Arab Revolutions that Shook the World.* Boulder, CO: Paradigm Publishers, 2012.

Khoury, Philip H. and Joseph Kostiner, eds. *Tribes and State Formation in the Middle East.* Berkeley, CA: University of California Press, 1991.

Khuri-Makdisi, Ilham. *The Eastern Mediterranean and the Making of Global Radicalism, 1860–1914.* Berkeley, CA: University of California Press, 2010.

Kienle, Eberhard. *Ba'th vs. Ba'th – The Conflict between Iraq and Syria, 1968–1989.* London: I.B. Tauris, 1990.

Kienle, Eberhard. *A Grand Delusion – Democracy and Economic Reform in Egypt.* London: I.B. Tauris, 2001.

Kirkpatrick, David D. *Into the Hands of the Soldiers – Freedom and Chaos in Egypt and the Middle East.* New York: Viking, 2018.

Killingsworth, Matt, Matthew Sussex and Jan Pakulsi, ed. *Violence and the State.* Manchester: Manchester University Press, 2016.

King, Stephen J. *The New Authoritarianism in the Middle East and North Africa.* Indianapolis: Indiana University Press, 2009.

Klaas, Brian. *The Despot's Accomplice – How the West is Aiding and Abetting the Decline of Democracy.* London: Hurst and Company, 2018.

Koselleck, Reinhart. *Le Future Passé – Contribution à la Sémantique des Temps Historiques.* Paris: Éditions de l'EHESS, 1990.

Krämer, Gudrun. *A History of Palestine – From the Ottoman Conquest to the Founding of the State of Israel.* Princeton, NJ: Princeton University Press, 2008.

Krasner, Stephen. *Sovereignty – Organised Hypocrisy.* Princeton, NJ: Princeton University Press, 1999.

Lacoste, Camille and Yves eds. *L'État du Maghreb.* Paris: La Découverte, 1991.

Laroui, Abdallah. *L'Histoire du Maghreb – Un Essai de Synthèse.* Paris: La Découverte, 1982.

Laurens, Henry, John Tolan and Gilles Veinstein. *L'Europe et l'Islam – Quinze Siècles d'Histoire.* Paris: Odile Jacob, 2009.

Leca, Jean. 'La Rationalité de la Violence Politique', in Baudoin Dupret, ed., *Le Phénomène de la Violence Politique – Perspectives Comparatistes et Paradigme Égyptien.* Cairo: CEDEJ, 1994, pp. 17–42.

Lenczoswki, George. *Political Elites in the Middle East.* Washington, DC: American Enterprise Institute, 1975.

Little, Douglas. *American Orientalism – The United States and the Middle East since 1945*. Chapel Hill, NC: University of North Carolina Press, 2008.

Lockman, Zachary. *Comrades and Enemies – Arab and Jewish Workers in Palestine, 1906-1948*. Berkeley, CA: University of California Press, 1996.

Longrigg, Stephen Hemsley. *Iraq 1900 to 1950 – A Political and Economic History*. Oxford: Oxford University Press, 1958.

Louis, William Roger, ed. *The End of the British Mandate*. Austin, TX: University of Texas Press, 1986.

Lowe, Robert and Gareth Stansfield. *The Kurdish Policy Imperative*. Washington, DC: Brookings Institution Press, 2010.

Luciani, Giacomo, ed. *The Arab State*. Berkeley and Los Angeles: University of California Press, 1990.

Luciani, Giacomo and Ghassan Salamé, eds. *The Politics of Arab Integration*. London: Croom-Helm, 1998.

Luizard, Pierre-Jean. *Le Piège Daech – L'État Islamique ou le Retour de l'Histoire*. Paris: La Découverte, 2015.

Maddy-Weitzman, Bruce. *The Crystallisation of the Arab State System, 1945-1954*. Syracuse, NY: Syracuse University Press, 1993.

Maddy-Weitzman, Bruce. *A Century of Arab Politics – From the Arab Revolt to the Arab Spring*. London: Rowman and Littlefield, 2016.

Mahler, Anne Garland. *From the Tricontinental to the Global South – Race, Radicalism and Transnational Identity*. Durham, NC: Duke University Press, 2018.

Makdisi, Ussama. *Age of Coexistence – The Ecumenical Frame and the Making of the Modern Arab World*. Berkeley, CA: University of California Press, 2019.

Malcolm, Noel. *Useful Enemies – Islam and the Ottoman Empire in Western Political Thought, 1450–1750*. Oxford: Oxford University Press, 2019.

Manela, Erez. *The Wilsonian Moment – Self-Determination and the International Origins of Anticolonial Nationalism*. Oxford: Oxford University Press, 2007.

Mann, Michael. *The Sources of Social Power, Volume 1 – A History of Power from the Beginning to AD 1760*. Cambridge: Cambridge University Press, 1986.

Marr, Phebe. 'Iraq's Leadership Dilemma: A Study of Leadership Trends, 1948–1968', *The Middle East Journal*, 24, 3, 1970, pp. 283–301.

Marr, Phebe. *The Modern History of Iraq*. Boulder, CO: Westview Press, 1985.

Masoud, Tarek. *Counting Islam – Religion, Class and Elections in Egypt*. New York: Cambridge University Press, 2014.

Masters, Bruce. *The Arabs of the Ottoman Empire*. Cambridge: Cambridge University Press, 2013.

McDougall, James. *History and the Culture of Nationalism in Algeria*. Cambridge: Cambridge University Press, 2006.

Meijer, Roel. 'Political Citizenship and Social Movements in the Arab World', in Hein-Anton Van Der Heijden, ed., *Handbook of Political Citizenship and Social Movements*. Cheltenham: Elgar Publisher, 2014, pp. 628–60.

Menza, Mohamed Fahmy. *Patronage Politics in Egypt – The National Democratic Party and the Muslim Brotherhood in Cairo*. New York: Routledge, 2013.

Ménoret, Pascal. *Graveyards of Clerics – Everyday Activism in Saudi Arabia*. Redwood City, CA: Stanford University Press, 2020.

Migdal, Joel S. *Strong Societies and Weak States – State-Society Relations and State Capabilities in the Third World*. Princeton, NJ: Princeton University Press, 1988.

Migdal, Joel S. *State in Society – Studying How States and Societies Transform and Constitute One Another*. Cambridge: Cambridge University Press, 2001.

Miller, Rory. *Desert Kingdoms to Global Powers – The Rise of the Arab Gulf*. New Haven: Yale University Press, 2016.
Miller, Susan Gilson. *A History of Modern Morocco*. Cambridge: Cambridge University Press, 2013.
Mitchell, Timothy. 'The Limits of the State: Beyond Statist Approaches and Their Critics', *American Political Science Review*, 85, 1, 1991, pp. 77–96.
Mitchell, Timothy. 'No Factories, No Problems: The Logic of Neo-Liberalism in Egypt', *Review of African Political Economy* 26, 82, 1999, pp. 455–68.
Mitchell, Timothy. *Rule of Experts – Egypt, Techno-Politics, Modernity*. Los Angeles: California University Press, 2002.
Mohamedou, Mohammad-Mahmoud Ould. *Iraq and the Second Gulf War – State-Building and Regime Security*. San Francisco: Austin and Winfield, 1998.
Mohamedou, Mohammad-Mahmoud Ould. *Contre-Croisade – Le 11 Septembre et le Retournement du Monde*. Paris: L'Harmattan, 2011.
Mohamedou, Mohammad-Mahmoud Ould. *Understanding Al Qaeda – Changing War and Global Politics*. London: Pluto Press, 2006 and Ann Arbor, MI: University of Michigan Press, 2007, expanded edition, 2011.
Mohamedou, Mohammad-Mahmoud Ould. *A Theory of ISIS – Political Violence and the Transformation of the Global Order*. London: Pluto Press, 2017 and Chicago: University of Chicago Press, 2018.
Mohamedou, Mohammad-Mahmoud Ould and Timothy Sisk, eds. *Democratisation in the 21st Century – Reviving Transitology*. London: Routledge, 2016.
Monroe, Elizabeth. *Britain's Moment in the Middle East, 1914-1956*. London: The Johns Hopkins Press, 1963.
Moore, Pete. 'QIZs, FTAs, USAID and the MEFTA: A Political Economy of Acronyms', *Middle East Report* 234, 35, 2005, pp. 18–23.
Morris, Benny and Dror Ze'evi. *The Thirty-Year Genocide – Turkey's Destruction of Its Christian Minorities, 1894-1924*. Cambridge, MA: Harvard University Press, 2019.
Mufti, Malik. *Sovereign Creations – Pan-Arabism and Political Order in Syria and Iraq*. Ithaca, NY: Cornell University Press, 1995.
Muñoz, Gema Martin and Ramón Grosfoguel, eds. *La Islamofobia a Debate – La Genealogía del Miedo al Islam y la Construcción de Los Discursos Antiislámicos*. Madrid: Biblioteca de Casa Árabe, 2012.
Muslih, Mohammad. 'Toward Coexistence – An Analysis of the Resolutions of the Palestine Council', *Journal of Palestine Studies*, 19, 4, 1990, pp. 3–29.
Nakash, Yitzhak. *The Shi'is of Iraq*. Princeton, NJ: Princeton University of Press, 1994.
Nimni, Ephraim. 'Stateless Nations in a World of Nation-states', in Karl Cordell and Stefan Wolff, eds., *Routledge Handbook of Ethnic Conflict*. London and New York: Routledge, 2011, pp. 55–66.
Nordlinger, Eric A. *On the Autonomy of the Democratic State*. Cambridge, MA: Harvard University Press, 1982.
Owen, Roger. *State, Power and Politics – The Making of the Modern Middle East*. Routledge: London, 1992.
Owen, Roger. *The Middle East in the World Economy, 1800-1914*. London: I.B. Tauris, 1993.
Owen, Roger. *The Rise and Fall of Arab Presidents for Life*. Cambridge, MA: Harvard University Press, 2012.
Pankhurst, Reza. *The Inevitable Caliphate? – A History of the Struggle for Global Islamic Union, 1924 to the Present*. London: Hurst and Company, 2013.
Parolin, Gianluca Paolo. *Citizenship in the Arab World – Kin, Religion and Nation-State*. Amsterdam: Amsterdam University Press, 2009.

Picard, Elizabeth. 'Nation-building and Minority Rights in the Middle East', in Anh Nga Longva and Anne Sofie Roald, eds., *Religious Minorities in the Middle East – Domination, Self-Empowerment, Accommodation*. Leiden and Boston: Brill, 2012, pp. 325–50.
Poggi, Gianfranco. *The State – Its Nature, Development and Prospects*. Stanford, CA: Stanford University Press, 1990.
Polakow-Suransky, Sasha. *Go Back to Where you Came From – The Backlash against Immigration and the Fate of Western Democracy*. London: Hurst and Company, 2017.
Potter, Lawrence G. and Gary G. Sick, eds. *Iran, Iraq and the Legacies of War*. London: Palgrave Macmillan, 2004.
Quinlivan, James T. 'Coup-proofing: Its Practice and Consequences in the Middle East', *International Security*, 24, 2, 1999, pp. 131–65.
Rabbani, Mouin. 'The Year of the Citizen', in Bassam Haddad, Rosie Bsheer, Ziad Abu-Rish and Roger Owen, eds., *Dawn of the Arab Uprisings – End of An Old Order?* London: Pluto Press, 2012, pp. 33–6.
Rear, Michael. *Intervention, Ethnic Conflict and State-Building in Iraq – A Paradigm for the Post-Colonial State*. London: Routledge, 2008.
Robin, Marie-Monique. *Escadrons de la Mort, l'École Française*. Paris: La Découverte, 2008.
Rodogno, Davide. *Against Massacre – Humanitarian Interventions in the Ottoman Empire, 1815-1914*. Princeton, NJ: Princeton University Press, 2012.
Rogers, Paul. *Irregular War – ISIS and the New Threat from the Margins*. London: I.B. Tauris, 2016.
Roll, Stephan. 'Managing Change: How Egypt's Military Leadership Shaped the Transformation', *Mediterranean Politics*, 21, 1, 2016, pp. 23–43.
Rosen, Nir. *Aftermath – Following the Bloodshed of America's Wars in the Muslim World*. New York: Nation Books, 2010.
Roy, Olivier. *En Quête de l'Orient Perdu*. Paris: Le Seuil, 2014.
Roy, Olivier. *Jihad and Death – The Global Appeal of Islamic State*. London: Hurst and Company, 2016.
Saccarelli, Emanuele and Latha Varadarajan. *Imperialism – Past and Present*. Oxford: Oxford University Press, 2015.
Sadiki, Larbi. *The Search for Arab Democracy – Discourses and Counter-Discourses*. London: Hurst and Company, 2004.
Sadowski, Yahya. 'The New Orientalism and the Democracy Debate', *Middle East Report*, 183, 1993, pp. 14–21, 40.
Said, Edward. *Orientalism*: London: Penguin, 1978.
Said, Edward. *The Question of Palestine*. New York: Times Book, 1979.
Said, Edward. *Culture and Imperialism*. London: Vintage, 1994.
Said, Edward. *Reflections on Exile and Other Essays*. Cambridge: Harvard University Press, 2000.
Salamé, Ghassan, ed. *The Foundations of the Arab State*. London: Routledge, 1987.
Salamé, Ghassan. *Democracy without Democrats? – The Renewal of Politics in the Muslim World*. London: I.B. Tauris, 2001.
Salvatore, Armando. 'Beyond Orientalism? Max Weber and the Displacements of "Essentialism" in the Study of Islam', *Arabica*, 43, 3, 1996, pp. 457–85.
Salvatore, Armando. 'Civility: Between Disciplined Interaction and Local/Translocal Connectedness', *Third World Quarterly*, 32, 5, 2011, pp. 807–25.
Salvatore, Armando. *Sociology of Islam – Knowledge, Power and Civility*. Malden, MA: John Wiley and Sons, 2016.

Salvatore, Armando and Dale F. Eickelman, eds. *Public Islam and the Common Good*. Leiden: Brill, 2004.
Satia, Priya. *Spies in Arabia – The Great War and the Cultural Foundations of Britain's Covert Empire in the Middle East*. Oxford: Oxford University Press, 2008.
Sayegh, Yezid. *Armed Struggle and the Search for the State – The Palestinian National Movement, 1949-1993*. Oxford: Oxford University Press, 1997.
Sayyid, Salman. *Recalling the Caliphate – Decolonization and World Order*. London: Hurst and Company, 2014.
Schlumberger, Oliver. 'The Arab Middle East and the Question of Democratisation: Some Critical Remarks', *Democratization*, 7, 4, 2000, pp. 104–32.
Schlumberger, Olivier. *Debating Arab Authoritarianism – Dynamics and Durability in Nondemocratic Regimes*. Stanford, CA: Stanford University Press, 2007.
Schmitter, Philippe. 'Is it Safe for Transitologists and Consolidologists to Travel to the Middle East and North Africa?' in Roger Heacock, ed., *Political Transitions in the Arab World, Part One*. Birzeit: Birzeit University Press, 2001.
Schmitter, Philippe. 'From Transitology to Consolidology', in Mohammad-Mahmoud Ould Mohamedou and Timothy D. Sisk, eds., *Democratisation in the 21st Century – Reviving Transitology*. London: Routledge, 2016, pp. 167–84.
Sharabi, Hisham. *Neopatriarchy – A Theory of Distorted Change*. Oxford: Oxford University Press, 1988.
Shenker, Jack. *The Egyptians – A Radical History of Egypt's Unfinished Revolution*. New York: New Press, 2016.
Shields, Sarah D. *Fezzes in the River: Identity Politics and European Diplomacy in the Middle East on the Eve of World War II*. Oxford: Oxford University Press, 2011.
Shlaim, Avi. 'The Rise and Fall of the All-Palestine Government in Gaza', *Journal of Palestine Studies*, 20, 1, 1990, pp. 37–53.
Sirrs, Owen L. *A History of the Egyptian Intelligence Service – A History of the Mukhabarat, 1910-2009*. London: Routledge, 2010.
Skocpol, Theda. 'Bringing the State Back In: Strategies of Analysis in Current Research', in Peter B. Evans, Dietrich Rueschemeyer and Theda Skocpol, eds., *Bringing the State Back In*. Cambridge: Cambridge University Press, 1985, pp. 3–38.
Slater, Dan. *Ordering Power – Contentious Politics and Authoritarian Leviathans in Southeast Asia*. New York: Cambridge University Press, 2010.
Sluglett, Peter. *Britain in Iraq, 1914–1932*. London: Ithaca Press, 1976.
Sluglett, Peter. *Iraq Since 1958 – From Revolution to Dictatorship*. London: I.B. Tauris, 1990.
Sluglett, Peter. 'The Historiography of Modern Iraq', *The American Historical Review*, 96, 5, December 1991, pp. 1408–21.
Sluglett, Peter and Marion Sluglett. 'Some Reflections on Sunni/Shi'i Question in Iraq', *British Society for Middle Eastern Studies Bulletin*, 5, 2, 1978, pp. 79–87.
Soliman, Samer. *The Autumn of Dictatorship – Fiscal Crisis and Political Change in Egypt under Mubarak*. Stanford, CA: Stanford University Press, 2011.
Stansfield, Gareth. *Iraq*. London: Polity, 2016.
Stohl, Michael, Richard Burchill and Scott Englund, eds. *Constructions of Terrorism – An Interdisciplinary Approach to Research and Policy*. Oakland, CA: University of California Press, 2017.
Strange, Susan. *The Retreat of the State – The Diffusion of Power in the World Economy*. Cambridge: Cambridge University Press, 1996.
Strayer, Joseph R. *On the Medieval Origins of the Modern State*. Princeton, NJ: Princeton University Press, 1970.

Suarez, Thomas. *State of Terror – How Terrorism Created Modern Israel*. Bloxham, Oxon: Skyscraper, 2016.

Sung, Il Kwang. *Mamluks in the Modern Egyptian Mind – Changing the Memory of the Mamluks, 1919-1952*. New York: Palgrave Macmillan, 2017.

Szmolka, Inmaculada, ed. *Political Change in the Middle East and North Africa – After the Arab Spring*. Edinburgh: Edinburgh University Press, 2017.

Tahtawi, Rifa'a Rafi Al. *An Imam in Paris – An Account of a Stay in France by an Egyptian Cleric (1826-1831)*. London: Saqi Books, 2016 [1834].

Tejel, Jordi. 'Beyond the Dichotomy of Accommodation versus Resistance: The Kurdish Minority in Iraq and Syria in Long-term and Comparative Perspectives, 1920-2015', in Michael M. Gunter, ed., *Kurdish Issues – Essays in Honour of Robert W. Olson*. Costa Mesa: Mazda, 2016, pp. 258–82.

Tejel, Jordi, Peter Sluglett, Riccardo Bocco and Hamit Bozarslan, eds. *Writing the Modern History of Iraq – Historiographical and Political Challenges*. London: World Scientific, 2012.

Thompson, Elizabeth. *Colonial Citizens – Republican Rights, Paternal Privilege and Gender in French Syria and Lebanon*. New York: Columbia University Press, 2000.

Thompson, Elizabeth. *How the West Stole Democracy from the Arabs – The Syrian Arab Congress of 1920 and the Destruction of Its Liberal-Islamic Alliance*. New York: Grove Atlantic, 2020.

Tibi, Bassam. *Arab Nationalism – A Critical Inquiry*. New York: St. Martin's Press, 1991.

Tignor, Robert L. *Modernisation and British Colonial Rule in Egypt, 1882-1914*. Princeton, NJ: Princeton University Press, 1966.

Tilly, Charles, ed. *The Formation of National States in Western Europe*. Princeton, NJ: Princeton University Press, 1975.

Tilly, Charles. *Capital, Coercion and European States AD 990-1992*. New York: J. Wiley, 1993.

Tilly, Charles. *The Politics of Collective Violence*. Cambridge: Cambridge University Press, 2003.

Toynbee, Arnold. *The Western Question in Greece and Turkey – A Study in the Contact of Civilisations*. Boston: Houghton Mifflin Company, 1922.

Tripp, Charles. *A History of Iraq*. Cambridge: Cambridge University Press, 2007.

Tuğal, Cihan. 'The Decline of the Legitimate Monopoly of Violence and the Return of Non-state Warriors', in Juergen Mackert and Bryan S. Turner, eds., *The Transformation of Citizenship – Struggle, Resistance and Violence, Volume Three*. London: Routledge, 2017, pp. 77–92.

Utvik, Bjørn Olav. 'The Modernising Force of Islamism', in John Esposito and François Burgat, *Modernising Islam – Religion in the Public Sphere in Europe and the Middle East*. London: Hurst and Company, 2003, pp. 43–68.

Uyar, Mesut and Edward J. Erickson. *A Military History of the Ottomans – From Osman to Atatürk*. Santa Barbara, CA: Praeger, 2009.

Vatikiotis, Panayiotis Jerasimof. *The History of Modern Egypt – From Muhammad Ali to Mubarak*. Baltimore: Johns Hopkins University Press, 1992.

Vergé-Franceschi, Michel, ed. *Guerre et Commerce en Méditerranée – IXe-XXe siècle*. Paris: Veyrier, 1991.

Vitalis, Robert. *America's Kingdom – Mythmaking on the Saudi Oil Frontier*. Redwood City, CA: Stanford University Press, 2006.

Vitalis, Robert. *White World Order, Black Power Politics – The Birth of American International Relations*. Ithaca, NY: Cornell University Press, 2015.

Walter, Dierk. *Colonial Violence – European Empires and the Use of Force*. London: Hurst and Company, 2017.

Waterbury, John. *The Egypt of Nasser and Sadat – The Political Economy of Two Regimes*. Princeton, NJ: Princeton University Press, 1983.
Watts, Nicole F. 'Institutionalising Virtual Kurdistan West – Transnational Networks and Ethnic Contention in International Affairs', in Joel S. Migdal, ed., *Boundaries and Belonging – States and Societies in the Struggle to Shape Identities and Local Practices*. Cambridge: Cambridge University Press, 2008, pp. 121–50.
Weber, Max. *From Max Weber – Essays in Sociology*. Oxford: Oxford University Press, 1946 [1918].
Wedeen, Lisa. *Ambiguities of Domination – Politics, Rhetoric and Symbols in Contemporary Syria*. Chicago: Chicago University Press, 1999.
Willis, Michael. *Politics and Power in the Maghreb – Algeria, Tunisia and Morocco from Independence to the Arab Spring*. London: Hurst and Company, 2012.
Wolf, Anne. *Political Islam in Tunisia – The History of Ennahda*. Oxford: Oxford University Press, 2017.

INDEX

Boldface locators indicate figures and tables; locators followed by "n." indicate endnotes

al Abadi, Haidar 104, 176
Abbas, Mahmoud 89
Abbed Rabo, Yasser 84
Abu Timmin, Ja'afar 72
Administrative Monitoring Authority 125
Afghanistan
    carpet-bombing of 160
    'consolidation' type 175
    NATO's intervention in 174–5
    Soviet invasion of 13, 150
age of imperialism 19
Al-'Arwi, Abdallah 49, 53
Alawi, Iyad 176
Albanians 30
Alexandretta, *sandjak* 105
Algeria 4, 9, 38, 75
    'children of the revolution'
        generation 17
    décennie noire (dark decade)
        civil war 18
    FLN 11, 15–16, 175, 186
    French torture in 6, 11
    Polisario Front (1975) 148
Algeria-Morocco war (1963) 148
Algerian crisis 150
Ali, Mehmet (Muhammad) 28–9, 117
    Egyptian state, foundation 117–20
Allende, Salvador 150
'All-Palestine Government' 82
Al Qaeda 10, 18, 147, 152–3
    Global War on Terror against 155
    regional franchises 157
    regionalization 150–1
    revolutionary approach 152
    sectarianism 156
Al Rihla al Bariziyya 39 n.10

Amar, Paul 52
    'parastatal' campaign 63 n.64
Amnesty International 130
Anatolian Christianity, destruction 30
Ancient Greece, resurrection 28
Anderson, Benedict, official nationalism 98
Anderson, Lisa 11
Anglo-French war 25
An-Na'im, Abdullahi 54
Ansary, Tamim 10
anti-Arab feeling 18
Arab emigration 31
Arabian Peninsula 21 n.16, 31, 34–5
    social strata 36
    US military intervention in 151
Arabism, principle 72, 149
Arab-Israeli war (1948, 1967) 13, 83–4, 151
Arabistan 31
Arabization 35
Arab nationalism 7, 16, 21 n.11, 32, 34,
    74, 83
    anti-imperialism of 36
    chauvinistic notion of 98
    collapse of 17
Arab Palestine 82
Arabs 9, 57, 71
    Albanians and 30
    Kurds and 98
    Turks and 31–3
Arab Socialist Union (ASU) 119
Arab Spring (2011) 3, 14, 18–19, 43, 108,
    117, 155, 158, 171, 188
Arab statehood 47–50, 57
Arab states 7, 14, 16, 38, 41, 49, 52, 57,
    150–1. *See also* Mashreq and
    Maghreb

Arab regional order 16–17
  crisis of legitimacy 34
  democracy 43–4, 59
  governance approach in 189
  old and new approaches **58**
  postcolonial 182
  socialization, traits 42
  state, concept of 187
  unitary legal code 42
  as weak and artificial creations 41
Arab Uprisings (2011) 43, 50, 57
Arab world 4, 17, 34, 36, 50, 59, 69, 82, 119, 150, 158, 181
Armed Forces Land Projects Organisation (AFLPO) 125
Armenian community 30
al Assad, Bashar 11, 18, 55, 106, 171
  'bulwark against terrorism' 19
al Assad, Hafez 11, 99, 105–7, 188
authoritarianism 4, 15, 17, 117. *See also* protection pact (Egypt's authoritarianism)
  crisis legitimacy 121, 133–4
  institutions 119–20, 122
  Islamism and 36–8
  'military option' and 16
  protection pact 121
  provision pact 121
  strongman protector 177
  uprising (2011) and 120–2
  weakness politics and 166–7
  Western demands 38
authoritarian modernism 37
authoritative political institution 62 n.45
Ayubi, Nazih 11, 47, 49–50
  Overstating the Arab State 49, 62 n.46
Al Azhar 132–3, 135, 137
Azzam, Abdullah 152

Ba'athist *mukhabarat* (intelligence services) 4, 99, 119
Ba'athist regime 74, 76, 153, 186
  ethnic chauvinism and sectarianism 99
  massive coercive campaign 103
Badie, Bertrand 19, 47
al Baghdadi, Abu-Bakr 54–6, 153, 155
Balfour Declaration 7, 13, 81–2
Balkanization 29
Balkan Orthodox 30
Bantustanization of the Occupied Palestinian Territories (policy) 151

barbarian 29
Barber, David, *Lawrence of Arabia* 15
Barcelona Process 51
Barkawi, Tarak, Orientalism 7
Barnett, Michael 16
Barzani, Idris 105
Barzani, Masoud 94
Barzani, Mustafa 101, 103
Barzanji, Sheikh Mahmud 101
Bashir, Tahseen 5
Battle of Chesme (1770) 26
Battle of Plassey (1757) 26
Bayart, Jean-François 47, 186
Bayat, Asef 57
Ben Ali, Zein Al Abidin 4, 18, 51
Berlin Wall, downfall 180
Bin Laden, Osama 18, 152–3, 156. *See also* September 11 (2001) attack
Bin Salman, Mohammed 20
Bishara, Azmi 44
Blair, Tony 172
Blumi, Isa 48
  Chaos in Yemen – Societal Collapse and the New Authoritarianism 61 n.34
Bolsonaro, Jair 185
Bonaparte, Napoleon 25
Bou Nassif, Hicham 122
bourgeois democracy 97
Bourguiba, Habib 48
Boycott, Divestment and Sanctions (BDS) campaign 89
Bozarslan, Hamit 95
Brown, Nathan J. 120
Brownlee, Jason 126
Bush, George W. 10, 18, 172, 174
Büssow, Johann 12

Caliphate 5, 10, 31, 33, 39 n.13, 41, 55–6, 94, 153
Cameron, David 174
Capitulations 10, 35
Catherine II, Empress 27. *See also* Greek Project
Chamoun, Camille 171
Chejne, Anwar 17
'children of the Arabs' 31
citizenship, concept of 189
civilization 28–9, 32, 102, 179
civil society 12, 49–51, 128–9
'civil state' (*dawlah madaniyya*) 43–4, 57
class and society 12, 26

INDEX   269

Clinton, Bill 152
Cold War 17, 35–6, 41, 51
    bipolar system 172
colonialism 7–8, 11–12, 58, 70, 161, 180
Committee of Union and Progress (CUP) 5, 70, 95
consensus democracy 97
Constantinople 14, 26
constitutional-parliamentary system 72
'consular illness' (*morbus consularis*) 30–1
continuous referendum 69
Copernican revolution 25
counterinsurgency 52
Crimean War (1854–6) 29
Cronin, Stephanie 12
cultural aggression 36
Curti, Giorgio Hadi 21 n.2

Dabashi, Hamid, *Authority in Islam* 55
Da'esh 63 n.66
'dark-skin immigrants' 185
Dawisha, Adeed 47
    Beyond Coercion 62 n.45
Dayan, Moshe, open bridges policy 89
'Deal of the Century' peace plan 3, 14
decolonization 16, 18, 48, 147–9, 166, 173
de facto veto power 54, 60 n.16
De Gaulle, Charles 15
democratic deficit 42, 45, 56
    Arab statehood 47–50
    neoliberalism and 51–2
Democratic Front for the Liberation of Palestine (PDFLP) 84
democratic state 44, 46–7, 60 n.16
democratization 60 n.16
al Dhawahiri, Ayman 152
'Dialogue of Civilisations' 160
al Din (Saladin), Salah 75

early mobilization 7
Eastern Crises (1832–3, 1839–41 and 1854–6) 28, 30
Eastern Question 25, 28
Edict of Gülhane (1839) 29
Egypt
    authoritarianism (*see* authoritarianism)
    Egyptian state, foundation 117–20
    extensive subsidy system 118
    income tax law 124
    politics and economy, military in 122–6

protection racket 145 n.115
repression 128–30
ruling party, elections and patronage 126–8
Egyptian Commission for Rights and Freedoms (ECRF) 143 n.82
Elias, Norbert 179
Emiliani, Marcella, *L'idea di Occidente* 61 n.30
enlightened despotism and reforms 27
Erdoğan, Tayyip, Democratic Initiative 108
e-revolutionaries 18
European Enlightenment 32
European Orientalism 32–3
European Union (EU) 51, 62 n.43, 86
    democratic package 108
Evans, Gareth 170
Evans, Peter 186
evolutionary synchronism 29–30
Executive Order 13769 Protecting the Nation from Foreign Terrorist Entry 20 n.1
expatriates 36
external control 6
Ezz, Ahmed 127

Faisal I, King 70–1
'Faith Campaigns' 77
Faraj, Abdessalam 159
'far enemy' (*al adou al ba'eed*) 147, 149, 156
Fascism 34
Fatah 83–5, 88, 91 n.6
Fatah–Hamas split (2007) 86
Fawzy, Muhammad 119
Faysal I of Iraq, King 25
Fayyad, Salam 86
    'statehood first' approach 86–7
Fayyadism 86–7
Fichte, Johann Gottlieb 68
fight against terrorism 19, 38, 51
First Coalition (1792–7) 27
First Gulf War 13
First Palestinian Intifada 13
First Republic (1958–63) 103
First World War 68, 180
foreign fighters 154, 157
France 10, 27, 30, 46, 93, 150
    ethno-naturalism 68
    Muslims in France 158, 160

radicalization of Islam 159–60
violent and manipulative campaign 150
Freedom and Justice Party 129
Free Syrian Army (FSA) 153–4
French Campaign of Egypt and Syria (1798–1801) 27
French Mandate (1920–46) 101, 105
Front de Libération National (FLN) 11, 15–18, 175, 186
Fukuyama, Francis 181

Gaddafi, Muammar 4, 11, 15, 18, 52, 171–2, 174–5
garbage collection crisis (2015) 42
Gellner, Ernest 68, 187
gender 12, 52
genocide 21 n.16
Georges-Picot, François 14. *See also* Sykes-Picot agreement
Ghalioun, Burhan 47
Ghani, Ashraf 176
globalization 31, 147, 157, 182, 186
    dynamism of 184
    as post–Cold War ideology 184
globalized transnationalism 7
Global War on Terror (GWOT) 3, 10, 13, 18–19, 155, 157, 160, 173
'good governance' agenda 51
Gordon, Alexander 9
Gramsci, Antonio 186
Grand Mosque in Mecca, seizure 13
Great Arab Revolt 11, 13
Great Britain 30, 35, 38
    France and 93
    occupation of Egypt 118
Greater Middle East 173
great game 9, 169, 172–6
Great War 33
    new states, emergence of 33–6
Greco-Turkish War 25
Greek Project 27
Greek Revolt (1821) 28–9
Grotius, Hugo 170
Gulf Cooperation Council (GCC) 50
Gulf War 3, 14, 38, 75–7, 80 n.20, 94, 104, 151

Habash, Georges 84
Haddad, Fener, sect-centric nationalism 80 n.23

Hadi, Abd Rabbo Mansour 169
Haifa Declaration 44
Halliday, Fred 13
Hamas rule in Gaza 87–8
Hamid II, Sultan Abdul 5
Hammoudi, Abdellah 53
Hanieh, Adam 12, 52
harratha 71
Hashemites 11, 34, 72
Hawatmeh, Nayef 84
Herder, Johann Gottfried 68
Herzl, Theodore, *Altnueland* 89
Heydemann, Steven 47, 49–50
Hiltermann, Joost 104
Hobbes, Thomas 179
    state of nature 167
Hodge, Jeremy 145 n.112
Hollande, François 174
Hourani, Albert 70
human community 45–7, 49
Human Development Index (HDI) 167
humanitarian interventions 19, 183
Human Rights Watch 124, 128, 142 n.65
Huntington, Samuel, *Who are we?* 184
Hussein, Saddam 11, 17, 36, 93, 99, 104, 151, 153, 157, 171–2, 175, 190
hyper-Jacobinist strategy 55

Ibrahim, Saad Eddin 187
ideal 'Sunnistan' 158
identical taxation system 29
identity politics 12
    rise and disintegration 76–8
illegal immigration 63 n.52
Illicit Gains Authority 125
Imbert, Paul 9
imitatio occidentalis 61 n.30
'imperial communication routes' 33
implication 33, 36–7, 39 n.14, 165. *See also* involvement
Industrial Revolution 27, 118
insecurity regional system 167
insurrectionary 7
'integration' policies 158
International Commission on Intervention and State Sovereignty (ICCS) 170
international community 43, 89, 155, 168, 170, 172
international Islamist terrorism 151
internationalization 35

international relations factor 26–8
International Security Assistance Force (ISAF) 174
intervention/interventionism 6, 18–19, 31, 167, 176
   'collective responsibility' principle 168
   failed states 183
   failing/collapsing state 168–9
   global responsibility 168
   humanitarian intervention 183
   international order 168
   international system and law 172–3
   power 172
   responsibility to protect 183
   restoring peace and security 168
   right to interference 170
   stability and peace 168
   threatened peace 168
Intifada (1987) 84
invention of tradition 28–9, 32, 37
involvement 33, 36–7, 39 n.14
Iranian revolution 13–14
Iran–Iraq war 75–6, 103, 105
Iraqi Coalition Provisional Authority 172
Iraqi Constitution 98, 103–4
Iraqi patriotism 75
Iraq (statehood) 4, 18, 55, 67
   attachment to empire 69–70
   British military campaigns in 11
   decline of nationalist-socialism 77
   detachment from empire 70–3
   dystrophies 6
   ethno-communal cleavages 67
   federalism 104
   identity politics, rise and disintegration 76–8
   'imagined community' 73
   invasion of Kuwait 3, 75
   Iraqi nationalism 67, 72, 74
   Kurds and Arabs 98
   long quest for autonomy 103–4
   praetorian societies 166
   United States to govern 76
Islamic Salvation Front (FIS) 18, 150
Islamic State in Iraq and Syria (ISIS) 8, 44, 52, 54–6, 63 n.66, 94, 104, 153–5
Islamic State in Iraq and Syria/Levant (ISIS/L) 153
Islamic State (IS) project 8, 18, 43, 54, 57, 147, 173

and confessionalization of resentment 153–8
Islamism 53, 149, 161
   and authoritarianism 36–8
   Janus-faced ambition 7–8
'Islam is the solution' (*al islam huwa al hal*) 36
Islamist revolution 53
Islamophobia 18, 37
Ismail, Salwa 42, 59 n.7
Israel-Egypt Peace Treaty 13
istikhbarat 11

Jewish emigration 31
jihadi Salafism 8
jihadism 37, 147–8
   of few 159–62
   'liberation' movements 148
   post-colonial order to 148–52
   struggle against fundamentalism 150
al Jolani, Abu Mohammad 153
Joseph, Suad 59 n.9

Kaczynski, Jaroslaw 185
Karer, Haki 102
Karzai, Hamid 174, 176
Kemal, Mustafa 25, 95, 97
Kemalism 37
Kemalist revolt 93
Kepel, Gilles 159–60
Kevin 161
Khaldun, Ibn 185, 189
Khalidi, Rashid 21 n.8
al Khalifa, Hamad bin Isa 171
Khan, Reza 95
Khomeini, Ayatollah 54
Khoybun Committee (1927–43) 101
Kienle, Eberhard 51
King, Diane 15
Krasner, Stephen, organized hypocrisy 180
Kurdish issue, evolution 94
   Anglo–Iraqi statement 98, 100
   'democracy for Iraq, autonomy for Kurdistan' (slogan) 102
   intellectuals 101–2
   Kurdishness 95, 98–9
   minorities (*see* minority rights (Kurds))
   national identity fiction 100, 105
   'national rights' 103

Rojava 94
  in Turkey 106–8
Kurdish Question 93, 108, 110. *See also* Kurdish issue, evolution
Kurdistan Democratic Party (KDP) 101, 103–5
Kurdistan Workers' Party (PKK) 94–5, 102, 105–7
  national liberation movement 107
  radical ideological re-orientation 108

Laurens, Henry, 'great game' 9
League of Arab States 6, 16, 42, 82, 91 n.2
League of Nations (LoN) 14, 93, 100
  Mandate System 6, 87
'Learned Arms' 27
Lebanese Christians 33
Lebanon War (1982) 84
Lenin, Vladimir 70
Levant 5–6, 8, 14, 70, 101, 170, 175, 186
Lewis, Bernard 159
liberal era 34, 37
Libya 156, 166, 170, 190
  intervention 19, 46, 174
    Italian concentration camps in 6, 11
  post-Gaddafi chaos 20
Long Revolt (1961–70) 101
Louis XVI, King 27
Louis XVIII, King 168
Love of Egypt (*Fi Hubb Misr*) 127–8
Luciani, Giacomo 47, 62 n.45, 187, 192 n.19
Luizard, Pierre-Jean 55

Maastricht Treaty 51
Mahmoud II 28–9
Mali, French interventions 175
al Maliki, Nouri 104, 153–4
'management of savagery' 56
Mandate System 6–7, 33
Manek, Nizar 145 n.112
Mann, Michael 62 n.47
Mansour, Adli 133
Marxist fringe 84
Masaryk, Tomáš Garrigue 25
Mashreq and Maghreb 3–4, 71, 173
Masoud, Tarek 143 n.90
mass mobilization 7
Mauritania 6, 21 n.3
Mazower, Mark 100
McMahon-Hussein correspondence 7, 13

Meier, Astrid 12
'MENA,' idea 9–10
mercenarization 36
Migdal, Joel 49
  state-in-society 96, 111 n.11
migration crisis (2014) 19
Mill, John Stuart 170
minority rights (Kurds) 93
  accommodation *vs.* resistance 94, 96
  continuity and change 96
  contradiction and mimesis effect 100–2
  dealing with minorities 97–100
  federalism and de-centralization 97, 101, 109–10
  fragmented tyranny 96
  image of homogeneity 96, 100
  interactionist approach to 94–7
  mimesis process 100
  particularism 95
  'Syrian Kurdistan' 101
  universalism 95
Mitchell, Timothy 45
modern civilization 32
Mohamedou, Mohammad-Mahmoud Ould 58, 159
Mohammed, Prophet 55, 77
Morocco 6, 21 n.3
Morsi, Mohammed 122, 132–5, 138, 143 n.89
Mubarak, Gamal 127
Mubarak, Hosni 4, 11, 42, 51, 62 n.41, 117, 119–20, 123, 135, 171
Mubarak era (1981–9) 122, 125
  protection pact 130
  repression 130
  ruling party, elections and patronage 126–8
Muhsin, Jabar 80 n.21
mukhabarat 11, 50, 57, 99, 119
Muslim Ban 3, 19–20, 20 n.1
Muslim Brotherhood 83, 128–9, 131–3
myth and history 17, 74–5
  national integration 105
  political-security myth 21 n.16

al Nahyan, Mohammed Bin Zayed 20
Nasser, Gamal Abdel 37, 95, 103, 117–19, 135
nation, defining 68
national community 67–9, 72–3, 75

National Defence Council (NDC) 123, 126, 145 n.107
National Democratic Party (NDP) 119, 126–8, 141 n.57
nationalism 75, 78
    centralism, constitutionalism and 70
    state, nation and 68–9
nation-building 67, 72, 78, 98, 100, 109, 176
    modern centralization and 70
    non-ethnic 68
nation weakness 166
Nazi Germany 34, 39 n.16
neo-authoritarianism 15, 19
Neo-Conservatives (Neo-Cons) 176
    'regime change' strategy 173
neoliberalism 51–2
neo-nationalisms 184–5
Netanyahu, Benjamin 58, 92 n.12
    economic peace 87, 89
new nation states (Europe) 69
New World 26
nizam-e-jedid (new order) 5
non-Christians (Jews), emancipation 29–30
non-ethnic nation-building 68
non-Muslims 33, 55, 75
    consular protection 31
    emancipation 29–30
    Muslims and 28–9
al-Nur party 132, 143–4 n.91

Obama, Barack 174
Öcalan, Abdullah 107–8
old orders
    dismantling 28–9
    and statehood 4–8
'open-ended' regime 85
Orbán, Viktor 185
Organisation de l'Armée Secrète (OAS) 15
Orientalism 7, 32–3
Orientalist depictions 43
Oslo agreement (1993) 85
Oslo Peace Accords (1993) 151
Ottoman Empire 8–9, 39 n.3, 55, 148
    active diplomacy 28
    administrative reforms 5
    attachment to 69–70
    authority and administration 11
    decentralization 26, 33
    defeat during First World War 13
    detachment from 70–3
    effective tax system 28
    fall of 10–12, 110, 191
    French and British mandates 13
    imprint 6
    military reforms 28
    non-Muslims, question 29
    pacification process 31
    powers, alliances 26
    rescue operation 29
    'slow end' of 5
'Ottoman-ness' 26
Owen, Roger 62 n.45

Palestine/Palestinians
    Arabs' aspiration 82, 90
    British occupation of 81
    challenges 90
    dislocation and protest 88–9
    great revolt 82
    independent Arab state 82
    national movement 81, 84, 89, 91 n.1, 92 n.10
    Palestinian identity 88
    peace process 51, 90
    pragmatism 83–5
    revolution and 'return' 82–3
    self-determination 84, 89
    state-building 86
    United Nations partition plan 13
Palestinian–Israeli settlement 86
Palestinian Liberation Organisation (PLO) 48, 83–4, 86, 151
Palestinian National Charter (1968) 44
Palestinian National Council (PNC) 84
Palestinian 'Zionism' 87
pan-Africanism 16
pan-Arabism 98, 147
    inferiority 187
    rapprochement 149
pan-Islamism 5
Pape, Robert 169
Partition Plan (1947) 82
Pasha, Ibrahim 28–9
Patriotic Union of Kurdistan (PUK) 101, 104
Peace and Democratic Party (BDP) 108
Pearl Harbor factor 155
Peel Commission (1937) 82
peripherality and malleability 6
Peter the Great 27
Picard, Elizabeth 97

Pilsudsky, Józef 25
Pir, Kemal 102
Pitt, William 25
Polisario Front (1975) 148
political and national unity 68
political economy 12, 43
  mercenarization 36
political educators 49
political future (Africa) 14
political Islam (Egypt) 128, 131
  extent of threat 132
  types of threat 132–4
Popular Front for the Liberation of Palestine (PFLP) 84
'Ports of the Levant' (*Échelles du Levant*) 26
positive neutralism 35
post–Arab Spring movement 6, 18
post–Cold War ideology 184
post-colonialism 17
post-colonial state 165
  'centre' of international system 165
  international relevance 165
  weakness politics and authoritarianism 166–7
  weak structure 165
post-1979 Iranian state model 53
post-neoliberalism 52
post–Second World War 34, 95
pragmatism 83–5
protection pact (Egypt's authoritarianism)
  economic reform 136–7
  fragmentation of politics 130–4
  generals' bargaining leverage 135
  governing coalition 135–6, 138
  historical impact 134–8
  managing mass politics 134–5
  political and institutional bargains 137–8
Putin, Vladimir 14, 19, 185

Qamishli revolt (2004) 106
Qassem, Abdul Kareem 95, 103
Qutb, Sayyid 52, 159

radicalization of Islam 159
  approaches 161–2
  political causes of 160
  spatialization of trajectories 159
reformers of Islam 32
'regime change' strategy (Neo-Cons) 173
regional crises 35

regionalization of exasperation 150
Renan, Ernest 68–9, 73
  constant 'referendum' 73
  French model 78
repression 11, 99, 106, 121, 138
  domestic security, military in 129–30
  international cooperation in 150, 152
  outside legal system 130
  strategic installations 129
republican era (1958–1968) 73–4
  national edifice during 67
responsibility, concept of 168
responsibility to protect (R2P) 170, 183
restorative conservative movement 8
retribalization 77
Rojava 94
Roy, Olivier 160, 163 n.21
  Jihad and Death 160–1
al Rundi, Abu al Baqa, 'Lament for the Fall of Andalusia' 186
Russo-Turkish war (1768–74) 27

al Sadat, Anwar 117, 119, 135
  strategy of 'limited war' 119–20
Sahnoun, Mohamed 170
Salafi-jihadism 159
Salamé, Ghassan 12, 47, 61 n.33, 62 n.45
  Democracy without Democrats 59 n.9
  Foundations of the Arab State 61 n.30
Saleh, Ali Abdallah 18, 172
Salvatore, Armando 53
Samet-Marram, Oren 120
Sarkozy, Nicolas 174
Saud, Ibn 21 n.16
Saudi Arabia 19, 53, 171, 173
  coexistence/cooperation 150
  creation 34
  transfer sovereignty 133
Sayigh, Yezid 122, 145 n.114
Sazonov, Sergei Dmitrievich 14
Second Coalition (1799–1802) 27
Second Gulf War 36, 76, 151
Second World War 34–5, 82, 180
sect-centric nationalism 78, 80 n.23
secular Arabism 147, 149
Sela, Avraham 17
Selim III 27–8
Semitic 32
September 11 (2001) attack 3, 10, 14, 18, 151, 157, 160, 173
Seven Years' War (1756–63) 26

shari'a 54, 143 n.91
Sharif, Safwat 127
Shi'a militias 153–4
Shia Muslims 56
Shi'i–Kurdish alliance 76
Shi'is and Sunnis 71–2, 76, 153–4
Shishakli, Adib 98
al Sisi, Abdelfattah 20, 117, 120, 122, 124–31
    coup-proofing features 135
    enforced disappearances of citizens 130
    political and institutional bargains 137–8
    political Islam 131
    renew Islamic discourse 133
Slater, Dan 121, 131
Soliman, Samer 62 n.41
Somalia
    'consolidation' type 175
    Islamic Court Union (ICU) 175
    US intervention in 169
Southeast Anatolia project (GAP) 112–13 n.39
sovereign state/sovereignty 88, 104, 106, 148, 167–70, 180–1, 184
    classical definition of 185
    crucial domestic dimension 181
    domestic prerogative 183
Soviet Invasion of Afghanistan 13, 150
Stambolisky, Aleksandar 25
Stanski, Keith, Orientalism 7
state-building 16–17, 33, 58, 72, 165, 182, 188
    failures of 21 n.8
    history of 8
    intra-society relations 190
    Islamic solutions 53–6
    project 6, 15, 43
state (*dawla*) 12, 54, 61 n.32, 180. *See also* Arab states
    Arab specificities 44–7
    conceptualized and perceived entity 180
    emergence of new 33–6
    fragility and mortality of 185
    as idea 188
    inevitable international dimension 181
    inferior entity 187
    ingrained vulnerability of 186
    as instrument 188
    modernization 69–70
    nation and nationalism 68–9

    of *omnium contra omnes* 179
    par excellence 72
    sense of longing for 179
    Westphalian in essence 181
state-formation 5, 72
statehood 5, 12–13, 18, 34, 85–8, 165, 180
    Arab 47–50, 57
    constrained sovereignty and limited 176
    cultural commonality 7
    historical developments 4
    invention of tradition 32
    modernization dynamics and demand 20
    old orders and fleeting 4–8
state-making 42, 45–6, 49, 50, 57, 186
state nationalism 67, 71, 73
    war and failure of 67, 74–6
stateness deficit 5
state of nature, concept of 167
state–society gap 190
Strange, Susan, 'retreat of the state' 184
Strayer, Joseph 179
structural adjustment programmes 51
subnational identities, politicization and militarization 67
Suez Canal Regional Developmental Project 125
Sufism 53
Sunni Ashraf 72
Sunni Islam 30, 33
Support Egypt Coalition (*I'tilaf Da'm Misr*) 128, 133
Supreme Council of Armed Forces (SCAF) 123, 127, 132
al Suri, Abu Musa'b, *Da'wat al Muqawama al Islamiyya al 'Alamiyya* 157
Sykes, Mark 14
Sykes-Picot agreement 6–7, 13–14, 48, 54, 189
Syria 174
    cultural to political claims 104–6
    intervention in Lebanon 171
    Jabhat al Nusra 153
    minorities 98
    mukhabarat 99
    praetorian societies 166
Syrian War 38

Tahtawi, Rifa'a Rafi al 39 n.10
Tajdeed movement 61 n.30

Talabani, Jalal 105
tanzimat (reorganisation) 5
taqiyya 105
theory of rights 53
Third Gulf War 36
Thomson, David 161
Thomson, Elizabeth F. 24 n.62
Tilly, Charles 49–50, 165–7
   'state as criminal scheme' 192 n.17
Toshka project 125
totalitarian-patrimonial model 74
Toynbee, Arnold 26
   nation-state formula 25
   'The Patriots' 25
   A Study of History 25
   The Western Question in Greece and Turkey – A Study in the Contact of Civilisations 25
traditional power politics 166, 169
transnationalism 7, 21 n.11
Treaty of Lausanne (1923) 93
Treaty of Sèvres (1920) 14, 93, 98
tribal-clanic systems 5
Trump, Donald J. 3, 14, 19, 184–5
Trump Plan 91
Tsar 19
Tuğal, Cihan 52
Tunisia 6, 18, 32, 62 n.43
   economic crisis 42
   neoliberal policies 51
Turanian whole 32
Turkey 69
   cycle of demobilisation 106
   democratic autonomy 108
   Kurdish issue, solution 93, 106–8
   repression 101
Turkish–Israeli alliance 107
Turkish 'nation-state' 97–8
Turkish Workers Party (TIP) 99
Turks, Arabs and 31–3

United Arab Emirates 19–20, 184
United Arab Republic (UAR) 98
United Nations Development Programme (UNDP) 167
United Nations General Assembly (UNGA) 84, 170
United Nations Military Staff Committee 172
United Nations Partition plan 13, 91 n.4
United States
   Central Intelligence Agency (CIA) 150
   to govern Iraq 76
   invasion (2003) 54
   against ISIS 94
   militarization of foreign policy 151
   military aid 123
   September 11 (2001) attack 3, 10, 14, 18, 151, 157, 160, 173
UNSC resolutions 170, 174
USS Cole vessel 152

Venizelos, Eleftherios Kyriakou 25
Vergennes, Charles Gravier de 27
violent extremism 159, 162
Von Metternich, Klemens 168

Walter, Dierk 19
war society 166, 172
Washington Consensus 51
weakness politics
   and authoritarianism 166–7
   parameters of intervention 167–72
   power politics and 169
Weber, Max 180
   From Max Weber – Essays in Sociology 61 n.23
   Politics as Vocation 45–6
Western empire
   imprints 8–9
   inevitable 30–1
Western Question 25, 27, 35–6, 38
Westphalian State
   international politics of power 165
   parameters of intervention 167–72
White Man's interventionism 182
Wilson, Woodrow 70
window-dressing 175
World Trade Centre's Twin Towers 152

Young Turks movement 5, 11, 95
Young Turks Revolution (1908) 33
Yugoslavia, collapse 29

Zainab, Sayeeda 154
al Zarqawi, Abu Mus'ab 153, 156, 170
Zartman, William 47
   Beyond Coercion 62 n.45
al Zawahiri, Ayman 159
Zionism/Zionist movement 16, 33, 82, 85, 87
al Zur, Dayr 113 n.42

www.ingramcontent.com/pod-product-compliance
Lightning Source LLC
Chambersburg PA
CBHW051805230426
43672CB00012B/2638